1996

Teacher Cognition in Language Teaching

THE CAMBRIDGE APPLIED LINGUISTICS SERIES

Series editors: Michael H. Long and Jack C. Richards

This series presents the findings of recent work in applied linguistics which are of direct relevance to language teaching and learning and of particular interest to applied linguists, researchers, language teachers, and teacher trainers.

Teacher Cognition in Language Teaching

Beliefs, decision-making and classroom practice

Devon Woods

 CAMBRIDGE
UNIVERSITY PRESS

Published by the Press Syndicate of the University of Cambridge
The Pitt Building, Trumpington Street, Cambridge CB2 1RP
40 West 20th Street, New York, NY1001–4211, USA
10 Stamford Road, Oakleigh, Melbourne 3166, Australia

© Cambridge University Press 1996

First published 1996
Printed in Great Britain
by Cambridge University Press

Library of Congress Cataloguing-in-Publication Data

Woods, Devon.
    Teacher cognition in language teaching :beliefs, decision-making, and classroom practice /
Devon Woods.
        p.   cm. – (The Cambridge applied linguistics series)
    Includes bibliographical references and index.
    ISBN 0–521–49700–0 (hc). – ISBN 0–521–49788–4 (pb)
    1. Language and languages–Study and teaching. 2. Language teachers–Psychology. 3.
Curriculum planning. I. Title. II. Series.
    P53. W66 1996
    419.007–dc20   95–37618
                                                                               CIP

A catalogue record for this book is available from the British Library

ISBN 0 521 49700 0 hardback
ISBN 0 521 49788 4 paperback

We have been trained to think of patterns, with the exception of those in music, as fixed affairs. It is easier and lazier that way but, of course, all nonsense. In truth, the right way to begin to think about the pattern which connects is to think of it as *primarily* (whatever that means) a dance of interacting parts and only secondarily pegged down by various sorts of physical limits and by those limits which organisms characteristically impose.

Gregory Bateson: *Mind and Nature*

Contents

Series Editors' Preface

A dominant paradigm in research on teaching over the last two decades has been characterized as process-product research. In this research paradigm, teaching is approached from the outside, that is, from the perspective of a researcher or observer looking at observable classroom teaching processes or teaching behaviours, such as strategies used in opening lessons, questioning behaviours, ways of giving praise and feedback, error correction, and other quantifiable aspects of classroom interaction. This approach has attempted to understand the nature of teaching through identifying and describing sets of discrete teaching behaviours. The assumption is that specific teaching behaviours could be identified with particular learning outcomes and the teaching behaviours characteristic of effective teachers could be used as a basis for the training of other teachers.

A different research paradigm is illustrated in the present volume by Devon Woods, an approach which is based on a qualitative or interpretive approach to teaching research and which seeks to understand teaching from the inside rather than from the outside, that is, from the point of view of the participants themselves. Rather than depending on quantification of teaching behaviours, Woods focuses on how teachers' knowledge systems, beliefs, attitudes, values, and experience shape their understanding of teaching and how they arrive at planning and instructional decisions in teaching. Through interviews with teachers, analysis of the stories they tell about their teaching, and through exploration with them of video recordings of their lessons, Woods presents a fascinating account of the pedagogical reasoning and action processes employed by second language teachers in their work.

This book therefore adds an important dimension to our understanding of second language teaching, one which enables us to recognize the limitations in conceptualizing teaching only in terms of teaching methodology or teaching behaviours, and one which emphasizes the importance of understanding the cognitive dimensions of teaching and the ways in which beliefs, attitudes and experience shape teachers' classroom actions and perceptions

Michael H. Long
Jack C. Richards

Thanks

I would like to thank the many people whose inspiration, contribution and support have been very important over the ten years that this study has been emerging. Any errors of misjudgment or oversight in the manuscript, however, are solely my responsibility. First, I would like to acknowledge the eight teachers involved, who allowed me into their lives and their thoughts and contributed greatly to my thinking about the work of teachers. For them I have the highest admiration and respect. In my professional past, I would like to acknowledge a number of people who played an important role in the evolution of my thinking about the subject of understanding the work of ESL teachers. Michael Massey, at the University of Ottawa, encouraged me to take the teacher's perspective at a time when much of the field considered it a peripheral area. Graham Smart, at the Bank of Canada, introduced me to a process perspective in writing and encouraged my explorations of it with teachers' work. At Middleton Hall in Scotland, Hugh Trappes Lomax, Henry Widdowson, Alan Davies and others taught me about Blake. In return, I taught them about blowing in beer bottles. In Edinburgh, Ginny Swisher, Fernando Castaños, Trevear Penrose, Howard Thomas and many others pushed my thinking and my improvisation to extremes that I otherwise could not have reached. In Ann Arbor, Larry Selinker encouraged and helped create an environment that included, among many other important influences, Virginia Samuda, Pat Rounds, Carolyn Madden, Sandy Urquhart, and Robert Bley-Vroman. There, as well, I was introduced to Charlotte Linde and her work, and to the work of Michael Agar and Gregory Bateson, all of which had a pivotal place in developing my thinking and giving me a feeling of its professional legitimacy. Also in Ann Arbor, Brad Arthur, Kathleen List, and Jim Runner played an important role in my being able to make connections between areas of life where connections are not usually made. In Lancaster and at Carleton, many discussions with Dick Allwright challenged my thinking and my models and pushed them forward. Also at Carleton, the extended support and inspiration of Ian Pringle made a difference at a time when it seemed like the study would never be completed. In Utrecht, support and inspiration came from Mike Sharwood Smith, Wolfgang Herrlitz,

Theo Wubbels, Paul van Buren, Eugene van Ervin and the rest of Simon Smith and the Dancing Bear. I would like to acknowledge the contributions of Renata du Pourbaix, Andy Gray, Richard Kidd, Fran Manning, Ian Dale, Donna Fairholm, Suzanne Liddell, Tracey Poirier, Kumiko Murasugi and Sue Burhoe who all helped me with different aspects of carrying out the project. I would also like to acknowledge the Social Science and Humanities Research Council of Canada who funded the initial research out of which this book grew. The final realization of the projects in the form of this book was assisted greatly by the constructive comments of three anonymous reviewers, by Liz Serocold who suggested many improvements to my convoluted syntax but allowed me poetic license in a number of cases; and especially by my editor at Cambridge University Press, Alison Sharpe, whose encouragement and patience during the delays caused by my perfectionist tendencies, my publophobia and my motorcycle mishap were so important. I also appreciate the on-going support of Jack C. Richards, including his suggestion for the title. My feeling that 'understanding' is an important process in life goes much further back, however, to my family life of continual moves to new places and new 'cultures'. For their support during that life, I am enormously indebted to my parents, Jack and Joan Woods. In the intervening years, Chris Woods, Joan Hughes, Vesna Scott, Maria Helena Kubrusly, Alan Watts, Robert Fritz, Albert Hofmann and John Coltrane all played an important role in helping me learn what it means to understand.

This work is dedicated to Xan, Emily and Penny, who are for me, what understanding is about.

1 *Why study the teacher?*

My interest in studying the role of the teacher in the second language learning/teaching process stems from two sources. The first was an experience in teacher evaluation at the English Language Institute of the University of Michigan a number of years ago. I had the opportunity of observing a number of different classes, sometimes ones in which teachers were giving the same lessons, using the same materials and textbooks, sometimes even the same pages and exercises. It struck me that although the students were ostensibly doing the same thing – i.e. the same activity or exercise – there seemed nonetheless to be basic differences in what was 'really' going on. There was somehow important differences in what they were *doing* these activities *for*, and therefore a difference in what they were *doing*. It was almost as if the textbook item, instead of being the essence of the content being taught, only constituted the surface level of the lesson – an excuse, as it were, for the real learning that was occurring as a result of the interactions among the students and teacher. At some deeper, underlying level there seemed to be things happening of which I, as an observer in the classroom, only got brief glimpses.

For example, in one case, two teachers were carrying out their lessons involving the same reading passages and related exercises from a textbook. However it seemed that, in addition to the assigned work in the textbook, one teacher was using the passage in an informal way to deal with the issue of accepting cultural differences when you arrive in a new, seemingly hostile environment, whereas the other teacher seemed to be using the same passage and exercises as a means of reinforcing some grammatical points that had been introduced in another lesson (and in neither case were these uses of the passage explicit in the textbook itself).

In another case, in a textbook lesson on vocabulary and word formation, one teacher seemed to use the lesson in such a way as to get across the idea that dictionaries can be very misleading and that one does much better by guessing from context – and so students should

1

learn to avoid them. Meanwhile another teacher used the passage and the related exercise to teach students techniques for using a dictionary (and by implication to use a dictionary). I was curious to know what was 'really' being taught and what was 'really' being learned.

The second source of this interest was what seemed to me to be an implicit neglect and disregard for what the individual teacher brings to the learning experiences of the students in the field of second and foreign language teaching. In fact, at one time – when there was a push to make language teaching a scientific endeavour – this disregard was explicit. Fries (1945), in discussing the importance of linguistic analysis in preparing teaching materials wrote:

It is true that many good practical teachers have, out of their experience, often hit upon many of the special difficulties and some of the other important matters of learning a foreign language that would be revealed by scientific analysis. Usually, however, such good results from practical experience alone are achieved by chance; are not related to any principle and are thus unsystematic and uneven. (1945:5)

This feeling can be recognized in the methods and teacher training methods through the years that followed which downplayed the role of the teacher, in order to have the teacher follow the teaching method prescribed, and not meddle with the 'what' and 'how' of the teaching (let alone the 'why'). Although this attitude has been changing over the years, and textbooks now often invite the teacher to pick and choose or resequence, there is still relatively little research on what the second language teacher brings to the process of second language learning. As Larsen-Freeman (1991) has noted, there has not developed a theory of second language teaching. The role of the teacher has remained a relatively peripheral component of language teaching research through the years, and of current theories of classroom second language acquisition.

The interest in language teaching theory and research is based on the perception and observation, on the part of testers, teachers and the learners themselves, that there are language learning successes and language learning failures. These successes and failures occur at the level of the individual learner (some seem to learn very efficiently and reach a high level of ability in the second language, while others seem only to achieve a very high level of frustration), at the level of the lesson (lessons are evaluated by teachers themselves, by learners, and by outside evaluators, who often use an evaluation of a lesson as an evaluation of the teacher), and at the level of a course (evaluations of success and failure in a course are carried out by researchers investigating the effects of different teaching practices, by institutions, by teachers who evaluate their students' progress, and by learners). In addition to formalized evaluation procedures, which use standardized tests or specific *a priori* criteria to make decisions regarding success, these participants involved in the teaching process generally have perceptions about success and failure, and discuss these concepts informally: teachers often talk about good courses, good activities, good classes, good learners; learners talk about good courses, good activities, good classes, good teachers.

There have been many debates over the years, both in the literature, and over coffee, about what makes language learning successful and what makes it unsuccessful, and what makes the classroom teaching of it successful or unsuccessful. The central concerns of research in the area of language learning/teaching have shifted over the years, from a focus on the method of teaching, to a focus on the learner and learning processes, and more recently to a focus on the classroom setting in which formal learning is taking place. These are all attempts to evaluate the success and failure of the process, to determine the factors that lead to success, and to render it more successful.

Research and language teaching

In the past fifty years, there has been an immense amount of research aiming – or, according to discussions of its 'pedagogical implications', claiming – to extend our knowledge of second language learning and teaching in order to exert an influence on the practices of second/foreign language teaching, and in particular the teaching of English. (The extensive body of literature in the field of education is not discussed in this chapter, but rather under each of the specific topics dealt with in later chapters.)

For a period extending over several decades, language teaching methods were examined, evaluated, tested, and compared. During the 1970's the focus shifted to an attempt to examine the learning or acquisition processes of the second language learner. During the 1980's the emphasis again shifted, to the classroom and classroom interactions. In the discussion below, each of these research areas will be summarized in turn, followed by a proposal for a type of research focusing on the perceptions of the participants in the learning/teaching process. This proposal sets the stage for a study of language teaching from the perspective of the teacher.

The method debates

Over the years, decades and even centuries according to Kelly (1969) and Howatt (1984), the second language teaching literature has examined the question of teaching methods. A large number of articles, papers and theses have been devoted to comparing approaches to and methods for teaching a second language. The ways in which the comparisons have been made, and by which approaches are evaluated and advocated can be categorized into two groups.

First, a large number of authors have attempted to delineate the distinguishing characteristics of particular approaches to second language teaching and to advocate one approach over another on the basis of a conceptual comparison. For example, in the 1960's and 1970's, a great many articles appeared which attempted to compare, from a conceptual point of view, the 'audio-lingual habit-formation' approach and the 'cognitive-code transformational-competence' approach (Carroll, 1966; Diller, 1971; Chastain, 1976; among others). Prior to this, in the 1940's, 1950's and 1960's, many authors compared the 'oral' approach or 'audio-lingual' approach to previous 'grammar-translation' approaches (for example, Fries, 1945, Moulton, 1962). Fries had also compared his 'oral' approach to the 'direct method' of teaching, which had previously been contrasted to 'reading' approaches. Further comparisons followed in the 1970's: 'functional' or 'notional' approaches versus 'structural' approaches (Wilkins, 1976; Allen, 1977; Rutherford, 1979). A number of authors have advocated listening before speaking approaches (for example, Nord, 1980). Terrell (1977) and Krashen and Terrell (1983) advocated a 'natural' approach. In the area of specific purpose teaching, there appeared in the early 1980's, articles comparing teaching a 'target repertoire' versus teaching 'underlying abilities' (Hutchinson and Waters, 1980; King, 1980). Widdowson (1981) argued for the notion of 'process' in ESL teaching, in contrast to a 'product' based approach. In the areas of second language writing instruction (stemming from earlier work in mother tongue writing instruction) authors have also compared process and product approaches (Woods, 1984; Zamel, 1982).

Secondly, a number of attempts have been made to advocate one approach over another on the basis of an empirical or quantitative study. This trend was very evident in the 1960's and early 1970's as a strongly-held tradition of quantitative empiricism in research was applied to the language teaching field. For example, the Pennsylvanian Project (Smith, 1970; Smith and Baranyi, 1968), and the GUME Project (von Elek and Oskarsson, 1972) were large scale studies attempting to compare the results of teaching programs based, on the one hand, on an inductive audio-lingual approach, and, on the other hand, on a deductive cognitive approach. Several other studies attempted similar empirical comparisons (Scherer and Wertheimer, 1964; Creore and Hanzeli, 1960; Chastain and Woerdehoff 1968; among others). Hauptman (1971) attempted to compare an approach presenting structures grammatically with an approach presenting structures situationally. Further attempts were made to compare inductive and deductive approaches (Politzer, 1968; Seliger, 1975). Fathman (1976) attempted to compare a number of factors, including 'method', affecting the learning of English as a second language in schools. A number of studies compared traditional oral or audio-lingual approaches demanding early production (through repetition in the early stages) to approaches which encouraged a silent period on the part of the students in the early stages (Postovsky, 1975).

Although some of these authors made stronger claims for their results than others, studies of this type have typically been subject to many objections which call into question the validity of the conclusions that were drawn. The number of interrelated variables makes it extremely difficult to attribute the results to the method variables in question. None of the findings of these studies have been accepted in the field as unambiguous, and with few undebated results, these attempts to compare methods quantitatively eventually died out.

One difficulty in both types of comparison is that the criteria for success and the type of tools used for measuring success reflect one or the other of the theoretical approaches chosen for comparison. Since the approaches often make specific assumptions about what language is (the target of the learning), and what learning is (what the processes are by which the language is acquired), each operationalizes success in different ways. In choosing what criteria to use for measuring success, a researcher automatically and implicitly makes some choice about what success means and how it progresses. For example, success as measured in a grammar-translation approach was not considered success by those advocating oral approaches in the 1960's. The criteria for success for a functional approach (where the use of the language in certain specific contexts is the target) are difficult to compare to the criteria used for a structural approach (where the target is knowing and applying certain grammatical patterns). Communicative success is usually considered to be different from knowledge of the language; and academic success is not considered the same as fluency in the language.

Even more crucial than the relativity of the notion of success is the relationship of language teaching activities to the theory they are intended to represent. Are the activities what they are intended by the theory or theorist to be, or are they what they are perceived by the teacher and/or learner as being? For example, in the inductive/deductive controversy, an inductive approach is meant to have the learners draw a generalization from a number of examples, whereas a deductive approach starts with a generalization which is tested through examples. However, in such a distinction, the learner's state of mind and previous background is crucial. For example, a learner who has already been given a rule or has developed a personal explanation may treat the examples which initiate the inductive approach as illustrations of his explanation or as tests of his hypothesis. On the other hand, learners may prefer not to develop an interpretation when the rule is initially stated, or they might not be listening at all, so that the ensuing examples are not illustrations of the rule, but rather the raw data which they treat inductively. Similarly, a learner may be attending to language data presented in a communicative activity as form, or may focus on the communicative value of language presented in a structural approach. Under actual conditions, then, the relevant conceptual distinction may disappear.

With the lack of results in determining the approach or method which produces success in language learning, the field turned its focus to the learner, learner language and the processes of second language acquisition in order to shed light on the essential factors.

Focus on the learner

Sparked off by early articles on learner language (Corder, 1967; Selinker, 1969, 1972), and benchmarked by a book entitled *Focus on the Learner: Pragmatic Perspectives for the Language Teacher* (Oller and Richards, 1973), the developing area of research on the second language learner was intended to reveal the processes and causal factors in the acquisition of a second language in the hope that this would provide not only theoretically interesting conclusions, but also practical applications to the field of language teaching. This discussion briefly considers the issues and trends which were considered particularly relevant to second language teaching, and notes a number of reviews of the literature which have appeared through the years.

Research in the field of second language acquisition has examined various hypotheses accounting for learning. One of these was the natural order hypothesis. This began with a study by Dulay and Burt (1973), inspired by the research of Brown (1973) for first language acquisition, to determine if there was any regularity to the order in which particular language items (grammatical items, especially morphemes, such as third person singular '-s', or progressive '-ing') are acquired. This notion of regularity (both in first and second language acquisition) developed out of Chomsky's assumptions about an innate language ability, which allows a child learning a language to determine very quickly how the particular language they are exposed to symbolizes universal relationships, such as actor, agent, object, spatial relationships and so on. The important question for researchers in second language acquisition was: does this innate ability (if it exists) play a role in how a second language is acquired? A regularity in the order in which the child's grammar is acquired (across social and environmental differences) could be treated as evidence for this.

In addition to this theoretical importance, it was claimed that such a discovery had important pedagogical implications.

> Similarities in the acquisition of structures by different L2 learners in different settings would justify looking further into the ways in which learners' internal mechanisms seem to affect what is actually learned ... Over and above the provision of theoretical guidance, acquisition order studies could provide practical guidance in the development of curricula, materials and assessment instruments. (Burt and Dulay, 1980:266)

Burt and Dulay's first study was followed by others by them and by numerous other authors, producing what were subsequently known as 'the morpheme studies'. These studies gained a certain amount of notoriety in the field. The proponents claimed what seemed to be an uncanny regularity in studies comparing L2 learners in different settings, L2 learners of different L1 backgrounds, and L2 learners of different age groups (including child and adult). Correlation coefficients were often in the order of .9 or more. Burt and Dulay state: "it seems clear that children of different language backgrounds learning English in a variety of host country environments acquire 11 grammatical morphemes in a similar order" (Burt and Dulay, 1980:276). This was quite clearly an exciting time for the researchers engaged in these studies. But just as clearly, the results were intuitively troubling for many other researchers in the field, and these morpheme studies have been the subject of a great deal of criticism. Subsequent summaries of this criticism include Hatch (1983) and McLaughlin (1987) who argue that scoring and methodological factors involved in determining what is acquired and what is not may influence the interpretation of the data. Although the issue was never unequivocally resolved, the discussion has died down in recent years. One reason is because these particular language items, although posing a few intriguing question marks, are no longer considered an important enough part of the process of acquiring the overall ability to function in a language to place such an emphasis on. This is an interesting case where our changing definition of what language, language use and success in language acquisition are, rather than empirical results, has changed our conception of what relevant research is.

One author, however, took the work on this natural order and expanded it into an overall philosophy of language acquisition and of language teaching practice. Krashen was one of the researchers impressed by this notion of regular acquisition and the notion of an inner mechanism governing acquisition. This combined with his appreciation (one that many second language teachers also express) of the fact that error correction rarely works, and that learners often either speak the language well without consciously knowing the rules or know the rules but do not speak the language fluently, led him to make certain assumptions about second language learning. One of the main assumptions of his monitor model was that the 'natural' process of acquisition and the conscious process of rule learning are two independent and separate processes, ones which do not interact (Krashen, 1981). (An assumption implicit in his discussion is that the term 'second language' primarily refers to the syntax of the language.) A further assumption was that acquisition of new grammatical items occurs when a learner is exposed to meaning which he can understand couched in language which is syntactically just beyond his current level. When this occurs, the learner is 'ready' to acquire these items. Exposure, in particular in the form of explicit teaching, before this period of readiness will result in either no effect, or in conscious 'learning', which can only be used in situations where the language use can be consciously monitored and controlled.

Krashen's work has been critiqued from a theoretical perspective elsewhere (see, for example, Gregg, 1984, McLaughlin, 1978, and Seliger, 1988), but its influence on second language teaching was pervasive. The influence of his work was felt strongly in the area of pedagogy for one important reason. Instead of taking the (perhaps very logical) view that a language teaching syllabus should be organized around this invariant acquisition order that was being proposed, he suggested that the classroom should be much like life outside the classroom – very communicative and with lots of language. The role of the teacher in this setting was to make what was said understandable, through context, gestures, pictures, and through naturally simplifying the language (tempo, repetition, pauses, simplified syntax) to make the meanings understood. To many teachers, especially those moving toward a reduced focus on syntax and an increased focus on communication, this made intuitive sense. There was suddenly a view of acquisition of grammar which provided an argument allowing the teacher not to teach grammar explicitly. Many teachers who were interested in communicative teaching, functional teaching, needs analysis, teaching for specific purposes and, later, content teaching, but were worried about not including explicit grammatical content in their teaching, could organize their classes around real discussions and real communication and still feel they were taking care of grammar. From this pedagogical perspective, Krashen's 'comprehensible input hypothesis' was an important insight, and one that influenced many teachers.

Krashen's position with regard to second language acquisition fit in with a growing interest among researchers in the relationship of the learner's developing system to the language data that the learner gets. This interest stemmed out of claims that the linguistic input which is understood by the learner, or 'intake' (Corder, 1967) is the primary data that learners use for the acquisition of the target language system. An assumption that follows from this is that modifications to the input to the learner (by native speakers), such as slower speed, clearer articulation, simplified syntax, less reduced phonology, and so on, make it comprehensible. These modifications were observed in a number of empirical studies (for example, Arthur et al, 1980).

Long (1981) took this claim one step further by examining the interactional structure of conversation. He argued that it is the conversational adjustments – the 'negotiation of meaning' – in conversations between native and non-native speakers, rather than the adjustments to the speech addressed to the non-native speaker, that produce the modifications necessary for acquisition to occur. By focusing on the functions of utterances in conversations between native and non-native speakers, rather than the form of the speakers' utterances, Long (1983) noted a number of 'devices to modify interaction'. For example, he noted functions such as requesting clarification, confirming comprehension, repeating own utterance, repeating the other's utterance, as well as strategies for avoiding trouble, such as relinquishing topic control, and selecting salient topics. He concluded that it is the function of the utterances in modifying the conversation more than the simplified form of the utterances *per se* that makes them (both the individual utterances and the conversation as a whole) comprehensible and thus usable by the learner for acquisition.

Many studies, including Varonis and Gass (1985), then looked at non-native/non-native conversations, and found them also full of interactional modifications. They concluded that NNS/NNS interactions allow learners "a non-threatening forum in which to practise developing language skills" and "an opportunity to receive input which they have made comprehensible through negotiation" (1985:87).

Although for many years there had been a somewhat implicit argument that an understanding of the processes of second language acquisition was essential for improving classroom language learning, over time there was a growing acknowledgement that for the second language teaching profession a more directly relevant research focus was second language acquisition in formal environments – in the classroom.

Classroom-centred research

A recently developing focus of language teaching research is termed classroom-centred research. There are two threads in the development of this research. One is an extension of the focus on second language acquisition described above. The other stems from work occurring meanwhile in the areas of discourse analysis (as exemplified by the work of Sinclair and

Coulthard, 1975, and as summarized by Cazden, 1986), and mother tongue education analyzing classroom interactions using grids of analysis (brought into the second language classroom by Fanselow, 1977).

As noted above, second language acquisition research had moved from looking at the learner's order of acquisition of linguistic elements to comprehensible input as a factor in the learner's acquisition, and then to interaction as a means of getting the required input, i.e. from the learner *per se* to the learner's interactions. Eventually researchers, while still retaining the focus on the learner's acquisition processes, began to look at the modifications and negotiation of meaning that occur in the classroom. An example of this type of classroom-centred research is the work of Pica (1987) and Pica and Doughty (1985), who found that there is little negotiation of meaning in traditional teacher-centred classrooms, and little as well in group work involving consensus activities, i.e. where the task requires students to come to a consensus. In this latter case, for example, one participant can dominate an activity with little comprehension on the part of other participants and with few interactional adjustments and yet complete the task with what appears to be a consensus. The researchers found that most conversational adjustments occur in information gap activities, activities where every participant has unique access to information required by each of the other participants. These results, combined with the twofold assumption that language modification makes language comprehensible and comprehensible language produces acquisition, led the researchers to recommend the use of information gap activities in the classroom.

The conclusions for teachers and for how teaching drawn from the results of such studies should take place, therefore, hinge on two crucial assumptions. The first is that the primary data for language acquisition is comprehensible input. As noted by Long, "... one of the main goals of research on NS-NNS conversations, as on linguistic input to non-native speakers, is to determine how input is made comprehensible to the acquirer, and thereby (presumably) usable for second language acquisition" (1983:131). One of the reasons that this is an assumption, and not an empirically tested hypothesis, is due to the difficulty of determining operationally what the term 'comprehensible' means. The second assumption is an unstated one – but one clearly implied in many publications: that the primary goal (for learners and teachers) of second language classes is the acquisition of syntax by the learners. As the following chapters show, this is not necessarily how teachers see it (and perhaps learners as well – that has to be another study).

Interestingly enough, however, it seems these kinds of suggestions were not accepted and embraced by language teachers for the research results. Rather, these suggestions, very concrete as they were (even offering certain specific types of classroom activities), fit in with a developing 'common sense' approach of language learning for communication, part of the *Zeitgeist* which had been evolving over the previous ten years or longer.

A second thread of classroom-centred research is the attempts to examine what is happening in the second language classroom independent of the second language acquisition perspective. There has developed a focus in research on the classroom and what is going on in the classroom, which is summarized and analyzed in detail in Allwright, 1988. The goal of such research, which stems from classroom analysis in first language education (for example, Bellack et al, 1966 and Flanders, 1965), was to remove the bias of the observer from the observations and conclusions by using standardized observational methods. The article by Fanselow (1977), 'Beyond Rashomon' was a key article in this trend, arguing that it is by the use of such grids that we can avoid the bias of personal perceptions. A more recent attempt by Fröhlich, Spada and Allen (1985) uses a grid of characteristics to produce a continuum of communicative orientation in classroom teaching.

However, as recent work in cognitive psychology and in the philosophy of science has argued, the observer's perceptual and interpretive biases are still at play in any observation. An *a priori* grid, while reducing some biases, introduces others by eliminating from consideration contextual factors related specifically to the current lesson being observed, factors which may be as important to the processes occurring in the lesson as the pre-selected factors.

Gaps in our understanding of language teaching: three research questions

The research in the three areas described above has contributed not only to our understanding of classroom teaching and learning of a second or foreign language, but also to our methods for examining it. However, in my view, there are three important gaps which are relevant to the theory and practice of language teaching. It is these gaps, and the interrelationships among them, that have guided the setting of the research questions for the study described in this volume.

1. Research has not described the structure of classroom language teaching in pedagogical terms, i.e. in the context of the larger units of course structure and the underlying objectives.
2. It has not examined the processes by which language teachers plan and make decisions about their teaching (both for and in the classroom).
3. It has not examined the language teaching/learning process as it is perceived and interpreted by the participants themselves – in particular the teacher.

Let me discuss each of these points in turn.

The structure of classroom teaching

The focus of attempts to understand the structure of classroom inter-actions and classroom discourse has generally been isolated from the context of larger structural units of the course. Most classroom research, with either an educational focus (such as Bellack et al, 1966, and Fanselow, 1977) or a linguistic/discourse focus (such as Sinclair and Coulthard, 1975, and Coulthard, 1977) has analyzed the teacher-learner exchanges occurring in the classroom into a classification of types of interactional 'moves'. A major focus of both types of research has been the recurring three-part pattern (teacher initiate, student respond, teacher evaluate) that occurs between teacher and learners. Sinclair and Coulthard's (1975) discourse analysis placed this pattern within a structured hierarchy of 'ranks', including 'acts', 'moves', 'exchanges' and 'transactions', the latter rank of 'transaction' being the most inclusive unit in their analysis. They did not find discourse-type rules to link these superordinate units of discourse to higher level classroom structures. Coulthard (1977) states:

> Sinclair et al emphasize that they have been 'constantly aware of the dan-ger of creating a rank for which there is only pedagogical evidence.' In fact for the largest unit, *lesson*, they are unable to provide a structure, and it thus has the same status as *paragraph* in grammar. (1977:101)

For teachers, however, there are larger units which are relevant to how they operate in class and what goes on in the classroom, concepts which they express in a number of ways, such as 'theme', 'unit', 'exer-cise', 'task', 'activity', and so on. What needs to be done is to describe classroom discourse and classroom processes in terms of the larger units which make up the course, a point argued by Germain (1990).

This issue provides the *first research question* addressed by this volume: *what are the structural units of teaching a second language course, and, more specifically, what are the relationships of more local units (such as units of classroom discourse) to the more global organiza-tional units used by the teacher to accomplish the course?* This issue is the focus of Chapter 4.

Teachers' planning processes

As described in the previous sections, the thrust of research related to language teaching moved from a focus on the *product* of teaching – analyzing the outcomes of different methods – to the *process* of teach-ing – analyzing the classroom interactions which lead to these out-comes. An important purpose underlying this research shift was to determine what are the classroom processes that lead to successful learning of the language.

However, when we take into account in our analysis the decision-making processes which are involved in creating and structuring the classroom interactions and events which comprise the course, the distinction between process and product becomes more complex. In this sense, classroom discourse can be considered the *product* of the decision-making *process* that creates it. We can then distinguish between the *structure* of the course – the events and actions of which the course can be said to consist, and the *structuring* of the course – the process of decision-making which results in the above product.

These two equally important aspects – the structure and the structuring – are crucially interdependent. Although the responsibility for the structuring of the course lies, in most settings, partly with an education ministry, board or institution, partly with the textbooks or materials that are provided for the course, and partly (and ultimately) with the learners in using the course to activate their own learning, the teacher usually plays a particularly crucial role in determining what happens, on a moment-to-moment basis, in the classroom implementation of the course. The structure of the course that results, then, is dependent on the process of course creation which occurs through a series of decisions made by the teacher in conjunction with and through interaction with the other participating agents. The course is the trail that the decision-making process leaves behind.

There is a sense in which the second language teaching field is currently in a position analogous to that of the field of writing before research began on the processes by which writers create written text. Our observations and evaluations of teachers are primarily based on what they do in the classroom. Although, as noted above, in one sense this is the process of teaching being looked at, in another important sense it is still a product – the ultimate manifestation of a process of planning, preparing, organizing, creating, structuring. This latter process we know very little about except anecdotally. Yet a very important part of understanding teaching is understanding these processes – how teachers plan.

This issue provides the *second research question* addressed by this volume: *what are the procedures that the second language teacher uses to structure (plan and organize) the course of teaching?* This is the focus of Chapters 5 and 6.

Teachers' interpretive processes

There is a sense in which what is happening in the classroom is what the *participants* – the learners and the teacher – perceive is happening within the larger context of the course and their intentions and goals. This perspective, which may be quite different from what an outside analyst concludes is happening, has not been taken into account in any systematic way in research related to second language teaching.

There are a number of reasons for broadening the research to include the understanding of the participants of the events which make up the process of the classroom learning/teaching, ones which are related to the difficulties that arise in observing 'success' and 'failure' solely from the perspective of an outside observer. For example, in the evaluation of the learning and/or teaching, the perceptions of these three groups may differ in important ways. The researcher's view of what and how much the learners learned (based on pre- and post-tests, for example) may not correspond to the teacher's view of what they learned, nor with the learners' views of what they learned – in particular what they learned that was important to them. Nor may the observer's view of an effective lesson, effective teaching or an effective teacher (based on whatever observational criteria are used) correspond to the teacher's own view or the learners' views.

If for example, a learner comes out of a learning experience feeling that she has achieved success, this is a sign of success, independent of whether or not she has passed the exam that the teacher set and improved according to the researcher's pre- and post-test. Similarly, if a teacher feels that a course or lesson was successful, this is also important, independent of whether this success matched an outside evaluator's criteria; and it is important even if it does not match what the learners feel. There are different sets of criteria and different types of validity (theoretical and personal) related to each perspective. If we are interested in determining the factors involved in success and failure, then it is important to examine all facets of this complex picture of success and failure, including what is seen as success and failure by the participants and how classroom events relate to it.

There has been some research in the field of second language teaching which attempts to take into account the perceptions of the participants in the learning/teaching process, most of them focusing on the learner. For example, Allwright's (1984) approach to the classroom and to classroom interaction is one based on the notion of 'learning opportunities' that are created in the classroom through interactions that learners are party to (through participation or observation) with the teacher or among learners. Slimani (1989) has attempted to determine what these learning opportunities are by eliciting the views of the learners about what they think they have learned. Cohen and Cavalcanti (1990) have examined teachers' written comments to learners by eliciting from teachers what the comments were intended to mean, and from learners what they understood by them. Both these types of studies, however, were done without taking into account the context of the course and the evolving relationships between teachers and learners.

In addition, there have also been a number of attempts by researchers to include the perceptions and insights of learners in our understanding of language learning success by looking at the strategies used by successful second language learners (Rubin, 1975; Stern, 1975; Wenden, 1986; Oxford, 1989). Although these studies represent a form of looking at learners' perceptions, they generally have not been done in an on-going manner during the process itself, but rather as a one-shot retrospective. Language-learning diary studies of the type reported by Bailey (1983) provide some insights into the on-going attempts and difficulties of language learners in natural and classroom situations. This kind of work needs to be done with learners who are not linguists and researchers themselves.

Work which focuses on the perspectives of teachers has recently begun to develop in the context of teacher education (for example, Freeman, 1990; Johnson, 1992; Nunan, 1992; Richards and Lockhart, 1994; Spada and Massey, 1992).

This issue relates to the *third research question* addressed by this volume: *what are the processes by which a teacher interprets classroom events and information about teaching, and how do these interpretations influence the teaching practices of the teacher?* These issues are the focus of Chapters 7 and 8.

In order to pursue these three questions, it is important to begin to see the whole process through the eyes of the teacher. Although such a goal is ultimately never possible, there are some steps that can be taken to move in this direction. To do so, I am proposing the following type of research.

Participant-centred research: focus on participants' understanding of events in context

In the research described in the above sections of the chapter, attempting to determine how second language learning takes place and what produces successful learning, the process has been observed from the outside. In other words, an outside observer examines the events occurring in the classroom, and interprets their significance within the hypotheses that make up a particular theoretical construct.

There are three important ways in which this type of research differs from the research I am proposing here – research on participants' understanding of events in context. These differences relate to the notion of 'context'. The first is the focus on the significance of events within the context of the *course* and the *curriculum* – how the interactions which make up the lesson play a role in the accomplishment of the course and the curriculum that the course embodies. The second is a focus on the classroom teaching within the context of the *processes of planning* of which it is the culmination. The third is the focus within the context of the *interpretations and understanding of the participants*: i.e. the context that the teacher and learners bring to bear in terms of their knowledge, assumptions and underlying beliefs, and their perceptions about how classroom events play a role in accomplishing (or failing to accomplish) the teaching and the learning.

These three aspects of contextualization play an important role in our understanding of the meaning of events (both verbal and non-verbal) that take place in the learning/teaching process. For example, events which may seem to make no sense when examined in terms of their formal meaning (i.e. out of context), become coherent when looked at in terms of their functioning within the larger context of the course. In fact, as is discussed in Chapter 4 on the structure of classroom decisions, it is precisely the function of these formal elements within the context of a course that gives them meaning for the participants. However, when as an outside observer, we attempt to make sense of the elements in a narrow context (for example a lesson or part of a lesson), rather than the broad context, we only get a partial sense (or perhaps a misrepresentation of the sense) of the elements.

Walker and Adelman (1976) demonstrate the point with the example of the following exchange in a British (mother tongue) classroom.

Teacher: Wilson, we'll have to put you away if you don't change your ways and do your homework. Is that all you've done?

Boy: Strawberries, strawberries.
(laughter)   (1976:134)

To understand the meaning of this, one needs to have experienced some of the recurring patterns in the classroom over time, and to know how these patterns evolved to function in the accomplishment of the learning/teaching that occurs there. By asking the classroom participants, Walker and Adelman discovered that one of the teacher's favourite expressions was that the students' work was "like strawberries – good as far as it goes, but it doesn't last nearly long enough". However, to understand the functioning of the student's comment, it is necessary to look yet deeper, within the context of the course and the relationships of the participants in the unfolding of the course. Walker and Adelman see this exchange as a reflection of the "underlying means of social control". The student's response, in addition to being a joke, is a signal that he and the class know what is expected of them in terms of the work they are to produce in this class by this teacher.

As outsiders, when we look at lesson transcripts, what we tend to see is the bare bones of meaning – the universals freely available within our culture – not the full richness of talk, which is what makes a relationship

valuable and unique to its participants. What we miss is the
subcultural experience of the group and its associated private and
personal meanings ... . (1976:139)

Including the contexts of the course and the participants makes it
possible to recognize that what are observed as the same events *formally* may be quite distinct when perceived *functionally*. In other
words, what on the surface seems to be the same event may be viewed
by the participants as being different because of its relation to their
goals, intentions, assumptions and beliefs. This notion is central to the
discussion in subsequent chapters.

This point is illustrated by the following example (provided by
Virginia Samuda, personal communication). In one class, an activity
perceived by an outside observer as a teacher-directed grammar activity may, according to that teacher, function as a component of a
structurally-organized syllabus. In this case, the activity functions to
teach students the use of, for example, the past tense as one component of the knowledge they must explicitly learn and internalize in
order to master the language. In another class, for a teacher whose syllabus is organized around communication tasks, the same grammar
activity may have a quite different function. In this case, the teacher
may hold the belief that students used to a structural approach must
be introduced to a communication-based approach gradually, and uses
the grammar activity as a means of fostering the students' sense of
trust in the teacher and security in the course. For this teacher, the
function of the grammar activity is the first step in a gradual introduction to her approach, based on group work and cooperative learning,
all of which is unfamiliar to the students. We see in this example how
the context of the overall course, of the students, and of the perceptions, assumptions and beliefs of the teacher play a role in the meaning
of classroom events.

From these examples it can be seen that what is 'actually happening'
in the process of language learning, and in second language classrooms
is in some important ways related to the perceptions and interpretations of the participants in the process within the overall context of
the course. This is not to deny that the observer or researcher who ana-
lyzes classroom data from the outside has a valid perception, and
through the analysis may see things that neither teacher nor learners
perceive (a good example of this is the phenomenon of teachers being
inaccurate judges of how much talking they do in class). John Fanselow
(personal communication) has noted "We have to realize that the participants do not necessarily know very much about what actually happened ... if we ask a person in prison about the experiences we need to
listen to the views of course, but few will provide insights such as those

provided by a person like Genet, for example." Nevertheless, the data provided by participants in the process, data which includes their perceptions of what they are doing within the larger context, is an important aspect of an outsider's understanding of the events.

The figures in the following diagrams contrast the traditional model of classroom-centred research to a model focusing on the perceptions and interpretations of the participants. The traditional approach to classroom-centred research can be illustrated by Figure 1.1. (The diagrams below are not intended necessarily to represent a teacher-fronted classroom.)

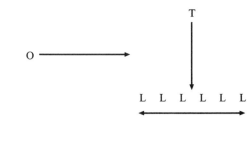

O = observer
T = teacher
L = learner

Figure 1.1 Classroom-centred research

On the other hand, teachers have access to perceptions and insights based on their intentions, their knowledge of the students, and their perceptions of the overall dynamic development of the course and its continuity, perceptions which an outside observer can only get glimmerings of. Research which taps the teacher's understanding of the classroom can be diagrammed as in Figure 1.2, where the observer attempts to trace the teacher's perspective of what is occurring in the classroom.

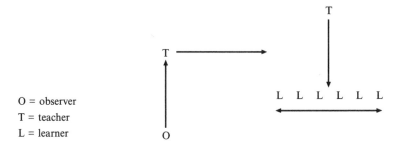

O = observer
T = teacher
L = learner

Figure 1.2 Classroom-centred research: teacher's perspective

Neither observer nor teacher, however, can be fully cognizant of the perceptions of the learners. The learners' classroom experiences include their overall goals and intentions, their interests, their background and previous experiences, and their view of how what is going on in the class relates to their overall situation and their out-of-classroom life. The researcher's or teacher's view of what a learner is getting out of a lesson may be quite different from the learner's view. Research which taps the learner's view of the process can be diagrammed as in Figure 1.3, where the researcher attempts to trace the learner's perspective of what is happening in the classroom.

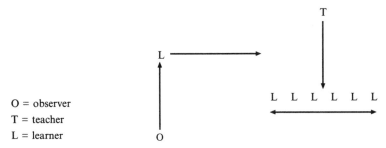

Figure 1.3 Classroom-centred research: learner's perspective

However, a discussion of the teacher's (or learner's) perspective requires some clarification of the semantic area normally and non-technically referred to by the terms 'teaching' and 'learning', in particular clarification of the roles of the learner and teacher in the process. 'Teaching' – usually considered the role of the teacher in the classroom – is traditionally associated with presenting information (deductively or inductively) in terms of target language items or generalizations, providing directions and guidance for the activities and exercises to be carried out so that the items or rules will be practised and remembered, and, when necessary, providing inspiration so that the students will be motivated to participate in the activities and exercises. 'Learning', in the context of ESL teaching, is often considered the converse of 'teaching'. 'Learning' is what the students are expected to do – at least partially in the classroom where they are expected to grasp and remember the information provided, to carry out the activities and exercises, and to study and practise what has been taught.

Over the years, an awareness has developed of the active (even when covert) role played by the learners in selecting and structuring, in their own ways, the language data which is available as input to their learning. Since the activities of selecting and structuring language input are traditionally considered responsibilities associated with teaching, the learners are, in a sense, taking partial responsibility for the 'teaching'. Thus, it is no longer clear where the line is to be drawn between the responsibilities of the teacher and the responsibilities of the learner. Based on this reasoning, Allwright (1981) developed the term 'management of language learning' to refer to the process of deciding upon, carrying out, and evaluating activities intended to lead to language learning, whether done by the teacher, the learner or through a collaboration.

Examining the possible roles of the learner and teacher in the learning/teaching process, we find that it is conceivable to have a situation in which the learner makes all decisions in learning the language – i.e. the learner is the primary manager of his own learning, and makes, acts upon, and evaluates decisions about what to do, who to interact with, what to study, how to practise. The learner may, for example, move to the country where the language is spoken and attempt to find situations and opportunities to interact with native speakers, or buy a textbook and study its contents, or make a list of words he would like to know and ask someone for target language equivalents, or tape record and transcribe conversations with target language speaking friends.

We frequently find, however, that a learner makes the decision to engage the services of a second party (a teacher or institute) to aid in the management of his learning. This results, in traditional terms, in a 'teaching situation', where the teacher or institute assumes responsibility for the teaching. In Allwright's terms, negotiation is formally opened for a collaboration in the management of the learning. In such a situation involving a second party, the responsibilities for the management of the learning assumed by the learner and by the second party will vary from case to case. In some cases the learner will use the second party as a guide and informant; in other cases, the learner may leave virtually all the decisions up to the second party. But, as Allwright (1981) has noted, the negotiation between the two parties is an on-going process, continuing right into the classroom.

In the cases mentioned above, it would be informative to investigate the kinds of management decisions made, the attitudes and negotiations influencing those decisions, the activities carried out for learning, and the feedback received on such activities. In both cases mentioned above, it would be informative to explore these aspects of the process from the *learner's perspective* – in terms of the learner's view of his objectives and expectations, and in terms of the learner's own view of success. In the second case mentioned above, it would be informative, as well, to explore the learning/teaching situation from the *teaching perspective* – in terms of the objectives, expectations and view of success of those engaged to aid in the management of the learning. This perspective involves not only negotiation with the learner, but also potential negotiation among various participants on the teaching side – teacher or tutor, materials writer, curriculum developer, textbook author, program organizer and so on. It is out of these negotiations, as well as negotiations with the learner, that come what we traditionally know as lesson plans, course plans, curricula, textbooks, and so on. (We might note at this point, that some teaching perspectives take the learner's perspective carefully into account, while other teaching perspectives seem to operate almost independently of the learner's perspective.) Within the teaching perspective, we have the *teacher's perspective* – the point of view of the teacher of the above interaction and negotiation. It is this latter perspective of the overall processes of teaching and learning that is the focus of this study.

Conclusion

One might argue that it really makes no difference, as far as learning the language goes, what an activity is done for and how it is perceived by the participants. Perhaps the important thing is only that certain essential elements are there, for example that comprehensible input is there, or that interaction is there. Perhaps how participants perceive or interpret what is going on is irrelevant to learning.

However, as we will see in the case studies reported in this book, the teachers' interpretations of the process – including the method, the curriculum, learners' behaviours – affect in many ways what class-room activities are chosen and how they are carried out. There are many subtle ways in which teachers' interpretations are displayed to students. Although the interpretation of these subtle signals by any particular learner may not correspond to the teachers' conceptions, the signals and messages undoubtedly play a role in the formulation of what is going on by the learner, and in the motivations and strategies for learning the language which do affect the learning. As noted above, the mechanisms involved in learner perception or understanding of what is going on, and how it affects learning is outside the scope of the present study. This study of teachers is intended to contribute to our understanding of the processes of second language learning and teaching by examining the perspective of the teacher, and by taking some initial steps toward an understanding of second language teaching on its own terms.

There is a practical reason for developing such an understanding. The training for becoming a language teacher, where one learns how to go about doing the job, has typically focused on theory and class-room technique. Information about teaching has generally been nor-mative rather than descriptive, and when descriptive then based on categories external to the situation and to the participants. Teacher education lacks a description of the structure of second language courses, and the lessons, pedagogical activities and classroom moves and discourse that make them up which is situated within the larger context of the participants. In looking at teaching and learning from the viewpoint of the teacher, and within the context of the course, we are centrally concerned with classroom events – the product of teaching decisions. However, for teacher education there has to be a focus on the processes by which these events come into being. We need to know more about the nature of goals, subgoals and means, and their relationship to the dynamic, interactive, negotiated processes of decision-making in teaching.

There are two key aspects of the picture of the language teaching/learning process that are important to elicit. One is the planning process of the teachers, dealing with how teachers go about preparing for what goes on in the classroom, and how events which are part of this preparation process relate to success in the classroom: i.e. how teachers' current behaviour is projected forward to future classroom events. The second aspect is the teachers' perceptions and interpretations of the classroom events that their behaviour is part of: i.e. how teachers' current behaviour is projected backward to include their background knowledge, assumptions, beliefs, goals and prior plans.

This study of language teachers' decision-making, which I have termed an 'ethno-cognitive' one, consists of a description of methodology, the development of a model or framework, and discussion of several areas of results. The study is ethnographic in orientation with regard to its research methodology – attempting to use informants as a source of information about the culture of language teachers and the ways of communicating and thinking of members of that culture. The study is cognitive in terms of what it is seeking to describe – the cognitive processes of teachers' decision-making. Chapter 2 describes the methodological details of this participant-centred study: the subjects, methodology for data collection and analysis, and theoretical considerations of validity of the methodology. Chapter 3 presents a cognitive framework or model for the study of teachers' decision-making by synthesizing selected relevant literature related to planning and interpretive processes in the areas of cognitive psychology and linguistics.

Chapters 4 to 8 discuss the results of the three research questions posed above in light of theoretical notions developed in discourse analysis and in research on teaching (however, I want to stress that this is a study of language teaching and is not framed specifically to respond to theoretical questions in discourse analysis or education generally). Chapter 4 uses the data of classroom events as reported on and reflected upon by the teachers, rather than a predetermined set of categories, to describe the structure of a language course. Chapters 5 and 6 describe the processes by which the structure is arrived at – teacher decision-making, both in preparation for the classroom and in the classroom. This is a projection forward, relating current actions and events to future actions and events. Chapters 7 and 8 describe teachers' interpretive processes. This is a projection backward, relating current actions and events to prior actions and events through the teachers' evolving network of beliefs, assumptions and knowledge.

Chapter 9 uses the notion of 'coherence' as a basis for synthesizing the findings of the two previous chapters and for discussing the processes of curricular change, teacher change and teacher expertise. Chapter 10 summarizes the major results and discusses the theoretical and practical relevance of this study in terms of (i) program change: curriculum development, and program implementation and evaluation, and (ii) teacher change: teacher education and professional development, and teacher evaluation.

There is a sense in which the outside observer looking at classroom events only sees the tip of the iceberg; the purpose of this book – even though the view will inevitably have distortions – is to have a look under the water.

2 *The study*

This volume is based on a study of the planning and interpretive processes of eight teachers of English as a Second Language. The broader research plan of the study was to follow each of the teachers through their course of teaching, from the time that they were given the course assignment until the conclusion of their course responsibilities. The teachers were tracked in order to determine the processes they go through in planning a course curriculum and turning the curriculum into lessons and language learning activities, and in order to examine how information about teaching, learning and language is related to the actions and events that the students face in the classroom.

This chapter deals with the research methodology used in the project: the subjects and the data collection and reduction. A number of steps were taken to enhance the validity of the analysis. Nonetheless there are important *caveats* to be considered when assessing the results of this study. These *caveats* are discussed in terms of each of the types of methodologies used. In the description of the methodology, as well as in the discussion of results in subsequent chapters, I have provided quotations from the data using examples of different teachers in order to exemplify the points at issue.

Subjects and classes observed

The subjects for the study were eight teachers of English as a Second Language, seven female and one male, at four different university settings in three cities in east-central Canada, teaching in credit or non-credit programs for adults. The teachers were all experienced ESL teachers recommended to me by the program head at the different institutions as being among their best. They had relatively homogeneous current teaching situations (types of students, types of programs), but relatively heterogeneous backgrounds in terms of education, teacher training, and previous language learning/teaching experiences. For example, four had originally come from outside North America (Britain, Morocco, Sweden and Switzerland), three being non-native speakers of English. As a group, they had a wide variety of previous teaching experience (children vs adults; ESL vs EFL, homogeneous vs heterogeneous groups of students, rigid vs free curricular guidelines).

Of the classes observed, all were for adults or young adults. Two (Courses G and H) were part of a six-week summer bursary program for young, mainly francophone, adults, most of whom were high school students. These two low intermediate level classes, whose curriculum included all skills and was primarily determined by the instructors, met daily for three hours. The remainder of the classes consisted of university students of various linguistic backgrounds. Three of the classes (Courses A1, A2 and B) were advanced credit courses, including all skills, but primarily academic, with set objectives and syllabus, and with recommended but not required materials. Two were pre-academic integrated skills courses (Courses C1 and D). The others were specific skill-based courses: two writing (Courses F1 and F2), two vocabulary (Courses E1 and E2), and one oral skills (Course C1). One of the teachers (Teacher A) was teaching two sections of the same course, one was teaching the same skill-based course at two different levels of proficiency (Teacher F), and one was teaching two different courses (Teacher C). In addition, two sections of the same course (and course content) were being taught by two different teachers (Teachers A and B). A total of twelve courses provided data on the eight teachers. Information about the courses is included in Table 1.

Research methodology

Data collection

On the basis of a prior pilot study, a methodology was developed which incorporated three complementary approaches: ethnographic interviews, modified ethnographic observation over time, and a video-based method of eliciting introspective data. These three approaches provided data to capture aspects of the teacher's decision-making process on three levels: an 'abstract level' not based on events in a particular time period, a 'course level' covering decisions occurring within the time frame of a course, and a 'lesson level' covering decisions made in the classroom during the time frame of a single lesson. Varied methods of elicitation, consisting of interviews, logs, video-based recall, and collection of lesson plans and rough notes constituted an attempt to produce data in different contexts and modes and thus provide some degree of triangulation of the data. The issue of triangulation is discussed below.

TABLE 1: TABLE OF INFORMATION ON COURSES/TEACHERS TRACKED

Teacher	Course	Type of course	Length of course	Lessons per week	Hours per lesson	Total hours	Skills	Level	Class size
A	A1	credit	13 wks	3	1	39	academic	advanced	18
A	A2	credit	13 wks	3	1	39	academic	advanced	20
B	B	credit	13 wks	3	1	39	academic	advanced	16
C	C1	intensive component	12 wks	2	1.5	36	conversat'n oral skills	elementary	19
C	C2	intensive component	12 wks	2	3	72	integrated pre-academ.	intermed.	18
D	D	intensive component	12 wks	3	3	108	integrated pre-academ.	low intermed.	17
E	E1	int. comp. (elective)	12 wks	1	1	12	vocabulary	intermed./ advanced	18
E	E2	int. comp. (elective)	12 wks	1	1	12	vocabulary	intermed./ advanced	12
F	F1	int. comp. (required)	12 wks	3	1	36	writing	intermed.	14
F	F2	int. comp. (required)	12 wks	3	1	36	writing	advanced	15
G	G	summer intensive	6 wks	5	3	90	integrated	intermed.	16
H	H	summer intensive	6 wks	5	3	90	integrated	intermed.	16

First, open-ended interviews were carried out with the subjects, which elicited their perceptions of themselves as teachers, their views of the nature of language and language learning, and information about what they considered to be the important aspects and concerns in second language teaching. The content of these interviews resulted in a number of explicit statements of belief and implicit presuppositions and assumptions, and provided a basis for cross-checking findings at the course and lesson levels. The interviews were carried out by the author and two other researchers in other research locations.

These statements of belief were not elicited explicitly by the interviewer. For example, in the early interviews about the teacher's background, questions like "Do you believe ...?" or "What is your approach ...?" were to be avoided. Generalizations and information about beliefs and assumptions arose when volunteered by the teacher. Instead, questions were to be formulated in order to elicit anecdotes about the subjects' previous language-learning/teaching related experiences, and the influence of these experiences on their current practices and views. Questions such as "Have you learned any languages other than English?" ... "Tell me about your experience learning this language" ... and, later, "Did this experience have any influence on the way you teach?" were intended to elicit personal narratives or stories about concrete events and experiences. (The use of narrative accounts as a source of data has a long history: relevant discussions of this procedure include Agar, 1980; Connelly and Clandinin, 1990; and McCracken, 1988.)

The attempt to elicit data in the form of 'stories', rather than in the form of generalized statements of belief was done for two reasons. First, personal narratives have been analyzed in other areas of study, for example in the work of Agar and Hobbs (1983), which would aid in the analysis of the data from the teachers. Second, beliefs (and their interrelationships) may not always be entirely consciously accessible, and teachers may, in responding to questions about generalized beliefs, answer according to what they would like to believe, or would like to show they believe in the interview context. When a belief or assumption is articulated in the abstract as a response to an abstract question, there is a much greater chance that it will tend more towards what is expected in the interview situation than what is actually held in the teaching situation and actually influences teaching practices. A belief articulated in the context of a 'story' about concrete events, behaviours and plans, is more likely to be grounded in actual behaviour. (This phenomenon has a parallel in the case of monitored speech discussed by Labov (1972) and Tarone (1982) in research on phonology, sound change and interlanguage.) The assumption underlying the data collection is that language teachers know a lot about themselves in language teaching situations, but although they have had the experiences, they may not have categorized and labelled them. Therefore using abstract questions, symbols and categories that the interviewer might feel comfortable with may not allow them to express what is important to them. Instead, it was considered important to talk in concrete terms, and use the answers to 'construct an understanding'.

Second, each of the eight teachers was observed within the time frame of a course. The teachers were interviewed on a weekly basis at which time they discussed what had occurred in their previous lessons, as well as their options and choices about upcoming lessons, and their thinking about the teaching in general. These interviews were complemented by written logs kept by the teachers about what they carried out related to planning, organizing and teaching their course (including thinking and talking about it), and by copies of the materials that they used in the classroom and any lesson plans or rough notes that they produced related to the course.

Third, teachers were observed during the time frame of a single lesson, and their comments about the options considered, decisions made and actions taken during the period of the lesson were elicited and recorded using the following method. The lessons were videotaped and subsequently watched and commented upon by the teacher. By pressing a remote pause button to stop the video and then making the comment, the teacher provided unstructured commentary regarding thoughts, plans and decisions that were related to the classroom events on tape. Whenever possible, it was left to the teacher to initiate the comments, although teachers varied a great deal in their tendency to explain what was going on from their point of view. However, until the teacher got used to the process, and in particular cases where no teacher commentary seemed forthcoming, the interviewer, in order to get the teacher talking, pressed the pause button and elicited a comment, saying something like: "What was going on there?", or "What were you doing here?" The point at which the tape was stopped was a point at which the interviewer sensed that there might be something to say (and therefore these points were not in an experimental sense repeatable). However, the goal was not to find out specifically about what the teacher was thinking at that particular moment, but rather to use the moment as a concrete point to elicit talk about the teaching in general. In fact, many of the subsequent verbalizations of the teachers expanded into discussions of other lessons, other studies, their planning, their beliefs, and so on. The specific moment at which the tape was stopped, therefore, is not a crucial element of the research. A composite videotape containing both the lesson and the teacher's metacomments was produced at the same time. The composite tape was then analyzed for further information about the teacher's process of decision-making during that lesson.

The data from this technique was contextualized through a pre-lesson interview (in which the teacher's plans for the upcoming lesson were discussed), and a post-lesson interview done prior to the video-tape watching session (in which the teacher's spontaneous evaluation of 'how things went' was elicited). These additional interviews may indeed have affected the content of the lesson somewhat: the teacher may have been more organized and followed the planned lesson more than would otherwise have been the case by virtue of being more explicit about the planning for the lesson. On the other hand, the context provided by the interviews allowed for deeper understanding of the decisions made and the activities carried out. The data from the videotape watching session was examined for indications that the videotaping and the pre- and post-lesson interviews may have had an effect. In addition, the results from the videotaped lesson were compared to data throughout the course for correspondences and inconsistencies.

It is important to acknowledge, however, the imperfect 'human' side of the data collection as well. For example, two of the final tapes for one teacher disappeared during the period of the study. In addition, three audiotapes were never completely transcribed, but rather just summarized to save time in the early part of the study before the researcher came to grips with the idea that the project (and the tran-scribing) was going to take several years. Also, one videotape captured the voices of the class and the view of a wall, as the researcher left the camera running unattended to go and interview another teacher. In another case, in one post-lesson videotape viewing session, the recording equipment failed to record, necessitating that the session be redone, and clearly affecting the nature of the interaction between subject and interviewer and the nature of the data produced.

The resulting data was approximately 60 taped interviews, lessons and commentary, the teacher logs (often recorded in chart form), and the materials that were used in the classes. The combination of the research methodologies provided data in the following areas for each of the teachers: first, an overview of their previous second language learning, second language teaching and teacher training, and their conception of its role in their perceptions of themselves as teachers; second, a procedural summary of the strategies, decisions and actions used in planning and preparing for the course and the factors influenc-ing them; and third, a mapping of the strategies, decisions and actions used in carrying out a lesson and the factors influencing them. The purpose of examining all three levels for each subject was to allow us to clarify the relationship between experience and abstract knowledge and beliefs, and between longer term planning and moment-to-moment decision-making.

The research methodologies described here stem both from ethnography and from research on such cognitive processes as problem solving, reading, learning and writing. This latter type of research attempts to reconstruct the process of cognition in these areas from the behaviour and verbalizations of human subjects, using the subjects' own insights and conscious awareness of the processes as a basis for reconstruction. There are a number of discussions of the pros and cons of this type of methodology in the literature. Some other studies which used this kind of approach to the study of how a particular ability is acquired are Dias (1987, on students reading poetry), Emig (1971, on writers), Flower and Hayes (1980, on writers), and Hosenfeld (1977, on readers of a foreign language).

One subcategory of this research is the use of videotaped events which the participants subsequently view and comment on. For this study, the inspiration for such a technique came from the work of Frankel and Beckman (1982), which focuses on the process of communication and interaction. Frankel developed the research methodology called IMPACT, an interaction-based method for preserving and analyzing clinical transactions (based in turn on the work of Erickson, 1982), which he used to examine patient-doctor/resident interactions and interactions occurring in clinical settings. The methodology was used as follows: the interaction was videotaped, and the resulting videotape was played separately to the patient and the resident doctor. Using a remote control pause device, whenever the viewer felt the urge to comment, the videotape was stopped (placed on freeze action pause) and the comment made. Another machine recorded the comment as a voice-over on the frozen frame of the original. Frankel's procedure was an attempt to examine closely what was occurring in the interaction as perceived by the participants, and to compare those perceptions, and produced interesting data about how particular critical moments or 'hotspots' in the interaction were perceived and interpreted differently by different participants.

This technique has also been used in many studies of teaching. It was used for example in the study by Mehan, Hertwick, Combs and Flynn (1982), where the teacher watches the videotape and stops it to report on 'anything interesting', or to identify particular student behaviours the teachers associated with particular students. They note (1982:304) a number of other researchers who have used this 'reconstructive' approach. In addition, reviews by Shavelson and Stern (1981), Clark and Yinger (1979), Clark and Peterson (1986), and Leinhardt and Smith (1985) note a number of research studies employing this technique of 'stimulated recalled'. Verloop (1989) gives a summary of the history and current discussions of the use of this technique.

Data analysis

The first analysis of the data examined the statements made by the teachers in the interviews, in the logs, in the videotaped lessons and in their comments on the videotaped lessons, for instances of the following types (related to each of the three research questions outlined in Chapter 1):

i)   statements which reflected the teachers' understanding of the conceptual structure of the course, and of the lessons and the sub-lesson units that made up the course (which can be considered, in a sense, the product of teaching decisions);
ii) statements which reflected planning procedures and strategies used by the teachers in preparing for the teaching (which can be considered the process of decision-making carried out by the teachers); and
iii) statements which reflected factors underlying the decisions, including the teachers' background knowledge, assumptions and beliefs.

The second stage of data reduction was to note recurring themes in the data and the relationships among these themes. This focus on themes and their relationships stems from the work of Linde (1980a, b, c) and Agar and Hobbs (1983). In their work, Agar and Hobbs use the term 'coherence' to describe the relationships among themes. This concept is discussed in detail in Chapter 3.

Linde notes that it is possible to posit underlying knowledge, beliefs or assumptions implicit or explicit in discourse, and by comparing instances occurring in different situations and at different times, to look for consistencies and patterns. It is when we note the recurring instances of beliefs and perceptions about the culture and its situations, and when we can deduce the consistences and relationships among them, that we can perceive the 'coherence' that underlies the culture.

Agar and Hobbs discuss three types of coherence in narrative accounts. The first of these is 'local coherence': coherence within the narrative itself in terms of the relationships of elements of the story to each other. The second is 'global coherence': the relationship of elements of the story to the broader, more generally understood cultural situation in which the story is being told and to the overall point of the story. The third type of coherence is 'themal coherence': the recurrence of themes in the story that tell us something about the underlying values and beliefs of the culture and about the narrator's perceptions of it. In our analysis, although the first two types of coherence are relevant to our understanding of how the data represents both the culture of teachers and at the same time the interview situation, it is this third type of coherence that plays the most important role in connecting what happens in the classroom (number i) above) to the teachers' planning processes (number ii) above) and the teachers' underlying knowledge, assumptions and beliefs (number iii) above).

There are several ways to locate such recurring themes. One way is to locate the explicit statements of teachers about their beliefs and assumptions. We have to be wary of such explicit statements because they can be easily monitored – a teacher may state a belief (such as "I believe in the communicative approach", or even "I usually don't talk so much in class") which may not coincide with what other evidence suggests, and even though the teacher may change his or her mind with more evidence to the contrary. However, we can take such statements as hypotheses to be supported or contradicted by subsequent evidence. This cautious perspective implies that beliefs may not always be held consciously, and may be 'discovered' or brought up to a level of consciousness later. It also implies that they are dynamic, and always changing, both in terms of their specific details and in terms of the relationships among them. This point is illustrated in later chapters.

A second way to locate such themes is by looking for recurring issues in the teachers' discourse (in class, or in the interviews about the course and its lessons), and specifying the implicit beliefs which are embedded in recurring mention of particular issues and concerns. These issues are signalled by recurring use of certain terms to express concepts important to the teacher, by explication and elaboration of those terms, by opposition to other terms, by causal and part-whole relationships among concepts, by implicature and linguistic signs of commitment and distance (Stubbs, 1986), and especially by evaluative comments about the concepts the terms refer to and about the relationships among them. The importance of the issues to the teachers is signalled by the frequency of their occurrence, their centrality with regard to other issues, and by explicit mention, by tone of voice and other signals of highly loaded issues, and other means of evaluation. The relationships among themes are signalled and can be deduced by the way in which the themes are embedded in sentences and contexts which include mention of other themes. For example, the following comment, made by Teacher G in the context of a discussion on lesson planning, raises a possible hypothesis about the relationship of 'student needs' and 'success in learning'. (This example is discussed in more detail in Chapter 6.)

G: I'm convinced that the more the teaching responds to the needs of the student, the more motivated the student is going to be, and the more motivated and successful he's going to be in his learning.

Several types of discourse were analyzed to make hypotheses about such themes. The examples provided below are designed to indicate the intertwined nature of descriptions of what happened and 'naturally occurring' evaluative comments about what happened.

One type was the discourse produced in the background interviews about the subjects' experiences in learning and teaching situations, and in particular language learning and teaching situations. For example, in the background interview Teacher A described the importance of different teachers she had as a language learner:

A: ... I didn't mention this in my educational background, but I did study languages, a few different ones and some with more success than others, and it had a lot to do with the kinds of teachers that I had ... and those teachers had a lot of influence on my wanting to teach initially ... I realized which teachers I enjoyed taking courses with and felt that I made a lot of progress with, and which I didn't,,, so that's one thing that influenced my decision to teach and the kind of teaching that I think is good.

She later described a good teacher she had, "very personable, very energetic" and "the atmosphere that he created was something that I thought was very positive", and related this to her progress in that course. In contrast

A: ... I had a terrible Spanish teacher when I took my Spanish course, and he's also a model for me, one not to follow. He went very much by the book, page by page, reviewing because people were asking constantly so that we never got very much past the second chapter of a book of I don't know how many chapters and we made no progress. It was very dull and very little explanation, just, you know, do the exercises ... .

This 'Spanish teacher' recurred as a label – a kind of metaphor – later in making evaluative comments about her evolving abilities as a teacher:

A: I felt that I didn't know very much about what reading was and what happened when someone read and I felt that was the weakest part of my teaching. I just really didn't know what to do with my students and when I followed my textbook I felt like my Spanish teacher ... I felt that I was following along and doing the exercises and I know that I was supposed to be improving their ability to predict things and inferencing and stuff like that – I knew the skills that we were supposed to practice but I really didn't know how it was going to help their reading.

A second type of discourse in the data was the on-going interviews which described what happened in the previous lessons and what the plans were for upcoming lessons. For example, in an interview in which Teacher E links the last lesson with her upcoming one, the concepts of 'quiz', 'threatening', 'review', 'practice', 'strategy' and 'learning from context' are all themes which occur in different linguistic contexts in this and other interviews, and which allow hypotheses to be made about Teacher E's course structure, her planning procedures, her interpretive procedures and the coherence underlying her beliefs, assumptions, knowledge and actions.

E: ... when I left the last class I thought a bit more about the quiz and I knew I wanted to give them a quiz although I don't want this to be a serious thing/I don't want it to be threatening. All I want them to do is to review their affixes ... and I also want to go on with the practice of strategy we've been talking about, learning from context. So those are two things that I wanted to do and I decided that at the end of last class.

A third type of discourse was the discourse that occurred in the classroom as part of the videotaped lessons. For example, Teacher D made this comment to her class as she handed out some articles and gave instructions about an upcoming assignment. In this comment, phrases such as "should be able to", "main point", "supporting points", "do a good job", "up to you" and "tools" are related to concepts which are frequent themes in her discourse.

D: You should be able by now to analyze the article, to look at all the paragraphs, figure out what the main point is, figure out what the supporting points are. If you really want to do a good job, you should make a skeleton of the article, but it's really up to you. You've got the tools now to do this. Okay. So you do it on your own ... .

A fourth type of discourse was the taped commentary made by the teachers while watching the videotape of the lesson they taught. For example, Teacher B made this comment while watching the videotape of his lesson, a comment which reflects the theme of overpreparing for lessons (described in more detail in Chapter 6) which occurs frequently in the interviews.

B: I didn't close that [activity] off because I didn't have time. I went over by ten minutes what I had anticipated this activity to take. You know I was going to say it's partially because I wasn't familiar enough with the article. I had read it a couple of times and had gone through basically what I thought was the structure of it. But on the other hand I don't feel that badly about that because I feel the more time you spend on doing that work yourself the more reluctant you are to give it to the students, you've got your own ideas then and you will try to bash those in.

A fifth was the logs that the teachers kept, either in the form of a narrative or in the form of a chart. The teachers were free to keep these logs, intended to fill in the gaps between interviews, in whatever format suited them best. One teacher even tried a taped log – describing on tape what happened. Teacher E wrote a comment in one log that foreshadowed her view of learner autonomy:

E: I like the idea of trying to end activity or a session with a summary of what happened during the session – a bit of a conclusion maybe. I think I should get students to do this for themselves rather than me doing it for them.

A sixth was the written notes and lesson plans that the teachers made in preparing for their normal lessons, which gave another means of determining how the teachers perceived structural units of the teaching, and of determining what aspects of planning occurred when.

Although the data analysis was described above in terms of stages, in practice there was a constant moving back and forth between the data and the evolving 'construction of an understanding'. Each fresh look at the data led to a further evolution in the construction; and with each change in the construction, the data became fresh again and new relevant issues, comments, and relationships became apparent. The most vivid example of this was provided by the transcript of Teacher C's lesson, which the researcher examined (for an upcoming conference presentation) without having analyzed any of the other data for Teacher C's course. In the margin, I wrote "Not much here!". However, months later, when looking at it again after having become very familiar with Teacher C's transcripts, I could not believe I had written that comment, as every utterance seemed laden with significance, and previously invisible relationships to other utterances were suddenly clearly apparent. In addition, the construction of the understanding was helped by enforced periods of incubation. At one point I had to let the whole study drop for a 12 month period, after which the resolutions to several what had seemed insoluble conceptual problems were suddenly very obvious.

The overall attempt was to come to what Gumperz and Herasimchuk (1972:81) called the "situated meaning of a message" or, as they describe it, "its interpretation in a particular context". The interpretation, in this case, is of the classroom messages situated within the context of the teaching situations in which the teachers were taking part.

Validity and the research methodology

The data collection methodology

There are a number of potential issues to be raised in considering the validity of the collection and analysis of the data and the presentation of the results, with regard to the research questions being posed. These research questions relate to the structure of classroom events, of the teachers' processes of planning, and the teachers' interpretive processes. These questions are all viewed through the 'lens' of the teachers' perceptions as represented in their verbalizations.

A variety of means to achieve triangulation to enhance the validity of the data to similar types of studies have been suggested in the literature (see, for example, van Lier, 1988; Herrlitz and Sturm, 1991). Below, I consider the dangers inherent in this type of study, and examine a number of ways to take them into account.

Although the attempt in the study was to intervene as little as possible, both in the overall teaching process as well as in the individual interviews, in order to elicit as much as possible a record of what normally transpires, it is nonetheless clear that what was studied was a classroom under observation, and interactions between teachers and the researcher clearly affected the evolution of the courses and teachers' decisions. The subjects noted instances when they felt that the activities required by the study affected their normal behaviour. In the analysis of the interviews and the transcripts, inconsistencies in behaviour that might be attributable to the study were also noted. This interaction of researcher and teacher has implications for the role of research in teacher development, and this topic is discussed in Chapter 8.

The research methods for data collection described above rely on techniques which elicit self-reporting and introspection on the part of the subjects. There are two major dangers of the kind of research which asks subjects to introspect and self-report in order to recount their actions and their motivations. The first is the possibility that the process of verbalization could alter the process we are interested in studying. The second is that the data resulting from the verbalizations of the subjects may not reflect precisely what was going on. These dangers have been downplayed by some researchers (Flower and Hayes, 1980; Hosenfeld, 1979) and stressed by others (Cooper and Holzman, 1983). Mehan, Hertwick, Combs and Flynn (1982) conclude, for example, that this method of 'stimulated recall' strikes a balance between "fidelity to and control over the spontaneity of the original situation".

Ericsson and Simon (1980) and Cohen (1984) have explored the issue further, and delineated circumstances in which this kind of research method provides data which cannot be obtained by observational techniques used alone. It is clearly the case that in several fields which have become fertile areas of research employing a variety of research methods (including the composing process and miscommunication), an initial surge of insights and hypotheses was set off by introspective and ethnographic methods such as those outlined here. The authors (such as Cooper and Holzman) who stress the dangers, suggest not that such research methods be abandoned, but rather that researchers take into account these dangers both when carrying out the research and when making claims based on the results.

For example, Verloop (1989) restates Yinger's (1986) argument that the videotaped replay is not the original situation, but only 'related' to it. This is an important point to keep in mind in terms of this study. However it is also worth noting that the focus of the present study was not to track the teachers' moment-to-moment classroom thinking, but rather to determine the perceptions underlying their teaching in general. As a result, the discrepancy between their actual thoughts in the classroom and their insights about their teaching as they see it on videotape (or about their planning and classroom decisions stimulated by the videotape) is less crucial than in studies that have used this method of data collection to reconstruct teachers' classroom thinking.

As suggested above, the investigation is based on three specific methods having some characteristics of an overall ethnomethodological approach. This reflects an important characteristic of the approach: that of observing the planning and decision-making process as it naturally occurs in its regular contexts; intervention on the part of the researcher was intended to elicit observations and not restrict or guide behaviour. There are instances on the tapes where this intention was not always entirely successful. Several of the teachers commented at some point during the study that the interaction with the interviewer had some effect on their behaviour.

The effects can be categorized into three types: (1) those resulting from carrying out such a study as a whole with teachers as subjects, (2) those resulting from asking specific questions in the interviews, and (3) those resulting from videotaping the lesson. In the first case, having to keep track of their behaviour may have made some teachers feel that they had to be more organized (and less spontaneous) than they would otherwise be, and may have inhibited their more natural planning tendencies. In addition, the constant discussion of their behaviour may have made the teachers more insightful about their course and their students than they would otherwise have been, causing more evolution in teachers' thinking and behaviour than would otherwise have occurred. In the second case, specific questions asked by the interviewer, and the manner in which they were asked, may have resulted in answers more connected to the interview situation than the teaching situation being studied. In the third case, the videotape machine in the classroom may have made teacher and students more self-conscious and restrained than they would otherwise have been. I will comment in more detail on each category below.

1. Differences in teacher behaviour caused by the study as a whole

Differences between the behaviour surfacing as a result of the study and the usual or desired teacher behaviour (such as being more organized, or less spontaneous) seemed eventually to lead to a realization of this on the part of the teacher, and to some commentary on this effect. We attempted to take this into account by noting instances in the data where the study seemed to affect teachers' behaviour and verbalizations. As in any observation study, however, we can not be entirely sure in what ways the 'observer effect' influenced the data collected.

However, from the analysis of the data through the course, each teacher's 'natural tendencies' gradually became clear. These tendencies turned out to be extremely powerful, and after a lag, quite evident in the data. When circumstances (the interviewer's questions, or the process of interviewing itself, or institutional circumstances surrounding the organization of the course) contradicted these tendencies, the teachers signalled their discomfort through 'hotspots' (explicit and implicit) in the interview data. These hotspots gave a strong indication of the subjects' 'normal' behaviour; however they were evident as hotspots only after a lapse of time. This indicates the importance of the longer term study in getting a more valid picture of what the momentary processes were. For example, Teacher B, as he was describing his plan for an upcoming lesson two weeks into the course, said:

B: ... it's funny I/ perhaps because of this study that you guys [the researchers] are involved in, I've tried to be more prepared than I usually am, and I find that I'm less organized. You know what I mean? I'm making a conscious effort to prepare things more systematically and as a result I feel less organized. I feel like I'm trying to do too much in a space of time. Usually the way I would teach/ ... it's difficult to say that you can do x amount of material in an hour because if the students want to talk about it or if they want to go off on a tangent that's interesting to them ... I can't see pedagogically why you wouldn't want to ... .

This expression of discomfort was found to be consistent with issues and concerns expressed throughout the course relating to institutional curricular constraints and the teacher's philosophy of planning.

In another example, Teacher H, after a week of the study, said:

H: You asked me if I thought it (the study) was having a big effect on me, but only/ not in terms of getting me to do things, but just making me paranoid,,, so I decided on Thursday that I would refuse to be paranoid ... I don't know why I was feeling paranoid. I wasn't having a good week, and I decided to go back into my/to teach in my usual way, as I did on Friday.

In this case, the teacher had become somewhat self-conscious ("paranoid") about her teaching because of the interviews, but only became aware afterwards that she was teaching differently, and brought it up in a subsequent interview. It was only at this point that she became able to assess more consciously whether or not her behaviour was what she considered 'normal'.

It is probable that teacher awareness, reflectiveness and insightfulness were enhanced by the study. However, these effects were not critical to the validity of the study since 'degree of insightfulness' was not a teacher characteristic being assessed as such. The fact that several teachers commented that they were more insightful about their teaching due to the discussions does tell us something about teacher change: that talking about the details of one's teaching can be a factor in encouraging change to happen. This aspect is discussed further in Chapter 8.

2. Differences in teacher responses caused by the interviewer's questions

In terms of the questions asked, the ethnographic part of the study involved the initial interviews and the on-going interviews with the teachers throughout the term to elicit what they were doing, and what they thought about what they were doing. As noted above, certain ethnographic precautions were taken to elicit stories, and not to bias the data (although it is recognizable in the data that the researchers' abilities in these areas improved with experience).

This reason for eliciting stories was based on the assumption that it is possible for individuals to utter belief statements which they feel they should utter (or even believe) which are not consistent with what they do believe (i.e. monitored speech occurs not just at the levels of syntax and phonology, but also at higher levels of meaning in discourse). In such cases, we might find hotspots or inconsistent beliefs.

As Edgerton and Langness (1974) states, there may be a discrepancy between what people say and what they do:

As the fieldworker observes and participates, he becomes aware of the complexities and contradictions in what people say and in what they do. What people say is right and proper and is referred to as 'ideal culture', and these ideals, or values as they are sometimes called, are an important insight into how and why people behave as they do. Yet the fieldworker will also discover that many people do not behave as their ideals would have them do. This behaviour is also important not only because it points to the realities rather than the ideals of life, but because it can give insights into areas of change or tension in the culture. (1974:31)

This notion of 'hotspots' – areas of tension between what people say and what they do, or what they say and do on different occasions – is relevant not only to the question of possible future changes (a point which is discussed in detail in Chapter 9), but also to the question of interviewer interference in the data elicitation. There are a number of examples in the data of leading questions which limit the possible responses of the teacher. In cases like this it is extremely important to examine the response critically, for signs that the subsequent verbalizations of the teachers are being guided more by the interview setting than the teaching setting they are reporting on.

In some cases of blatant leading questions, even the subject noticed:

I: You said you were going to do this with the groups. Would it not be maybe a better idea to talk to the class for a few minutes first?

E: You're putting words into my mouth.

Other cases were much more subtle. One of the important areas of concern is the imposition of the interviewer's use and interpretation of particular terms. For example, in the following exchange, the interviewer (I) asked a leading question, first imposing a particular term, 'syllabus', then imposing a refinement of the teacher's term, before allowing the teacher to refine the meaning in her own words. Somewhat later in the interview, the teacher, perhaps feeling that it had been adequately defined, also began to use the term 'syllabus'.

I: Will you actually, at any point in the next few days, uh, actually sit down and plan a syllabus?

E: That is what I am going to do. Uh, perhaps syllabus is not the right word for it, uh, although a syllabus could be just a description of activities/

I: /a general description/

E: /yes, yes, uh. However, I/the planning I'm going to do is listing these general things and trying to think of activities that go along with that, I will try not to be too specific and I don't get tied down by that.

The subsequent evaluation of the data attempted to take such uncomfortable moments, or 'hotspots' into account, and to focus on the subject's elaboration of his or her choice of terms.

On the other hand, it is also unnatural to ask questions as if there is no implicit shared knowledge at all. There are cases in the data where the interviewer asks for a degree of detail or blatantness that is abnormal, and this is also evident in the response. It is a fine balance, and one which is learned through experience. Later interviews are better in this regard than earlier ones, both in the naturalness of the conversation, and in the amount elicited. There are also many examples in the data of questions which are open-ended and allow the subject relative freedom to pursue a teaching-based answer and not an interview-based answer. For example:

E: ... it actually worked nicely in pairs as well although I like the feeling of the group[work] because a lot of things go on there that I really value.

I: Like what are the things that you value?

E: A lot of it/ for example for the kind of activity I'm going to do today if I put them into groups and I only give them one [work]sheet and have a recording secretary as opposed to everybody writing down their own things, that gets them more involved in the discussion. If I get everybody to write [on their own worksheet in pairs] they get worried, they get caught up in writing, putting things down into words and sentences and stuff like that and the focus is away from where I want it to be.

3. Differences in classroom processes caused by the videotaping

With regard to the videotaping, the teachers in general claimed that the videotaping had little effect on the classroom processes. Several teachers, nevertheless, considered the videotaped lesson somehow 'atypical', as illustrated by Teacher E's response:

I: Did you have any perception of either you or the class being different because I was there than it would be normally?

E: I thought it was very unobtrusive. I thought/ the machine and stuff is very small. I forgot you were there. I really did. I don't think the students/ maybe in the second class when we used you in a way [to contribute a native speaker opinion], they probably were more aware of you being there, but in the first class I think the students probably forgot as well. So I believe that particular class would have been the same way whether you were there or not. However, I don't think that it was like the regular class, the kind of class that I usually give, with that particular group anyway, because they weren't all there. There was a slightly different feeling. I noticed that but it didn't have anything to do with you being there. It was something else.

It is not clear whether this is an indication that the process of videotaping did have an effect, or whether teachers are wary of being 'rubricized' (Maslow, 1968:126), and of having generalizations made about their teaching on an insufficient sample. There may also be social reasons related to the carrying out of the interview which would encourage the teachers to downplay the effect of having a camera in the classroom (the learners' view was not elicited in this study), and we have to accept some level of 'observer effect' on the classroom data and attempt to triangulate it with other types of data. Ultimately it is important to retain a constructively sceptical attitude about the conclusions drawn.

It is evident when looking at the transcripts that the skill of the interviewer in all types of data collection improved as the study progressed (the period of data collection lasted one year), producing longer and more natural narratives in later cases. This is evidenced for example by the researcher's frustrated scrawl beside a section of an early transcript that looked more like a game of 'Twenty Questions' than a narrative: "Why didn't I just ask her to tell me about any

experiences learning a second language that were significant to her???"
In addition, some teachers had a knack for relating long anecdotes
while others answered the questions very briefly. As a result, some
interviews and some subjects produced a great deal more data than
others. It was not possible to judge unambiguously whether or not
some subjects were more insightful about their teaching processes than
others, and if so whether it was these teachers who had more to say.
As a result I attempted to take verbalizations at face value and avoid
judging the data of some as more valuable than that of others. The
caution with which the data was treated depended more on the context of the interviewer's particular prompts, as noted above. In this
regard, it is important to note as well that the data for analysis
included not only the teachers' verbalizations, but also the interviewers' verbalizations.

In addition, the types of questions pursued in greater depth also
evolved 'emically' as the study progressed. For example, after Teacher
B had expounded at length about his 'philosophy' of spontaneous
planning, more questions to Teacher A (who was being tracked
concurrently) of the type "When did you decide to do that?" became
evident in the data.

Validity and the analysis of the data

There are also a number of dangers inherent in analyzing narrative
data to specify the perceptions of the subjects. These must be taken
into account in the presentation and discussion of the results.

In the analysis of the statements by teachers that made up the data in
the interviews, logs and taped commentary on the videotaped lessons,
an attempt was made to have the patterns and categories emerge from
the data (in the tradition of Emig, 1971, and Dias, 1987, and as noted in
van Lier, 1988:16), as opposed to using an *a priori* set of categories
related to theoretical approaches to teaching as a basis for examining
the teachers' assumptions. However to some extent, implicit *a priori*
assumptions on the part of the analyst will inevitably exist. In order to
minimize them, the following heuristic was used as a guide in the analysis. Each expression (by a teacher) of the factors related to a decision, of
strategies used for planning, or of important concerns or issues reflecting
underlying beliefs was taken as a hypothesis. Further instances of similar
points were taken as support for the hypothesis or suggestions of a new
or refined hypothesis. Particular care was taken when beliefs and
assumptions were implied, because what they imply could be what they
imply to the researcher, based on his own beliefs. In these cases, the
researcher looked for evidence that these implications corresponded to
or were inconsistent with beliefs expressed elsewhere and in other ways

in the data. A goal of the analysis was not just to identify beliefs, but rather to characterize the relationships operating among them.

In analyzing course and lesson structure, the teacher's categorizations were used wherever possible, as well as the teacher's labels for these categories. For example, although different teachers used the term 'theme' in a similar way – to relate to a high level organizational unit that usually covered several lessons – they based the themes on a range of concepts. Some teachers used the term 'theme' to refer to a unit based on a content area, others to units on strategies or functions, and so on. In analyzing the data, an attempt was made to identify what the term meant to each teacher according to the data.

In addition to using the teachers' verbalizations as a basis for hypothesizing the meaning of terms, formal markers were also sought in the interview data and in the videotaped lesson to hypothesize the boundaries of structural units. For example, in responding to a question in one interview, Teacher E categorized an activity (in which the students made a quiz for each other) into three parts, and then relabelled one of the parts, and categorized it into further subparts. Again, corroboration was sought in other sections of the interview, and in other data (such as the teacher's lesson plan).

I: How long did it take?

E: It took the whole time. I mean the whole quiz, preparing it, taking it and correcting it.

I: I'm just asking about preparing it.

E: Making up the quiz? It took about / with me coming in and talking about the quiz and then them doing it and going from one group to another and all that it took about half an hour.

When these formal categorizations were not evident, the intuitions of the researcher and colleagues were used. As practising teachers, it can be said that we have 'member's competence' (this term was suggested by Charlotte Linde, personal communication), in the sense of being members of the same professional community as the teachers being observed. Although this has the advantage of providing a member's understanding of the issues and the language used to express these issues, there is also the danger of assuming that another teacher's use of a term is equivalent to ours. Therefore, an attempt was made to unravel and take into account the teachers' perceptions and their ways of verbalizing them, following Kelly's (1955) advice (but not using Kelly's Repertory Grid). For instance, particular attention was paid to how the teachers verbalized concepts and what they opposed them to, in order to avoid jumping to conclusions about how technical terms were intended.

No attempt was made to validate the categories through inter-rater reliability measures for several reasons, both pragmatic and philosophical. First, what emerged as the most important aspects of the analysis was not the specifics of the categories themselves, but rather the structuring of the relationships among them, which emerged gradually as the analysis and the description of results proceeded. Secondly, I would argue that there is a theoretical difficulty associated with looking for inter-rater reliability in a case like this. If we consider training of raters to be required (which we do since the 'member's competence' of a teacher is required), this implies that one possible reason for disagreement among raters is inadequate understanding of what is being looked for, or, in other words, inadequate training. When what is being looked for is subtle enough to require training, the implication is that the more training, the greater the understanding of what is being looked for, and the greater the reliability. The ultimate case of an understanding of what is being looked for, and therefore of reliability, is having identical raters – or a single rater. This is not to say that input and discussion from colleagues about methods, categories and relationships did not or should not play a role. The on-location interviewers listened to and summarized each interview for 'salient issues' before carrying out the next one; and these notes were used as a check on the themes posited as relevant by the author. However, a formal reliability measure was not carried out in this study, and, as noted above, the arbitrariness of the analysis was countered by the focus on relationships among factors rather than the factors themselves, by appeal to teachers' formal categories, and by the presentation of examples and data to support the generalizations made.

One type of triangulation would have been of great interest – to contrast different views of the researchers and the teachers (and perhaps even with individual learners) by letting each participate in the drawing of conclusions from the data (a variation on a type of triangulation described by van Lier, 1988, and suggested by Freeman and Allwright, personal communications). This would have entailed a discussion of results and categories emerging from the analysis with the subjects themselves to see if these results and categories 'resonated' with their own understanding of their behaviour. This type of validation would include the perceptions of the subjects not only as data but also as part of the process of data analysis. This was not formally done for primarily pragmatic reasons – the time lag between the data collection and analysis was so long that any such 'resonance' would have been diminished and a further process of re-interpretation would occur, involving a whole new set of data and a new set of relationships in the data (across time). However, several of the teachers have had a chance to hear presentations of aspects of the results at conferences and in lectures. They informally indicated that the information presented was consistent with what they remembered, but also noted that they had in some ways changed since then. It can be said, then, that the teachers described in this study no longer 'exist', both in the sense that the representations here are the researcher's hypothetical constructs, and in the sense that the teachers who were the subjects of this study have evolved beyond what is described here.

Throughout this volume, specific results and generalizations are exemplified by excerpts from the transcribed data. In some of these cases, the aspects of meaning of the teachers' verbalizations being focused on are obscured when all the hesitations, pauses, restarts and asides are included in the example. As a result, I have altered the examples in the following ways. In cases where asides and false starts are not relevant to the point being made, they have been ellipted, and the ellipsis, no matter how long, indicated by three dots: ... . In cases where the pronoun referents may not be obvious from the excerpt, they have been specified between square brackets: [ ]. Although there is a danger that the alterations to the data could give a false impression of the meaning of the verbalizations, there was also a danger that the exact rendering would do the same or at least make the meaning difficult to discern. The intent in the rendering of the examples was to make the meaning that was evident in listening to the tapes as clear as possible, and to use several examples to back up the generalization.

In making the transcriptions themselves, the following rules of thumb were used. Clear sentence junctures are indicated by periods. Other syntactic junctures not accompanied by a pause are indicated by a single comma (,). Short pauses (approximately a second or less) are indicated by a double comma (,,), and all longer pauses, no matter what the length, have been indicated by a triple comma (,,,). Cases where the speaker or another person interrupts the anticipated syntax are indicated with slash (/). The teachers were assigned letter names (Teacher A, B and so on) rather than pseudonyms, with the risk of being 'dehumanized', to avoid the connotations that names seem to carry.

Conclusion: generalizability of results

There are of course also dangers in case studies in terms of the generalizability of the results to other situations. In the most narrow sense, this research is on eight ESL teachers who were under study. For the reasons discussed above, the results cannot be entirely true of even those teachers. It is also important to note that the teachers who were the subjects of this study were teaching in a particular kind of cultural and institutional setting, and so the results can only be generalized with caution to ESL or second language teachers in other settings. For various other situations, for example, foreign as opposed to second language teaching settings, settings where the students are children rather than adults, settings where the curriculum is strictly imposed by the institutions, settings where the teachers are not virtual native-speakers of English, and indeed, settings where teachers do not keep track of their behaviour throughout the term, the results reported here should be seen only as possible hypotheses, ones which may or may not be consistent with actual practice. In summary, this study is primarily a study of ESL teaching which could be seen as having some relevance for language teaching in general. It may have something to say about teaching in general, and it could also be looked at as a study in 'applied cognitive science'. However, these links are more tenuous and such speculations lie outside the scope of the study.

However, there is in any case an important epistemological question related to replicatability, validity and generalizability regarding what is found in the data and who finds it. An analyst may discover evidence for certain findings (for example, relationships among beliefs) that a teacher may be completely unaware of, or perhaps loath to admit. On the other hand, the way the analyst interprets the data is clearly in the light of his own theoretical constructs (which may not be entirely con-scious). This is an important issue in this study. The notion of validity which underlies this study is not based upon generalizability of results to other settings, but rather on a more dynamic notion of 'resonance' to individual readers of the study who process the resulting discussion according to their own interpretive processes (this notion of resonance comes from Freeman et al, 1991), and look for their own coherence. In other words, if a study can be seen to be one 'turn' in an on-going professional discourse (as Reither, 1985, has suggested), in this case on the subject of language teaching, then the reader can (and undoubtedly will) have the opportunity to participate in 'dynamic triangulation' by comparing the results presented here with her or his own experiences, and by seeking to understand the differences. Subsequent research will provide a better triangulation not if it tries to replicate this study identically (which as we know from the literature on research itself, rarely happens anyway), but if it uses other means of determining whether these results can contribute to the on-going 'construction of understanding' of language teaching.

3 An ethno-cognitive model of language teachers' decision-making

As discussed in Chapter 2, this study uses methodological and analytical techniques which have evolved in the areas of ethnography and cognitive science (and the overlap between the two areas). From ethnography comes the notion of the study of culture and the discovery of the values of a culture or subculture and their conventions for communicating those values during their normal daily activities (Garfinkel, 1967). The field of ethnography also inspired the choice of research methodology for the elicitation of the data. From cognitive science comes the notion of cognitive processes underlying (i) the procedures for planning and carrying out 'normal daily activities' and the processes of interpretation used in those activities. The evolving field of cognitive science has produced a number of concepts which are basic to the model (developed below) used to provide a framework for the analysis and interpretation of the data in this study. This attempt to graft the two fields was inspired greatly by the work of Agar and Hobbs, who have been working on combinations of ethnography and artificial intelligence. However, the precedent for this type of cross-fertilization was already set in Frake's (1968) article entitled "The ethnographic study of cognitive systems". In addition to the above-mentioned two fields, the fields of linguistic analysis and discourse analysis form an important basis for the study in that they underlie a notion of how language and discourse are structured to represent and convey meaning.

This chapter first describes ways in which this study might be considered an ethnographic study of teachers. Then it provides a description of the areas of cognitive research which are particularly relevant to the teachers' decision-making processes – including processes of planning and processes of interpretation. Finally, the chapter describes the concept of 'coherence', which has been used in ethnography, artificial intelligence and discourse analysis, and uses it to tie these strands together. The discussion culminates in a model which is used in subsequent chapters to 'construct an understanding' of the practice of the eight teachers from the data. The concepts described in this chapter have been increasingly used in the educational literature of the past two decades; the remainder of this volume focuses on their application to the context of language teaching.

The ethnographic study of teachers

This study has a tradition of anthropological, ethnographic and ethnomethodological research which feeds into it. Anthropology and ethnography involve the study of 'tribes' and their cultures. Ethnomethodology as described by Garfinkel is the study of everyday life and the way language is used by a members of a culture to represent the world to themselves and to others in normal patterns of communication. This notion provided the impetus for treating ESL teachers as a 'tribe' or subculture with shared behaviours, shared language and shared understandings of the concepts referred to by that language, and also for researching the 'normal daily activities' that are characteristic of that subculture.

The culture of language teachers, then, involves a set of basic issues around which their beliefs and actions fill a particular spectrum. They share a common vocabulary of language teaching, including terms such as 'proficiency', 'grammar', 'cloze' and 'input', and such phrases as 'information gap activity', 'communicative approach' and 'it's like pulling teeth' – although, as with any culture, the precise understanding of what is referred to by such terms will vary. They also have common concepts of appropriate behaviour patterns related to particular social situations, for example the classroom, the teachers' meeting, the after-class student consultation, the resource room browse, the hallway gossip, and so on. Of course, as within any culture, there are related subcultural groups, and related larger cultural groups. For example, a particular group of teachers (who may describe themselves as 'progressive') may have their own subset of shared understandings and responses (for example, unstated assumptions about how to respond to students who say "we want verb tenses") that operate within the larger set of shared understandings of language teachers, who in turn share certain understandings with teachers in general. But all would nevertheless agree that they fall into a culture of teachers, and that their particular assumptions and behaviour are related in important ways to the larger or traditional culture (even as a reaction against it).

There is also a relationship between the study reported here and ethnographic research in terms of 'participant observation'. Although this study is not strictly participant observation (the author was not actually participating with the subjects in the course), the author is nonetheless a member of the culture of language teachers (and has 'member's competence', i.e. an ability to interpret teachers' statements within the range of meanings normal to the language teaching profession), and ask questions like "What did you do today?" and "How did it go?" in a way somewhat like a colleague might.

Although it is perhaps technically not an 'ethnography' or an 'ethnomethodological study' (it uses methods which are not strictly ethnomethodological), this study is nonetheless trying to get at some of the same aspects of the subculture: the way members of the 'tribe' of language teachers use language to represent what they are doing and how they communicate it (or miscommunicate it) to others. However, this study is not ethnographic in that it does not attempt to describe that shared culture and processes among groups; rather it focuses on processes within the individual. This gives the study a more cognitive focus.

A cognitive model for the study of language teachers

A model of language teachers' decision-making processes needs to include three essential elements. The central core of such a model is what we observe in the classroom: decisions being carried out as classroom actions and events. By projecting forward to planned future lessons, we can focus on the planning processes by which future events and actions are chosen and organized. By projecting backward from the classroom events to previous lessons, courses and other relevant experiences in the life of the teacher, we can focus on the interpretive processes, including background knowledge, assumptions and beliefs, by which these classroom events and actions are understood and evaluated.

The field of cognitive science, an important area of literature related to this study but lying outside the fields of language teaching and second language acquisition, has elaborated a number of these concepts over the past several decades. However, many of its themes and findings have not been reflected in the literature on language teaching. By synthesizing the most influential of this work, we find a basis for a framework or model which fits our requirements. The description below includes a step-by-step visual representation of the overall model. It is important to emphasize that any two-dimensional sketch of a complex set of concepts and relationships is bound to be to some extent helpful and to some extent simplistic. I am using the set of diagrams here as a heuristic to demonstrate how the crucial elements in this study have been central concepts in the field of cognitive science which have evolved historically, and to demonstrate how the present study builds on this tradition. They are not intended to be an empirically testable model. The terms I have chosen to use in this synthesis, of the myriad of possibilities, are ones which occur quite consistently throughout the literature, and ones which appear to have relatively common referents when used by different authors.

Plans and action

The evolving theoretical work on plans and action discussed below gives us a theoretical rationale for studying teachers' decision-making behaviour in terms of plans and intentions or goals. The making explicit of variables such as those mentioned below provides a framework for looking at the more specific case of language teachers' planning. Examination of the data from teachers in the process of planning their courses can show whether similar factors are at play in the less formal ill-defined circumstances in which teachers plan. The combining of the findings of the work in artificial intelligence with the findings regarding teachers' planning can give us insights and information which are relevant to the development of professional knowledge for teaching. The planning process is one aspect of the overall process of classroom teaching/learning that we know little about, in particular the relationship between planning and what goes on in the classroom.

The development of the concept of planning

A pioneering work on the relationship between plans and action in the field of cognitive science is a book by Miller, Galanter and Pribram (1960), entitled *Plans and the Structure of Behavior*, which, in an era still primarily devoted to stimulus-response conceptions of behaviour and learning, began to elaborate the inside of the 'black box' of the mind by exploring notions of understanding, goals, intentions, knowledge and plans. Miller, Galanter and Pribram cite work evolving out of older philosophical and psychological discussions by a number of authors such as Bartlett (1932) and Lewin (1951) in pointing out the importance of the broader context rather than the narrow stimulus in explaining behaviour.

The evolution from the stimulus-response conception of behaviour to one which included an initial conception of goals and background knowledge such as that described by Miller, Galanter and Pribram is illustrated in Figures 3.1, 3.2 and 3.3.

The authors introduced the notion of a 'central control room'. This central control room plays a role in understanding events and in guiding behaviour via a 'cognitive map of the environment', which includes representations both of background knowledge and of intentions or

S (E) ──────────────► R (A)

S = stimulus (or E = event)
R = response (or A = action)

Figure 3.1 Stimulus–response model

S (E) ──────────────► BB ──────────────► R (A)

S (E) = stimulus (or E = event)
R (A) = response (or A = action)
BB = 'black box'

Figure 3.2 Stimulus–response model with the 'black box'

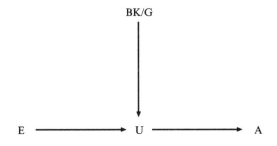

E ──────────────► U ──────────────► A

E = event
A = action
U = understanding
BK = background knowledge
G = goals

Figure 3.3 Inclusion of background knowledge and understanding of event

goals (see Figure 3.3). In doing this, they implicitly introduced a 'top-down' conception of behaviour, also an important part of the early work in cognitive psychology done by Ausubel (1963), and evolving out of the Gestalt tradition (Köhler, 1947). This conception contrasted with the 'bottom-up' conception suggested by behavioural notions of conditioned responses to individual stimuli.

The authors note that although these previous attempts to look at the larger context to explain behaviour attributed importance to understanding (in the sense of the overall mapping in the control room), nevertheless a gap remained between understanding and action. By this they mean that no mechanism had been developed to explain how the two are linked. To do this, they introduce the notion of

E = event
A = action
P = planning
U = understanding

Figure 3.4 Inclusion of planning mechanism

'plan', and develop it so that it plays a central role in their model of behaviour.

Figure 3.4 illustrates the inclusion of the notions of the understanding of events and the planning of subsequent actions in the model.

Planning and feedback

The major focus of their book is to develop characterizations of plans and the process of planning. Planning occurs when an individual's 'current state' is different from a 'desired state' or goal. One important element which is characteristic of a plan (and thus of the planning process) noted by Miller, Galanter and Pribram is a 'central feedback loop' which links this goal state and current circumstances. In other words, there is a constant monitoring of the current state and the difference between it and the goal state, which affects subsequent choices in behaviour. A second important characteristic is that these comparisons of goal states and current states can be embedded. In other words, the ultimate goal state can be broken down into components, creating subgoals, and sub-subgoals, and producing a hierarchical organization of goals. A third characteristic is that plans include a meta-planning function. In other words plans can include plans for making plans. When this characteristic is taken together with the monitoring and feedback characteristic, it means that it is possible to monitor and evaluate plan-making, and thus develop improved plans over time. An important aspect of Miller, Galanter and Pribram's work is the assumption that people are always operating according to plans, even when non-verbalized, ill-defined and perhaps contradictory (in the latter case, the authors speculate, plans can become a source of frustration and even serious illness).

The inclusion of the feedback loop has an important consequence for our conception of the process by making it recursive: one action leads to another through the processes of planning and understanding or interpreting. At this point we can see more clearly that the individual plays an active role in the process, both in the sense that there is an active interpretation of the event and in the sense that the action taken becomes part of the event that starts the next cycle. The notion of the

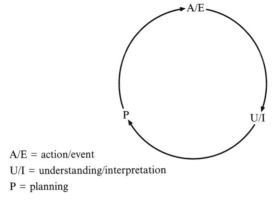

A/E = action/event
U/I = understanding/interpretation
P = planning

Figure 3.5 Inclusion of planning mechanism with feedback loop

feedback loop also points out the relationship between 'action' – with its connotation of intentionality and goal orientation – and 'event' – with its connotation of lack of intentionality. An individual's action is a part of a larger event which results, and which also includes others' actions and unforeseen consequences. Figure 3.5 illustrates the inclusion of the feedback loop and the notion of the recursiveness of actions and events.

Further work in the area of artificial intelligence elaborated these characteristics of plans and planning. Sacerdoti's (1977) work produced a computer program (called Network of Action Hierarchies, or NOAH), which was explicit enough to model the planning process including several crucial characteristics suggested by the Miller, Galanter and Pribram work. In Sacerdoti's system, knowledge units are schemata corresponding to actions at different levels of generality, and thus generate a plan hierarchy rather than a single level plan. Each action schema includes information about consequences of the action and about conditions that are prerequisites for the action. Plans are formed by comparing goals to consequences of actions, and then by choosing actions whose consequences match the goals and whose prerequisites are satisfied in the current situation or become goals that can be achieved by further planning. In a sense, then, subgoals act as a means of achieving goals, and become part of the plan.

As a result, plans are represented as a partially ordered sequence which specifies high-level steps and then the major components, and suppresses details until they can be considered in their proper context. The ordering of the sequence of steps is tentative, and made explicit only to the degree that is necessary before moving to the next level of planning. In addition, the planning system includes a mechanism that enables the monitoring, evaluating and adjusting of plans on a continuous basis.

An important aspect of Sacerdoti's 'procedural network' for representing hierarchical plans is the inclusion of both 'declarative' and 'procedural' knowledge bases.

> Knowledge about a task domain is supplied in two ways. Knowledge about the actions that may be taken in the domain is specified in procedural form. Knowledge about the particular state of the world in which a particular problem is to be solved is given to the system as a set of declarative expressions. In addition, knowledge about the ways in which actions and subplans can interact is embodied within the system itself. (1977:2)

By including both types of information, procedural and declarative, the system is able to criticize and modify its plans. Sacerdoti found that the organizing principles which create the structure of the planning process are relatively simple, yet support a performance of surprising complexity. (See Figure 3.6.) These characteristics – the feedback loop, plan hierarchies, the relationship of goals and means, the tentativeness of detailed planning, and the procedural and declarative specification of knowledge – are crucial notions in the description of the processes in teaching, and are elaborated in this context in Chapters 4, 5 and 6.

Top-down and bottom-up planning

One characteristic of the early theoretical discussions of planning (perhaps as a reaction to previous behavioral models) was an emphasis

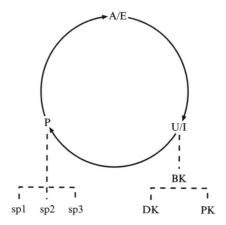

A/E = action/event   BK = background knowledge
U/I = understanding/interpretation DK = declarative knowledge
P = planning   PK = procedural knowledge
sp = sub-plan

Figure 3.6 Elaboration of background knowledge and of hierarchical planning

on top-down directionality – there was an implication that lower level planning is controlled from higher level structures and not the other way around. However, subsequent work by Hayes-Roth and Hayes-Roth (1979) studied the process in the context of planning a series of errands, and developed a model of interacting knowledge and decisions that includes a bottom-up component, which they call 'opportunistic planning', where higher level plans are formulated and evolve in response to decisions made to take advantage of 'opportunities' at lower levels of the process. Similarly, research by Flower and Hayes (1980) on the composing process noted the interrelationships among decisions made in planning, where choices made about one component of the plan imply constraints on other components.

Figure 3.7 illustrates the inclusion of both the top-down conception of planning, and the bottom-up conception of opportunistic planning.

Planning in language production

In the anecdote at the beginning of the book, I noted that from watching what was being said and done in two classes, it seemed that in the two classes, different 'things' were happening on an underlying level. In order to explore this idea further, we need to be able to look at the relationship between what is said in classroom interactions, and the higher level plans around which the course is structured.

By looking at the ways in which teachers' classroom verbalizations

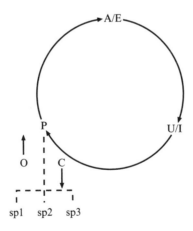

A/E = action/event
U/I = understanding/interpretation
P = planning

sp = sub-plan
O = opportunistic planning
C = constraints

Figure 3.7 Two-way elaboration of planning to include 'opportunistic' planning and constraints of prior plans

are related to their plans, we can establish a link between planning in verbal behaviour and planning in the broader sense of accomplishing educational objectives. We can also determine to what degree carrying out the plan is a top-down instantiation of the plan, or a bottom-up development of the plan through lower level opportunities. This work is also relevant to teacher planning in the classrooms – the 'on-line decisions' that a teacher makes, including the verbalization of instructions, explanations and feedback. Through this work with teachers in the context of the course they are teaching, we can see how language production (utterances) in the classroom is linked to longer term plans and goals. Although investigating the planning of speech production in teachers' verbal behaviour (at a sub-utterance level) is not part of this study, examining the relationships between verbal behaviour and higher levels of structure in the teaching/learning process is. The research described below illustrates the importance of hierarchies in this type of planning.

With advances in psycholinguistics, an important subset of this research on planning developed almost independently: how planning occurs in the production of language. Although there is an obvious connection between planning in speech production and the more general (or 'higher level') planning discussed above in terms of the accomplishment of more general goals through verbal behaviour, the main interest of psycholinguists was how the verbal behaviour, or speech production, itself is planned and carried out: how people plan and formulate their utterances. This area was introduced by Miller, Galanter and Pribram, using Chomsky's (1957) *Syntactic Structures* as a basis, and followed up by Minsky and Papert's (1972) work in artificial intelligence using Halliday's systemic grammar as a basis. These discussions assume hierarchical relationships in language, where immediate constituents (starting with articulatory features) combine to form functionally meaningful units at a higher level (phonemic, then morphological, then syntactic).

Clark and Clark (1977) link the higher and lower levels of planning in verbal behaviour with what they term a 'production hierarchy', made up of discourse plans, sentence plans, constituent plans, and an articulatory program. They treat the goals that the verbal behaviour is intended to accomplish also as hierarchical, starting with local communicative goals and moving to global ones. Faerch and Kasper (1983) deal with plans and strategies in foreign language communication, presenting a model based on Clark and Clark's (1977) discussion of planning in speech production. According to Faerch and Kasper, there are two phases in the process: planning (consisting of goal, planning process, plan), and execution (plan, execution process, action). In both phases, monitoring and feedback take place, allowing for repair or self-correction (similar to the feedback mechanism suggested by Miller, Galanter and Pribram, and the one by Sacerdoti). They describe the production plan as being designed to achieve a goal through verbal action, and as based on an analysis of the given situation and its resources with respect to the goal (1983:23). Faerch and Kasper also discuss the characterization of the first phase in intellectual behaviour as comprising "the orientation about the situation and the conditions of the task", which they see as the first phase of the planning process, and which as we will see later has an interesting parallel to teachers' planning. Implicit in this discussion is the assumption that there are important similarities between linguistic behaviour and non-linguistic behaviour, in this case similarities between the planning mechanisms. In this study, these similarities allow us to relate local levels of classroom verbal behaviour (production and comprehension of utterances) to broader levels of course structure and pedagogic goals.

This aspect of the model is illustrated in Figure 3.8.

The aspects of the model discussed above are connected through the process of planning to the relationship between present actions and

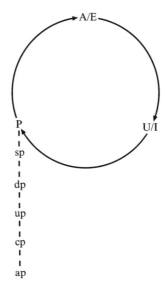

A/E = action/event   dp = discourse plans
U/I = understanding/interpretation   up = utterance or sentence plans
P = planning   cp = constituent plans
sp = subplans   ap = articulatory plans

Figure 3.8 Inclusion of planning in verbal behaviour and speech production

events (both verbal and non-verbal) to future actions and events. The next section deals with the relationship of present actions and events to past actions and events: the prior experience and background knowledge that the individual brings to bear in coming to an under-standing and interpretation of these present actions and events.

Interpretation of events: background knowledge and belief systems

In the past two decades, there has been a great deal of work in the area of the cognitive processes underlying text comprehension and the roles that an individual's background knowledge structures and beliefs play in this. The discussion below reviews this literature as it applies to our framework. It then extends the concept of background knowledge structures in two important ways: to include belief systems and working assumptions, and to include the interpretation both of verbal texts and non-verbal events.

There are three levels at which the discussion of theoretical concepts below is relevant for this study of teaching and decision-making. First, it allows us to take into account the different legitimate ways in which both learners and teachers are interpreting events (including language events) in the classroom. If teachers are making plans and carrying out decisions to transmit learning through language, then our understand-ing of how ideas are transmitted and perceived by the participants is important in how we analyze classroom processes. How teachers, in particular, interpret the events and actions that occur in a classroom will clearly influence subsequent planning processes, and affect what subsequently happens in the classroom in the following moments, days and weeks.

Second, it allows us to treat teachers as comprehenders, whose views about language teaching and what goes on in the classroom are influenced by the ways in which they have interpreted what they have learned as they became teachers. Teachers themselves have been encul-turated according to these processes of transmission and interpretation through language (reading articles and texts, and listening to lectures, talking to professors and peers, as well as experiencing classes), and, as with any listener or reader, comprehension processes will play a role in a teacher's interpretation of texts that she reads or hears, including curricular information and directives, discussions of peda-gogy and methods, research reports and articles, conference presenta-tions, things other teachers say, and even specific terminology.

Third, it makes us aware that in interpreting as researchers what is happening, we are also using the same processes. This phenomenon needs to be taken into account in the discussion of the research and the results.

Background knowledge structures

In the mid-1970s, the developing field of artificial intelligence and the developing sophistication of computers led to some notions that have been particularly helpful in modelling the role that background knowledge plays in behaviour, especially in cognitive behaviour and in language behaviour. One important notion in the modelling of plans and behaviour is that of 'background knowledge structures'. In order to take appropriate action, people need to understand; and to understand they need knowledge about the world and specifically about the situation they are in. Researchers have attempted to characterize the nature and form of that knowledge, how it is organized, and when and how it is brought to bear for understanding to take place. The emphasis in this research, then, is on the understanding and interpretive aspects of the process as opposed to the planning aspects emphasized by the previous authors mentioned, and the main thrust of the work shows the role of the individual in actively shaping the 'meaning' of the events observed. This section discusses a selection of theoretical and empirical studies which illustrate our developing appreciation of the role of background knowledge in understanding.

There have been a number of terms used in the cognitive literature to represent the concept of background knowledge. Miller, Galanter and Pribram (1960) discussed "world knowledge plus self knowledge" (upon which plans depend) using the term 'images'. This term had been used earlier, for example, by Bartlett (1932) and in Gestalt theories of perception. The idea that the individual takes an active role in interpreting incoming sensory data was an important psychological basis for the distinction between phonetics and phonology developed in the Prague School of Linguistics and represented by Bühler's 'Prinzip der abstraktiven Relevanz' (1965:42). The term 'schema' was used in 1932 by Bartlett in a study referred to frequently in cognitive literature starting with Miller, Galanter and Pribram (although, as Rumelhart, 1980, notes, the term goes back to Kant, 1781/1963, while Bartlett himself attributes the ideas to Head, 1920) to account for how background knowledge structures influence the understanding of stories. This concept has been an important one in cognitive research and theory since the mid-1970s.

The inclusion of background knowledge structures playing a role in understanding, planning and action can be diagrammed as in Figure 3.9.

However, as Schank and Abelson (1977) noted, it is a big step from asserting the importance of background knowledge to describing the elements of this knowledge and the role these elements play. An important part of the empirical and theoretical work in the evolving field of artificial intelligence was to refine and explicate this notion to

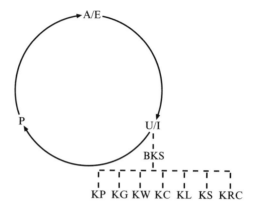

A/E = action/event
U/I = understanding/interpretation
P = planning

BKS = background knowledge structures
KP = knowledge of plans
KG = knowledge of goals
KW = knowledge of the world
KC = knowledge of the culture
KL = knowledge of the language
KS = knowledge of scripts
KRC = knowledge of relevant contexts

Figure 3.9: Inclusion of notion of structured background knowledge and its different facets

provide the background knowledge structures that would allow a computer program of planning to operate (for example, in the work of Sacerdoti).

Schank and Abelson (1977) introduced the notion of scripts, along with related notions of plans and goals, in order to specify the details of the most appropriate knowledge structures that underlie understanding. They distinguish general knowledge of the world that enables us to understand texts in terms of general human needs and the means of fulfilling these needs (for example, we do not need to inquire why someone has asked us for a glass of water), from specific knowledge that is used to interpret events that we have experienced many times (for example, what we are to say when a waiter comes to our table). This latter knowledge is termed knowledge of 'scripts'. When someone tells a story they make reference to a script which enables us to interpret the story even though many details are missing. Schank and Abelson give the example of the restaurant script – for example we understand about waiters, menus and ordering even if it's not mentioned explicitly in someone's story about a restaurant. Scripts are also organized hierarchically; and so a restaurant script includes such variations as fancy restaurants and fast food restaurants as components. We know then that "I ordered a cheeseburger and took it to the park" makes sense in a way that "I ordered a coq au vin and took it to the park" does not.

They note that people can adapt to scripts that they have never heard before, making sense of new connections among sentences by using their knowledge of plans and goals. Part of our understanding is also an understanding of the nature and intentions behind plans and goals – i.e. purposive behaviour. For example, to make sense of the text "Willa was hungry. She took out the Michelin guide", we need "knowledge of a generalized plan or group of plans that can connect the goal state to a set of possible actions to realize that state" (1977:71). We also need to understand that the plan is based on a goal, and that goals can be stacked in a hierarchy with many levels. When a higher level goal is blocked, a lower level goal with many similar attributes may be substituted, or an even lower level goal may be chosen which prepares the ground for the prerequisites for achieving the higher level goal.

Bruce (1980) elaborated this notion further. "Viewing an action as a step in a plan provides an organizational schema for events in the social world ..." (1980:367) and helps us to structure and understand what we see, hear and read. Understanding plans is a critical part of understanding actions, but it has to be done inferentially. To understand a story (with purposive actors), one needs to link together actions at different levels. In order to interpret actions at the intentional level, one needs to be able to recognize a plan, a sequence of actions leading to a goal, and to recognize the actions of others in terms of their presumed goals (i.e. why people do things), and to have knowledge about how actions are typically carried out, what typical sequences are, what the preconditions and outcomes are, as well as about the roles and attitudes of the actors (1980:370). Conditions change as sequences of actions unfold, and previous actions play a role for subsequent ones (1980:373).

Agar developed a number of terms which relate to notions evolving in cognitive science and artificial intelligence. Agar (1982:788) uses 'schema' as a general term to include the notions of goals, frames and plans. He uses 'strip' to refer to a social act, recognized as a unit by the nature of its characterization in the informant's language (or an interview, or a document – any bounded phenomenon against which ethnographers test their understanding of the group). Schemata are by definition anchored in the strips which they are abstracted from. "In cultural anthropology, there has always been an emphasis on the development of higher order schemas that show the relations among several lower order ones" (1982:791).

Rumelhart and Ortony (1977) described schemata in terms of memory: "Schemata are data structures for representing the generic

concepts stored in memory. They exist for generalized concepts underlying objects, situations, events, sequences of events, actions and
sequences of actions ...", and "the network of interrelations that is
believed to generally hold among the constituents of the concepts in
question" (1977:101). The notion of structure and interrelations is
important here. It implies that bits of knowledge are interrelated in
structured ways, and thus that one piece of knowledge cannot be
changed without having effects on other pieces of knowledge in the
system. The growth of knowledge, then, implies a reorganization of the
system – a reanalyzing of wholes into various components and a resyn-
thesis in a new form. They identify four characteristics of schemata: (i)
they have variables, (ii) they can be embedded and recursive, (iii) they
can vary in abstraction and (iv) they represent knowledge. Schemata
include 'generic knowledge' (knowledge we have of concepts abstracted
from the memory of particular events), and 'episodic memory' (memory of events we have directly or indirectly experienced) and their relationships. We interpret events and remember not the event but the
interpretation. We may only remember fragments of this interpretation;
and to recall, we may need to reinterpret. Anderson (1977) characterized schemata as abstract structures containing a 'variable', 'slot' or
'placeholder' for each constituent element in the knowledge structure,
which are 'instantiated' in any particular case of comprehension, allowing that situation to be made sense of. "Abstract schemata program
individuals to construct concrete scenarios" (1977:429).

    Rumelhart (1980) summarized the evolving thinking on the role of
schemata in cognition: schemata play a role in perception, comprehension, remembering, reasoning (problem solving) and learning, which
are all, according to this view, goal directed activities. All of these
depend on an individual's construction of an interpretation of an
event, object or situation. "The total set of schemata we have available
for interpreting the world in a sense constitutes our private theory
of the nature of reality". Rumelhart described a schema as a personal
theory, and comprehension or interpretation of events as testing a
theory: "... the fundamental processes of comprehension are taken to
be analogous to hypothesis testing, evaluation of goodness of fit and
parameter estimation" (1980:38). If the schema fails to fit a situation,
we can ignore (or misread) the data, or restructure the schema. He
gives the following passage to illustrate an evolving restructuring of a
schema as the reader interprets the situation, tests the interpretation,
and perhaps reinterprets it during the process of reading the passage.

Business had been slow since the oil crisis. Nobody seemed to want anything elegant anymore. Suddenly the door opened and a well-dressed man
entered the showroom floor. John put on his friendliest and most sincere
expression and walked towards the man. (1980:43)

Rumelhart illustrates how people arrive at a clear interpretation of this passage, not all at once, but gradually. "As sentences are read, schemata are activated, evaluated, and refined or discarded." As readers describe what they think the passage is about while reading through it, "a remarkably consistent pattern of hypothesis generation and evaluation emerges." The first sentence is usually interpreted to mean that business is slow because of the oil crisis, and leads to a hypothesis about selling cars or gasoline. The second sentence leads to a weakening (although not necessarily a rejection) of the latter hypothesis, and a more elaborate representation of the first to include luxury cars as an element. The showroom cue allows a more particular representation of the selling hypothesis, the last two sentences allow the slots of potential customer and salesman to be filled.

There is, in addition, a paralinguistic aspect of the process of comprehension included in Rumelhart's definition. He discusses the notion of interpretation of events, indicating that actions and events are viewed as meaningful, and are interpreted in terms of background knowledge structures. For example, we can make sense of the following sentence only because we accept that events have meaning, and that they are interpreted: "He didn't come today; that means he's not interested." In this case, we understand that the referent for the word 'that' is the interpreted event of 'his not coming'.

Underlying people's actions and behaviour are their interpretations of the situations they are in, including the texts and events which occur in those situations, and the prior texts and events they have experienced which are related to those situations. There is a dynamic interaction between schema and event. The schema influences the perception of the event; and the perception of the event influences the evolution of the schema. This is a crucial aspect of our examination of the interpretation of classroom actions and events, including, but not limited to, verbal actions and events.

The concept of background knowledge structures has played an important role in theories of text comprehension. Anderson and Ortony (1975) stated that reading includes both top-down and bottom-up processing, and that a top-down interpretation may develop which is contradicted by the precise information in the text. Anderson, Reynolds, Schallert and Goetz (1977) demonstrated that much is 'read into' sentences, supplied by the reader (and the reader's knowledge of context and culture).

Carrell and Eisterhold (1983:556) also used the term 'schemata' to refer to "previously acquired knowledge structures". This concept involves background knowledge that has been integrated into a structured organization with a systematic working relationship among its different aspects. It implies that a new item of knowledge will cause a restructuring of the knowledge that was previously there. To illustrate how we use background knowledge to understand a text, and to supply implicit aspects of the events being referred to by the text, Carrell and Eisterhold used the example (discussed in Rumelhart, 1977:267, and originally taken from Collins and Quillian, 1972) of the sentence 'The policeman put up his hand and stopped the car'. In order to make sense of this sentence, the reader brings to bear on this text a number of unmentioned aspects involving a driver of the car, and the relative positions and roles of the officer and the driver, the braking system of the car, and the means that the driver uses to activate the braking system, as well as probable motivations for the actions by the police officer and the driver. The reader uses this information to make sense of the text and of what comes next in the text. The world knowledge activated to make sense of this text is then contrasted by Carrell and Eisterhold to the world knowledge used to make sense of another occurrence of the same sentence occurring in a larger text from which the reader knows that the car is an empty car rolling down a hill and that the policeman is actually Superman in disguise. (Consider, for example, the types of information needed by a visitor to the United States from a culture which does not include knowledge of Walt Disney nor North American values and lifestyle to explain the bumper sticker "I owe, I owe. It's off to work I go.")

Anderson and Schiffrin (1980) indicated that the process of understanding the meaning of words in context is also an aspect of interpretation in light of background knowledge structures. They stated that meanings of a word are like 'family resemblances' – there are characteristic features but no necessary defining features. Each word has an infinite number of instantiations or 'meanings in use' (1980:333). This phenomenon is illustrated by Anderson and Ortony's (1975) and Anderson's (1977) example of the word 'eat', normally considered to have a straightforward meaning abstracted from any instance of its use. However, in phrasal contexts such as 'eat steak', 'eat soup' and 'eat an apple', the word includes in its meaning the suggestion of different utensils, and different actions of the lips, tongue and teeth. When the context is extended to a sentence and an agent is considered, "observe what happens to 'eat' and also to 'steak' in 'The executive ate the steak', 'The baby ate the steak' and 'The dog ate the steak'. Each of these sentences gives rise to different suggestions about location, circumstances, manner, instrumentality, and antecedent and consequent conditions" (Anderson, 1977). The meaning of a word in any particular instantiation will thus depend on the comprehender's knowledge of the world. In describing the process of comprehension, they say that any instantiation may be deep or shallow: any narrowing of the meaning of a term in a particular case counts as an instantiation.

This implies that in any particular case of communication, the degree of instantiation will depend on what is needed to satisfy the demand of the situation. Consider, for example, how many ways (including deep or shallow) a learner's comment "I don't understand" could be interpreted.

These notions led to a shift in our understanding of comprehension of texts as not being exclusively a bottom-up process, i.e. not a process of decoding the language from the smallest items to a complete understanding, but rather an interactive process of matching expectations from context with data on lower levels. A number of empirical studies, a selection of which are presented below, have examined the role of background information on the comprehension and recall of texts, and have contributed to the development of these theoretical concepts and the understanding of the processes they represent.

Bransford and Johnson (1972) and Bransford, Stein and Shelton (1984) carried out a series of studies in which subjects were given different amounts of contextual background information to determine what effect the contextual information had on comprehension and recall. One such text was:

Sally first tried setting loose a team of gophers. The plan backfired when a dog chased them away. She then entertained a group of teenagers and was delighted when they brought their motorcycles. Unfortunately, she failed to find a Peeping Tom listed in the Yellow Pages. Furthermore, her stereo system was not loud enough. The crab grass might have worked but she didn't have a fan that was sufficiently powerful. The obscene phone calls gave her hope until the number was changed. She thought about calling a door-to-door salesman but decided to hang up a clothesline instead. It was the installation of the blinking neon lights across the street that did the trick. She eventually framed the ad from the classified section. (1984:32)

Subjects who were told before reading the text that this text was about Sally's attempts to get her neighbours to move scored much higher both in comprehension and in recall than subjects who had no information about the context, and also higher than subjects who got the contextual information after reading the passage. This was interpreted as meaning that the prior information provided a framework or schema within which the details of the text made sense and could be remembered.

Anderson, Reynolds, Schallert and Goetz (1977) compared the recall (both free recall and scores on multiple choice questions) of subjects who were grouped according to their academic backgrounds and areas of interest and familiarity. The subjects all read the following passage:

Every Saturday night, four good friends get together. When Jerry, Mike and Pat arrived, Karen was sitting in her living room writing some notes.

She quickly gathered the cards and stood up to greet her friends at the door. They followed her into the living room but as usual they couldn't agree on exactly what to play. Jerry eventually took a stand and set things up. Finally they began to play. Karen's recorder filled the room with soft and pleasant music. Early in the evening, Mike noticed Pat's hand and the many diamonds. As the night progressed the tempo of play increased. Finally a lull in the activities occurred. Taking advantage of this, Jerry pondered the arrangement in front of him. Mike interrupted Jerry's reverie and said "Let's hear the score." They listened carefully and commented upon their performance. When the comments were all heard, exhausted but happy, Karen's friends went home. (1977:372)

In addition to the free recall, subjects answered multiple choice questions such as:

What did the four people comment on?

a) The odds of having so many high cards.
b) The sound of their music.
c) The high cost of musical instruments.
d) How well they were playing cards.

The two groups of subjects, one of which consisted of music education students and the other of physical education students, tended to remember the above passage, which could be interpreted as a card game or music rehearsal, and a second passage that could be interpreted either as a prison breakout or a wrestling match, according to their backgrounds and areas of familiarity and interest. The authors conclude: "evidence ... indicates that people's personal history, knowledge and beliefs influence the interpretations that they give to prose passages" (1977:376).

Steffensen, Joag-Dev and Anderson (1979) tested the hypothesis that culture-specific background knowledge affects the interpretation of texts. They gave subjects from the United States and India letters describing weddings in each of those countries. They measured reading time, had the subjects recall and write down everything they could remember about the descriptions, and answer some inferential questions about the descriptions. Each group read faster and recalled better the description of the wedding from their own culture. In addition, the subjects writing about the wedding from the other culture introduced distortions into their versions reflecting interpretations of the text which reflected their own cultural background knowledge. For example, a section of the letter describing the American wedding stated:

Did you know that Pam was going to wear her grandmother's wedding dress? That gave her something that was old, and borrowed too. It was made with lace over satin, with very large puff sleeves and looked absolutely charming on her. (1979:20)

One of the Indian subjects restated this as:

She was looking alright except the dress was too old and out of fashion. (1979:21)

On the other hand, the description in the Indian wedding of the dowry was recalled incorrectly by some of the Americans, for example, by changing the wording from the "agreement about the gifts to be given to the in-laws" to the "exchange of gifts", and by identifying the gifts as "favours" given to the attendants by the bride and groom:

There was some discussion of what the favours would be but they settled on silver cups for the men and saris for the ladies and toys for the children. (1979:21)

In addition, readers in each of the two groups included in their own descriptions information about the wedding from their own country which was not explicitly included in the text, indicating their background knowledge of traditions regarding rings, family roles, and the reception.

Recent work on human information-processing, called parallel distributed processing (PDP), has argued against the notion that higher level mental structures such as schemata are stored in memory. Attempts to implement models of the human information-processing system have found that large scale schematic structures are not flexible enough to adapt easily and readily to new situations and new configurations of events. In order to achieve this goal, Rumelhart, Smolensky, McClelland and Hinton (1988), propose mental building blocks at a much more micro level. In their view,

... schemata are not 'things'. There is no representational object which is a schema. Rather, schemata emerge at the moment they are needed from the interaction of large numbers of much simpler elements all working in concert with one another. Schemata are not explicit entities, but rather are implicit in our knowledge and are created by the very environment that they are trying to interpret – as it is interpreting them. (1988:20)

When input comes into the system, a set of mental units is activated, creating a network based on the satisfaction of certain constraints related to that input, and leading to a 'goodness of fit' with that input.

Certain groups, or subpatterns of units tend to act in concert. They tend to activate each other and, when activated, tend to inhibit the same units. It is these coalitions of tightly interconnected units that correspond most closely to what have been called schemata ... In those cases in which there are coalitions of units that tend to work together, we have a rather close correspondence to the more conventional notion of a schema. In those cases in which units are more loosely interconnected, the structures are more fluid and less schema-like. Often knowledge is structured so that there are relatively tight connections among rather large subsets of units. In these cases, the schema provides a very useful description. (1988:20–21)

According to the authors, the difference between the conceptualization of schema and that of 'micro-units' is that schemata, as such, are not stored in memory. What is stored, according to theories of PDP is "a set of connection strengths which, when activated, have implicitly in them the ability to generate states that correspond to instantiated schemata". In other words, although the advances in theoretical work in the area of PDP represent a major departure from our previous conception of the details of mental processing, the authors state:

Thus, the language of schemata and schema theories should be considered an approximation to the language of PDP. (1988:21)

In our discussion of the decision-making of ESL teachers, the specific *manner* of activation of structured knowledge is not at issue. However, *what* knowledge is activated and *how* it is used by teachers in making decisions about their day-to-day and moment-to-moment activities is crucial to our understanding of what teaching is. The weighting of different factors in the decision-making process of teachers, and the flexibility with which patterns of units of teaching are combined and adapted, makes the metaphor of PDP particularly appropriate to the discussion in the following chapters.

This discussion of patterns of connection is also raised by Bateson (1979) as a more general process:

The division of the perceived universe into parts and wholes is convenient and may be necessary, but no necessity determines how it shall be done. (1979:38)

In a footnote to this statement, Bateson elaborates in a way consistent with the principles of perception and interpretation in the theory of PDP:

Evidently, the universe is characterized by an uneven distribution of causal and other types of linkages between its parts; that is, there are regions of dense linkage separated from each other by regions of less dense linkage. It may be that there are necessarily and inevitably processes which are responsive to the density of interconnections so that density is increased or sparsity is made more sparse. In such a case, the universe would necessarily present an appearance in which wholes would be bounded by the relative sparseness of their interconnections. (1979:38)

This idea of more densely and sparsely connected units is an important one in considering how background knowledge structures change or evolve over time, and is raised in the discussion of teacher change in Chapter 9.

Belief systems

The work described above relates to the structuring of background knowledge – i.e. what a person knows that affects thinking, interpretation and planning action. There has also been some work on the structuring of what people believe – i.e. 'belief systems'. This notion of belief systems is also relevant to this study. Teachers 'interpret' a teaching situation in the light of their beliefs about the learning and teaching of what they consider a second language to consist of; the result of this interpretation is what the teacher plans for and attempts to create in the classroom.

The notion of belief system has been developed in an original way, one particularly relevant to this study, in the work of Linde (1980a, b, c). Linde characterizes a belief system as a "set of beliefs which is coherent, which is focused around some central issue, and which is not held by everyone in a given culture" (1980a:13). In her use of the term, it is a social system of beliefs shared by more than one person. Her work examined written texts in order to determine "how we display and negotiate our values and beliefs, how we demonstrate that we have acted in accordance with them, how we negotiate shared acceptance of a proposition, etc." (1980a:3). This is done through an analysis of the propositions in the text, and the presuppositions and implicatures that link them, in order to specify the beliefs that underlie the propositions. Linde exemplifies this with the following text, taken from a booklet on rape prevention.

The city attracts all kinds of people. Most of them are law-abiding citizens. But there are exceptions, and you have no way of knowing who is and who is not law-abiding.

In today's society, rape has emerged as one of the most serious crimes against women. In recent years, this crime has escalated at an alarming rate. For this reason, it becomes imperative that women realize the increasing potential danger to themselves from a rape attack. Rape is one of the most frightening and violent of all crimes against women. The experience of being raped is a shock from which the victim never completely recovers.

The most important thing to remember is that the rapist frequently plans his crime; he looks for the right chance and the easiest victim. Your best defense is to minimize his opportunity to attack you. Play it safe! (1980a:handout)

Linde specifies a number of implicatures inherent in the propositions of the text, for example, that 'all kinds of people' implies that some of these people are not 'like us', and by saying 'the city attracts all kinds of people' the text implies that these people are newcomers and not the original inhabitants. She posits a number of beliefs upon which these implicatures might be based, that:

1. rape is a problem of cities,
2. rape is committed by newcomers,
3. rape is committed by people who are not like us,
4. rape was once less of a problem than it is now,
5. rape is to be prevented by changing the behaviour of the potential victim,
6. rape is the problem of the woman as an individual, not of women collectively.

She notes that "these beliefs are coherent; they do not contradict one another, and they represent a recognizable position on the spectrum of positions on rape" (1980a:12). In this way, this written text represents 'a belief system'.

A belief system deals not only with beliefs about the way things are, but also with the way things should be; and a belief system includes "beliefs about values, that is about what ought to be the case". For example, "a particular belief in the area of language teaching might be 'A teacher ought to speak as little as possible during a lesson'" (Linde, 1980b:2). In her research, "belief systems have been represented as having a tree-structured organization. This is an attempt to capture the intuition that different beliefs may represent different levels of generality, and may be related via logical implication" (Linde, 1980b:2). Linde gives the following example:

Someone may hold the following two beliefs: 1) A teacher ought to speak as little as possible during a lesson. 2) A student learns by doing (speaking), not by listening. I would claim that these beliefs are related in the following ways. (1) is less general than (2). (1) and (2) are consistent with one another. Someone holding (1) must believe (2), but the opposite is not true. (1980b:2)

Linde's analysis of documents for the overt semantic structure, and for the system of covert values, presuppositions and beliefs about the world which underlie them, is based on a variety of concepts taken from linguistics and artificial intelligence. The semantic structure of written texts is often signalled by overt markers such as titles and headings, and by overt discourse markers such as 'first', 'second', 'most importantly', 'in conclusion' which function to mark parallel units of discourse, to 'push down' the discourse to subordinate semantic units, or to 'pop up' the discourse to higher level semantic units. The linguistic notions of presupposition and entailment allow us to specify the underlying propositions which must be assumed for a particular sentence to be interpreted. For example, the sentence "John stopped smoking" has the presupposition that John used to smoke, and the sentence "John killed Fido" has the entailment that Fido is dead (Linde, 1980c). Assumptions about the author (or speaker) and the situation of utterance can be based on our knowledge of 'speech formulas' – fixed phrases such as 'Gentlemen, start your engines' evoke an image of a particular speaker and situation of utterance. Similarly,

... a phrase like 'law-abiding citizens' evokes as its speaker someone who is either a member of a law enforcement agency, or has a strong identification with such agency. Speech formulas allow us to specify a 'default author' and a 'default intended use' of a text. (1980c:2)

In addition, the relationship between the author and audience may be marked by lexical choice and syntactic structure, and the amount of directness or indirectness in the text. This allows the audience to identify who the author wishes to present himself or herself as, and also to identify which arguments in the text the author wishes to be more closely identified with. Similarly it may be possible to identify points in the argument with which the author is uncomfortable being identified, either because of the nature of the content or because the argument is weak at that point. "Sudden increases in markers of distance indicate a problem point in a text, one to which the analyst should pay the closest attention" (1980c:2).

This relates to an important aspect of Linde's work in studying belief systems: the notion of 'hotspots'. It is at points in a text where there seems to be a conflict between what is stated and what is believed, that beliefs more clearly and less consciously appear. This notion is particularly important in the study of teacher beliefs where teachers (often in a subordinate power relationship with supervisors, evaluators, theorists, and researchers) may prefer to claim allegiance to beliefs consistent with what they perceive as the current teaching paradigm rather than consistent with their unmonitored beliefs and their behaviour in class.

Linde also describes the importance of the concept of evaluation in determining aspects of belief systems in the analysis of narratives:

Narratives are seen as divided fundamentally into orientational material (information about where, when, and why the events of the narrative occur), narrative material (the events themselves), and evaluative material (material which tells the audience what the events mean, and how they are to be understood). The evaluative material expresses the author's opinion of what the audience should believe about what is heard or read. Linguistic markers of evaluation include morphological choices such as 'one' or impersonal de-stressed 'you'; overt lexical markers of evaluation such as 'fantastic', 'terrible', 'the best part', etc.; iconicity of syntactic placement of evaluated items; use of negation as an indirect marker of the expectations in a given situation; etc. Because the evaluative structure of a text shows what the author wants us to believe, it therefore indicates what he himself considers to be important. (1980c:3)

An important aspect of Linde's discussion is that beliefs can only be hypothesized according to cues, and supported (but not confirmed) or contradicted by other cues. Even when the beliefs are overtly stated, they must be taken as hypotheses, because they may not correspond with what the author or speaker really believes, but rather with what they would like the audience to think they believe. However, when examined over longer texts, over longer periods of time and in different circumstances, structured patterns of beliefs clearly emerge.

As Linde notes, belief systems are part and parcel of our language, and are signalled by different aspects of our language. She states that the term 'belief system' refers to social structures (and therefore not to an individual's idiosyncratic network of beliefs), and, like language and culture, is negotiated and shared through interactions. With regard to the subculture of teachers, there is a dynamic interaction between socially shared (with groups and subgroups) and idiosyncratic systems – each evolving from and through the interactions. In this regard, what we see mirrors the evolution of language and culture in their broader sociological and psychological conceptions.

Knowledge structures versus belief systems

Abelson (1979) discusses the differences between knowledge systems and belief systems. He points out seven distinctive differences between knowledge systems and belief systems. Although none of these are defining features, taken together, he suggests, they provide an overall sense of a belief system.

1. Belief systems are non-consensual: not everybody agrees on the belief, and there is an acceptance of alternative beliefs around the same issue;
2. Belief systems often include a notion of 'existence', that something exists;
3. Belief systems are highly evaluative: states are considered as being good or bad;
4. Belief systems contain a high degree of episodic (anecdotal) material;
5. Belief systems have differing degrees of strength (i.e. strong beliefs);
6. Belief systems have unclear boundaries and a high degree of overlap with beliefs in other areas.

Abelson suggests that the features he notes make belief systems much harder to model in artificial intelligence than knowledge systems. However, in practical studies, the notion of belief systems plays an important role. For example, in the field of medicine, Dielman et al (1980) propose an 'HBM', a health belief model, which focuses on the current dynamics acting on the individual and postulates that the likelihood of an individual undertaking a particular health action aimed at preventing or curing some disease or condition will depend at least partially on the individual's perceptions and beliefs regarding his own health, the condition, and the cure; and it will not simply depend on the recommendation of the health professional.

From Abelson's discussion, it is clear that there is no qualitative distinction between knowledge systems and belief systems. He states that the more these seven features are present, the more we can think of the structure as a belief system rather than as a knowledge system. This blurring of the concepts of knowledge structures and belief systems is also reflected in the extensive work in this area in the literature on education and teacher cognition (which is discussed in detail in Chapter 7), and is relevant to the concept of beliefs, assumptions and knowledge (BAK) developed in Chapter 7.

Including the notion of belief systems in conjunction with knowledge systems gives us the diagram in Figure 3.10.

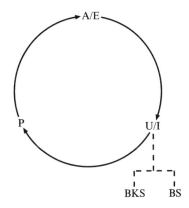

A/E = action/event   BKS = background knowledge structures
U/I = understanding/interpretation   BS = belief systems
P = planning

Figure 3.10 Inclusion of background knowledge structures and belief systems

Linguistics, discourse analysis and the study of language in context

In the areas of cognitive research described above – the process of planning, carrying out and interpreting actions – language and discourse play an important role. It is through language that an individual's plans and interpretations are labelled, represented and shared with others (whether in daily life or in experimental situations). The theoretical underpinning of the field of discourse analysis is that language use is a form of action. Conversely, in the practical area of teaching, the actions and events that make it up are primarily linguistic. In order to look at how the language which occurs in the classroom is related to the accomplishment of the teaching/learning process, we need to include two important concepts from the fields of linguistics and discourse analysis, the concept of context and the concept of function.

An important assumption of the field of linguistics is that language has structures which can be described independently of the mental processes of the users. Thus the traditional linguistic fields of phonology, morphology, and syntax developed as independent areas of study, with the object of study – language – idealized from particular contexts of natural occurrence (Lyons, 1968).

However, in 1935, Firth argued that:

the complete meaning of a word is always contextual, and no study of meaning apart from a complete context can be taken seriously. (1935, reprinted in 1957:7)

The notion of context, although not in the sense of Firth's "complete context", has always been a central aspect of the study of the functions and meanings of language. The notion of meaning was invoked in phonology to show how sounds, in the context of surrounding sounds, produce meaningful units of language (morphemes), and to deduce the phonemes of a language through substitutability for others in phonological contexts. In the study of morphology and syntax, the notion of meaning was invoked to show how morphemes function in the context of surrounding morphemes to produce words, how words function in the surrounding context to produce meaningful grammatical categories (for example, subject, or agency), and how these function in combination in particular ways with surrounding grammatical units to produce sentences. In all these cases, there is an important distinction between form, the description of the elements at any of these levels, and function, the way in which they combine with other elements in the surrounding context to produce elements at a higher level. This discussion is not meant to imply that the relationships are identical at all levels. Halliday (1961), for example, makes the opposite argument: that there are 'levels' (for example, phonology, morphology and syntax) and 'ranks' within levels (categories of organization within the level of syntax, for example). The point I wish to make here is only that the notions of form and function apply both across as well as within traditional linguistic categories such as phonology, morphology and syntax.

Firth's arguments were brought forth again by Coulthard in *An Introduction to Discourse Analysis*:

Firth urged linguists to study conversation for "it is here that we shall find the key to a better understanding of what language is and how it works". (1977:1)

Coulthard and other linguists and applied linguists were interested in examining how syntactic structures, such as sentences, function in combination with others in the context of surrounding sentences to produce discourse structures. Out of this study came a number of discourse categories (for example, 'act', 'move', 'exchange', 'transaction'). The notion of meaning was invoked to identify categories of intended meaning or 'illocutionary force', producing a classification of speech acts and rules for how utterances and sentences in continuous texts are related to each other.

Widdowson (1978) also distinguished between the relationship of formal elements in a text (sentences or utterances), and the relationship of the functions of those elements:

Where we can establish a propositional relationship across sentences, without regard to what illocutionary acts are being performed, by reference to formal syntactic and semantic signals, then we recognize cohesion ... Where we recognize that there is a relationship between illocutionary acts which propositions, not always overtly linked, are being used to perform, then we are perceiving coherence. (1978:29)

He used the following example to illustrate this meaning of coherence in discourse:

A: Doorbell.
B: I'm in the bath.
A: O.K.

It is by understanding that in this exchange, A's first remark functions as a request, that B's response is a reply to A's implicit request and functions as an excuse for not complying with A's request, and that A's second remark is an acceptance of the excuse and a statement of an undertaking to carry out the originally requested task, that we can make sense of this exchange. It is by looking at the functions of the formal elements in discourse in terms of the intentions of the participants that we make sense of it. Discourse analysis thus works at a higher level of idealization, looking at utterances within a context of surrounding utterances or exchanges.

Halliday and Hasan (1989) use the term 'coherence' to include the context not only of the surrounding discourse, but also of expectations, background and culture:

A text is characterized by coherence; it hangs together. At any point after the beginning, what has gone before provides the environment for what is coming next. This sets up internal expectations; and these are matched up with the expectations ... that the listener or reader brings from the external sources, from the context of situation and of culture. (1989:48)

By including the cultural background of the participants (in addition to the intentions or plans) in our formulation of coherence, we acknowledge that it is more than illocutionary force which makes an exchange such as the one above coherent. There are variables related to the background knowledge, assumptions and beliefs of the inter-locutors that connect what is being discussed to the larger cultural and situational context. When Widdowson's example was translated into Spanish to illustrate the notion of coherence in the context of a Mexican article on discourse analysis, it was rendered as:

A: Tocan. (Someone's knocking)
B: Me estoy bañando. (I'm taking a bath)
A: ¡Chin! A mi se me van a quemar las tortillas. (Darn. My tortillas are going to burn.)

(Castaños, 1984:23)

In other words, in the context of this article in a Mexican journal, the phrase "O.K." has been rendered by "My tortillas are going to burn." The translation of this text functioning as an exemplification in this context demonstrates coherence not only as a phenomenon related to 'making sense' in terms of illocutionary force (in which case the two phrases are equivalent), but also to 'making sense' in terms of cultur-ally appropriate and culturally relevant meaning (in which the trans-lated phrase is appropriate in the Mexican rendition in a way that would be considered odd in the English version).

At each of these levels of linguistic and discourse analysis, the term 'context' is usually considered to consist of the surrounding elements, and the term 'function' taken to refer to the relationship of an item to a higher level of structure. The term 'meaning', in parallel fashion, is taken to be the meaning of the item being considered at a particular level of idealization and decontextualization: the meaning of /pɪn/ ver-sus /bɪn/ or the grammatical versus semantic meaning of 'colorless green ideas'. These are meanings inherent in the language – meaning as denotation, which is of course an important element of what any language user knows – but idealized and decontextualized from a larger picture of the situation of use and of what is brought to bear in a participant's interpretation in that instance. Similarly, at the level of discourse, the notion of 'language in use' is an idealization of categories of speech acts (such as requests, for example) common to examples of language use at a particular level of decontextualization. The generalizations, patterns and rules coming from each of these lev-els of study are part of what a language user knows and an essential aspect of our understanding of how language works, and of how meaning occurs in particular instances of use; however, as noted by Firth, this knowledge does not account for the "complete meaning" in any instance of use.

In the study of language in classrooms, for example, what is important is how the language and the discourse are structured at yet higher levels to produce events that we can perceive and label as a 'course' of teaching. To arrive at this point we need a greater sense of how meaning is created and interpreted in yet larger contexts. The assumption underlying the preceding statement is that the gap between the (relatively) decontextualized verbal events described by linguists and discourse analysts and the completely contextualized instantiations of meaning used by the participants in the accomplishment of a course of teaching is structured and can be described.

This assumption, and a similar line of reasoning, has been also extensively pursued in the work of van Dijk (for example, 1977, 1980, 1981) and in his work with Kintsch (for example Kintsch and van Dijk, 1978). These authors posit the notion of semantic 'macrostructures' referring to a more global organization of discourse, which includes the type of discourse and the relationship among discourses. Their work is also concerned with relating sentence and sequence structures to macrostructures and discourse and, in particular, with how these relationships affect strategies of comprehension.

This notion of meaning within the structure of higher level contexts allows us to see the distinction between 'denotation' and 'connotation' as a spectrum rather than as two distinct components of meaning. This is an important point for our discussion of teachers' interpretive processes. This point becomes more evident when we note that, although the above discussion relates to the meaning of *verbal* events, which have been the focus of linguistic and discourse analysis, the notion of function also allows us to include *non-verbal* events in the discussion of meaning in context. This point has been developed in Sperber and Wilson's (1986) discussion of "conditions for relevance". All perceived events, including both verbal and non-verbal, can be interpreted as meaningful; and the meaning can be labelled and used in subsequent exchanges. Consider the sequence "I see Marc is absent today. That means he won't know about this assignment which is due next class. Danielle, could you give him this worksheet?" In this example, the word "that" refers to an event, albeit a negative one (someone's absence from class), perceived by the speaker and being interpreted as being meaningful. It is this interpretation which provides the basis for the subsequent sentence. This event (and its perceived meaning) is not contained and decoded linguistically as in the case of a verbal event. Nonetheless, the relationship of this event to the context in which it occurs would be the same as that of a verbal event such as Danielle saying "Marc is not coming to class today". The meaning of the non-verbal event is at the connotational end of the connotation-denotation spectrum. However, in an important sense it is the connotation – the situational interpretation of meaning – which is superordinate to the denotational or idealized meaning. Our understanding of this relationship allows us to make sense of a sentence like "He said he's not interested in her. That means he is interested." It is the context which allows us to interpret the narrower denotational meaning of the utterance "I'm not interested" as an event whose meaning in that utterance is the opposite of its denotational meaning. Although non-verbal events, and those at the connotational end of the spectrum, do not have a structure which is describable in linguistic terms, they can be said to be part of a larger structure of events that is interpreted and that guides behaviour.

The parallel between the semantic representation of social behaviour (including non-verbal events) and the semantic representation of linguistic structures (verbal events) has also been noted by Clarke (1983), in developing a more generalized "structural model of behaviour":

If, however, we are to consider the semantics of behaviour, the tendency for one sequence of behaviour to lead us to one set of inferences about the actors, while another behaviour sequence leads us to another, we shall have to consider the possible relations between the observed behaviour stream and the *semantic representation* which the observer erects from it. There may be a *deep structure* to social behaviour in the same way as there is said to be a deep structure to a sentence ... . (1983:16)

There are three problematic areas in determining how language becomes meaning in use, and these involve three aspects of context: (i) the context in terms of the surrounding elements in which the actions and events occur, (ii) the context in terms of the goals and intentions of the participants, and (iii) the context in terms of the background knowledge structures and beliefs which represent the participants' prior experiences. This brings us back to our model and the assumptions that underlie it. One assumption is that the contexts surrounding and 'above' the levels traditionally analyzed as language and discourse are also structured. The second is that the structuring is perceived actively according to the goals, intentions and background knowledge structures and beliefs of the participants. What we want to do is to elaborate on the teacher's perspective of (i) the structure of the events in the context of the course which gives those events meaning, (ii) the planning process within which those events have meaning, and (iii) the interpretive process which attributes meaning to the events, and then, finally, examine how these three aspects of context fit together to produce what the teacher calls a 'course'. It is these notions of context that bring us back to ethnography and the ethnographic notion of coherence. It is through the study of teachers carrying out their normal daily activities within the context of their course of teaching, their planning processes, and their background knowledge and beliefs, that we can look for the coherence in the decisions they make.

The concept of coherence and the overall model

The way all the elements of the model described above fit together – including the relationships among goals, plans and the interpretation of verbal and non-verbal events – is what in this study I have termed 'coherence'. As noted above, the term 'coherence' has been used extensively in the literature on discourse analysis to account for the way language elements are related to each other and to an outside context, and how a language user employs the knowledge of the way these relationships work to formulate and make sense of propositions. The term 'coherence' has been used in ethnography to describe the social aspects of 'making sense' in terms of belonging to a culture. In cognitive science and artificial intelligence, coherence refers to the psychological aspects of 'making sense' in terms of relating concepts: an important element of the work on comprehension described above relates to making sense of spoken and written texts – attributing meaning to them in light of what we know of the world, of people, of everyday scripts and people's goals and plans. The work of Agar and Hobbs (1982, 1983) has attempted to link these two aspects of coherence, the social and the psychological, and forms an important basis for this study.

Agar (1982:786) provided a description of coherence within an ethnographic framework, which includes a relationship between background knowledge and planning – i.e. how knowledge is reorganized in order to carry out a 'projected act'. Individuals have goals or intended purposes behind actions they carry out. They use plans to lay out the actions to achieve a goal. The plan includes the notions of a purposive actor with goals, operating in a specific world which constrains and is modified by an executed plan. The background knowledge involves generalized but flexible knowledge structures with variables that are filled in particular instances of their use and is encoded and restructured in and through language. Coherence is achieved when an individual makes sense of an observed event, seeing it as part of a larger goal-driven project or plan, in terms of background knowledge frames.

In applying the notion of coherence to ethnographic interviews and narrative accounts, Agar distinguishes among: (i) global coherence: relations among lower level events mentioned in the narrative, and a higher level 'overall picture' or 'global plan' in the narrative; (ii) local coherence: sequential relations making one event follow coherently from a previous one (where, as he notes, local coherence may be pursued by the narrator to the detriment of global coherence); and (iii) themal coherence: recurring content themes and implicit underlying assumptions inherent in the discussion but not related to local or global coherence. Themal coherence serves as a pointer from the specific text (with its associated textual goals, etc.) to the more general properties of the speaker's world, i.e. the 'relevant cognitive worlds' of the speaker.

An important aspect of the study of coherence and culture is participants' perceptions:

Rather than focusing on the way social scientists segment behaviour, perhaps the actors themselves have a working knowledge whereby they segment the on-going interaction. To the extent that they learned to do so, it must have been communicated to them as they learned the culture ... . (Agar 1975:42)

He suggests that the participants' working knowledge can be accessed through their representation of event structure. For example, in his attempt to understand the world of the street junkie, he learned the 'addict argot': the terms and sentences used by the junkies in the street culture, but says:

I remained confused about the overall meaning [in the "subculture of addiction"], partly because I did not understand the larger 'unit' of which the sentence was a part. (1975:43)

Agar's notion of coherence, which includes the actor's goals, is related to cognitive concepts implicit in Widdowson's (1978) discussion of the notion of illocutionary force (i.e. what is being done with what is being said) in discourse. As Widdowson notes, cohesion is the relationship among formal elements in discourse and coherence is the relationship of formal elements to their functions and the relationships operating between functions. The discourse notion of illocutionary force (or 'function'), implicitly includes the cognitive notion of goals and plans, which thus must be a part of what makes up coherence in discourse.

The notion of coherence is relevant to our study in a number of ways. First, it allows us to explore (in Chapter 9) how the notions of goals and plans in the process of planning and structuring a course (Chapters 5 and 6) are related to the notions of background knowledge and beliefs in the process of interpreting and understanding actions and events that occur in the course (Chapters 7 and 8). In addition, the discussion of form and function of elements in a hierarchical structure is a key aspect of the description of event structure in a course (Chapter 4).

Conclusion

The developments in cognitive science provide us with a model with three components: (i) the classroom events/actions, (ii) the planning that precedes these events and actions, and (iii) the understanding/interpretation that follows them. These are the central parts of the loop in Figure 3.5. In addition to the interaction among these components, there are interactions within each one (as described from a theoretical perspective above). Each of the components is structured (with subcomponents and relationships among the subcomponents), and each component proceeds and evolves through a number of processes. Understanding these structures and processes is essential to an understanding of second language teaching. This study, through the analysis of eight cases, is an initial attempt to extend our understanding of these structures and processes.

There are two important features implicit in the model so far that are crucial to the discussion of teacher decision-making in subsequent chapters. It is therefore important to make these features explicit. First, the model does not represent the hierarchical aspects of the process: it does not show how the interpretation of a particular event plays a role both in making decisions about immediate subsequent actions, and also in planning at other levels, for example immediate subplans or longer term superordinate plans. For this we need a more complex version of the model. After discussing the hierarchical aspects of the structure of teaching decisions/elements in Chapter 4, I will return to these further developments of the model in the discussion of the planning process in Chapter 5.

Second, there is an important distinction implicit in the pairs of terms used in the above model, specifically in the pair of terms 'action' and 'event' and in the pair of terms 'interpretation' and 'understanding'. The term 'event' implies something that happens to someone rather than being done by someone. In other words, there is the implication of passive reception rather than active production of a conscious or deliberate act. Similarly, in the pair of terms 'interpretation' and 'understanding', there is a parallel distinction. The term 'understanding' implies what happens to someone – a relatively more passive role – whereas 'interpretation' implies a relatively active role of the participant in shaping or affecting the outcome. Absent in the model is a parallel opposition for the term 'planning'. The term 'planning' implies an active engagement on the part of the individual in formulating future actions. However, an important facet of teachers' decision-making processes is expressed by the term 'expectation' – implying a relatively passive role of the teacher in affecting what will happen. In order to relate present processes to future lessons in the discussion of the planning process in Chapter 5, I will include in the

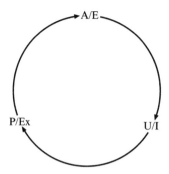

A/E = action/event
U/I = understanding/interpretation
P/Ex = planning/expectation

Figure 3.11 The three main components of the model

model both the concepts of 'planning' and 'expectation'. The model in Figure 3.11 includes this alteration.

I should note that these pairs of terms imply binary distinctions. However, it is clear from the way in which the words are used and the existence of other words, that individuals strive to fill the gap with a range of intermediate possibilities. For example, between planning and expectation there is prediction, which implies a more active kind of expectation on the part of the individual. Also, we can say "I understood that differently from you", which has the implication of a more active role of the individual in coming to an understanding. In the model, I simply wish to make it explicit that both ends of the spectrum should be included. The issue of deliberateness and consciousness is explored further in Chapter 5.

This model forms the basis for the analysis of the teaching process which is done in the following chapters. Chapter 4 elaborates the structure of the actions/events that make up the course that the learners experience. Chapters 5 and 6 deal with the teachers' processes of planning. Chapters 7 and 8 describe the processes by which teachers understand and interpret the teaching events, and how these interpretations feed back into further planning and subsequent events.

4 The structures of teaching: units and relationships in a course

The model developed in Chapter 3 contains three main areas: (i) the structure of the actions and events which occur in the classroom and which taken together can be said to comprise the course, (ii) the planning process through which the teacher plays a role in creating the course and provides input into the events which actually occur, and (iii) the process of interpretation by which these actions and events are understood and evaluated and then fed back into the planning process. Although these three aspects of the teaching are interwoven, they are nevertheless distinguishable. Hence, although a discussion of any of the three entails mention of the others, it is possible, for purposes of analysis, to focus on each of the three separately.

This chapter deals with what is usually considered to be the central aspect of teaching – the actions and events which occur in the classroom. Considered together, these classroom actions and events are structured in such a way as to make up a 'course', the largest unit of analysis in the study. In this chapter, I distinguish between the structure of the classroom events and the processes and procedures of decision-making that produce that structure. This chapter focuses not on the processes of planning and thinking that produce the course structure, but rather on the product: the resulting structure of the course itself. In order to explore the question of the structure of a course, it is necessary to explore the relationships between the actions and events that take place in the classroom and the larger context of the course that they comprise.

Although I referred to the course structure as a product – the outcome of the structuring process – there are processes of another sort which must be taken into account: the processes of interpretation that must have taken place in order to posit such a structure. As described in Chapter 1, there are two ways in which the problem of positing structures of teaching can be handled. One way is to attempt to establish an external framework to analyze classroom events, producing a classification of the types of events that occur. An alternative way is to examine the structures as they are perceived, interpreted and labelled by the participants. This type of analysis follows the example of Erickson and Schultz (1982) who use the perceptions of the partici- pants to determine what points in the continuous behaviour stream were regarded as especially salient and to posit the relationships among those events.

This study, then, instead of creating a framework based on class- room discourse alone and representing an external perspective, uses a *participant-centred view of course structure*. Since the role of the teacher is a particularly crucial one in determining the classroom actions and events that occur, this study focuses on the perspective of the *teacher*. In order to posit the structures linking the classroom actions and events to higher level course structures, the study uses, in addition to the videotaped classroom discourse, the on-going discus- sions of the course which occur in the regular interviews with the teachers, and in written documents such as the teachers' logs, notes and lesson plans. In the discussion below, in order to emphasize that the generalizations described are represented in the data of all the sub- jects, I have provided a number of verbalizations by different teachers to exemplify the structural aspects of the course.

A participant-centred view of course structure

Under normal circumstances, determining what a course 'is about' involves experiencing the events which occur as part of the course, and making some generalizations about the 'meaning' of those events. Such an interpretation takes place presumably on the part of each of the learners in a course – the ones at whom the course is targeted. Similarly, an interpretation of the course structure takes place on the part of the teacher. In the case of an analysis involving an outside observer such as a supervisor, a teacher evaluator, a materials writer, or as in this study, a researcher, the outside observer interprets the events taking place. In this section, I wish to discuss this process briefly, contrasting the interpretation process of the learner, the teacher and the researcher.

The interpretation of the learner

From the point of view of the learner, how is the structure of a course arrived at? How does the learner in a course develop an understanding of what the course is all about? In the classroom, what is perceived at the level of the senses is sound and movement. Everything 'above' this level – everything that we understand and make sense of – is an inter- pretation or abstract construction (as described by Bühler, 1965). This includes, at levels normally associated with psycholinguistic analysis, the interpretation of sounds into phonemes, phonemes into morphemes, morphemes into lexical and phrasal components in syntax, and these into utterances or sentences. As we move to the level of discourse, utterances combine to become moves with illocutionary or 'pragmatic' value. Since we are in a classroom, and since we are familiar with second language courses, we can recognize recurring structures above the level of moves. There are exchanges which we recognize as components of exercises or activities, which when taken together become units of study and lessons, which in turn make up what we know as a course (which, when taken in the context of the learner, is a part of the learner's broader second language and life experiences).

Of course, this bottom-up description of the process does not mean that the learner's process of interpretation is bottom-up. On the contrary, there is a great deal of evidence from research on comprehension processes of top-down processing (as noted in Chapter 3). The learner's goals, knowledge and beliefs, and plans and expectations both at higher and lower levels (what this course is going to be about, what today's lesson will be about, what we are going to do now, or what the teacher is going to say now, what the first part of an utterance leads me to expect about the rest of it) play an important role in determining how we interpret what is perceived at the level of sound and action. It may also mean that the learner may not attend carefully to lower level features when there are strong expectations at higher levels, and may not notice cases where the lower level 'data' violates higher level expectations. This process affects the learner's interpretation of the course structure.

The interpretation of the teacher

From the point of view of the teacher, the process of interpretation is similar, except that the teachers' plans and expectations of what is going to happen are usually stronger than the learners'; and the interpretation of what happened will generally be seen in the light of what the teacher planned. For example, what a learner interprets as a 'great conversation' may be for the teacher an 'exercise gone astray'. In other words, for the teacher, the interpretive process may be more top-down than for the learner. From the point of view of the teacher, as well as the materials writer, supervisor or teacher evaluator, the interpretation of what happens is to a greater extent coloured by their view of what *should* happen.

The actual course which occurs will not be what has been planned in advance or expected by any particular participant. The exact way in which a curriculum is instantiated will be different from the curriculum as laid out by an institution or textbook. The interactions which occur will not be the same as the teacher's plan for a lesson, nor exactly what a learner plans for a lesson. This point was exemplified by the first five minutes of the videotaped lesson of Teacher C, which involved a discussion by the teacher on the current issue of acid rain, sparked off by a student noticing the words 'acid rain' on the board (left there from a previous class) and asking the teacher what it meant. This aside, which the teacher regarded as a valuable part of the lesson (she ended the aside by saying "I don't remember who asked that question but I'm glad you did"), was clearly not in the teacher's agenda and likely not in any student's agenda, at least until the class was beginning. However, it definitely became an element that would have to be accounted for in the course structure, providing some 'learning opportunities' (Allwright, 1984), and used by the teacher and perhaps some learners, as a source of linguistic input and an exercise to develop listening fluency and cultural familiarity.

The interpretation of the researcher

How then can the researcher or analyst explore the structure of a course and the events that make it up? As noted above, the researcher can take the role of an outside observer and use methods of discourse analysis or grids of analysis to examine the structure of the interactions which take place in the classroom. Alternatively, the researcher could explore the structure of the course by being a participant (learner or teacher) and interpreting the structure from this point of view. A participant-centred approach to course structure adopts the categories and structures inherent in the interactions with and among the participants and relevant to their purposes. This approach can begin to give us a view of how the classroom events, actions and interactions play a role in the broader picture of the accomplishment of the course. In this approach, the researcher is an observer who tracks and interviews the course participants (learners or teachers, or both), using their verbalizations as a basis for 'reconstructing' their interpretations.

For a researcher to "locate, perceive, identify and label a seemingly infinite number of concrete occurrences", it is necessary to determine what are perceived as the boundaries of these occurrences (Goffman, 1974:21). For these boundaries, Goffman used the term 'frame'. This term has been used analogously in many fields (see Tannen, 1979, for a review), to refer to such boundaries. This term has also been used with a connotation of hierarchical structure, in terms of levels of abstraction or 'logical typing', by Bateson (1972:190) to explain how individuals exchange signals that allow them to agree upon the level of abstraction at which any message is intended. This notion of hierarchy is also important in the subsequent discussion in this chapter. In this study, it was necessary to identify boundaries through the teachers' verbalizations in the interviews, in the classroom discourse on the videotape, in the teacher's commentary about the videotaped lesson, and in the accompanying logs and notes.

As the researcher, my 'reconstruction' of the course structure was also made in both top-down and bottom-up fashion. The top-down deductions were evoked by the interviews with the teachers, their logs, written notes and lesson plans, and were inherent in their language in discussions about what they would do and what they had done. The bottom-up deductions came mainly from what they said in class while carrying out the lessons captured on videotape. The two types of deductions were then matched and compared during the analysis. In other words, the notion of course structure as presented here is the structure seen in classroom discourse between the teacher and learners, and in the discourse of the teacher talking retrospectively about lessons which occurred and what occurred in them.

Types of course structure

From the verbalizations of the teachers about the courses they were teaching, it became clear that there are two types of co-occurring course structures that are an inherent part of the course. First, there is the *chronological structure*: the formal schedule in terms of the calendar and the clock. Second, there is the *conceptual structure*, consisting of the conceptual units being taught. This inherent dual structuring is evident in the meaning of the word 'lesson'. The Oxford English Dictionary defines 'lesson' both as "a continuous portion of teaching given to a pupil or class at one time", and as "one of the portions into which a course of instruction in any subject is divided". These two meanings are evident, for example, in textbooks, where a lesson (conceptual unit) may take longer than a single lesson (calendar unit) to cover. The term 'course' can also refer to either the chronological course occurring in calendar time, or the overall conceptual whole to be covered.

Chronological (calendar/clock) structure

The first sense in which the teachers' verbalizations in the data imply a course structure is in terms of its chronological structure – its formal schedule in terms of the calendar and the clock – which is not usually a result of teacher decisions, but which plays a crucial role in the teachers' decision-making process. The chronologically scheduled units have formal boundaries which are relatively inflexible: courses must begin and end on scheduled dates, lessons are expected to end within a short time (five or ten minutes perhaps) of their scheduled period. Breaks within a lesson, such as a coffee break, also have certain expectations related to their timing, although a teacher may have more flexibility there, as noted by Teacher F.

F: When we came back from the break we had exactly one hour left. I timed it so that the break took place before the one hour mark rather than after. That's because I wanted them to have 20 minutes to write on each topic when they were writing.

These chronological boundaries generally had very clear signals in terms of labels and verbalizations in the interviews. They were also signalled in the classroom indications and student behaviours, both verbal, such as explicit announcements by the teacher, or non-verbal, such as the students putting away their books or getting up and leaving. In addition, teachers referred readily to the chronological units of the course and the component lessons in their discourse both in the interviews ("On Tuesday, I'm planning to ..."; "The course began last Tuesday"; "We meet on Mondays and Wednesdays for two hours"; "Before the break, I plan to go over the assignment ..."), and in the classroom ("On Wednesday, we will continue this unit ..."; "Let's take a break now and after we'll correct the exercise you did for homework ..."). In addition, teachers in their discourse tended to group activities and conceptualize the course weekly: "This week we'll do ..."; "In week three, we'll do ...". Within a lesson, activities and parts of activities were grouped in terms of blocks of clock time: "In hour one, we'll do ..."; "It took ten minutes to ...". This calendar/clock structure is hierarchical in the sense that a component at one level consists of subcomponents. These components are largely independent of the characteristics of the concepts being taught. So, in this formal sense, a course that students enrol in, such as Course C, can be illustrated in a tree-like fashion as in Figure 4.1, below.

In many cases, there were also institutionally imposed restrictions on the chronological structure of the course. For example, Course H was an intensive course for French-speaking students learning English, consisting of approximately 180 hours of class time, divided into 30 lessons of three hours each, five days a week over six weeks. The first and last days of the course were scheduled for orientation and testing. Within this chronological map were a number of institutionally-imposed 'regularly scheduled events'. One of these was a once-weekly meeting with the counterparts in the corresponding class of English-speaking students learning French. A second regularly scheduled event was a language lab period.

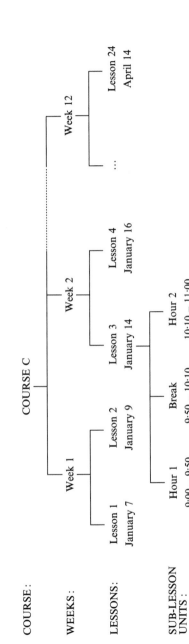

Figure 4.1 Chronological (calendar/clock) structure

In addition to the in-class time, the teachers also considered time between classes as potential learning time, and frequently assigned (conceptually based) activities for the students to carry out during the interim (chronological) period. These assignments were often an integral part of the course, and also served to link the activities of one chronological lesson to those of another. For example, as Teacher D described her Monday and Wednesday lessons, she included mention of the between-lesson period:

D: I asked them to take ... the course outlines home and read them carefully. And then when they came in the next day, I said I would go over it again and "if you have any questions, if there's anything you don't understand, we'll take it up on Wednesday".

Conceptual structure

The teachers' verbalizations made it clear that the course also has a conceptual structure, in addition to the chronological structure described above. The conceptual structure is made up of conceptual units or elements at different levels of abstraction. The possible range within which these units can be posited ranges from the highest or most global unit of the study, i.e. the course, to the most local and concrete level of sound and movement at which categories of experience are perceived. The terms 'unit' and 'element' in this study refer to the structural categories perceived by the participants, in this case the teachers. In an attempt to avoid reaching *a priori* conclusions about the nature of the structure – how to label the units, which units to categorize as more global (or higher level) versus more local (or lower level), and how to analyze linguistic versus non-linguistic units – the study takes as the primary criterion for positing categories and positing relationships between them the labelling and phrasing used by the teachers as they talked about their courses.

The conceptual structure can be looked at as content, as goals, or as methods. On the one hand, it is a structure of the units of content to be taught. This conceptual structure of units of content is intimately related to a goal structure, as these units represent what students are to learn, either as terminal goals or as enabling goals. The conceptual structure of units of content is also intimately related to instructional methods, as these concepts also become means for achieving higher level goals. The relationship among goals, content and methods is discussed in more detail later in the chapter.

The notion of goals is crucial in the distinction between the conceptual structure of the course and the chronological structure. The goals in the conceptual structure are inherent, linking lower level actions and events to the accomplishment of higher level units, and these goals play an integral role in the ultimate conceptual structure of the course. The chronological structure, however, contains no inherent goals because chronological units are simply a set of bounded time-frames within which the teaching occurs. Goals related to chronological units involve only whether or not the conceptual goals are accomplished in the appropriate time-frame. In other words the chronological goals involve getting the job done, but say nothing about *how* the job will be done.

The distinction, in terms of goals, between chronological and conceptual units is also evident from the videotaped lesson of Teacher G. It begins with the continuation of a lab activity begun during the previous day's lesson and carried over. In this case the goal of the first chronological section of the lesson, i.e. until the break, is the completion of the (conceptual) lab activity. In contrast, the goal of the lab activity (stretched across two chronological lessons) is to achieve a higher level conceptual goal (in Teacher G's words, to develop the students' "processing skills").

All teachers discussed their courses in terms of both the conceptual structure and the chronological structure. While each element of the conceptual structure was expressed in terms of a goal inherent in its superordinate element, the calendar and clock units of the courses were expressed in terms of serving the conceptual goal structure: to cover a particular conceptual unit. Teacher F realized that

F: ... certain segments are going to take a given time, and for instance with the sample writing, I may well allow the elementary group a bit less time than the advanced group as they seem to do more pen-chewing but on the other hand have less to put on paper. I think also with the elementary group it's going to take them longer to introduce themselves and it's going to take me longer to explain to them in a comprehensive fashion what we'll be doing, so say for the advanced group I might have an hour and 15 minutes for the sample writing, for the elementary group I might just have 45 minutes for the sample, say about 15 minutes per sample, and maybe just hope to collect a paragraph from each, whereas with the advanced group I'll hope to collect a page from each.

This is not to say that there are never occasions when teachers think in terms of a chronological goal of 'filling time', rather than in terms of conceptual learning goals to be accomplished by the course, where the teacher's goal becomes one of having enough material to get through part of a lesson or a lesson. In such a case, the conceptual planning serves the chronological planning, instead of the other way around. It is even possible to imagine courses which are primarily intended, even by the institution, as time fillers or as 'babysitting'. In such cases, the goals are 'chronological' rather than 'conceptual', and the analysis of the course structure would take on a non-pedagogical slant.

The discussion below exemplifies the conceptual structure of courses in the study. The discussion is divided into (1) overall conceptual goals, (2) global conceptual units (such as themes or chapter), (3) intermediate conceptual units (such as activity clusters, activities, or subactivities), and (4) local conceptual units (such as verbal units of discourse and language). However, it is important to note that from the point of view of the relationship between levels as expressed in the teachers' verbalizations, these are not discrete categories; rather the number of levels perceived or organized by the teacher expands or contracts depending on the complexity of conceptual structure.

Overall conceptual goals

A course, when considered in terms of its overall conceptual organization, is made up of one or more overall conceptual goals, or purposes. This was evident in some cases in the study from the name of the course and from teacher references to the overall course. Most teachers expressed an overall purpose or conceptual goal for their course(s), although in a number of cases it was vague, delimiting the area but not specifying the details. In these cases, the overall goal usually limited the type or area of English and/or the skill: Courses A and B1/B2 were called "academic English", Course C1 "conversation", Courses C2 and D "pre-academic English", Courses E1 and E2 "vocabulary", and Courses F1 and F2 "writing". For some teachers, the overall goal was taken for granted and implicit, as in the case of Courses G and H, where the goal was the most general possible – to improve English. However, there were often implicit aspects of the goals that teachers, if they were new to the course or institution, discovered as they went along, or, if they had experienced the course or institution, revealed as they went along. The expression of the goals often included mention of the current state of the students in light of those goals.

Course C, for example, had only a very general goal imposed by the institution, according to the teacher: "the focus of the course is to be on conversation, strategies ... on talking, anything related to talking ...". From this, the teacher extrapolated a number of more specific sub-categories of objectives for the course:

I: So how would you describe your general objectives now – once you found out it was conversation?

C: The overall objectives of what I would try to do? Well, I want to facilitate their ability to speak in a variety of different contexts – that's probably as vague as any objective I've ever read – which means that I want to put them in a number of situations, a number of different contexts, both the academic context as well as the social context, to identify the kinds of language that they would require for those situations, which is basically the functional thing, and then to contextualize it in terms of something that is a common occurrence for them ... .

Teacher D discussed the overall goal of Course D in terms of how she interpreted the requirements of academic study: being able to recognize the structure of a written or oral text, extract the main and supporting ideas and integrate them into an organized piece of academic writing.

Teacher E verbalized the overall goal of her vocabulary course by contrasting it to traditional vocabulary courses. In this case, she took an active role in reinterpreting the goal of a course limited only by its name: "Vocabulary".

E: ... instead of saying that [vocabulary] is the content of the course and that we're going to be focusing on words – the focus will not be on "I want you to learn these particular words"– what I want to do is "I want you to learn from the experience of learning those words. I want you to generalize on to how to learn other words on your own without me" – so the skill of how to learn vocabulary instead of vocabulary, okay, so that will be the main focus of the course.

Teacher F stated that the overall goal of Courses F1 and F2 was "to improve their writing – for some students it's passing the test into university, for others it just means better writing".

Further discussion of the teachers' processes of interpretation of the curricular goals is in Chapter 6. In this chapter, the relevant issue is the structure of the perceived goal in terms of the components perceived as making it up.

Global conceptual units

The teachers all discussed these overall conceptual goals in terms of a curriculum to be covered, consisting of a number of global conceptual subunits. These subunits were often expressed by the teachers as "components", implying a structure with a part-whole hierarchical organization. However, the source of the structural breakdown varied from case to case: in Courses A and B the breakdown stemmed primarily from the institution (a curriculum committee), in Courses F1/F2 from a textbook, and in the others, primarily from the teacher, with the proportions differing in different cases. The breakdown into components is evident in their discussions of the course, and in the labels that they gave these components. In the examples below, the categories can be seen as conventions: they are arbitrary, but shared among members of a local teaching group.

For example, Teacher A, in discussing the content of a previous course which had been changed, described it in terms of four main categories (grammar, writing, reading and listening), and described the categories in terms of a breakdown into subcomponents:

A: ... you do subordination, and coordination and you do a review of the tenses for grammar, and for writing there was summary and for reading it was, you know, the main ideas and things/ and skimming and scanning and vocabulary ... and listening was taught by a monitor rather than by the teacher ... .

Because this is similar to a standard 'four skills plus grammar' break-down common in the field, one might hypothesize that Teacher A inadvertently omitted the category of 'speaking'. However, when this above statement is posited as her perception of the goals of this partic-ular course, and compared with other comments found in the data, a consistency emerges. For example, this breakdown is consistent with a statement made in another part of the interview where she discussed a technique that one of her own teachers had used:

A: ... I don't find that [technique] is that relevant to the type of teaching that I'm doing now unfortunately, because what we're doing here is not really oral skills at all ... .

As the discussion continues, each of these conceptual components is assigned certain conceptual subcomponents. In different versions of a course, the subcomponents can be assigned to different superordinate components, depending on how the structure is perceived. For example, in Teacher A's description of the new version of the institution's courses, where the conceptualization had changed, it was evident that the subcomponents had been assigned to different categories. In one case certain sub components can be seen as being a part of grammar, while in the other case they are seen as part of writing:

A: ... so all the components got reorganized in a different order with the emphasis changed from one course to the next, so [the elementary course], instead of doing all that sentence level grammar in writing, changed to a review of the verb system in English ... subject-verb agreement, pronoun antecedents, just those kinds of very basic things ... no subordination, coordination, anything like that ... and [the more advanced course] is going to have coordination, subordination, sentence combination techniques and ... different rhetorical patterns, cause-effect, classification ... .

Teacher D, in an interview in which she discussed her previous and upcoming lessons referred to the conceptual units of Course D, expressing them by using terms for ways in which academic texts are organized (for example, chronological and spatial order, generalization and support). These were the major organizational units of the course.

D ... I had just/ I had decided to do chronological and spatial order together, to get rid of it. And, uh, so I did. ... anyway, uh, looks like this group will need more challenge, so I'm beginning generalization and support next week ... .

Many of the teachers used the term 'theme' to denote the larger units of curricular structure (especially the teachers who developed the units themselves rather than being provided with them by the institution). However, the types of content included within themes varied greatly. Teacher G labelled her major course units 'themes' in the more traditional sense of content topic areas. Her course included major units such as "travel", "money", and so on. Similarly, the organization of Teacher H's course was also based on themes, starting with "Me; my interests; my classmates; my anglophone counterparts [in the equivalent section of the French course]; the campus; and [the city] – what's cooking". Following this were other themes including "personality", and "marriage and divorce".

Teacher C discussed Course C1 in terms of thematic and functional units, stating that "the course is starting to take shape in terms of an organizing principle – I'm going to be working thematically, but I'm going to be working in terms of language function". This resulted in a theme of "parties" in which language functions such as "introducing yourself" and "engaging in small talk" occurred. In some cases, the theme and function were the same, as in the case of "giving and understanding directions". These units are evidenced by announcements made in class, and from the teacher's discussions of planning throughout the term.

The organization of Course C1 into some of its conceptual components is illustrated in Figure 4.2.

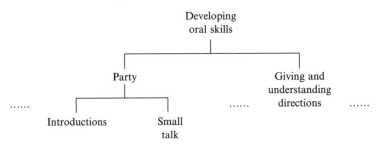

Figure 4.2 Organization of major conceptual components

Teacher E described the two major goals for Courses E1 and E2 (two sections of the same course).

E: ... there are two things I am trying to do in the overall course. One is the monitoring and becoming aware of the strategies that you are using.

That is one major thing that goes on that is a thread in the course. And the other thing is my attempts to provide the students with different strategies too ... .

The second of these goals produced the organizational units of the course, while the first was built into each unit. Teacher E sometimes labelled these units "strategies" and sometimes "themes". Examples of such units were "using dictionaries", "word analysis" (also called "using affixes" and "the strategy of guessing the meaning of words by cutting them into pieces and trying to find out what they mean"), "learning from the context", and "memorizing words" (also called "the strategies you use to remember words").

For Teacher F, who used textbooks to teach the writing courses F1 and F2, the high level units were based on textbook chapters (and referred to as "chapter one", "chapter seven", and so on). The two textbooks split the conceptual curriculum up in different ways. The elementary book was based on topic areas that the students were to write about while, in the teacher's words,

F: ... the advanced one is more structurally oriented dealing with the writing task per se, starting on the paragraph level, then to essay format and research format in a kind of spiralling curriculum fashion.

In contrast to the chronological units, the occurrence of the conceptual units in the course was relatively flexible and more or less under the control of the teacher. The 'frames' for these units are evident in the teachers' discussion of their plans and in retrospective accounts of what transpired in the classroom, in the interviews, the logs, and their written lesson plans. They are also evident in the classroom discourse. One way they are signalled is by teacher discourse markers in the classroom interaction: "Okay, now we are going to start the unit on generalization and support."

There was no set number of levels inherent in what I, for the purpose of presenting the information, have called 'global conceptual units'. The more complex the conceptual content, the more levels of subcomponents might be conceptualized to aid in the organization. The larger units of organization flow into what I am calling the 'intermediate conceptual units'.

Intermediate conceptual units

Within each major conceptual unit a number of smaller units were discernable: the verbalizations of the teachers referred to activities or clusters of activities framed in terms of accomplishing one of the higher level conceptual goals. These subunits were described in a similar fashion in terms of their goals whether they were called activities, exercises, explanations, short lectures, or a combination of these.

These varied types of units were discernable both in the lessons reported on in retrospect by the teachers in the interviews, and also in the lessons which were videotaped. For example, the major conceptual activity in Teacher A's videotaped lesson, one that in fact spanned two lessons, was a presentation by the teacher on the subject of definitions. Teacher B's lesson included a drawing activity and a task to analyze the organization of an article. Teacher D's lesson included a discussion of ongoing assignments, and a videotape activity. Teacher H's lesson included a "song activity" and a "three-way listening activity on weddings".

However, certain units in the lesson were also related to the chronological, as opposed to conceptual, organization of the course. For example, lessons included greetings, announcements of the break and end of the class and leave-takings, which are units not at all related to the conceptual structure of the course. Other units in the lesson had to do with the relationship of the conceptual structure to the chronological structure, for example, organizational discussions of the content or activities planned for the lesson, or of the assignments to be done between lessons in order for the conceptual activity to be completed in the next chronological lesson.

The subunits themselves were broken down into smaller components (which included both 'things to talk about' as well as 'things to do'). For example, Teacher A's presentation on definitions had two clear major sections: one on "formal definitions" and one on "stipulated or extended definitions". Teacher H's song activity included (i) listening to a song on tape, (ii) writing the story the song tells in subgroups, and (iii) reporting to the whole class on the subgroup's version of the song.

In Course C, the unit on "giving and understanding directions", which occurred over three class periods, included a number of activity units: for example, in one lesson there was (i) a brainstorming activity, (ii) an "artist game", and (iii) a map activity. Each of these components had subcomponents as well. For example, the artist game included an introduction and instructions from the teacher, then a demonstration or practice game, and then the actual game, before the transition to the next activity. Teacher C used the marker "okay" in conjunction with a particular falling intonation at each of these junctures, making a transition from one subcomponent to another.

This conceptual structure is illustrated in Figure 4.3.

Local conceptual units

One of the important issues in the analysis of classroom discourse raised by Coulthard (1977:101), discussing Sinclair et al (1972), is the

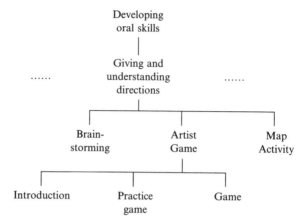

Figure 4.3 Organization within a major conceptual unit

difficulty of relating linguistic and discourse structures to higher level pedagogic structures, such as lessons. The analysis in this study suggests that the reason that discourse structures resist being connected to the higher level unit of the 'lesson' is that linguistic and discourse units are conceptual units while the lesson, as it is discussed here, is a chronological unit. In the interviews, teachers consistently talked about lower level conceptual units (i.e their utterances and speech acts) as having the function of accomplishing the *goals* represented by higher level conceptual units. Lessons, as chronological units, cannot act as goals for subordinate conceptual units, nor as the means to accomplish superordinate conceptual goals, and therefore do not fit into the conceptual structure. The data in this study, in contrast, allows us to create a connecting link between the more local conceptual levels of language and discourse and more global levels of conceptual course structure.

Teachers described the units of activities and subactivities in terms of utterances or exchanges, i.e. they described what they were trying to *do* by *saying* certain things. This relationship between the local units of the course and the more global units is discernable in the interviews, in the teachers' comments made while watching the videotaped lesson, and in the classroom discourse itself. In the interviews with the teachers, there was frequent reference to the role of particular utterances in accomplishment of higher levels of the conceptual structuring of the course. The teachers very frequently expressed their accomplishment of the more local level goals in terms of what words they said (or should say or should have said). Such comments indicate that they view their utterances as functioning to accomplish specific rhetorical or discourse goals, which in turn function to accomplish pedagogical goals.

For example, Teacher E discussed an activity she used at the beginning of the lesson to link the current lesson with the previous lesson (and to link for the students the calendar units and the conceptual units). In discussing this activity, she uses a report of her utterances to show the linguistic realization by which this was accomplished:

E: ... I started the class with / I very often do that / "What did we do last week?" It just gets students to think about what they did and make a link between what we've got to do next. So I asked/ I was by the board and what I said was "What we are going to do is a review of the prefixes" that they had studied in order to do the homework and so I'd say "Give me one that you learned about during the week" because of the homework, so they would say "pre-, the prefix pre-".

This comment mixes indirect speech and what represents actual classroom discourse, and shows how the teacher considers the introductory section of the class to be made up of the smaller moves and verbalizations which are intended to accomplish it.

In a later comment about the same lesson, she talks about two levels in the structure: the concept of "working on affixes" consisting of two subunits, "giving examples" plus "practising". Then, in response to the interviewer's query about how the topic of affixes was introduced in this lesson, she explains its accomplishment through the verbalizations that were made.

E: ... These are the affixes that I want them to work on and I want them to give me a whole bunch of examples and I want them to practise these by doing the exercises.

I: I'm just wondering how you introduced that particular topic ...

E: ... what we did was "okay you know what prefixes are now, you know what suffixes are, you know the exact meaning of some of them" what I said was "... understanding the meaning of these little words can help you in understanding the meaning of many other words", so that's how I introduced it as a continuation of the last activity.

Teacher C also describes the accomplishment of a subgoal – the institution in one of her classes of a news reporting activity – in terms of the utterances she used:

C: ... the first thing I said to my [class] when I met them yesterday was "With my other class, first thing in the morning I am bringing them information about the news, and then they are going to take it from me and talk about what's happening in the news", and I asked them "How would you like that? Do you think that would be interesting?", and they all said "Yes!", ... and so I said "okay", so I told them at that point what was happening in the news, and there were a number of interesting stories that related to some of the students in the class.

Teacher F discusses "phrasing" (presumably the choice of words and sentence structure) in terms of accomplishing the goal of getting across a particular point:

F: I'll remind them of having used 'who' and 'that' in relative clauses before ... that they were restrictive in the sense that they limited the scope and made the definition more precise. And I'll try and phrase that in a way that they would understand. I mean, usually you can try once and see if you get a lot of question marks in their faces and re-phrase it.

There is evidence of the local organizational units of the course in the comments the teachers made about the videotaped lesson while watching it subsequently. Teacher A made comments, in fact, about the boundaries between 'units' of content (what she called "ideas") that she wanted to get across to the students. In the case exemplified below, she was explaining the concept of 'formal definition' (one of the rhetorical patterns to be taught) by using the example of a wristwatch. At one point in the explanation, she stated: "... so those are the distinguishing features of a wristwatch. Okay, now, let's see/".

At this point, she stopped the videotape and commented:

A: I guess I paused very quickly to look at my notes and kind of see where I'm going next. I don't know. There seems to be a real break between finishing an idea and going on to the next idea. I'm conscious of that from watching it. I don't even know why I stopped to say that ['okay, now, let's see'].

At another point in the interview, she said:

A: ... I'm conscious of it from watching this, that I say "okay" fairly often. I think I say "okay" when I've ended one point and I'm going on to another point, and I guess it's a signal to them that if it's not okay they should say something now before I go on ... .

In addition, the more local levels of course structure can be posited by examining the discourse occurring in the lessons for categories, units and boundaries. This relationship of local levels of classroom discourse to higher levels of conceptual course structure is evident in the videotaped lessons, where a particular activity gets carried out through verbalizations and interactions.

The following example taken from the transcript of a taped lesson taught by Teacher C, illustrates how we can posit elements of a higher level structure from the classroom discourse. (Of course, by virtue of transcribing the lesson, I have already interpreted the perceptual level of sound to phonological, morphological and syntactic, as well as orthographic, levels of categories.)

C: just as a warm up for what we are going to do today, why don't we brainstorm again/we'll take time/let's just write some instruction words on the board, just to refresh our memory. When you are giving directions or giving instructions to someone, what words would you say? Can you just give me some words that you might use?

S1: For directions?

C: Yes, related to directions.

S1: Next to,

C: [while writing the words on the board] Next to,

S1: Close to,

C: Close to,

S2: Beside,

C: Beside ... good.

The teacher's first comment, made up of a number of utterances and syntactic units, included several moves related to the accomplishment of the activity: (i) it introduced and named the activity, (ii) it gave a reason for doing the activity ("just as a warm up for what we are going to do today"), (iii) it explained how it would be done ("let's just write some instruction words on the board"), (iv) it requested the students to participate ("can you give me some words that you might use?"), and (v) it explained how to participate ("when you are giving directions or giving instructions to someone, what words would you say?"). Student 1's first comment was not a response to the teacher's request for participation, but rather a comprehension check; and this is followed by the teacher's response to that check, a confirmation. These two utterances make up an exchange that Gass and Varonis (1985: 152) have termed a 'push-down': a short exchange which functions as a subordinate exchange not directly related to completing the exchange that had begun, but rather to achieve a pre-condition (in this case, his understanding of what was required) for it to be carried out. When the 'push-down' was completed to the satisfaction of the participants, the conversation 'popped up' to the previously initiated exchange, which then continued with the students suggesting words, and the teacher repeating them and writing them on the board.

This local functioning of utterances within the context of the course can be illustrated diagrammatically as in Figure 4.4.

This example illustrates the way in which pragmatic categories from discourse analysis such as 'request' and 'respond' function in a capacity of accomplishing particular tasks in the context of the

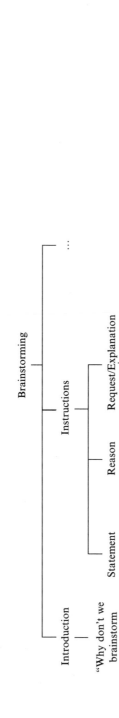

Figure 4.4 Local functioning of utterances

activity, which in turn are part of accomplishing the conceptual lesson, and the conceptual course.

The example below of a "three-way listening activity" carried out by Teacher H in her course illustrates how the structure of an activity becomes more layered as the procedures for carrying out the activity grow more complex, and yet how the relationship of goals and means in the structure remains.

This activity included (i) a warm-up section, where the teacher elicited terminology and information about weddings, (ii) a group work section, (iii) a re-grouped group work section, (iv) a whole class correction, and (v) a completion statement. The first section, the warm-up, included elicitations about terms in the semantic field of weddings ("what are the man and woman called?"), and information related to weddings ("what does the bride do with the bouquet?", and "what other superstitions are there?").

The second section was more complex, and had several subsections: (i) instructions for forming groups and carrying out the task, (ii) getting ready for the task: forming groups, receiving the worksheet, and finding a location to work (involving going to nearby empty class-rooms), and (iii) carrying out the listening task, involving listening to the tape and filling in the worksheet. This latter subsection involved a number of interactions. For example, there were interactions among group members to work out how to operate the tape machine, and to negotiate procedures for getting the information from the tape (i.e. which bits to replay), and to work out the informational content of the tape required to answer the worksheet questions. Each group's experience with the task ultimately involved different sub-structures, as one group played the tape through several times before attempting to answer while others stopped the tape frequently and discussed one answer at a time. In addition, there were different individual interactions with the teacher, queries from the students about the task, and comments initiated by the teacher related to carrying out the task ("Don't get hung up on the statistics, just get the general idea") and to elicit elaborations from the students.

The third section of the activity was the regrouping of the students (i.e. one person from each of the three subgroups joined a person from each of the other subgroups, each representing their group's understanding of the taped information). This section was broken into the following components: (i) exchange of information, (ii) a true-false exercise on the combined information, and (iii) 'take-up' exercises. Each of these sections had a subsection. For example, the second section had two parts: (i) answering the true-false questions, and (ii) correcting the false sentences. The final subsection ("taking up the exercises") included (i) instructions to write the answers on the board,

(ii) putting answers on the board, and (iii) checking agreement of other students.

The different subsections were often marked by transition comments. For example, the transition to the latter part of the activity was marked by the teacher saying "okay, we seem to want some discussion". This latter subsection was carried out by the teacher via a complex set of subordinate structures. First, the teacher determined which questions there was disagreement for, which she achieved by calling out question numbers and asking for choral answers, listening for dissenting voices, and marking the numbers of the questions with disagreement on the board. Then she elicited from the students evidence based on the listening passages to support their answers. This she accomplished sometimes by open-ended questions to the whole class, and sometimes by specific questions to particular individuals. Within this structure, there were also instances of a substructure for focusing on the meaning of vocabulary items: for example, Teacher H asked the students if they knew the meaning of 'newlyweds', then proceeded to analyze the meaning of the individual parts of the word, and put those meanings together to guess at the meaning of the whole word. She signalled the end of the overall activity with an evaluative comment: "Very good explanations", and a statement that it was time for the coffee break.

To summarize, the crucial pattern for this study is not found in the characteristics of the units on their own, but rather in the characteristics of the relationship among the units. It is these characteristics that allow us to link the actions and events that occur in the classroom at the most concrete and local level to the most abstract and global level – what the course is all about.

Characteristics of the structures
Relationships among units: sequential and hierarchical

This section of the chapter discusses in more detail some essential characteristics of the structures of teaching, in particular, ones related to relationships among the units that make up those structures. Evident in the above discussion of the structure of the course and its components are two types of relationships: sequential and hierarchical. In other words, a unit of a course (at any level, for example, a thematic unit, a chapter, an activity, an utterance) can be seen as one of a sequence of units with specific relationships to those occurring after and before, or as a node in a hierarchical structure with relationships to its superordinate and subordinate nodes. The argument that I wish to make here is, first, that course structures above the level of discourse are discernable, and, second, that some of the relationships that are characteristic of linguistic and discourse structures also exist with regard to these higher level pedagogical structures. The emphasis in this study, and the relevance to the processes of planning and interpretation described in the following chapters, is on these similarities across levels rather than on the differences.

One way in which units of a course are related to each other is sequentially: a unit followed by a subsequent unit at the same level. For example, a teacher might say "After the listening exercise is finished, we will do the interview activity". Or, "After the theme on Winter, we'll do a theme on the Inuit". A bounded sequence of units on the same level, when taken together, comprises a unit on a higher level. In some cases, the order of the units in a sequence, according to the perspective of the teacher, may be variable and permitted to change, while in other cases the order may be fixed. For example, it may be considered acceptable by a teacher to interchange the Inuit theme and the theme on Winter, whereas the listening activity may be seen as a prerequisite to the interview activity.

The notion of sequential patterns of units has been posited in research on classroom discourse. Bellack et al (1966) described a particular type of recurring tripartite sequential pattern occurring in classrooms, consisting of teacher elicitation, pupil reply and (optionally) teacher evaluative comment. Coulthard (1977), following Sinclair and Coulthard (1975), elaborated on this pattern of teacher-pupil 'exchange' taking a discourse focus, and extending the analysis to a higher level of organization: that of a classroom 'transaction'. This latter superordinate category included a similar kind of patterned sequence consisting of a 'frame' (a boundary marker between transactions), followed by a 'focus' (a metastatement indicating what the transaction is going to be about), followed by the transaction itself, and an optional close or subsequent frame.

Although the specific pattern of teacher-student exchange noted by Bellack et al was not the norm in the classroom teaching of many of the teachers in the study (perhaps due to the frequent use of group work by many of the teachers), the more general pattern of opening, body and close noted by Coulthard, and the notion of frames or boundaries between elements in a sequence was evident both in the conceptual and chronological structuring and at the different levels of the structure of the course.

For example, in terms of the overall course structure, each of the courses in the study had particular conceptual elements which typically occurred at the beginning, supporting the notion that there are implicit or explicit rules guiding the structuring of the course, and that some sequences are, by convention, not 'permitted'. One element characteristic of the opening of the course was the handing out and discussion of a course outline. It seemed that if this course outline activity was delayed very long past the first lesson, it would be considered a 'violation' of the conventions guiding course structure. Such a course-initial unit could include a number of substructures, such as overview of the content of the course, description of the assignments required, the expectations of the teacher, the marking scheme, and so on. Other specific elements included in the first lesson(s) are discussed in Chapter 5. The course end also typically had some characteristic concluding elements, although they were not required. These might include an exam, a final social gathering, or at the least a verbalization such as "Bye. Good luck."

Larger conceptual units, such as themes, chapters, rhetorical patterns, and so on were also marked by boundaries and contained frames, introductory subunits, the core of the unit, and an explicit or implicit close. For example, many teachers discussed "introducing" a particular theme or major unit, although the particular means by which the introduction took place (for example, through a 'lecture' or 'discussion' or 'brainstorming' or 'group activity') differed from teacher to teacher and unit to unit. Similarly at the sublevel of activity units, the three-part structure is also evident, and supports Germain's (1990) notion of an ordered sequence of components within didactic activities. Teacher A, for example, in viewing the videotape of her lesson, noted that her reading out a definition to the class (combined with the word 'okay' and a noticeably clear and careful enunciation) functioned as a conclusion to an activity in the 'definition' unit:

A: This was an attempt to just close the whole thing off. I read the definition and that meant 'And this is what it was. It contains some of the things that we have done. I think now I can just finish it. We don't have to discuss it further'.

The second type of relationship that occurs among units in a course is hierarchical. In the case of hierarchically related units, a unit (or decision) can be made up of subunits (or subdecisions) which flesh out the details of the superordinate unit. For example, "in order to do this interview activity, first I'll provide a model of how it is to be done, then we'll practice it once all together, then they'll get into groups to do it". Any of the component subunits can also have its own sub-subunits. For example, "to get them into groups, I'll ask them to find two other people in the class who they haven't worked with before".

The relationship between different levels of the hierarchy is of particular importance to the discussion in subsequent chapters of the planning and interpretive processes of teachers. The lower level decisions which constitute the higher level decisions are the *means* by which the higher level decisions are carried out. Conversely, an element at a lower level has as a function the accomplishment of the *goal* represented by its superordinate element.

The notions of levels and relationships among levels evolved from the verbalizations of the teachers and in response to particular linguistic cues in the interview questioning and the teachers' interview narratives. The question word '*what*' and the word '*then*', (or '*after*' or '*before*') as in "what did you do then?" led to a focus on a series of decisions related sequentially. The question word '*how*' as in "how are you going to do that activity?" led to a focus on the relationship of higher level decisions to their subordinate nodes: "I did the verb tense exercise by first giving them the handout, then putting them in groups ...". Generally, when answering such a question in practice, however, the teacher did not explain all the details (which would be impossible anyway), but rather explained what was not taken for granted: i.e. the particular conscious decisions that had been made, perhaps different from what had been done before, in order to make the superordinate decision succeed. What was clear was that success of the subordinate elements represented the accomplishment of the superordinate element. The question word '*why*' led to a focus on the relationship of the subordinate levels to their superordinate nodes. Again, the teacher's answers to '*why*' questions often implied rather than stated this relationship and included other situational factors and background variables – this issue is developed in Chapters 5 and 6. Nonetheless, the teachers' comments clearly and continually pointed to a relationship between the '*what*' (the content) and the '*how*' (procedures for implementing the content), and the '*why*' (goals of implementing the content). In this way the linguistic and propositional structures occurring in the classroom were related to larger pedagogical structures mapped onto the lesson and the course.

One of the interesting consequences of this view is related to the distinction between content and method (or in cognitive terms, between declarative knowledge and procedural knowledge). The literature on curriculum and syllabuses (both mother tongue and second language) usually treats content and method as separate entities, but typically characterizes the whole area as one of confusion. For example, Stenhouse, Rudduck and MacDonald (1971) illustrate the problems of defining curriculum by listing a range of definitions from the educational literature, many of which include concepts such as "principles for the selection of content, what is to be taught and learned" and "principles for the development of method, how it is to be taught and learned". Similarly, among the wide array of perspectives and characterizations of curriculum described by Schubert (1986), the "paradigm of perennial analytic categories" of purpose, content, organization and evaluation (1986:188, 212, 233, 261) plays an important role.

White (1983) notes:

Traditionally, the syllabus has been regarded as the content of a course, the subject matter to be covered ... whereas the curriculum is a statement of what the course is trying to do, as stated in its objectives. Exactly what a curriculum is, however, is not easily defined ... . (1983:71)

He states that "there is considerable variation of views on the issue of objectives in the curriculum" and "similar variation when it comes to the question of content", and that in recent innovative approaches to language teaching, "the separation of content and method is no longer clear cut" (1983:77). Yet he argues that the three, although closely related, can be treated independently:

There is also a close relationship between methods and objectives, and although all three elements – objectives, content and methods – can be treated separately and independently, the realization of intended learning outcomes (i.e. objectives) may depend upon using one set of methods rather than another. (1983:77)

However, as Barnes notes:

It would be a mistake to think that what a teacher teaches is quite separate from how he teaches. Books on curriculum planning often show the selection and ordering of subject matter as a separate stage from the planning of learning activities or teaching methods. (1976:139)

The source of the confusion, and the difficulty in defining 'curriculum' in terms of separate notions of objectives, content and method, becomes more obvious when we take into account that each unit or element in the conceptual structure is *at the same time* content, method and goal. These are not three different entities, as the educational literature implicitly assumes, but rather the same entities looked at from three different angles. An element at any level of the hierarchy can be seen as content (the 'what' of the teaching) when considered from the perspective of its own level. When looked at from the perspective of its superordinate node (or any nodes in the superordinate structure), it can be seen as method or procedure (part of the 'how' or means employed to carry out the higher level). When looking from subordinate levels to the higher levels, we have a perspective in which the superordinate level can be seen as the 'goal' (or 'purpose' – from the *a priori* or planning perspective of the model – or 'rationale' – from the *a posteriori* or 'interpretation of events' perspective of the model) for the lower level structure. As demonstrated above, these relationships seem to be relevant for all levels of the hierarchy, from verbalizations (perhaps even articulation) to the major conceptual units of the course.

There are two additional theoretical notions which are important in this regard: the notion of function (versus form) and the notion of context. In the field of linguistics, the notion of function has been used to characterize relationships among units, while the notion of form characterizes the unit itself. Both structural and transformational grammar distinguish between grammatical categories or forms (for example, 'noun' or 'noun phrase') on the one hand, and grammatical functions (for example, 'subject') on the other. Function, according to Chomsky (1965:68), is "an inherently relational notion". It refers to the role of the item in question (for example, a particular noun phrase) within the superordinate structure (in this case, within the sentence). In Chomsky's example, "Sincerity may frighten the boy", the noun phrase 'sincerity' functions as the subject of the sentence. In discourse analysis, the notion of function has been extended to relate what is said to what is done with what is said. The function of the utterance is the role it plays in combination with other utterances and is related to its illocutionary force – what it is doing in the discourse. In the example described in Chapter 3, the formal utterance "the doorbell" functions as a request for action within the context of the exchange of which it is a part. The sense of the term 'function' which these examples have in common is the role that a particular element plays in the occurrence of its superordinate structure. In the case of this study, the meaning of the term 'function' can be generalized to refer to the role of an element or unit in the higher level structures of teaching of which it forms a part.

The view of course structure described above also helps us to take into account in a more principled way another crucial concept discussed in the literature on curriculum in ESL, as well as in linguistics and discourse analysis – that of context. The literature on second language curriculum (for example, White, 1983) treats context as a separate entity (for example the context of the culture and the context of the school) and an independent part of the process. However, we can treat context as part of the system of structures being posited here by extending the use of the term in the study of language and discourse. At the levels of the structure normally associated with linguistics, for example in discussions of phonology, the context of a phoneme (which qualifies its function) includes the surrounding phonemes plus higher levels of structure within which the phoneme occurs. In the areas of morphology (a word in the context of surrounding words) and syntax (the grammatical context), a similar concept of context is used (specifying the grammatical function, for example). Similarly, in discourse the notion of surrounding utterances is used (to specify the discourse function). To generalize in terms of the model being posited in this study, the context for any element includes the surrounding elements at the same level and the superordinate structure of which those elements are a part. Because higher levels represent the reason for carrying out the lower structures (i.e. intentions), context in this sense also includes the idea of goals or intentions. The higher the level of contextualization that we take into account in our analysis, the closer our account is to the actual instance of occurrence, and the more the perceptions and intentions of the participants are an essential aspect of the account. When our analysis is restricted to lower levels of contextualization (for example, the level of phonology or of syntax), the easier it is to posit generalized and abstract rules governing formal relationships without taking into account the perceptions and intentions of the participants.

In the model of the teaching process developed above, context is seen as a perception of individual participants, and is treated either as an aspect of planning (looking forward), or as an interpretation of events (looking backward). These latter two perspectives are discussed in Chapters 5 to 8.

Course structure as an evolving dynamic entity: tangled hierarchies and heterarchies

The hierarchical relationships noted above as operating among course components do not imply 'pure' hierarchies, in the sense that each node is uniquely connected to a single superordinate node. Rather we are dealing with what Anderson (1983) refers to as 'tangled hierarchies' and multiple hierarchies, or – following de Mey's (1977) use of the term (and Sharwood Smith's personal communication) – 'heterarchies'. These are cases in which a subordinate node can be related to more than one superordinate node resulting in cases where the relationships are 'tangled', or cases where more than one hierarchy seems to be operating.

There are a number of reasons for this phenomenon. One is that because the teacher maps conceptual structures onto chronological (calendar and clock) structures, two different hierarchies are operating at once, and (as noted above) the teacher needs to signal different aspects of each. This leads to the case where a number of elements have a double function – a function with regard to each of the two structures. This double functioning can be seen in Teacher C's labelling of components of the course. For example, in her introduction to the brainstorming activity, C states that it is also "a warm up for what we are going to do today", i.e. an introduction to the day's (chronological unit) activities, as well as the conceptual units of activities.

We find, as well, that in a linear sequence of utterances, some refer to the beginning of the lesson, while others refer to the beginning and ending of activities or other conceptual units, while others are concerned with the mapping of conceptual units onto clock time, i.e. explanations of where the class is picking up the activity begun last lesson. For example, C begins the lesson with:

C: Okay, on Tuesday, we started working on the language of instructions and giving directions. Remember that? We had our mystery island ... .

As this mapping process is being undertaken, lower level elements can be connected to higher level elements in different ways. For example, certain elements of a lesson may include higher level structures that occur on a regular basis as required by the institution. Courses G and H had several such units: a laboratory component functioned as one of the conceptual components of a listening comprehension section of a course. However, it was mapped onto the course in the form of a regular weekly component of the listening section, occurring as an hour-long component of a lesson each week. In this situation, a particular laboratory hour (occurring for example on March 14) functions at the same time as a one-hour component of a three-hour lesson occurring that morning, and as one part of a laboratory component of a course, scheduled weekly at the same time. The teacher takes into account both these functions in carrying out the course.

A second reason for tangled hierarchies is the fact that the conceptual content of the course is not linear, but the ultimate occurrence of classroom events has to be linear. It is in the mapping of abstract concepts to linear sequences – a major source of complexity for the teacher – that tangles may occur. Since one way to get around the constraint of being able to do 'one thing at a time' is by conflating two goals into one activity, a subordinate structure may be related to two superordinate nodes, causing a tangle in the hierarchy. For example, Teacher D used a regularly scheduled "writing journal" activity to function both as an opportunity to provide feedback on form (one of the conceptual goals of the course), and simultaneously as a means for the students to achieve greater fluency in writing.

The tangles occur not only during the mapping of conceptual categories onto chronological ones, but also during the transformation from the abstract conceptual entities which make up the course goals to the linear sequence of events which make up the teaching. As the process of course planning is under way, it occurs through a series of interim hierarchies. For example, Teachers D and H used a high level breakdown into the four skills as a planning heuristic. Verbalizations in early interviews reflected this breakdown; and in both cases it would be possible to account for the activities (and lower level structures) done in the course by categorizing them as one of the four skills. But as the courses were closer to realization, there were other hierarchies, related to thematic organization for example, that became salient in the verbalizations of the teachers.

The conceptual units are not necessarily organized sequentially across lessons. Many units succeed not only by virtue of being carried out, but also by virtue of their spacing in time (i.e. the non-activity time between them). As a result, there may be larger conceptual goals which are spread over the course. For example, the regular activity first thing Monday morning in Course D was a half-hour period when students wrote their journals. Each of these journal-writing periods was part of a larger unit that had the goal of developing students' writing fluency. Its successful accomplishment of that goal was partially dependent on the fact that it was carried out for a half hour a week over twelve weeks rather than for six hours consecutively. This activity co-occurred as a part of each Monday's lesson (in clock time) and yet was also part of a larger conceptual unit of the course.

Other activities are long-term activities, ones initiated by the teacher and carried on over a longer period of time. An example of this is discussed by Germain (1990) in the case of a teacher who, in one lesson, introduces an activity to go to the theatre to see a movie which occurs the following week, and which is discussed in another lesson the week after that. The exchange which makes up the initial discussion between teacher and students as to the best time to attend the movie functions both in chronological structure as one part of that particular lesson period, and in conceptual structure as one part of the movie unit. Such activities occurred frequently in the data in this study.

Because the hierarchies are pragmatic (both in the sense of what the learner needs to learn, and in the sense of making the course structure easier for both the teacher and learner to handle) rather than entirely logical, more than one hierarchy may operate without causing either the teacher or the learner serious problems. An example of this is Course A, where the structures of subordination and coordination can fit in as a component of writing or of grammar. According to Teacher A, they are placed under one or the other of the superordinate categories depending on the specification of the curriculum; but there is nothing to keep a teacher from treating them as part of both. In the example of Course C, neither the teacher nor the learners seemed upset that in some units, the function (for example, "introducing yourself") was a *subcategory* of a theme ("parties"), while in other units, the function *was* the theme ("giving directions").

Tangles may occur within the sequence of utterances or moves within a lesson. For example, a teacher may backtrack after starting a new unit of activity, saying something like "but before we do that, we'll do this". This produces a tangle in the way in which the conceptual categories are mapped onto the chronological sequencing of events. Teachers vary with regard to the degree to which their course maps and lesson maps are tangled. If the conceptual categories are plotted in time in a linear fashion, with little backtracking, the hierarchies will have fewer tangles. In a videotaped lesson taught by Teacher D, there was a great deal of backtracking and foreshadowing, which produced a number of tangles. For example, D stated:

D: Now we have our listening homework to check. But just before we begin that, how are your assignments?

In other words, after announcing the beginning of the section of the lesson in which the listening homework is going to be covered, D then backtracked to check on the progress of students' on-going assignments, which had been initiated the previous lesson, and which were due the following week. The discourse about the assignment turned out to be quite extended (more than she had planned, as she revealed while watching the videotape subsequently), as she involved all the students in describing their progress and their difficulties. Nevertheless, when this assignment check-up was completed, she had no trouble returning to the listening activity. In other words, although these two activities are conceptually separate, in clock time the progress check is embedded within the listening homework activity. (Interestingly enough, this kind of backtracking was part of her style, not only at the level of activities, but also on a discourse level in the interviews and the lesson, as she frequently began one sentence and then backtracked to start again in a different way.)

Tangles in the hierarchy may also occur because of psychological constraints (what could be considered the pedagogical equivalent of 'performance errors' in the study of syntax in normal speech). For example, Teacher A made this comment about the notes that she usually brought to class, indicating that there can be a 'tangle' in the 'course map' that the students have to make sense of:

A: ... I have them [my notes] there just in case.

I: Do you ever forget anything?

A: Oh yes ... I occasionally don't mention something which I feel later I should have mentioned and I'll bring it up again in a following class ... .

There is also evidence in the data that the linguistic performance errors (resulting in repairs which, in terms of the structural description here, can be seen as tangles at the linguistic levels of the hierarchy) are related to 'performance errors' (for example, psychological limitations of memory) at higher levels of the structure. In the example below,

Teacher A tells how the linguistic structure of her utterance is altered in mid-sentence due to a momentary difficulty in remembering the sequence of the information to be presented in the lecture.

A: ... I was going to say "I'm going to give you some words to define". Okay. Then I realized "Oh no, I didn't tell them about the problems yet. I've got to do that before I give them the words to define." So that's what/

I: /Okay. So you started to say "I'm going to" and then with a different continuation for the sentence and instead you continued that sentence with a different ending so it ended up being "I'm going to give you the/I'm going to tell you about some problems"/

A: /"Some problems". I think I continued it that way. Yes. But/I definitely was, at that point, looking down trying to remember what to do next and thinking "Okay. I'm gonna give them the definitions" and then sort of split second/ "no, no we're not ready for that yet".

This concept of tangled hierarchy or heterarchy does not negate the notion of hierarchical relationships operating, but rather points to the dynamic nature of the process we are investigating: the transformation through tentative hierarchies, which is described within the planning processes of teachers in Chapter 5. In this study, the use of the terms hierarchy and heterarchy is not meant to imply a strict set of formal hierarchical relationships, but rather structures with multiple or tangled hierarchical relationships.

Conclusion

The structure of the courses as described here does not necessarily correspond to the learner's view of what is happening. There is some evidence that certain elements of such structuring, which are in the categories and labels that the teachers use in discussing their plans and what happened in previous lessons, are perceived and used by learners in their 'making sense' of the course. For example, Teacher H addressed the students in her class with instructions and questions about related specific conceptual units such as activities. As the students worked in groups on filling out a questionnaire, H said "Are you finished?" The students had no trouble responding appropriately, understanding that the ellipsis in this question indicated that the referent was a previously set unit of activity.

The course structure discussed above also does not necessarily correspond to the teacher's pre-operational structure, which is the teacher's evolving course plan. As is described in Chapter 6, the teacher's plans are generally not well-defined, and are subject to many alterations as the term (and each lesson) proceeds. Early decisions are altered up to the moment of implementation, at which time they become 'the course'. Although we can use the teachers' discussions of their plans as evidence of course units which are relevant to them, in order to describe the course which occurred we need a retrospective structuring, based on classroom data and on the teachers' comments about what happened in class. The structure described here may not be identical to the teacher's later perceptions, as parts of it may be reanalyzed in light of later insights.

So, the important question remains of whether we can say that a course has a structure independent of the individual or idiosyncratic interpretations of different individuals. Perhaps (as the case is made about language) there may be some 'normal' or basic structure which would be perceived in common by all who participated or observed it. There is a sense in which this attempt to formalize the relationships that occur in the structures of teaching is akin to producing a 'grammar' of a second language course. Work along these lines has been initiated by Mehan (1979) and Cazden (1988) in the context of L1 classrooms. However, there are a number of issues that must be dealt with for this to be possible. A number of concepts must be evoked, such as 'functional equivalence', 'substitutability', and 'permitted', 'questionable' and 'non-permitted' sequences. These are concepts described by Sinclair and Coulthard (1975) as requirements for such an analysis, and are concepts used in linguistics for grammaticality and discourse appropriateness. In addition, it must be decided exactly what is the cultural community in which such conventions are currency; for example, does it include a subculture of all second language teachers, or does it include the subculture of all teachers and learners, or is it limited to the temporary subculture of a particular class of students and their teacher? These are also questions which must be taken into account in formulating the grammar of a language. Because this study is a study of individual cognitions and not of social conventions, this is an empirical question I have not attempted to answer. However, in this chapter, I have attempted to suggest characteristics of the course structure as revealed by the teacher-based data, and then show evidence to justify the structure.

The findings in this study suggest that what is crucial is not the specification of the levels in the system (i.e. the identification and labelling of a closed set of levels). In terms of a conceptual analysis, the types of units and the number of levels will vary: there will be more levels of subactivity when the complexity of the teaching increases. What is suggested by this study, is rather a closed set of 'patterns which connect' – the types of relationships between levels including goals, means and content.

There are a number of important consequences of the distinction made between chronological and conceptual units, and of the types of relationships connecting the conceptual units at different levels. These relationships involve theoretical notions which are common in discussions of teaching, and of research into teaching: the notion of 'goal' or 'objective', the notion of 'content', and the notion of 'method' or 'means'. Educational researchers and classroom discourse analysts, in their attempts to identify the structure and processes of teaching, have generally confounded chronological units (such as 'lesson') with conceptual structures (such as 'activity structures' and 'discourse structures'). Since a chronological unit such as 'lesson' has no intrinsic goal, it is not possible to relate lower level conceptual units to it using the notion of goal. Yet lower level conceptual units can be quite readily related to higher level conceptual units in this fashion. The implications for our understanding of the planning and thinking processes of teachers are discussed in Chapter 5.

One of the important aspects of this analysis is that the context (not only the context of the surrounding sequence of elements, but also of the hierarchy in which elements – including utterances – occur) plays an important role in our understanding of those elements and utterances. It is this context that gives the elements and utterances meaning. As formal elements, they only have meaning 'out of context' – the meaning given to such events in the culture at large. It is through their function in the context of the hierarchy as it is perceived in the plans and intentions of the participants, and interpreted in light of their beliefs, assumptions and knowledge that their full meaning is accounted for. It is from an understanding of this hierarchical structure that we know 'what is going on here' when we try to make sense of something that a teacher says or does in class.

Referring again to the model developed in Chapter 3, we can see from this chapter that the concept labelled 'event/action' has a complex structure. This structure is crucial to the discussion of a number of other concepts in this study. To understand the structure more fully, we must take into account not only the function of an element in terms of its relationship to superordinate units, but also how it functions in terms of the teacher's planning process and in terms of the teacher's interpretive processes. We need to examine how these classroom categories are produced through the teacher's processes of planning, and how they are attributed significance through the teacher's processes of interpretation and fed back into the planning process. These issues are developed in the subsequent chapters.

5 Decision-making in the structuring of a course: a model of the planning processes of teachers

Chapter 4 elaborated on the notion that a language course has a hypothesizable abstract hierarchical or 'heterarchical' conceptual structure underlying the linear sequencing of the classroom events and verbalizations that the participants experience in time. Out of this analysis arise some important questions. How does this linear sequencing and chronological organization evolve from a conceptual basis? What procedures and strategies does a teacher use to make this transformation? How does a teacher go about deciding what to do when? These questions are related to the issue of *planning*, one of the three main parts of the model developed in Chapter 3. This is an aspect of our understanding of the language teaching process as yet unexplored in the second language teaching field.

This chapter takes as a starting point the cognitive model of planning and action developed in Chapter 3. The chapter initially focuses on two important notions which were lacking from the model introduced there. The first is a broader notion of consciousness in the process of planning and decision-making. The second is the notion of relationships among decisions, both temporal and logical, which play an important role in the planning process. Then, using these notions, this chapter goes on to develop an elaborated model of the teaching process and the role of teacher planning.

Planning and decision-making in the teaching process

Clearly, the structure of events in a course is the result of a decision-making process. All participants are involved in making decisions about what will be done when in order to accomplish the course. Decisions lead to actions, which when carried out result in classroom events – ultimately in the form of a series of verbal and non-verbal events involving students and teacher. It is this series of events which, over the period of a term, we call a course. Decision-making is thus the cognitive work which culminates in a course. Decisions are based on knowledge and beliefs about the current state of the world (such as students' knowledge and abilities, the contents of the curriculum, and what is happening in the classroom), and about what is good and bad about this current state. Part of understanding a course therefore is understanding the decisions which create it (the planning part of the model, discussed in this chapter and Chapter 6), and part of understanding the decisions is understanding the knowledge and beliefs that underlie them (discussed in Chapters 7 and 8).

It is not necessarily the teacher, however, who is the prime decision-maker responsible for the structuring of a course. At one extreme, as in many teaching systems, the teachers' behaviour may be rigidly regimented by a supervisor and the method or materials may become a virtual script for the lesson. Teachers are held responsible for getting students through the material and exams that test whether the material was learned, and are observed and evaluated on their adherence to the method.

At the other extreme, it may be the learner who is responsible for structuring the course. For example in the case of my own saxophone lessons, my teacher normally greeted me with "What will we do today?", and I explained what I wanted to do or what I wanted to learn and he either did what I had decided, or he made decisions to help me accomplish what I said I wanted to learn. (Interestingly enough, however, he was aware that this procedure was not the norm in our society: the one time I kidded, "You're the teacher, aren't you supposed to decide?", he acted somewhat insulted and put me through an hour of rigorous, repetitive exercises in which I had no say at all.) This notion of learner responsibility is the model adhered to in some theories of adult education (for example, Knowles, 1975). The interesting feature of such a case is that while the teacher believes the responsibility lies with the learner, the learner may believe that the responsibility is the teacher's. This may lead to the paradoxical situation where the teacher asks "What do you want to learn?" or "What do you want to do?", the learner's response is "You're the teacher; you're supposed to know!" or "I want you to decide!" In other words, if the learner has the right to decide, this also includes the decision not to decide. Ultimately, there is no cause and effect: the relationship among the participants, and the learning itself, develops organically.

In the cases examined in this study, the key player in transforming the conceptual structure into classroom events was the teacher. The teachers all felt responsible either for creating the course or for organizing the curriculum for the students, i.e. for transforming the conceptual course into classroom events. As Teacher C noted at one point: "Teachers are the front-line generators of the curriculum."

Decisions about managing learning in the courses under study were made both by learners and teachers (together and individually), and by other individuals involved in developing the syllabus and teaching materials, and these decisions were produced through socially negotiated acts, as well as through acts of individual cognition. In this study, however, I am focusing on the teacher's perception of and contribution to the course: decision-making by the teacher. I will refer to the social and negotiated aspects of decision-making as they are discussed by the teachers from their own 'teacher's perspective' (as the term is defined in Chapter 1).

Before discussing what teachers do, we must establish what is meant by planning. The notion of planning is a particularly complex one. When we talk about planning, on the one hand we can be talking about decision-making as it occurs in time – some plans are made before others. On the other hand, we can be talking about decision-making at various levels of generality – i.e. planning for the overall course ("What can I do to develop their oral fluency?"), planning for individual lessons ("What will I do to get them to give each other feedback?"), planning moves or utterances in the classroom ("Should I give them instructions now for the whole activity, or just explain how to do the first step?"), and perhaps even planning the manner of articulation ("Maybe I'd better repeat what I just said but more slowly."). Planning itself can also be planned ("I think I'll plan the activity tonight, and then look for some good articles to go with it tomorrow.").

In addition to the question of time and levels, there is the question of consciousness. We can say that planning and decision-making involves thinking; and in the case of the most immediate classroom sense of planning, the distinction between planning and thinking is hard to perceive. It may seem like we are stretching the meaning of the terms 'planning' and 'decision-making' unnecessarily to include things like articulation or other actions which occur spontaneously in a way that does not seem to be consciously planned. Yet the overall model of the teaching process becomes much more powerful by taking into account two aspects of planning: (i) the different degrees of consciousness of decision and planning, and (ii) the distinction between decisions made at different levels (the hierarchical aspects) and decisions made at different points in time (the temporal aspects).

Planning and decision-making: the range of consciousness of decisions

In the research literature on teaching (the main thrust of this research has been that of teachers in mother-tongue primary and secondary systems – these issues are only beginning to become an important focus in the second language teaching literature), the concepts of decision-making and planning already have a history. Traditionally, teaching has been viewed as a decision-making process. For example, Leinhardt and Greeno characterize teaching as:

a complex cognitive skill requiring the construction of plans and the making of rapid on-line decisions. The task of teaching occurs in a relatively ill-structured, dynamic environment. Goals and problem-solving operators are not specified definitely, the task environment changes in a way that is not always under the control of teachers' actions, and information appears during the performance that is needed for successful completion of the performance. (1986:75)

Borko, Cone, Russo and Shavelson state:

Teaching, then, can be characterized as a process of decision-making: sometimes teachers are aware of their decisions, and sometimes they make them automatically. From this perspective each teacher has a repertoire of teaching strategies and materials that are potentially useful in a particular teaching situation. The choice of a particular strategy depends on the teacher's goals for the lesson, beliefs about teaching, and information about the students. (1979:138)

and then discuss the consequences of such a view of teaching:

When teaching is viewed as a decision-making process, the teacher is seen as an active agent who selects a teaching skill or strategy in order to help students reach some goal. The choice may be based on one or more factors. If all the types of information mentioned above were used, teachers would need to integrate the large amount of information about students from a variety of sources and somehow combine this information with their own beliefs and purposes, the nature of the instructional task, the constraints of the situation, and so on in order to select an appropriate instructional strategy. (1979:139)

There has been a certain amount of criticism in the literature describing what a teacher does using the notion of decision-making, with its connotation of conscious and deliberate reasoning (see Yinger, 1986, and Verloop, 1989, for discussion of this issue). However, the issue of consciousness is a complex one, and as Clark and Peterson (1986) noted, most researchers have avoided the issues of trying to locate "unconscious processes" by limiting their research to conscious, deliberate decisions on the part of the teacher.

The characterization of teaching by Borko et al (1979:138) quoted above distinguishes between making a decision while being aware of it and making a decision automatically (presumably, while not being aware of it). This discussion implies a binary opposition. Elsewhere in the education literature (for example, in Kagan, 1988:490, as well as Clark and Peterson), the opposition between conscious and unconscious is also often implicitly assumed to be binary – a decision is either conscious or it is unconscious. This assumption is consistent with the model of perceptual attention and perceptual learning (involving controlled and automatic processes) developed by Schneider and Shiffrin (1977) and Shiffrin and Schneider (1977), and discussed in terms of second language acquisition by Schmidt (1990). Schmidt (1994:11) went further in "deconstructing consciousness in search of useful definitions for applied linguistics", by distinguishing between consciousness as intentionality, consciousness as attention, consciousness as awareness and consciousness as control. His recommendations, which are articulated in terms of language learning, focus on alternative terminology which does not conflate these differing conceptions of consciousness. In the following discussion I would like to pursue this issue of the notion of consciousness as found in educational discussions of decision-making, noting ambiguities similar to those described by Schmidt, and also introducing the issue of the use of background knowledge in decision-making.

In the everyday use of the term 'decision', there is a usual implication of intentionality. However, in a teacher's statement such as "I asked George the question", it is possible that the action of asking George happened with a spontaneity and speed that left the teacher unaware of any decision-making going on. Yet, a teacher could still, retrospectively, characterize the action as a decision to ask George. The meaning of the term 'decided' in this example, however, sets up a contrast to a situation where circumstances controlled the outcome, such as in the statement "I didn't have time to give the test today", which would not be seen as a 'decision' but as an involuntary outcome. Decisions do have an implication of deliberate intentionality, yet because it is possible to talk retrospectively about an action that took place as if it was a result of a decision (even if that decision or the factors behind the decision took place below the level of awareness of the individual) we can say that as long as the action is seen as being attributed to the individual (whether or not it is seen as 'conscious'), and not to external circumstances, it can be characterized as a decision. This implies (as noted by Schmidt) that intentionality may not always be seen as conscious.

One way to look at the issue of consciousness in decision-making is to treat it not as a binary feature, but rather as matter of degree. In this view, teachers could be said to be *more or less* 'conscious' of their decisions. As is indicated in the next two sections of this chapter, a large number of elements are involved in any decision, including an important role for previous decisions and an important role for beliefs and assumptions. Also, particular decisions (or considerations underlying decisions) often evolve over an extended period of time. Because previous decisions as well as assumptions and beliefs can be more or less consciously in mind and/or used at any point in time, then it follows that a decision can be considered more or less 'conscious' simply from an awareness or use of more or fewer of the elements which underlie it.

In addition, teachers may become aware of the elements or aspects of a decision retrospectively (which happened often in this study). This can also be considered an aspect of the non-binary nature of consciousness and unconsciousness and the interwovenness of awareness and intention: a person's awareness of a decision and the elements in it can be raised in retrospect later – i.e. a teacher may not be consciously aware of all the factors he or she considered, but with further reflection this sense of awareness was increased. In cases where the teacher is aware of the intentionality behind a decision before (or as) it is being carried out, we can use the term 'purpose'; in cases where the teacher becomes aware of it after it is carried out, we can use the term 'rationale'.

The differing degrees of consciousness in the planning process are reflected in the terms 'planning', 'expectation' and 'prediction'. Planning (as with the term 'decision-making') normally implies an active and perhaps deliberate involvement on the part of the planner in determining what will happen. Expectation, on the other hand, implies a more passive role. The term prediction implies something in between – a somewhat conscious activation of expectations.

We can see from Teacher F's comments how expectations, in this case brought up to a level of explicit mention, play a role in her discussion of decisions for an upcoming lesson. It is likely that, whether or not brought to a level of conscious realization, expectations are a part of the process of becoming ready for teaching.

F: ... I'm going to finish off chapter 7 ... I'm probably going to briefly review the paragraph hook business again, which we have started to look at ... I think they're probably going to have/some of the students will know what's going on, some of them might not remember quite. I expect some of them will mix up transitions and paragraph hooks and I'll have to reinforce again the difference between the two.

I: How will you do that?

F: Well I'll probably remind them of some of the examples in the book and/oh yeah, probably if it happens, I'll basically just refer to what they were saying before about it that each has a job to do, that it makes it clearer for the reader and, you know, provide a few examples.

In summary, the very structuring of decisions is a dynamic process, involving a range of types of consciousness, logic and intuition, thought and action, and purpose and rationale. A goal of this study was to capture this dynamic feature. Including the notion of varying degrees of consciousness is an important aspect of our model of processes of planning, for example with regard to the teachers' use of 'experienced structures', discussed in the next chapter. Because the terms 'planning' and 'decision-making' were part of the teachers' discussion about their own teaching and thus cannot be abandoned, and because planning included activities decided at varying and unmeasurable degrees of consciousness, I am, for the purposes of this study, defining these terms to include a range of degrees of consciousness, and to include the notions of expectation and prediction.

Planning and decision-making: the relationships among decisions

The issue of *relationships* among decisions has not been a central aspect of research on teacher decision-making. The main emphasis, at least up until the major summary of research published by Clark and Peterson in 1986, has been on coding and counting *types* of decisions according to a categorization of the factors that they are based on (approximately 77% of the studies reported in Clark and Peterson on teacher planning and interactive decision-making were of this type).

The first important criterion used to distinguish types of decision in this body of literature is whether decisions are made in preparation for the classroom (i.e. pre-active decisions – an initial distinction between pre-active and post-active decisions was dropped as the cyclical nature of the process became evident), or whether they are made in the classroom (i.e. interactive decisions). This distinction played an important role in defining and delimiting areas for subsequent research. It is worth noting, in light of the discussion of course structures in Chapter 4, that the distinction between pre-active and interactive decision-making is related to the chronological structure of the course (i.e. when the decisions are made relative to the occurrence of lesson periods) rather than the conceptual structure of the course (i.e. when the decisions are made relative to the beginning and end of conceptual units being taught. Clark and Peterson's concluding encouragement to link the two areas, and to show how pre-active plans are "communicated, reconstructed or abandoned in the interactive teaching environment" (1986:268), nonetheless retains the implication that the two areas are in some important theoretical sense different. Recent work in the area of second language teaching (for example, Richards and Lockhart, 1994) has retained this dichotomy between planning decisions and interactive decisions, and does not distinguish between decisions having to do with the conceptual structure of the course from those having to do with mapping the conceptual structure onto the chrono-logical structure. This latter distinction, which became salient due to the longitudinal nature of the present study, is an important aspect of the discussion in Chapter 6.

In light of this initial distinction between teachers' pre-active decision-making and teachers' interactive thinking, researchers typically attempted to categorize the types of factors taken into account by the teachers. In both of these areas, four broad categories of types of decisions were identified – objectives, content, instructional processes and learners. Researchers tallied these to determine the amount of time spent on each type. According to Clark and Peterson's summary of this research, it was found, in pre-active decision-making, that content is primary followed by instructional processes and then objectives (learners not mentioned), while in interactive thinking, the order is reversed, with learners primary then instructional processes then content (objectives not mentioned).

The concepts of objectives, content and instructional processes are familiar ones in light of the discussion of the conceptual structures of teaching in Chapter 4. As noted there, each element in the hierarchical structure can be seen as a goal (or objective), as content, and as a means (or instructional process) depending on its *relationship* to other units. This analysis suggests that the research results summarized by Clark and Peterson do not distinguish different types of decisions as much as they present the same decisions viewed from different vantage points. This becomes more evident when we look more closely at several examples provided by Clark and Peterson (1986:269) to demonstrate the distinc-tions between types of teacher thinking in the classroom.

To illustrate a teacher statement categorized as an indication of a thought about objectives, Clark and Peterson give the following example:

Example 1: I wanted them to see the connection between the 'sh' sound and the S-H, that they all had S-H's in them.

To illustrate a teacher statement categorized as an indication of a thought about instructional processes, they give the following exam-ples (among others):

Example 2: I thought after I explained it to her, "I didn't make that very clear".

Example 3: I was also thinking that they needed some sort of positive reinforcement.

To illustrate a teacher statement categorized as an indication of a thought about learners, they give the examples (among others):

Example 4: I was thinking that they don't understand what they're doing.

Example 5: I was also thinking "Tricia's kind of silly right now. If I ask her, I probably won't get a straight answer."

Example 6: Nobody was listening at all.

In each of these statements, although the teacher may seem to be high-lighting one or other of the factors, when we take the relationship among decisions into account we see that the other factors are also included and underlie the statement. Example 1, referring to what the teacher "wanted" (presumably the objective), also refers to the learner ("them"), the content (the sound-letter correspondence), and the instructional process (the strategy or technique the teacher using to achieve the mentioned objective). Example 2, referring to the instructional process (the way the explanation was done), also refers to the learner ("her"), the content ("it"), and the objective (getting the point across). Example 3, in addition to referring to the instructional process and the learner, includes reference to the content (the positive reinforcement itself – probably an utterance – which is a unit of content at the linguistic level), and the objective (what the positive reinforcement was intended to accomplish). Examples 4, 5, and 6, in addition to referring to the learners, also refer to content ('what' is being done, 'what' they are being asked, or 'what' is being listened to). They also refer to objectives ('why' they are doing what they are doing, 'why' they are being asked, or 'why' they are listening). Also included are instructional processes (what is it about 'how' they are doing what they are doing that they don't understand, 'how' should I handle this next question so that I get a straight answer, and what is it about 'how' this activity of listening is being done which has resulted in nobody listening).

I would argue that all these factors are not just contained explicitly or implicitly in the statements, but are part of the teachers' evolving thinking about the moment being referred to, and taken into account on some conscious-to-subconscious level. Clark and Peterson do, in fact, acknowledge the importance of looking at the relationships among decisions when they note that "interactive decisions are pre-ceded by factors other than judgments made about the student" and argue that this conclusion must be taken into account for the model to "accurately portray the processes involved in teacher interactive decision-making" (1986:277). The only way to know how the teachers' classroom thoughts relate to the larger picture of accomplishing the course, and to the structures by which this is accomplished is by look-ing at the relationships among decisions via a longitudinal description of teachers' planning processes.

There is an important practical reason for focusing on the relationships among decisions. As many researchers have noted, the task of a teacher is inherently complex. There are several causes for this complexity: (i) there are a large number of factors to be taken into account in making decisions, (ii) decisions must be made on many levels, and (iii) although the possibilities for what can be done are unlimited, only one thing can be done at a time. The important issue is, how does the teacher manage that complexity? With all the possible things a teacher can choose to do (or say) at any given point in time, how is what is chosen decided upon? It is in this crucial aspect of managing the complexity that the relationships among decisions become relevant.

Teachers' planning: factors in the process

An immediately striking feature revealed in both the interview and classroom data was indeed the complexity of the process of the teachers' decision-making in terms of the wide range of factors which play a role in what is decided and the wide range of possibilities for what can be decided at any point in time. At each moment when the teachers were in action, this process of decision-making occurred simultaneously on many levels, from immediate to medium range to longer range, more or less conscious, balancing and weighing constraints, possibilities and options. In this regard, the teaching process for these teachers was reminiscent of Flower and Hayes' (1980) description of the writing process. They compare writers to switchboard operators trying to juggle a number of demands on their attention and constraints on what they can do. Kagan's (1988) description of cognitive processes in teaching supports this view.

It was tempting to approach the analysis of teachers' decisions by categorizing the specific factors which underlie particular kinds of decisions. Such an analysis would reveal, for example, which factors are important in the early planning process, and which factors play a role in decisions made during the lessons in the classroom. However, the data from the eight teachers led me to the conclusion that an attempt to categorize factors underlying decisions by their situational characteristics would produce biased results, and hide some of the more interesting aspects of the process.

The bias would result from the fact that the factors taken into account in any decision are multiple and interwoven; and thus it seemed impossible (or at least rather arbitrary) to isolate a single causal factor behind any particular decision made by a teacher in the study. In describing the decisions they made, teachers usually included a large number of reasons which were interrelated in complex ways.

These reasons were also often restated at different times in different ways with different emphases, and so the particular emphasis was very open to interpretation by the researcher. In addition, the factors brought up in a particular interview are only the ones the teacher thought of at that moment. There are many examples in the data of additional factors arising, almost by accident, at a later point in an interview, leading me to conclude that those mentioned initially were the ones which fit the context of the interview at that particular moment, and not the ones which were 'most central' or essential as a source of a particular decision. When attempts are made in interviews to elicit explicitly the most essential decisions, the responses by the subjects are very open to monitoring.

Such a categorization would also hide some of the interesting aspects of the process, in particular those regarding the relationships among decisions, and the patterns which connect the relationships. For example, categorizing the factors behind decisions does not tell us anything about the direction of the process of taking into account such factors – i.e. the connections among the temporal sequence of decisions and the hierarchical structure of decisions. The interviews revealed that the decisions were not always taken in a top-down, or predetermined goal-directed fashion. The traditional way in teacher education programs of thinking about making pedagogical decisions is from the top down, starting with the objective to be achieved, and then making decisions to achieve that goal. However, in many cases, teachers seemed first to make decisions about what to do, and perhaps only later realize or figure out why they made those decisions. In general, there was an interwoven process between the decisions and the reasons, and an interaction between 'purpose' – the preplanned reason – and 'rationale' – the *post hoc* reason. For example, a teacher could be considering a certain long term goal, but have a couple of administrative problems to solve and a few student characteristics in the back of her mind, and have a few possible ways of proceeding next (next class, or next minute) also in mind, and be looking though a textbook and discover an article that, combined with a prior tentative decision about exercise types, will deal with several of the issues on her mind, and after having decided on or even carried out the plan may discover a couple of other reasons why it was a good thing she did what she did (i.e. *post hoc* rationalization).

In addition, categorizing factors in decisions by situational characteristics shields an important fact that the interviews revealed – that in particular situations different teachers based their decisions on different factors depending on their background knowledge, assumptions and beliefs. Even if the factors behind decisions were straightforward enough to claim, for example, that early planning decisions primarily involve institutional and scheduling factors while in-class decisions primarily involve assessment of student abilities and class dynamics, this kind of categorization hides an important aspect of the decision-making process: how knowledge, assumptions and beliefs on the part of an individual teacher interact with the factors as the process is being carried out. (This aspect of decision-making is addressed in Chapter 9.)

Finally, we do not find out through such a categorization how the complexity of the decision-making process is made manageable. On the other hand, examining the relationships among decisions, as is illustrated below, allows us to see the processes by which all the teachers made the process manageable. (This point is made in a discussion of the initial results of the study in Woods, 1989.) It is in examining the patterns in the process from this perspective that we find aspects which are common across teachers – the tentativeness in decision-making, the alternate use of resources and constraints, and the use of explicitly and implicitly planned structures, discussed in the next chapter.

In this discussion, I am taking the terms 'external' and 'internal' to distinguish between two types of factors playing a role in the decision-making process. *External* factors are situational factors which teachers take into account in making decisions (or to be more accurate, what teachers know, assume and believe about these factors). *Internal* factors are ones internal to the decision-making process itself, i.e. the internal structuring of decisions and the relationship of decisions to each other. The wide range of external factors that teachers take into account or can take into account in the decisions they make is a major reason for the complexity of the teaching process. The internal structuring of the decision-making process provides the means for the management and coordination of this complexity, producing the structure of activities and pedagogical units that comprise a second language course. It is in the internal structuring that we have the two types of interrelationships among decisions discussed above: earlier versus later decisions (temporal relationships), and more global versus more local decisions (logical relationships).

External factors

The decisions made by the teachers in this study were based on their knowledge about many 'external' factors related to specific events and to the specific situation at hand. In the process of making the decisions, these factors appeared very much interwoven. For example, in one lesson (the videotaped lesson) given by Teacher A, the following factors were brought up and commented upon while viewing the videotape, as playing a role in her decisions:

- explicit lesson plan
- explicit curriculum and objectives
- class routines
- degree of investment in preparation
- the lesson so far
- the preceding discourse
- assessment of success of previous part of activity
- a student's previous utterance
- other prior utterances which are judged relevant
- spontaneous thought
- consideration of what task involves
- consideration of future aspects of course
- perception of students as individuals
- perception of students as a group
- assessment of attention of students
- assessment of understanding of lesson/information
- assessment of time in lesson
- assessment of time in course
- perception of own personality
- prior experience as a student
- underlying beliefs and assumptions

In planning the same lesson (i.e. pre-lesson decision-making), as revealed in the interviews before the lesson, Teacher A took into account:

- how many students will probably turn up
- availability of photocopying
- knowledge about students' prior course experience
- a recent conversation with another teacher
- estimation of the complexity of a task
- estimation of how well the students as a group are moving
- estimation of what the group can handle
- estimation of how well particular individuals in the class are moving
- estimation of what particular individuals can handle
- class dynamics and individual dynamics in class

The teachers' discussions about their decisions revealed that typically no single isolatable factor 'causes' a decision to be made. Rather, the factors operate more like weights which are applied in favour of or against various possibilities and alternatives. This weighting phenomenon is illustrated by Teacher G's discussion of the pre-lesson decision to select a particular article for use in the videotaped lesson (part of a theme on careers):

G: One of the things that came out from the initial needs analysis was that these people wanted to talk about work. The other thing that came out during conversations was that most of them had not yet decided what kind of career they wanted to choose. So [after choosing careers as one of the themes], I went to my [computer] data bank to find something on careers. There were several things for careers. That one [the article that I chose] was cross-referenced for comparatives. Also I had never used that one before, so it was more interesting. The other one [that I rejected], I had used it before ... We had already done a little bit on comparatives, and I like to bring things back, almost like in a cyclical way. I knew then that I wanted to get back to comparatives at some point or other. I had prepared a sheet where all the rules [for comparatives] are summarized and there are examples on it, and I wanted to use the two [the prepared worksheet and the selected article] together ... .

Later in the interview, she stated:

G: I had two or three different articles on careers to choose from. That one was more interesting also because it allowed a lot of class interaction rather than pair work. We hadn't done much class interaction, so that combined with the fact that we could use it for comparison made it the most attractive.

In this example, the factors which Teacher G mentions as playing a role in this particular choice of articles are:

- topic of article
- knowledge of what students wanted to cover in the course
- knowledge of students' lives
- prior decision about theme
- grammar points occurring in article
- previous grammatical work done in class
- teacher belief about 'spiral' presentation
- previously prepared worksheet
- amount of previous whole class work
- belief in value of some amount of whole class work
- article not previously used by teacher
- teacher interest in trying something new.

Teacher G's discussion demonstrates the critical way in which the factors interrelate. Her decisions are not based on a single factor; rather they evolve out of a process of weighting of factors. It is a gradual process involving prior considerations, prior decisions, and the various factors underlying the prior decisions. Teachers' discussions demonstrated the highly contextual nature of the relevant factors: each course (each class of students, each lesson) highlights different factors, and each teacher, in the context of that course, interprets these factors in an individual way. They also illustrated the temporal nature of planning and suggest that a particular decision may occur gradually over a period of time, and that only some of the relevant factors may be consciously in play at any point in time.

In summary, characterizing situational factors as 'causal' did not reflect the process of teacher decision-making as revealed in the interviews. In addition, with the idiosyncratic and highly context-specific nature of the external factors that play a role in teachers' decisions, grouping and categorizing these factors would seem to hide rather than reveal the actual process of decision-making, and to ignore the internal relationships operating dynamically among decisions, which are crucial to the planning and decision-making process of teachers.

Internal factors

When a teacher is making decisions about what to do in a particular course, lesson or classroom moment, a major constraint exists: only one thing can be done at any time. The abstract non-linear concepts, which are interconnected in many ways and at different levels of generality, must be transformed into a linear sequence which occurs in specified time slots. This constraint does not reduce the complexity of the process; it brings it to a head: "What will I do now?"

One important aspect of managing the complexity of "what to do now" is in the internal relationships among decisions in the process. Included are two types of relationships among decisions. The first is the temporal distribution or timing of planning decisions – that some decisions are made before or after others in time. The second is the logical relationships which arise because planning decisions produce course units of different logical types – or different levels of generality – with certain ones being superordinate or subordinate to others. This distinction with regard to planning decisions is related, but not identical, to the distinction made in the last chapter between the hierarchical structures of teaching and the linear sequence of teaching events occurring in time. While levels of planning refer directly to hierarchical levels of course structure, planning sequences will differ from teaching sequences, for example, in the case where an early planning decision affects a later part of the course.

It is the relationship between the logical and temporal aspects of planning that determine whether it is 'top-down' or 'bottom-up' (this point is discussed in detail in Chapter 6). When earlier (or longer range) planning for any part of the course is more global or 'higher level' and later (or more immediate) planning is more local or 'lower level', planning is said to be top-down. When teachers start with lower level units (for example ideas for activities or texts), and later piece them together to form higher level units, planning is said to be bottom-up. In fact, there is a constant interface between the two as each chronological lesson, with its immediacies and its input into the longer term plan, goes past.

It is also in looking at the relationships among decisions that the notion of assessment plays a role. The process of assessment is crucial in connecting the levels of planning. The assessment can be at any level, for example, at the level of an utterance or move (to get a particular response or reaction), or the level of a part of an activity, or an activity, or a larger level unit such as a theme. The assessment of more local levels is made in light of the goals represented by superordinate units in the teaching structure. The perceived discrepancy between the expectations and the outcome is assessed in terms of how the teacher's expectations are framed, i.e. in terms of prioritization of criteria of success, and also in terms of the teacher's openness to finding discrepancies. This discrepancy then becomes part of the teacher's experience, and is fed forward to play a role in subsequent planning.

This principle of the internal temporal relationship among decisions – the role that prior decisions play in reducing the complexity involved in making a current decision – is an important aspect of teachers' ability to take into account the large number of factors impinging on the structural and cognitive complexity of classroom teaching. When the temporal and logical relationships among decisions is taken in light of the overall planning of a course, it allows us to see the path that a teacher follows in moving from a conceptual basis through successive hierarchies to the actual classroom events which emerge into the course that one can observe or participate in. The next section provides an elaboration of the model developed in Chapter 3 to include these relationships. The next chapter describes the procedures and strategies used by the teachers in this process.

An elaborated model of planning and decision-making in the teaching process

The initial model developed in Chapter 3 provides a basis for a more elaborated model to serve as a framework in discussions of the planning processes of the teachers in this study. However, this initial model does not take into account the distinctions developed in Chapter 4 between chronological course structure and conceptual course structure. Nor does it take into account the distinction between decision-making at different levels of the course structure (the logical relationships among decisions) and decision-making at different moments in time as the course progresses (the temporal relationships among decisions). This section further develops the model; and the subsequent sections examine, in this light, the teacher data related to planning processes.

In the field of second language teaching, this question of teacher planning has not been broached in any detail. Allwright (1981) is one of the few attempts to begin to explore this process. In considering the question of "what is to be done" in the management of language learning, Allwright notes:

> 'To be done' suggests action, but in fact there are three phases in management, rather than one. There are things to decide, actions to be taken on the basis of those decisions, and a process of review to feed into future decision-making. (1981:5)

> After a decision has been taken – say to use a particular textbook for a particular course – some organization is necessary – namely the purchase and delivery of an adequate quantity of the books to the classroom – before the decision can be fully implemented. The use of the textbook, for a sensible review to be possible, has then to be monitored to permit evaluation of its use and effectiveness, and the result can then go forward to inform subsequent decisions. (1981:5)

Allwright proposes the model illustrated in Figure 5.1, with its overlapping phases to indicate the dynamic relationships involved.

This model does not explicitly deal with the role that planning plays in the process, although planning is implied in the decision stage. In order to account explicitly for the notion of planning in the decision-making process, I have altered Allwright's model slightly. His model shows a decision phase; I will consider this *planning* – the decisions and organization resulting in a plan. His action phase I will consider *implementation* – the actions and events which carry out the teaching. The review phase I will consider *assessment* – the monitoring, interpretation and evaluation of the actions and events resulting from the implementation. As in Allwright's version, there is overlap and

Figure 5.1 Decision, Action, Review (Allwright, 1981)

recursiveness in the model. Note that the difference is simply categorizing the components of each phase slightly differently on a conceptual level; in practice since there is constant overlap, there is no
difference between the two models. When this figure is rotated one-
third of a turn counterclockwise, it is strikingly similar to the model
developed in Chapter 3. Implementation is clearly talking about
actions and the resulting events they become part of. The monitoring
and evaluating included in assessment are part of the process of understanding and interpreting the actions and events in terms of goals. The
decision-making and organization is directly related to planning and
the activating of expectations. This links our model of the teaching
process to a more general model of cognition. This altered and rotated
model is illustrated in Figure 5.2.

The weakness of this altered model (and the original on which it is
based) is that although it illustrates the workings of a single particular
decision, it does not show how decisions relate to each other and to
other factors in the process. For example, it does not tell us how, in
Allwright's terms, a result can "go forward to inform other decisions"
(1981:5), nor how higher and lower level decisions are connected. This
points again to a crucial issue in the area of planning, one neglected in
the literature: modelling relationships among decisions.

The strength of the above model is that, although it does not explicitly include temporal and logical aspects of planning, it can be readily
adapted so that it does. It can be taken as potentially referring to a
decision made at any point in time in the course – before the course
begins, between the first and second lessons or in the classroom during
the last lesson. It can also be taken as potentially referring to a decision made at any level of the hierarchy – one about the entire course,
one about a subunit of the course (for example, a lesson or a thematic
unit), or one occurring within a lesson (for example, an activity, a
move or a particular verbalization).

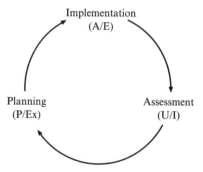

Figure 5.2 Planning, Implementation, Assessment

As a result, this model can be used as part of a larger model which includes these two types of relationships among decisions. We want the model to determine how decisions made at one level and at one time (for example, to use a particular activity in the first lesson) affect subsequent decisions. The model must take into account the fact that subsequent decisions may be at the same level (for example, the following activity in the current lesson), at subordinate levels (for example, decisions made about subparts of the activity and the utterances used to carry it out), and at superordinate levels (decisions about upcoming lessons, and the overall course). What we want is a model which combines the elements of the recursive 'altered Allwright model' with (i) the concept of levels of actions/events being related heterarchically which was developed in Chapter 4, and with (ii) the notion of planning procedures being related temporally. This would produce a kind of 'spiral' of contexts related to a particular 'moment of decision'.

Let me consider the temporal and logical relationships in such a model in more detail. In the case of implementation, the model would incorporate the factors described in Chapter 4 – the conceptual units mapped onto the chronological schedule, and includes the heterarchical structures presented there. The top level is the course as a whole. Each lower level describes in more detail the smaller sections of the course. The number of lower levels is indeterminate and potentially unlimited, possibly including multiple levels of major units and sub-units, activity clusters and activities, sub-activity units and moves, utterances, sub-utterance units, articulatory and paralinguistic features. The units at each level are perceived (along with their relationships to other levels) pro-actively in terms of planning and expectation and post-actively in terms of interpretation and assessment.

In the case of planning, the relationships are somewhat different. The chronological divisions of the course in fact provided a natural rhythm for the teachers' planning. There was a period of planning in preparation for the course that came to an end with the first lesson. There were periods of planning between lessons that ended with each new lesson. And there was planning activity that took place in the classroom as the lesson was being conducted. However, these divisions in planning periods related primarily to the planning or mapping of the chronological units of the course. In contrast, the planning procedures related to the conceptual structuring of the course (termed 'structuring' in the next chapter) seemed to span these boundaries, continuing into, through and across lessons, with a great deal of continuity and fluidity. In addition, the planning that took place at a particular time was often removed from the immediate chronological schedule; a teacher might consider a plan during the first lesson that related to another lesson much later in the course. (It is also important to acknowledge that the divisions in the planning periods related to the chronological schedule of the course are partially artifacts of the data-gathering process, which was carried out via pre-course interviews, weekly interviews between lessons, and videotaped lessons.)

The planning at different temporal points in the course (earlier and later), however, served different functions, as the nature of the information required and considered useable changed during the period starting from before the course and continuing through the course to its completion. In the most general terms, planning before the course involved higher level course structures, planning between lessons often had to do with more intermediate course structures, such as clusters of activities, particular activities and subactivities, while planning during the lesson focused on lower level structures: what to say (and how to say it) in order to accomplish the goals represented by higher levels. However, as noted in the examples in Chapter 6, there were many occasions where planning in the classroom included rethinking higher level structures, or where between-lesson planning was thinking about a recurrence of the course. Teachers' planning between lessons did not include explicit scripts for the words that would be used in the classroom to carry out an activity; however teachers often explained a planned activity (or how they were planning to accomplish a particular conceptual goal) with a simulated verbalization, suggesting that there is some implicit verbal planning done in advance of the lesson.

Because prior decisions served as constraints for the current situation, partially limiting the number of possible things that one could decide to do subsequently at any point in time, the set of prior decisions functioned as a kind of framework within which current decisions could be made. As a result, early planning was more tentative, with a lesser focus on constraints and a major focus on resources, and took a great deal of time. Later planning, on the other hand, was more a matter of refining, with a major focus on constraints and a lesser focus on resources, and took less time. However, the prior decisions were generally tentatively made, and functioned as a tentative framework, and at any point in time a teacher could decide to keep, alter or scrap a previous decision. Yet, without the framework provided by previous decisions, the almost infinite number of possibilities could seemingly paralyze the decision-maker. The planning behaviour of teachers in weighting factors discussed above was one way in which this relationship among decisions was played out. Teachers usually considered a number of options (tentative prior decisions) which limited the number of possibilities.

In this model, there is also no fixed number of levels that may be planned: the more complex the conceptual content is, the more subdivisions may be required in order to organize it for the classroom.

According to this model also, there are no unplanned structures. However, some structures (for example verbal structures) may be planned, in a relatively unconscious manner, virtually at the moment of implementation. The model also allows us to distinguish top-down from bottom-up decisions. When decisions move through time from higher to lower levels, they are top-down; when they move through time from lower to higher levels, they are bottom-up. Since implementation of one level may include planning for other levels, we can see that planning and implementation become intermingled – that implementation can include planning. And, finally, planning itself can be planned.

The temporal/logical distinction is also important in discussing assessment. Because the chronological structure of a course consists of a series of smaller units that are experienced through time (sometimes with pauses between them), as plans are implemented, their results can be assessed, and can feed into further planning of on-going and recurring units. The chronological structure of the course in lessons and weeks was a convenient way of thinking about and assessing the on-going course; however, these units often received a global assessment, for example "I had a good lesson" or "I had a bad week". Such global assessment, however, concealed two quite different types of assessments. On the one hand is the assessment of conceptual structures. This was described in terms of the evolution of the difference between perceived course goals and perceived learners' current abilities, and related to the linking activities of the teacher described in Chapter 6. The assessment of the conceptual structuring, in other words, influenced more directly the re-planning of the 'what/how' structuring in terms of conceptual goals. On the other hand is the assessment of the mapping activities of the teacher: whether the planned conceptual structures such as activities, thematic units, textbook chapters were completed within the planned time period. Such assessments led to re-planning the mapping of the course in order to compensate for what had not been covered in the preceding period.

Theoretically, the assessment process plays a role in linking the temporal and logical aspects of planning. The assessment can feed into and affect the subsequent development of the plan in three ways relative to the unit being assessed. It can directly affect the unit currently under consideration; or it can affect the subordinate structure of the unit currently under consideration; or it can affect its superordinate structure. I will use the analogy of learning to ride a bicycle to discuss these distinctions.

In the first case, at one extreme, if a particular unit is assessed as going well, there is no change made to it and its structural relationships and the teacher carries on as planned. At the other extreme, the teacher may decide to stop the unit and start over again, or to bail out and abandon the unit completely or replace it with another unit. For example, a teacher might start an utterance again, or repeat a set of directions a different way, or substitute an activity for another that is not working in the expected way. In the bicycle analogy, this would occur when the rider loses her balance and puts her foot down on the ground to start again.

In the second case, if the teacher comes to the conclusion that a unit is not working in light of the goals represented by the higher level structures, that teacher can make adjustments in the substructure in order to ensure that the unit is accomplished successfully. The adjustments can involve adding or removing or changing subunits (activities, moves, verbalizations, etc.). The discrepancy (lack of success) noted in the short term at one level of the hierarchy is taken as a signal for adjustment at lower levels aimed at avoiding a later discrepancy at a higher level. The difference between this type of adjusting and the restarting described above is that the adjustments are revised components of the 'unsuccessful' unit rather than a complete substitution. In the bicycle analogy, this is the case of the rider making constant assessments and adjustments of balance in order not to fall to the ground.

In the third case, the assessment affects the higher level structure. It may happen when the goals themselves are changed or refined so that the results of the unit become more in line with the superordinate structure. In this case the unit is 'reframed' in a new higher level structure. (In the bicycle analogy, this might be like deciding to try roller-blades instead.) Another way in which the higher level structure is changed is when the unit can be stored for later use so the next time, in another context, it can be done differently. This occurs when the assessment feeds back into higher level structures (other lessons, other courses) where the structures currently being assessed will re-occur. In this case, a revision is made to the unit of activity, both in terms of substitution of elements and in terms of elaborations of more refined 'enabling' activities so that its recurrence at another point in the teaching will be more in line with expectations. In this case, the higher level structure is replanned with different substructures. In terms of the bicycle analogy, this would be the more or less conscious realization, as you get up off the ground, that the next time you try to ride, you should not turn to the left when you are leaning to the right.

In practice, however, these different types of feedback processes occur simultaneously, as each level is thought about in a dynamic way as part of an overall structure. Assessments which connect certain levels are never totally independent of the other levels. In the next chapter, we will look at how the assessments and the planning link the levels of the course through time.

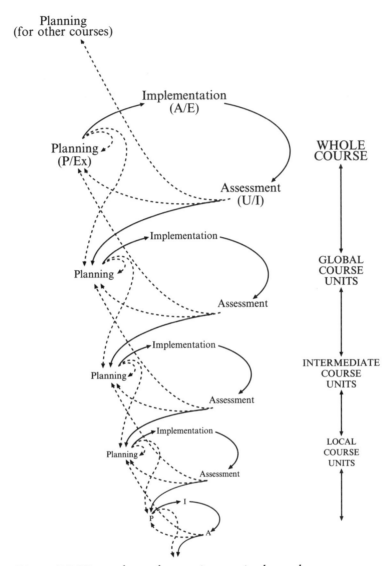

Figure 5.3 Hierarchy and recursiveness in the cycle

Conclusion: the model

With the two dimensions available on a page of paper, it is difficult to represent this concept diagrammatically. However, we can imagine a three-dimensional figure which represents the logical relationships where we look at planning and assessment in relation to the levels of the course being implemented. We can use the altered Allwright figure described above as a basis for these figures. By taking Figure 5.2 and tilting it on its side, we can then see the third dimension – the relationship of lower and higher levels of planning and decision-making. Figure 5.3 shows the relationships in terms of the logical levels, including planning, sub-planning and meta-planning, and including assessment feeding back into the same level, into subordinate levels, and into superordinate levels.

6 Procedures and strategies in the planning process

The model developed in the last chapter focuses on relationships among decisions in the planning process engaged in by the teachers. However, it does not specify the procedures and strategies the teachers use as they go through the actual process of planning in time. This is a crucial question, one which has not been examined in any detail in the field. As noted in earlier chapters, when ESL teacher education programs focus on process, the implication is usually classroom processes, not planning processes. In such programs, discussions of planning (creating lesson plans, for example) are often prescriptive rather than descriptive.

My initial curiosity about the question of teachers' planning stemmed from parallels I noticed while I was in the process of writing an article about the process of creating a writing process course (Woods, 1984). While in this vortex of meta-processes, I began to notice that there were interesting similarities between what I was going through in the writing of the article and what I had gone through in creating the course (not to mention what I had been asking my student writers to go through). Later, as I began examining the interview data for this study, the differences and similarities between what needs to be done in both cases became more evident. Clearly a written text is not interactive in the same way a second language lesson is, although Widdowson (1979) has argued convincingly that in the process of reading, a particular text becomes part of an interactive process with the reader. There is still an important difference – the interaction between author and reader is distanced in time and space whereas teacher and learners interact together – and this produces some interesting differences in the planning process of teachers as compared to the planning process of writers. However, there are a number of similarities. Both processes deal with the communication of conceptual and procedural information. Both processes involve considering an audience, applying constraints, and generating, organizing and sequencing ideas of different degrees of generality. And both processes involve turning abstract concepts into a linear sequence of language.

This chapter examines the issue of teachers' planning procedures in more depth and specifies a number of important distinctions relevant to the analysis of the planning process. The chapter first outlines the overall task that teachers face when given a course assignment. Second, it illustrates the procedures and strategies which the teachers in this study used to create the teaching structures that eventually made up the courses. Finally, the chapter specifies four factors that seem to be essential aspects of the process: (i) the tentativeness of planning decisions, (ii) the alternate use of resources and constraints, (iii) the use of top-down and bottom-up planning strategies, and (iv) the use of 'experienced structures'.

The task of the teacher

The overall task of the teachers in the study was to bring the learners from a perceived course-beginning state to a perceived targeted course-end state via a sequence of experiences. To accomplish this task, in principle, there are two requirements. First, the sequence must consist of events that the learners are capable of engaging in and will benefit from at any point along the course path. This means that the learners' current abilities are interpreted and taken into account in a dynamic fashion as the course progresses. Second, the sequence of experiences must lead the learners to the desired course goals. This means that the course goals are interpreted and taken into account in the teachers' planning.

When these two aspects are taken together, it means that the teacher uses the perceived differences between the learners' current abilities and the course goals in a dynamic on-going way in the planning process. This point is illustrated by Teacher D's comment at the outset of Course D:

D: The course I'm teaching I've done before and I feel, I feel I have a good sense of it, I feel I have a good sense of the students and a good sense of, um, where I pick them up and where I bring them and where I drop them off, and things like that ... .

Although the concepts considered to be course goals were usually not stated in behavioural terms, they were operationalized by the teacher (although often implicitly and gradually, as the course progressed) into behaviour – things that students are considered unable to do, and thus the reason that they are taking the course. Learners' current states were also generally interpreted in terms of behaviour and evaluated in terms of performance – how what they do reflects what they can do. In addition, the experiences that the learners engaged in as the course progressed were also viewed as things they do. In other words, there was a consistent focus on performance and on ability.

Interpretation of course goals

The teachers' interpretations of the course goals, as illustrated in Chapter 4, were expressed in a variety of ways. In some cases, the overall concepts were stated in terms of skills, for example, "oral skills", "writing", "vocabulary" and "academic skills". In other cases the overall concept was expressed in terms of language: "academic English", and in two cases, simply "English". Course goals varied from "improving English as much as possible" (according to criteria embodied in a pre- and post-course test, combined with personal views of what students needed) to quite specific abilities such as "write a paragraph on an academic topic using one of five rhetorical patterns".

Part of the interpretation was manifested in the ways in which the course goals are broken into subcomponents, i.e. the ways in which the units and their hierarchical relationships were determined. In some cases, some of the components were made explicit by the curriculum. For example, in several cases, there were several suggested textbooks from which the teacher had to choose one (or more than one) to be used. In one case, when a suggested textbook was used, the textbook itself broke down the concepts to be taught into units, lessons, activities for class and homework, and specific exercises. In other cases, the teachers had a great deal of freedom to work out the structuring of the units themselves. Often the teachers discussed the course goals in terms of their interpretations of what the students would have to do upon completing the course. In some cases this included what the teachers knew about the course (or even the specific teacher) that the students would move to after they finished the current course. Although the main emphasis on course goals occurred at the outset of the course, this process of interpretation and specification continued to evolve throughout the term through the refinement of subgoals and the overall goal structure of the course. This is evident in the comment by Teacher C overleaf.

Interpretation of learners' abilities

The teachers' interpretation of learners' abilities played an important role in their determination of course units, and their organization, sequencing and timing. These units, or events, had to be ones which the learners both (i) had the ability to engage in and (ii) would benefit from doing. Ability here related both to the students' ability to understand (whether they would 'get the point') and to their ability to perform (whether they could 'do the activity'). Part of the interpretation of learners' current abilities involved whether they were seen in terms of individuals or in terms of the whole class. Interpreting learners' current abilities depended on the monitoring and on-going evaluation of their classroom performance.

Teacher C exemplified this process in her description of an activity that she realized would not be accomplished without a more refined substructure. She did not think that the activity she had planned would be carried out in such a way as to help the students to move towards the course goals, and so she added a subactivity.

C: ... when I talked to you last time I told you I was going to go into the hidden information role play, but it occurred to me that maybe there was a step before that ... I rethought that because it seemed to me that I was jumping too much from the introduction [of the units] to the hidden information role play, which is where I want to go, ... but before we do that, I want to make sure that they can ask questions, so I've got another little activity built in/ ... there's quite an uneven ability range in that course where some people could ask anything in fifteen different ways, others I think would have a lot of trouble asking one question, so I've got to provide them with ... options, so I thought of one way of doing that would be by building in an interim step ...

Later she stated:

C: ... that will give them a little bit of practice in terms of asking questions because with the activities we were doing before, it seemed to me I was throwing it all into their laps, having them do it without having the stages, you know, giving them a little practice session to try and use it/ and for making sure in my own mind that they could in fact do it.

Teachers' procedures and strategies for planning

Overview

With the evolving interpretations of course goals and learners' current abilities occurring on a continuing basis throughout the course, the teachers then used a wide variety of strategies to plan the units at different levels of the course. Although the choice of strategies was quite idiosyncratic, and there were differences in the amount of planning done at different times; in sources and in emphasis, the strategies fell into a number of procedural categories that were surprisingly regular for the eight teachers included in the main study and, in addition, 14 others interviewed as part of a pilot project. These procedures are conceptually distinct, and recognizable as distinct in the data, but in practice there was a great deal of overlap from one to another, and a great deal of recursiveness in the process. Thus the use of the term 'procedures' in this chapter should not be taken as referring to a fixed sequence, but rather a generalized set of actions for approaching the teaching task involving a variety of flexible sub-strategies. The term strategies is used to describe the individual choices the teachers made for carrying out the procedures.

In general terms, teachers' planning involved the productive structuring of the course and its components through a series of decisions, connecting the conceptual goals of the course to the classroom events via a number of intermediary structures. The concepts inherent in the goals were identified and analyzed into components; meanwhile ideas for classroom events and their organization were generated. These together developed into a gradually evolving heterarchical and sequential structure with various superordinate and subordinate relationships, representing the 'units of the course'. As the planning process went on, the structure developed an increasing degree of linearity as the concepts and ideas were fit into the calendar and clock boundaries of an academic term. This transformation was a gradual one in which, during the process of course creation, the teacher went through many cycles of intermediate tentative hierarchical arrangements of the course. These tentative heterarchies served as instruments in the process. The gradual transformation into linearity culminated with the classroom: a sequence of actions and sounds for the learners to perceive, interpret and respond to. These transformations were carried out through a patterned set of strategic planning procedures.

In procedural terms, the task of the teacher can be broken down into two main components related to the chronological/conceptual distinction developed in Chapter 4. One component of the task of the teacher was to *structure* the conceptual units in order to link the overall course goals to a linear sequence of events to be experienced by the learners. The other component was to *map* this conceptual structure onto a series of bounded time frames – the chronological schedule of calendar and clock time. Both of these had to be undertaken by the teacher by making planning decisions over time and based on the on-going assessment of the results of prior decisions.

This first component – creating a conceptual structure to link the abstract goals of the course to a linear sequence of units that the learners experience – itself included two aspects: determining the units at various levels, and organizing the units in terms of their hierarchical and sequential relationships. Determining the levels, in turn, involved (i) constraining the possibilities, (ii) generating alternatives, and (iii) weighing and selecting.

The second component of the task relates to accomplishing the conceptual goals within the chronological structure of the course. It involves deciding on when particular units will begin, how long they will last, and how frequently they will occur (a one-time unit, or a repeating unit occurring at various points during the course). Teachers mapped conceptual structures onto the overall course period, onto particular lesson periods, and onto particular time slots within the lesson (for example, before or after the break, for the first hour, then

TABLE 2: OUTLINE OF PLANNING PROCEDURES

Definition of procedure:	Before course	Before lessons	During lessons
PLANNING			
Constraining: bringing to bear knowledge and information to reduce the range of current possibilities; at each point, the constraints are established very tentatively.	– activating what is known about the course from previous experiences; seeking specific information to constrain course plan possibilities.	– considering tentative course plan, updated by subsequent events and decisions, to constrain possibilities for next lesson and rest of course.	– considering tentative lesson plan and predicted responses, updated in light of on-going classroom events, to constrain moves and utterances.
Generating: expanding the resources that can be used within the current constraints. At any level of constraint, a number of alternatives are generated.	– within constraints, generating general tentative ideas for course, including textbooks, themes, activities, organizational structures.	– within constraints, generating ideas for activities or subactivity structures to fill holes or take into account changes in the plan.	– within constraints, generating ideas for moves and utterances to implement plan or for activity structures when plan changes.
Weighing & selecting: tentatively choosing, or giving positive weighting to specific units. This tentative weighing of possibilities sets up further constraints for subsequent decisions and for sub-decisions.	– tentatively choosing textbook (and relevant sections), themes, functions, written texts, tapes, activities, exams.	– tentatively choosing activities and subactivity structures for next several lessons.	– deciding on specific moves and utterances to implement activities.

Organizing & sequencing: linking conceptual units to higher and lower level elements in the overall structure by shaping the elements being considered as well as the overall structure; sequencing units with respect to each other.	– connecting overall goals of course, major organizational units, and activity groups and activity ideas.	– connecting activity groups, individual activities and sub-parts of activities and moves.	– connecting activities, subparts of activities, moves and utterances.
Mapping: adapting conceptual structure to fit into scheduled time slots and deciding what will be done in what periods of time.	– slotting major organizational structures, important dates, exams onto calendar of weeks and lessons.	– slotting activity and activity parts into, across and between upcoming lessons, and into timed parts of lessons.	– using moves and utterances to speed up, omit or slow down activity segments in light of class.
ASSESSMENT **Assessment:** assessing the results by monitoring and reflecting in light of the expected results and the higher level goals.	*After course* – assessing response to activity segments, activities, activity clusters, and larger organizational structures.	*After lessons* – assessing the response to activity segments and activities in light of goals.	*During lessons* – assessing the response to utterances, moves, activity segments and activities in light of goals.

the second hour, and so on). This aspect of planning specified what would be done when.

Although the cycle of constraining possibilities, generating alternatives, weighing the alternatives and making tentative selections occurred in all areas of decision-making, including the organization of the units, the mapping of the units, and even the planning of planning, it was most evident in the area of determining course units. It is in this area, therefore, that I have separated these procedures in the presentation below. The planning procedures, which occurred at all levels of course structure, and throughout the duration of the course, can be categorized as follows:

I. Structuring
   1. Determining conceptual units
      a. constraining the range of possibilities
      b. generating possible units
      c. weighing and selecting options
   2. Specifying relationships among conceptual units
      d. organizing and sequencing units

II. Mapping
      e. Setting the timing (onset, duration and frequency) of the conceptual units.

As units are implemented they are assessed, and the assessment can lead to any or all of the planning procedures described above: it usually provides new constraints; it may also lead to the generation of new ideas; it may result in a new decision regarding the selection of options; it may result in a reorganization of a structure, or it may cause a re-mapping of a particular time slot. As assessment becomes more immediate (for example, in the classroom) it becomes an integral part of on-going planning.

The procedures are summarized in Table 2.

Description of procedures and strategies

The chronological structure of the course provides a convenient way to describe the procedures and strategies for planning and assessment used by the teachers. This division indicates when certain procedures occur, but is not in itself meant to imply a categorization of types of procedures.

1. Planning before the course: overall course planning
2. Assessment after the course
3. Planning before the first lesson(s)
4. Assessment after the first lesson(s)

5. Planning during the course: between lessons
6. Assessment during the course: between lessons
7. Planning and assessment during lessons

Planning before the course: overall course planning

Although there is a sense in which the procedures described below are ordered, this ordering is somewhat flexible, as there was a great deal of overlap and recursiveness in the process. This flexibility is reflected in when different teachers began mapping the conceptual structures onto the chronological course schedule. Those teachers assigned a particular course for the first time focused primarily on structuring of the conceptual units first, and on mapping them onto calendar or clock time afterwards. However, the teachers who already had a good sense of the conceptual structure of the curriculum (for example, Teacher A who had developed the curriculum, Teacher D who had taught the course several times before, and Teacher F who was using a textbook) began focusing early in their planning on the chronological (calendar) structure of the course.

Constrain: The first step in course planning was to constrain the range of possibilities for the teaching. However, it was essential that these initial constraints still leave a great deal of flexibility in subsequent course creation. To do this, the teachers tended to look only for specific kinds of general information that could easily be adapted in light of later events. By creating a very general picture of the teaching situation, they were able to narrow it gradually as later events guided it. A too narrow or specific early 'instantiation' would have meant that later events might have contradicted the picture, and necessitated a more disruptive restructuring.

First, all the teachers indicated the need to get some initial information about the course as soon as they knew they would be teaching it. But the amounts of information required and demanded was very little, and brief and vague. This initial information that the teachers required consisted of three parts:

(a) a general idea of the level of the students, but only in the vaguest terms – a conception of whether they were beginning, intermediate or advanced.
(b) a general idea of the purpose of the course from the point of view of the institution, but again only in very general terms: academic, conversation, writing, etc.
(c) an indication of whether there was any required, suggested or previously used material for the course.

The teachers' interest in material seemed to have at least two functions: to find out if they were constrained by a particular institutional curriculum, and to get a more concrete sense of both the level of the students and the purposes of the course. A further reason for inquiring about required or previous course materials led into idea generating: to get ideas for what they could do in the course.

The teachers did not usually seek out much in the way of detailed information, even though they did have opportunities to do so. They usually took what they were told with a grain of salt at the beginning, including what was told to them by a supervisor, and waited to have these descriptions of the course, goals and students confirmed by other teachers, by the materials, and most importantly by the students themselves, before acting upon them. However, they did not explicitly indicate that they did not want more information, but rather they behaved as if the information could not be adequately transmitted through language – that it had to be revealed through experience. Teacher G was told that her upcoming class would be "a little lower" in level than her previous class, which she said was "helpful information" because the previous class was still "fresh in her mind", and it created a non-verbal image for her. Teacher F stated:

F: ... Once you see the students and get their writing samples, everything changes and starts from scratch again, so I've learned from past experience not to be too specific before I have any specifics to go by.

Teacher C did not start planning course content and activities in advance, but had a kind of general 'meta-plan' for how to proceed once the course was under way:

C: So what I have to do is find out who they are and what they want, and then look in my bag of tricks and see what I can find that satisfies me because it is psychologically sound and in tune with my philosophy of how things should work, and make a match.

Generate: This initial information about constraints allowed the teachers to move to their resources in order to generate ideas for course units. When the teachers went to their resources, they were guided by their conception of the purpose of the course and the level of the students. They began at various levels: from themes or larger organizational structures which would link activities together into larger units, to activities or smaller organizational structures which might be later fitted into a larger structure, to texts or worksheets which might be used as part of an activity. Almost all teachers (at least the non-textbook-bound ones) were continually on the outlook for ideas – reading, clipping, listening for and taping things that might one day fit into the current course, or perhaps even an unspecified course sometime in the future. These teachers were never fully 'off duty'.

The process of generating possibilities for course units seemed to be carried out at various degrees of consciousness. Sometimes the teachers had specific ideas of what they needed and they went consciously looking for those specific things. The teachers had a variety of such strategies for getting ideas in preparation for the course. In addition to their memory of past teaching experiences, they had a number of external sources of ideas, usually in the form of a collection of files and loose papers containing activities, exercises, handouts, and notes that they had used for previous courses or had collected from other teachers as well as books, journals, and other textual sources. They reported that once they knew they had a course to teach, they went to their collection, as well as perhaps to a library or resource centre, to look for specific items or to browse for ideas.

However, several teachers noted that this generation of ideas was often not a conscious process: the ideas seemed to spring to mind of their own accord once the initial constraints for the course were established and began to incubate. There was a sense that the ideas did not come *from* the teachers in the sense that they 'caused' them, but rather, that they came *to* them. The ideas evolved out of a combination of dynamic interaction between the teachers and circumstances and events; and the teachers showed an interesting awareness of the interaction between conscious and unconscious planning. One strategy that they used was to put themselves into situations where ideas would come to them. They did this both physically (like reading a newspaper, which might be a source of and/or spark some idea or other) and mentally (simply mulling things over in what seemed to be an aimless way, when suddenly specific ideas came to them), or a combination of physically and mentally (like going for a walk, leading to a mental state ready to receive ideas). One teacher mentioned that on the bus home after having been given the assignment to teach the course, her mind had already begun wondering about possibilities. In a sense the establishment of the initial constraints was both a pre-requisite and a catalyst for idea generation.

Weigh & select: As the teachers continued to generate ideas, they started to weigh and select them, as certain ideas were rejected outright and others were given a positive weighting. However, at this stage the selections were very tentative. The criteria for the initial selection of units were related to overall goals, characteristics of the students, and the constraints represented by previous decisions, for example, which themes had tentatively been decided upon. The main characteristic of this stage was to analyze the possibilities within the constraints established so far, but to leave open as many options as possible. This was exemplified by Teacher C's comments:

C: Before the course began, I learned that in fact the focus of the course was to be on conversation, strategies, therefore that narrowed the range considerably, because when I think we talked before it was unclear to me exactly what this course was going to consist of, but in speaking to [the coordinator] again, what happened was ... the focus was to be on talking, anything that related to talking, so that narrowed the focus considerably.

She then discussed what happened before the first lesson:

C: I often do this, I often prepare a number of things and then depending on my mood, the mood of the class, whatever/ I mean for me it was the phone call from [another teacher] and talking to her about the nature of the class and what they were doing in her class. That pushed me into the particular plan ... I had considered a number of options ... .

Organize & sequence: The organizing of the units in terms of their relationships to each other also phased in gradually as ideas at different levels were tentatively selected. Teachers focused both on elaborating the units downward, deciding on lower level units and how they would best be achieved (through substructuring). For example, Teacher H described the first steps for her in this process:

H: ... first one of the things I try and do is try and figure out the components that should make up the course/ that I want to teach ... For example, I wrote down the normal/ the reading, listening, speaking, writing, vocabulary, grammar/ all six main areas and then I just brainstormed on what I thought should go in and what kind of activities that I possibly could do in those areas.

Teachers also made connections upward, deciding that lower level units would fit into a sequence that comprises a superordinate unit. As this was being planned, the units were adapted and shaped in order to fit the evolving structures.

Map: Mapping the conceptual structure of the course onto the chronological schedule also began with constraints, in particular the calendar constraints the teachers knew or had learned about the course. There were a number of personal techniques for making what they termed "the plan". (When the teachers referred to their "plan", they typically meant the plan for mapping the conceptual structure onto the chronological schedule, whether it was for the overall course or for individual lessons.) Several of the teachers made a grid on a paper with the weeks of the course and the class days and then filled in the constraints and givens: holidays, final exams, other tests, regular lab or grammar periods, possible assignment dates; and then, as they developed conceptual units for the course, such as themes or activities, they tentatively 'pencilled in' possible units which would fit the overall purpose and level of the course. Other teachers followed a similar process in a list form, or with separate pages for separate weeks of the course. Several of the teachers did much of their mapping in their heads, and put little down on paper. Teacher C said that she had tried grids, but it didn't work. She said that her manner of organizing her course was a "weakness"; but it had clearly evolved in order for her to handle her courses in her own way. Teacher F said that if she "wrote stuff down it was bound to get lost and she would forget it", whereas if she committed it to memory she was less likely to "lose" it.

The major conceptual units were mapped onto the chronological structure of the course in a number of ways. Some were spread through the course in regular intervals (as noted in Chapter 4). Others were slotted into periods of several weeks or lessons. Teacher F, for example, in considering the textbook, noted that each of the textbooks falls into roughly twelve sections "which is kind of handy since we have twelve weeks to work with, so that is not too bad, so more or less I will go with that".

The available time plays a crucial consideration in this aspect of planning. Teacher F, in discussing the mapping of textbook chapters onto weeks of the course, stated: "Needless to say, one usually runs out of time, so I've looked at what I might be cutting in that case." She did this, in week 11, by replacing the chapter on research techniques with a guided tour of the library facilities: "It's not only a timesave, but also gives a real-life touch to the whole thing and it never hurts to get them out of the classroom at the end of the term anyway, everybody's bored and tired."

Teacher D, who had the most familiarity of any of the teachers in the study with the students she would have, planned the overall course structure and mapped it onto the schedule before thinking of specific materials that would be used:

D: What I've done is I've laid it out. I know everything that's going to be dealt with ... I know how the students are going to be assessed. I know how many assignments they're going to have, what dates those assignments should be due, what dates they should get things back. I've covered all the skills I think adequately, and there may be, once we get into the swing, some changes. But they won't be, they won't be really major changes. They may have one less assignment or something because of time problems, but I have to be very well organized in terms of knowing what's going to go on in the twelve weeks. And then we'll see. So to answer your question, I haven't got a clue what materials I'm going to use and I won't really think about that probably until, well, tomorrow or Friday and then I'll have Monday and on Tuesday I'm meeting one group.

I: The materials themselves aren't as important as what you're going to teach?

D: Well they really are important, but it was more important this week to get/ ... I had a lot of work to do this week, and I simply prioritized things and the actual materials wasn't high, although I wish it were done.

The teachers considered how many themes or units might fit into the overall time period for the course. They also considered whether any of their units would occur in regularly occurring slots throughout the course rather than in a sequence, as, for example, Teacher D's writing journals and oral presentation days:

D: ... I find I get into a pattern [in my teaching]. Monday morning we write. First thing is the writing journals. That kind of gives everybody a chance to wake up after the weekend. And then Friday is always orals. Of course it's not all Friday or all Monday. And then, sort of, the rest of Monday and part of Friday and all of Wednesday is working, if you know what I mean. So I sort of begin the week always the same way and end the week always the same way, and then do different things in between and I ... I like that.

Assessment after the course

The interaction among considerations, goals, content and procedures (described in Chapter 4) is clearly seen in teachers' assessments after the course was finished. These post-course assessments focused primarily on larger course units. The units were discussed as course content, expressed in terms of their recurrence in future courses. They were also discussed as goals to be achieved through a revised structuring of the subactivities that made it up. The assessment of these larger level units occurred in terms of how well they functioned in accomplishing the higher level (in this case, course) goals.

In the post-course interview, Teacher A's comment, below, demonstrates her perception of the links between levels in the goal structure, including high level goals of the course (enabling the students to function effectively in regular courses of study at the university) to a major subgoal (reading effectively), to a sub-subgoal (understanding what is required by an exam question), to classroom procedures (looking at the test question) even to a possible verbalization for carrying out the classroom procedure ("what are they asking you here?").

A: ... what I found in reading, something I didn't realize until the end of the course in the last exam and the last test I gave them, one big problem the students have in reading is that they don't know how to answer a question, they don't address the question, they give information that isn't being asked ... so I think a big part of their problem in reading and doing exams in other courses comes not so much from understanding the reading selection as much as they don't read the test question carefully and answer it, so that's something that I think I would like to work on with my students ... just to look at the questions and say "what are they asking you here?" I think that I've done a lot to help the students in reading, but I think that there's a lot more that has to be done ... .

These assessments also related to units that are mapped across lessons or throughout the course. For example, Teacher A considered changes in her method of marking writing, and of informing the students about this method, which is an aspect of providing feedback on writing mapped across the whole course. These potential changes evolved out of her assessment of the success of the current procedures in accomplishing the course's writing goals. Her evaluation of the writing part of the course was a theme that came up several times during the post-course interview:

A: ... now as far as the writing part of the course is concerned, I'm not as satisfied with it as I had been in the past ... .

In discussing the results of the final exam, she said:

A: ... I found they wrote a lot and the organization wasn't bad,, actually they did use the patterns appropriately and they did use the kind of lan- guage that was appropriate but there was something about the structure and the grammar that wasn't/ ... I guess it's not the patterns that was the problem as much as the grammar. I guess I'm disappointed in their ability to deal with the English sentence structures.

She viewed this assessment of the course results in terms of the fact that the course had been restructured by the institution, necessitating further changes on her part:

A: ... so I guess part of the problem is the restructuring of the course, and I have to figure out how to work that restructuring of the course in with- out having my students come out [of the course] with lousy sentence struc- ture.

This led her to some consideration of possible alternatives at the level of activity types, and a discussion of the potential for success of one of them in the light of her teaching experience:

A: ... . I want to spend more time I think trying to get them to rewrite or proof-read or analyze each other's sentences ... what I did a couple of times at the end of this semester was take students' actual essays and put them on the overhead and analyze the grammatical mistakes in them as a group, and the students found that to be very helpful ... I think I might do more of that in one form or another. When something works well I like to do it but then I don't want to get caught in the trap of doing it that way all the time ... / I think part of why it was interesting and it worked well was because the students hadn't done anything like that before, but if every week I put up on the board someone's paragraph and we analyzed it, I think it wouldn't be as successful.

She also considered changing her procedures for correcting students' work, so as to place less importance on the content of the writing compared to the grammatical structure, which was her area of concern:

A: I also wasn't happy with the way I marked it … I've decided that I'm going to mark it differently in the future … .

But her re-planning was still tentative as she said: "I'm teaching [the same course] again next winter, so I have enough time to think about it." This comment also indicates her awareness of the role of time in the planning process.

Planning before the first lesson(s)

Constrain: The initial constraints for the course – a general understanding of the types and levels of the students and of the goal or purpose of the course – were also the constraints for the first lesson (or lessons, if the introductory activities, which are planned on a conceptual basis, last longer than the first lesson). However the constraint that made the planning for this lesson concrete was not the information which teachers gained about the students and the course, but rather another part of their background knowledge: their sense of what a first lesson is for. The first lesson had a unique role in the teachers' planning process. Rather than being based on learning goals for the students as planning for the course and subsequent lessons were, the planning for the first lesson was based on the following three goals: (a) to get information about the students that would guide further planning, including information about the learners' interests, perceived needs, levels of proficiency and abilities in the language; (b) to introduce the course and course goals; and (c) to establish class dynamics. The role of this lesson was to provide information for planning for the teacher and at the same time to let the students know that this would be a good setting to learn in. These factors controlled the teachers' planning decisions about the first lesson.

   Generate: At the same time as they were looking for resources for the course, teachers began generating or considering possibilities for the first lesson that would achieve these three goals: allow them to find out more about the students, provide an idea of what the course would be like, and create a positive dynamic for the group. Although some teachers considered various possibilities for the first lesson, many teachers had in mind activities that they had used previously, because they had a sense of how they worked.

   Weigh & select: From their repertoire, they selected activities which they felt would do the best job of giving them the information in light of the initial constraints of the purpose of the course and the level of the students. The kinds of ideas for this first meeting varied, including such things as ice-breaking or introduction activities, needs analyses of various types, student interviews, student profiles, 'student I.D. cards', and so on. All were intended to reveal some characteristics of the students, who they were, what they wanted, needed and expected, and all were intended to get the students to perform in various ways so that the teachers could get a sense of their language abilities; only one teacher (in the pilot study preceding the main study) chose to use a standardized test or measure of any kind (although in many cases, the institution pre-tested the students for placement), and even then she paid little attention to the results once she had seen the students. It seemed far more important, for teaching purposes, to get a 'feel' for the level of the students.

In order to let the students know what the course was to be about, the teachers in the study provided (and the institution required) a course outline. This created a bit of a paradox for the teachers, as they generally had not planned the course in any detail before meeting the students. Several teachers had perfected the art of the vague course outline, one which satisfied the students and the institutional requirements, but left most of the important decisions about the course open. Teacher F treated this explicitly: she explained to the students her 'philosophy' of not giving them a course outline in the first lesson because she wanted "to find out what they know before sitting down to do one".

Organize & sequence: In this study, the teachers did not spend time thinking about the detailed ways in which the activities for the first lesson would be structured in order to be carried out, because the substructures of these activities had usually been experienced many times.

Map: The mapping of this first lesson was an estimate of how long the activities would take: whether they would all occur in the first lesson, and how they should be split into the chronological time slots (usually there was a break) that made up the lesson.

The before-course planning culminated with the implementation of the first lesson(s).

Assessment after the first lesson(s)

A crucial part of the course planning occurred after the first lessons, although the degree to which subsequent plans were directly based on the lesson varied from teacher to teacher. Teacher G, whose course was relatively unconstrained by an institutional curriculum, stated:

G: ... [the first lesson] affected very much what we did afterwards. As it turned out, the students want to do almost speaking and writing exclusively ... so then I could choose the precise activities and precise things I wanted to do when I knew that ... .

One of the aspects focused on was the students' abilities, both the range of individuals within the class and for the class as a whole. Teacher H reported on her first lesson:

H: Well I talked to them very briefly ... with these [low level] students it's difficult to [do] speaking very much, but they seemed to be well levelled. And then I did a dictation and that seemed to weed out quite a bit/seemed to show that there was quite a wide range of variation in the class ... I got them to work in groups, to speak to each other and so they had to pose questions to each other and so, you know, it's pretty obvious that they had a lot of trouble thinking of questions or formulating questions and getting the words together to ask an adequate question.

This result led quite directly into her planning of the subsequent lessons in a number of ways, including choosing activities to practice asking questions, and choosing a source textbook:

I: Are they at the level that you expected?

H: No, they are much lower than I expected.

I: How does what you know about them now/how will that affect what's coming in the future?

H: Well, in terms of the textbook, I had pretty well decided to use *Reader's Choice* as my main reading and vocabulary source ... and now I think it's way over their heads.

For all the teachers, the initial dynamic and attitude of the class was an important result of the first lesson. Virtually all the teachers commented on this both in terms of general enthusiasm, and in terms of specific attitudes sought by individual teachers. For example, Teacher G looked for interest in independent learning. Teacher E wrote at length in her log about students taking responsibility for their learning after the first lesson in which the students worked in groups to determine the problems they had in learning vocabulary:

E: ... . I felt uneasy when we finished doing this. What made me feel strange was that students looked so *relieved* and *content* because they had finished identifying all those problems and they almost looked like that was the end of their involvement or responsibility as far as the course was concerned. It was as if they had been to the doctor, talked about their symptoms and were simply expecting a prescription for medicine. I didn't like the idea of being perceived as a doctor who had the magical cure or potion.

This assessment of the students' attitudes led directly to subsequent activities (e.g. choosing dictionaries), parts of activities (verbalize criteria and monitor decisions), and accompanying verbalizations to encourage the students' acquisition of these attitudes.

Planning during the course: between lessons

Once the courses began to be implemented, planning was also tentatively done, most particularly in the earlier stages when the number of prior decisions made had not limited very much what would happen subsequently. The teachers continued to make frequent comments about not planning far in advance. For example, Teacher A, one of the teachers in the study most concerned with being well-prepared, when talking about plans for two weeks ahead, stated:

A: ... there's no point in planning that far ahead because so many things can change what I do. I have a very *general* idea (of what I will do) ... .

As the course went on, and the process of making on-going decisions progressed, there was less and less freedom to plan, but also less of a requirement for planning. As the constraints stemming from prior decisions gradually increased, there was less need to generate possible units in later lessons. Instead the focus moved to how to fit the remaining content into the remaining time. For example, Teacher B, a week before the end of the course said:

B: ... there's just trying to sort of get all those things finished up at the end, that I don't really have to plan, and I'm certainly not going to start anything new at this stage ... .

Constrain: The constraints on planning for each lesson were provided by prior course decisions that had been made (however tentatively) and the experiences of the lessons that had occurred prior to the lesson in question. These experiences updated the teacher's sense of what had to be done and what could be done. (The notion of revising the planning is discussed in more detail under 'assessment' below.) The 'course plan' up to that point – an evolving overall idea of the sequence of events (at the various conceptual levels at which they had been planned) became a kind of framework within which the next lesson, and the planning for that lesson, would fall.

Teacher C, in discussing her usual temporal planning procedures, indicated the importance of recently experienced classroom events in influencing subsequent decisions:

C: ... now when I get into the flow of the class, most of the planning for the next class will occur just after the class, because everything is fresh in my mind, the impressions are fresh, the needs are fresh, so that's when the planning takes place, basically I decide what the next direction is going to be ... .

Generate: Teachers mainly generated possibilities between lessons within the constraints of the previously established plan (or planned options), in order either to fill holes that the planning had left, or provide more options for what was already there. For example, Teacher B recounted that as he was reading a book out of interest on the bus, he discovered that it contained a passage that would be perfect for trying to get across the point of definitions he had targeted for the next lesson. Similarly, Teacher H, while embarking on a unit about banking for the accountants in her class, said:

H: ... I was reading the [newspaper] this weekend, and there was a lovely story about credit cards ... which I think I'll use as an exercise in reading ... .

A crucial part of the generation stage is the generation of options. This was an issue discussed by virtually all the teachers. For example, Teacher C stated explicitly "one thing I often do is give myself options when I plan".

In some cases, teachers' generation of ideas was clearly related not to the conceptual structure of the course, but rather to the chronological structure – in such a case the primary goal of the activity was to make sure the time slot was filled rather than to achieve a learning goal. Virtually all the teachers, at one time or another, expressed concern about running out of things to do with time still left in the lesson. In fact, this did not happen once during the period of the study with the eight teachers. Generally the opposite was the case, that the teachers had to creatively compress, postpone or eliminate units of teaching in order to achieve the conceptual goals within the chronological structure of the lessons and the course.

For idea generation, as before the course, teachers went to their own files, or to other sources. For example, Teacher H went to the resource centre to find an activity on directions for listening practice in the lab, found an appropriate written text and map, and had the written text read into a listening text by "somebody with a different voice" (her husband). Teacher B, at one point, tried a technique he had taught students of writing – brainstorm for ideas by using an "idea web" – and produced too much to be covered.

Some of the planning went on paper in the form of notes or a written lesson plan that was taken into class, although most of the teachers did not call it a 'lesson plan'. For some teachers, the stack of handouts to be used was the reminder of the structure of activities within a lesson. Teacher F said that she stored in her head what would be used, or had "little scribbles" as she called them (in one case, for example, on the back of an envelope). These props mainly functioned as reminders to refer to if necessary during the lesson.

Planning between lessons seemed to operate in an on-going and not always totally conscious process. Teacher C, for example, said:

C: .... shopping for me is a mindless thing ... you know, if I have to go in and buy meat, I go to the meat counter and I don't/ I'm not good at looking at prices ... because during that time that I'm selecting the hamburger I'm thinking "Okay, if I'd done this with Abdul, it would have worked a lot differently, now I need bread, alright now with Mohammed the strategy would be"/ I do that all the time ... .

Weigh & select: The options were considered within the evolving constraints, and eventually some of the options became more appropriate than others. The ultimate selection of the units to be used within the on-going structuring of the course was primarily related to filling the holes in the most recent conception of the existing structures, or reducing the options previously generated. In the following comment by Teacher E, we can see the tentativeness of the process of selection – the balancing and weighting of alternatives, the setting up of several possibilities and the incubation between lessons.

E: I think, as I said before, the whole monitoring of the week, I could set up an activity that concentrates on that, or I could just let that go and make up another activity that I've already thought about. We can already start talking about prefixes and suffixes and how that can help them. I've got activities all set up for that, if I want to do that. That particular activity is planned but I don't know if I want to do it next time or not. So I'm still thinking ... I have the possibilities, now I have to decide which is best. If I don't do it [decide] over the weekend, then I usually do it the day before, then if I need any materials or anything, that's when I do it. What usually happens is that I think about it, even if I don't do anything about it, I think about it seriously on the weekend, and then I do something about it the day before ... also because they [the ideas] change all the time, they don't change that much, but I like the idea of leaving myself time for other things to come to mind.

Organize & sequence: One way in which the teacher organizes the units on an on-going basis between lessons is by taking a higher level concept and developing a number of different alternative ways it could be developed at lower levels. For example, Teacher C described how a conversation in the classroom led to a consideration of various ideas for expanding the 'language functions' associated with meeting people into different situational possibilities that could be developed:

C: ... I talked to them [the students] about meeting people, and the way I used the party [introduced the party theme] was to say "One context in which you sometimes meet people that you don't know is the party." There were other contexts we talked about, like the wedding reception, a meeting,,, but those are all different sorts of things/ you know, the meeting especially, that's an important one. In the future I can see that being developed, you know, the language of the meeting.

Map: Planning between lessons included mapping conceptual units such as activities and parts of activities onto specific time periods. Teacher F expressed her expectations about covering what she had planned for a particular lesson:

F: Well hopefully before we actually take the coffee break we'll have a chance to go through the possibilities together ... Only I don't see any great room for individual freedom in this particular one since the essay is written for them and they just have to identify the various topics and determine the thesis statement and then the concluding statement and all that stuff. I mean, they can't really be too creative about that point. Let's put it that way ... .

I: I see. Well then do you think that would be done before the coffee break or will you have time?

F: It depends a bit how long the 'paragraph hook' review will take. Hopefully that's not going to linger on for too long.

One of the on-going challenges is mapping the units of teaching coherently onto the chronological structure of the course. In one case, Teacher C realized that her new idea would have fit better into the party theme which had already been completed.

C: ... another thing I want to do is work on ... information gap strategies. I think one thing they must be able to do is give and receive directions, so I'll be developing a whole unit in that area ... If I had more time, if I was writing this as a curriculum project ... I would have been able to fit all of this in, telephoning, directions, instruction, all in the context of the party. What is happening to me is that I know all of these things are important but I'm already moving beyond the party now. I haven't worked in these other things and I see they're important but I can't backtrack the theme. The theme is lost for me, so if I were to do the course again, then I could see how I could cluster more and build it into the theme. But it's all a question of time.

Deciding what to do next creates a particular type of conflicting pressure on the teacher. At any point in time, the teacher has the choice of moving on to a subsequent unit of activity in order to ensure that all of the required units will be covered in the course, or of spiralling down into the depths of detail subordinate to a current unit, in order to ensure that the particular unit accomplishes its superordinate goal. For example, Teacher E described this conflicting pressure in terms of continuing to develop activities involving strategies for using dictionaries, or moving on to the next theme in the sequence of vocabulary learning strategies.

E: ... I mean I saw certain [kinds of] dictionaries focusing on particular things, and all of a sudden a great idea about an activity just focusing on those particular things came to mind. I'd say "Oh, if I just put this one together with this, I can make up an activity just to focus on this particular area of lexical/words", and then I'd find something even more interesting and I'd say "Oh, now if I just add this and contrast this, and get them to see this", so I was just kind of going on and on,,, however, I went back home and when I planned my activity for the next day, I ended up coming back to the original idea, and I'll tell you what the main reason is ... I'm getting worried about time. I'm getting worried that we would be spending too much time on instruments and tools ... That's basically the constraint of time that put some restrictions on my designing of the activity there, although I'm glad that it happened.

Assessment during the course: between lessons

Assessment between lessons was considered to be an essential on-going part of the planning process. It included on-going assessments, similar to those after the first lesson, of units on a variety of levels: the overall units that occurred in the lesson, as well as a number of more local activities, techniques and interactions. Teacher C's questions to herself, reported as her "mulling" over what happened during the lesson, include both considerations of on-going units ("How did that work?" and "Where am I going to go from here?"), as well as analyses of the smaller sub-units ("What was it about the lesson ... . ?"), analyses that can result in revisions of those sub-units when used in the planning of future lessons.

C: ... I consider that my planning/when I was talking about planning, my mulling is actually my planning. "Okay, where am I going to go from here?" And "How did that work?" and "What would I do differently?" and ... "Who was happy in the class and who wasn't?", "Who participated a lot and who didn't?", "What was it about the lesson that worked for one person and didn't for the other?", "What can I do to remedy the situation so that everybody gets an equal go?", ... "How weak is he really? Is it fair to put him with this other student who's so good? Does it benefit him or is it inhibiting him?". All of these sorts of questions I consider planning.

Planning and assessment during lessons

As the cycle of planning/implementation/assessment becomes more immediate, it becomes more difficult in the analysis to separate the assessment from subsequent planning, and to separate the individual procedures. The constraints are used as input leading directly to a decision, the generating, weighing and selecting and organizing of units occurs in unison, and the mapping issue feeds immediately back into further planning. For example, the organizing of the structure downward in the hierarchy – into verbalizations – at this level coincides with the generation of lower-level structures. The assessment that occurs during the lesson becomes the final set of constraints that is applied to on-going classroom decisions.

Planning during lessons was primarily local planning – deciding on the level of moves and utterances – what would be done and said in order to accomplish the higher level structures that had evolved to that point in the on-going course plan and its component lesson plans. It involved elaborating plans into utterances – what would be said to accomplish certain sub-units. These usually were not pre-planned before the lesson, but rather 'shaped at the point of utterance'. However, teachers often described what they were going to do in terms of possible utterances, so there is an element of verbal planning or at least verbal expectations that may occur in advance. This type of verbal planning seemed to occur on a subconscious level, but it was accessible to later conscious reflection and discussion.

However, in addition to this type of immediate downward structuring, there were many cases where the stimulus for a restructuring of the long term plan came as an immediate response to what was happening in the classroom. This type of assessment and planning is illustrated in the examples below.

Constrain: The constraints operating on decisions made in the classroom were those established by the prior decisions made leading up to the moment of classroom decision-making. However, as the following example illustrates, there was a continuity between decision-making done between lessons and decision-making done during lessons. Teacher A's decision, moments before the lesson (in fact on the way up the escalator to the classroom) was a 'pre-active' decision, part of planning before the class. However, it could easily have been made as an 'interactive' decision only moments later, after the class had begun. The important thing, in either case, is that it was based on the constraints of previous tentative decisions: she knew "what I would base my decision on".

A: ... I think generally I like to leave it [not give them their handout until later in the class] because I don't want them reading the handout while I'm talking. The only reason I felt I might give it out before was because of the exercises on it and I realize that the exercises on it were simple enough that I could just write those dictionary words on the board and make a definition without having the handout ... I could get through everything on the formal definition before I reached that point so it wasn't important ... .

I: Okay. When did you make that decision?

A: On my way up to class after I picked up the handouts from printing and just briefly looked up at them going up the escalator. I knew what I was looking for at that point. And I knew what I would base my decision on. I just wanted to make sure that they didn't need the handout before the end of the lecture or almost at the end of the lecture.

However, in many cases the final constraint is related to an assessment of classroom events; it is this assessment which results in a number of strategies for further in-class planning, as in the examples below. In these cases, the assessment leads immediately back into the decision-making cycle and further decisions are implemented right away. Some of these are related to the conceptual structure while others are related to the mapping process.

Generate/Weigh & select/Organize & sequence: Many of the teachers discussed ideas which were generated during the classroom teaching. On some occasions these ideas were related to the success of the particular lesson or activity under way. On other occasions they were related to and therefore part of the planning for future lessons, and in a couple of cases, for future courses.

Teacher C indicated how her assessment of a component of an activity as it was occurring in class affected her thinking about the on-going activity. This assessment occurred at the close of a group activity in which she was working with one of the groups. In this case, she wanted, but was not able, to adjust the on-going activity so that its conclusion would be successful (or at least not 'uneven').

C: One bit of unevenness was that ... the first group finished before the second group and I was with the second group at the time they were finishing, so there were a few dead minutes there, so I would/ if I do this again I would somehow devise a strategy either to give them something else to do following the completion of the introduction or keep my eyes open more/ my eyes were open but .... I couldn't leave. I knew the other group had finished but I just couldn't leave.

This interpretation of a particular classroom event (the silence that occurred when one subgroup finished the activity before the other) also fed back into the higher level planning structure – "a lesson in chit-chat" done within the theme of the party – which itself was one aspect of the overall course goal of "conversation". This in-class assessment immediately fed into her planning for the subsequent lessons, which occurred tentatively within the context of larger planning units:

C: ... once that assignment was finished, unlike normal interaction, that table that had completed the assignment just suddenly fell silent, ... that triggered for me the next lesson, which was a lesson in chit-chat and small talk, and I did it in the context of the party.

In the following series of comments, Teacher C interpreted the silence in her more advanced class (Course C2) not as a lack of linguistic ability that a subsequent activity could have as a goal to remedy, but rather as a lack of knowledge of particular 'content', the news. The interpretation and assessment of this silence provided her immediately with an idea for an on-going activity which promoted presentation skills (one of the course's higher level goals) and student responsibility for learning (one of her higher level goals).

C: ... I asked them what was going on in the world, you see, what was happening outside, if they knew of anything interesting,, and there was absolute silence, there was nothing, and I mean these people usually talk so it wasn't a question of ... feeling shy or intimidated ... .

The outcome of this questioning first led to a further set of classroom decisions, and a sequence of subsequent verbalizations in the classroom:

C: ... then I asked/ I went into that, so "Do you watch television?", "Do you read the newspaper?", "Yes sometimes, but,,,". Anyway, as a result, I said, "Okay, well it's important to keep in touch ...".

These verbalizations led to an on-the-spot creation of a new regular activity that eventually became a recurring feature of each lesson through the entire course:

C: ... I told them that I would bring in the news the following day, then I was going to pass [the responsibility for] the news on to somebody else in the class, who would in turn pass it on to somebody else who would pass it on to somebody else ... .

The fact that a substructure (such as a news reporting activity) can be interpreted as having many different goals and be carried out for many reasons allowed her to transfer it to her other course (C1), where it helped in the accomplishment of the conversational goal of the course, and in the more specific goal related to the current theme of 'parties'. In this case, it is an example of a recurrence of an activity which has been used successfully in another set of circumstances.

C: ... it worked in perfectly because one thing that people often talk about at parties, superficially, is the news.

An important part of in-class generation involved on-going decisions about what to do before what. Some of the evidence for this kind of decision comes from the 'tangles' in the hierarchy of decisions in the classroom, as described in Chapter 4. The example noted there of Teacher D's decision to check the assignments rather than begin the listening is an example of a sequencing decision made in the class-room. This type of in-class planning is also evident in Teacher A's comment:

A: I don't think I really planned to talk about the problems next ... I think I was going to have them define those words ... before I gave the problems and as I was glancing at my notes and teaching it suddenly occurred to me that I should go on and discuss the problems and then have them do the definitions so that they could be conscious of what to avoid. But I really hadn't thought about it and planned that out carefully before.

In the example below, Teacher F described an in-class decision made during the introductory subsection of an activity, based on her inter-pretation of the students' current state. An additional 'substructure' was included in the introduction, that of using the blackboard, to help accomplish the objective of having the students understand the intro-duction.

F: But anyway, because I decided to do the introduction on the black-board, which I think was decided sort of half and I didn't necessarily know if I was going to do it or not ... there were kind of a few question mark faces, sort of looking back and forth and not seeming really to know how to get started and with that I felt that maybe it was a good thing to get them started with the blackboard support. So it was, to some extent, an *ad hoc* decision. It was a possibility, it was in my mind and I decided to use it sort of more or less on the spot.

Map: Teachers' planning during lessons in the classroom also related to getting certain units covered during the clock time of the lesson. The mapping of activities onto chronological time during the lesson was primarily a question of deciding what could be fitted into the remaining time before the break and especially before the end of the lesson – how the structures should be compressed, postponed or elimi-nated in order to achieve the goals of the superordinate structures within the time frame of the lesson and ultimately the time frame of the course. In the classroom, the teachers monitored the passage of time and the requirements of getting conceptual units accomplished. For example:

F: ... so then we returned to the classroom after the break and they fin-ished their outlines. They spent about between five and ten minutes on that. And then we came back together as a class and filled in the blanks on the blackboard.

In Teacher F's discussion of her in-class thinking, she indicated a change in plan based on a complex set of factors, but intended mainly to complete certain aspects of the planned conceptual structure during the lesson period. After describing an issue that the class raised regarding her emphasis on academic writing, she stated:

F: ... I decided to make [writing] the abstract a kind of individually based choice that they can just as well do on their own and that I wouldn't spend class time on.

I: So you decided/ obviously decided that right in the class/

F: /Well because there wasn't/I had to cut something because of the time factor if I wanted to get to the response [the next part of the activity], and I wanted to get to the response because I want to give them that option in the essay on Thursday. And since there had been questions raised about the appropriateness of over-emphasizing academic writing, I decided that I'll leave that [writing the abstract] as an elective activity for those who feel the need for it.

Features of the decision-making process

In this section, I want to focus on a number of generalizations and patterns which emerged from the analysis of the data within the framework of the model. The first was the extreme degree of tentativeness exhibited in the teachers' planning. The second was the alternate use of resources and constraints in planning. The third was the use of top-down and bottom-up planning. The fourth was the use of experienced structures (or 'implicit' planning) in the planning process.

Tentativeness of planning

One noteworthy phenomenon was how tentatively the course was planned, even by the most organized and prepared of teachers, and how much of what was planned was scrapped or altered as further information became available (which made depending on a textbook or set curriculum very difficult according to most teachers in the study). This finding has surprised virtually every ESL teacher with whom I have discussed these results: they said "I thought I was the only one who was like that!" This phenomenon of tentativeness occurred in the course planning both before and during the course.

For example, Teacher A, who described herself as a very organized person:

A: I like things to be organized or else I feel out of control and nervous ... I'm one of those people who spends a lot of time organizing and planning ... .

Nonetheless, she never planned in any detail far ahead; when talking about her plans for the following weeks, she stated:

A: There's no point in planning that far ahead because there's so many things that can change what I can do. I have a *very* general idea.

She expected that things would change:

A: I have ideas but they might change a lot once I start doing it.

Decisions for late in the course were initially left entirely open. When describing her plans for the end of the term, Teacher A said:

A: ... The last few weeks of the course are always like completely/like I never know until close to the end how far I'm into and whether I'm going to have time to review certain things or just be teaching right up to the last day. So the last few weeks I often don't even pencil in [on her calendar] until I get very close to the time ... .

This tentativeness also occurred in the on-going decisions at the level of lesson planning. Lessons were planned in detail only a few days ahead. For example, Teacher G, one of the most organized of the subjects (to the point of keeping a computerized cross-referenced list of all her teaching materials), was asked about her planning for the beginning of a subsequent week of the course:

I: At what point do you start doing [planning] Monday?

G: Not until the Wednesday before. That would be the earliest day ... I find it really frustrating to plan really far ahead because it's all going to change anyway.

This comment, with others made by other teachers, implies that teachers have tried planning more carefully in advance, but have learned from experience that this does not work, and have given it up. Yet in some cases, they feel that this is a weakness in their teaching. For example, Teacher C responded to a question about how she viewed her teaching:

I: What about your weakest point, things you'd like to change,,,

C: Probably my weakest point would be,,, I think the planning aspect is probably a weakness, I still feel guilt over not being able to predict, not being able to fix a plan ... I mean that is a weakness.

In addition, there was a surprisingly high degree of tentativeness within the lessons of the teachers in the study. Very often lessons were tentatively planned, with many choices and changes made as the lesson was unfolding (a frequent change for almost every teacher was to postpone or scrap the final part of the lesson which there was not enough time to complete). Teacher A, for example, reported making decisions related to certain elements of a lesson as she was going up the escalator to the classroom just before the lesson began, as noted above (page 165).

This finding was initially surprising because it seems to go counter to the traditional wisdom of teacher education programs of top-down setting of goals, of being 'organized' and well planned. However, in light of the finding about prior decisions providing a tentative framework for subsequent decisions, it is not surprising at all. The previous framework must be there to constrain current decisions, but there are new factors being considered on an on-going basis. So previous decisions must narrow and constrain current possibilities, but must allow the new factors to determine the final shape of the decisions. Since a number of the teachers considered themselves very organized but planned very tentatively, the implication is that being organized does not mean making definitive plans far in advance. Rather, being organized means having a range of possibilities and an understanding of the criteria needed for reducing these to the final decision.

Resources and constraints

With the large number of external factors which potentially need to be taken into account, the teacher must have some process for dealing with them. One way teachers seem to do this is by treating them as 'resources' and 'constraints'. These terms are used in the education literature; for example, in describing the cognitive skill of teaching Leinhardt (1989) refers to the complex task facing the teacher, including both resources (knowledge of subject, knowledge of students, text materials and time), and constraints (the need to keep people active and engaged in learning, time, environment), and notes the flexibility needed by teachers to balance different constraints and resources. However what is not emphasized in the literature is the complementary and systematic role these concepts play in the planning and decision-making process, and their relationship to top-down and bottom-up planning. It was through the use of resources and constraints that the top-down and bottom-up aspects of the planning occurred, as the top-down perspective began with constraints and attempted to fill the lower level 'slots' with appropriate resources, while bottom-up planning involved expanding resources and making them available for slots that appeared or were created.

We can take the term 'resources' to refer to factors which increase the number of possibilities or options open to a teacher. The most stereotypical type of resources are those found in a resource centre, but resources also include the teacher's own mental resource centre – memory of past experiences. In addition, for these ESL teachers, resources also included a personal collection of resources that they had filed away, as well as all kinds of objects in the world around them (newspapers, magazines, libraries, radio, television, labels, maps, photographs, friends, and so on). The concept 'resource' implies a hierarchy, since, for example, a resource centre can be considered a resource, and includes textbooks, which are also resources, each of which includes activities, which are also resources, each of which may include, perhaps, photographs or ideas, which can also be resources. The fact that teachers think of resources as hierarchical fits together well with the fact that they express their actions as having hierarchical interrelationships. As mentioned above, all teachers discussed using resources to get ideas and possibilities.

The term 'constraints', on the other hand, refers to factors which narrow, limit or decrease the number of possibilities or options open to a teacher. These may be external or internal to the decision-making process of the individual teacher. In the case of external factors, a number of institutional and situational constraints play a role, both chronological constraints such as time and schedules (how long there is to do something, when it can and should be done), and conceptual constraints such as the institutional curriculum. For example, in the case of Teacher A, a number of constraints were predetermined by the nature of the course: the fact that it was an academic course for academic credit at a university; the fact that it was for adults, including French-speaking Canadians, immigrants who are speakers of French and of other languages, and international students who are speakers of other languages. There were also constraints arising out of departmental policy and prior curriculum decisions. For example, aspects of the marking scheme were predetermined by the curriculum and director: a division between marks for class work and a final exam that was common to all sections of the course. There was also a departmental structure which constrained her mapping of the course schedule: a weekly laboratory hour for listening.

However, the most important constraint in the planning process was internal to the decision-making process: the constraint of tentative prior decisions. Prior decisions made by the teacher constrained the possibilities for subsequent decisions and provided a framework for subsequent decisions to be made. For example, the decision to use a particular resource (a textbook, a unit, a chapter, an activity, an utterance) also implied constraints on other levels. In other words, deciding to activate a particular element (for example, a reading activity) restricted to some extent the possibilities for action on lower levels, i.e. the means by which it would be implemented.

These two concepts, resources and constraints, are inversely related, since a lack of resources acts as a constraint (i.e. limits possibilities).

Nevertheless, both resources and constraints are necessary for planning and decision-making. Almost all the teachers indicated that many resources are desirable – with many resources, there are more likely to be effective possibilities and appropriate choices for the situational characteristics at hand – and teachers worked at maximizing their resources. However, without constraints, there is no basis for making choices among ideas from different resources. Constraints made some resources and some ideas more possible or appropriate than others. The teachers not only spent a lot of time looking for resources, but also spent a great deal of time studying and considering the constraints. In a sense (although this may seem contradictory given the above definitions), experienced teachers treated constraints as a type of resource, using them creatively to shape their decisions and the course. The experienced teachers in this study used a number of techniques for orchestrating resources and constraints in order to deal with the complexity of teaching their course.

One of the most important characteristics of the temporal aspects of teacher planning was the alternation between a focus on expansion (use of resources) and a focus on contraction or restriction (use of constraints). As noted above, when assigned a particular course, teachers immediately looked for constraints (although minimal). This was followed by an expansion (generating ideas for the course). Then followed a further limitation – selecting ideas for content and activities, adapting and shaping them, ordering them sequentially and mapping them onto conventional time. At the level of the lesson, we see that the course plan provided the initial constraint, from which alternatives and further ideas were generated, which were then constrained as they were mapped onto lessons.

This alternation between expansion and contraction can also be seen in Teacher G's discussion (page 129–30) of the factors that led to the decision to use a particular article with her class, first limiting the areas of interest of the students, then collecting possible themes, then choosing careers as a theme, then looking for possibly relevant articles, then choosing the particular article.

In the classroom, this process also occurred, and situational demands on the teacher's attention could be seen as immediate constraints: for example, when Teacher A heard a student say "What's a device?" (see the example on page 181) as she was discussing formal definitions, she was constrained to a more limited set of possibilities for the next decision (which did not necessarily involve a particular response to the student, but which did involve consideration of the student's utterance in determining what to do next).

What is left out of this description of resources and constraints is the initial expansion of the resources (both mental and physical) themselves that teachers gain from prior teaching experiences. As described in Chapter 8, this should be one important function of teacher education.

Top-down and bottom-up planning

In the education literature, research on teacher planning has stated that the instructional activity is the basic instructional unit of planning (Shavelson and Stern, 1981:478), in opposition to the traditional top-down conception of curricular planning which starts from goals or objectives:

One of the main findings of research on teacher planning is that teachers do not follow the traditional model for instructional design by specifying objectives, creating step-by-step procedures for moving students with certain entry skills and knowledge of these objectives and evaluating the effectiveness of instruction after implementing it. Rather, teachers focus on the activities – content, material – not which students will be involved ... . (1981:461)

Clark and Yinger's (1979) summary of research on the planning process of teachers makes the same point that teacher planning starts not from goals but rather from 'instructional activities', which are "self-contained, organizational units functioning as 'controlled behavior settings' that were shaped and molded by the teacher to conform to her perceptions and purposes" (1979:237).

The data from the teachers in this study shows a more interactive process, including both top-down goal-directed procedures for generating and considering activities for the course, and bottom-up 'opportunistic' procedures for taking advantage of whatever comes up during the planning process. This interactive process is consistent with the notion of the relationships between levels of the structures of teaching, where a level may be seen as a goal to be achieved by lower level units, as a 'content unit' (where an activity would be one example), or as a means of achieving higher level units.

Examining the teaching process in the context of a whole course, the teachers did use the notion of 'activity' as an important unit of planning. However, their planning was also initiated at higher structural levels, for example, with a theme rather than an activity, or at lower structural levels, such as a new way to handle correction. The state of the previously set plan determined to a great extent the level at which subsequent planning would occur, i.e. the 'holes' left in the prior plan shaped where the next stage of active planning would begin (or even subconscious planning, when the solution appeared out of nowhere).

There is an important relationship between, on the one hand, constraints and resources, and on the other hand, top-down and bottom-up planning. In the case of the eight teachers in this study, top-down planning often began with a set of established constraints. In the case of the course, this involved the very vague constraints of the purpose of the course and level of the students. In the case of lesson planning, the top-down structure was provided by the most recent version of the course plan, which provided a more local set of constraints: the teacher chose certain activities or sequences within a particular lesson to achieve certain course goals specified by the course plan. In other words, top-down planning began with constraints and then looked for resources.

Bottom-up planning, on the other hand, generally started with resources and then secondarily matched them against constraints. Bottom-up planning involved moving from seemingly randomly occurring 'ideas for things to do' to putting them together in particular ways so that they became 'plans looking for a goal'. The bottom-up process occurred primarily through idea generation, as the teacher browsed without a particular goal in mind through activities, texts, idea sources, seeing what might fit into the overall course in an as yet unspecified way. Teachers often came across good ideas that were put in storage for possible future goals. For example, Teacher C talked about an idea she had been saving for an appropriate goal:

C: ... that I've never tried before, that I've always wanted to try, never been daring enough to do. It's called 'conversation circle' and it's an idea I stole from an article in *Forum* ... I collect these ideas, I have a little collection that I keep and I must have read this about five or six years ago but never had the right context to try it. This is the first sort of class I've had in a long time which focuses directly on conversation strategies which is what this falls into.

It was notable as well that in a number of cases, the elaboration of course goals occurred in a bottom-up manner. In the early stages the teachers often did not know in detail exactly how the vague course goals were to be interpreted; they worked that out as the course evolved. Certain planned units and activities led to the emphasis of certain goals rather than the other way around. In this sense, the activity shaped the goal.

At times top-down and bottom-up planning seemed to occur very distinctly. There were cases where teachers were clearly looking for a means of achieving a certain goal. There were other cases where they were just as clearly collecting activities and ideas with no specific goals in mind. However, in many cases both seemed to be occurring in concert: what was noticeable was a constant alternation between consideration of constraints related to higher level conceptual structures and consideration and expansion of lower level available resources, and the search for matches between the two.

Taking into account the task of the teacher to create a multi-level structure that connects the conceptual goals of the course to the classroom events in order to create and implement a course, it makes sense that teachers use whatever resources they have and work both upwards (in order to connect what they have to the higher level goals) and downwards (to connect what they have to the verbalizations and actions that must occur linearly in the classroom).

Implicit planning: activating experienced structures

Part of the complexity of teaching is reduced by explicit planning, carried out in the ways described above, where some parts of the structuring between the overall conceptual goals and classroom events are explicitly worked out using various procedures and strategies. The purpose of such explicitly planned structures is to reduce the number of connections that have to be made and the number of possibilities, factors and criteria that have to be considered or remembered during on-the-spot decision making in the classroom. However, for the reasons discussed above, teachers' explicit planning only covers a portion of the connections that have to be made, and even then in a very tentative manner. With deadlines for lesson performance constantly looming, teachers have to have a way to handle the complex decision-making demands of the classroom. The way in which the teachers did this was by depending on a form of implicit planning – activating a structure that they had previously experienced, once or many times. To refer to such an entity, I am using the term *experienced structure*.

The notion of levels of units of teaching developed in the model in Chapter 5 helps to clarify the idea of an experienced structure. For any particular unit of teaching, one aspect of what a teacher experiences is the creation of the downward connections – from the level at which a unit is activated down through the various levels of substructure to the sound and movement that the classroom participants perceive. Having this experience allows the teacher to label the structure and insert it as a whole into a higher level structure without having to make the detailed decisions that would otherwise be required to plan it explicitly. In addition, the teacher also experiences the upward connections – as teachers use a structure in different circumstances and with different students, they expand their knowledge of the range of ends to which it can be put. They learn what it can be adapted to, when it can be adapted, and how to adapt it. Teachers develop the ability to create expectations out of matching the substructure to new circumstances, a very important part of the planning process, and develop a sense of what substructures are necessary to link what a current group of students know or can do (the task of the teacher described above) to the accomplishment of the superordinate units.

A good example of the importance of having previously been through the substructuring of a particular unit is Teacher C's outline of the planning for an upcoming lesson:

C: ... then that will lead us into the 'hidden information role play' ... and what it is basically/ I've done this one before and this one I really like, again it's an idea that I got from *Forum* many years ago, and it involves ... Mrs. Komer's dead dog and Mrs. Komer is talking to her neighbours in order to find out what happened to her dog, Mr. Green I think is the guilty party ... .

She already knows a great deal about the possible substructuring of this activity, including criteria for the decisions necessary to accomplish it (for example, she knows what she wants to get out of the students she chooses for the "first go"):

C: ... there'll be one group who will perform the hidden information role play, and I'll select them very carefully so that I can get as much out of them as possible. I'll probably use [higher level students] for this first go, and also to a certain/ extroverts as well, people that I know/ like Betty for example, the ones who really enjoy performing ... .

Part of this knowledge of the substructuring of the activity (what it consists of at lower levels) also plays a role in her confident sense of how this activity fits into the higher level course goals:

C: ... the class will be divided into five groups so they will each write their own hidden information role play using that as the model ... and the reason why I want to go in that direction was because I tried to get them to write a role play, to write something, an interaction based on the party, and it's obvious that they have no experience doing this at all ... so what I'm doing now has a dual purpose. First it's training them how to/ you know you can do it in terms of writing a role play because I see drama as a major ingredient in this course in terms of the interaction, a lot of what we're doing is actually drama, so it's important for them to have that as something they can draw on, ... it also gives them strategies for questioning.

The fact that experienced structures are less explicitly and deliberately planned than non-experienced structures does not mean that they are inaccessible consciously or that they cannot be analyzed and adapted for use in other circumstances. The downward adaptability allows the means of carrying out the structure to be changed to fit a new situation. The upward adaptability refers to connections higher in the hierarchy and means that it can be adapted for different purposes. They can also be nested, and can be connected with other experienced structures on different levels. For example, in the case of C's map activity, she planned a warm-up activity to lead into the actual map activity. To accomplish this she used an 'experienced structure', a brainstorming activity taken from another source, that fit into her overall approach in terms of coherence. As a result, a larger conceptual unit was experienced, with components that could be used at another time.

The metaphor arising from the study of parallel distributed processes in cognitive science (as noted briefly in Chapter 3) seems to be a useful way of thinking about this notion. Rather than describing such structures as having 'open slots' or 'variables' as in the language of schema theory, it is more consistent with the findings of this study to state that structures, when experienced, develop connections of varying degrees of strength to surrounding structures.

Experienced structures versus routines

In the education literature, the term 'routine' has been used to denote a similar concept. Shavelson and Stern (1981) state that a mental plan for carrying out interactive teaching, based around an instructional task or activity, becomes 'routinized' so that once begun it is usually played out unless something is not working; conscious decision-making in the classroom takes place when the activity is *not* going as planned. Clark and Yinger (1979) state that routines minimize conscious decision-making during interactive teaching, and reduce the information processing load on the teacher by making timing and sequencing of activities and students' behaviour predictable. Leinhardt and Greeno (1986:76) describe routine as a characteristic of skilled performance, where many component actions have become automatic through practice and are performed with little cognitive effort. Leinhardt, Weidman and Hammond (1987) point out that routines at lower levels allow more cognitive effort to be available at higher levels. They emphasize the importance of classroom routines shared between teacher and pupils in allowing for efficient use of class time.

There are two important characteristics of experienced structures apparent from this study, however, which differ from this notion of routine. First, while routines have been primarily linked to activities or parts of activities, experienced structures refer to all levels of the hierarchy of units of teaching. Second, while discussions of routines emphasize automaticity, the concept of experienced structures emphasizes different degrees of internalization.

1. Experienced structures refer to all levels of the hierarchy

In the education literature, then, the concept of automatic routine is associated primarily with activities or particular subactivity procedures

(such as correcting homework or handing out papers). In psycholinguistics, the concept of 'automatic' relates to the phenomenon of
normal speech: with little cognitive effort (although we can increase
the attention when we need to, to monitor or alter what we are saying)
we say things using language. The notion of an 'experienced structure'
links and broadens these concepts by referring to elements at all levels
of the heterarchy from a whole course to a particular phonological
feature. (In this discussion I am drawing a number of parallels between
using language and using higher level cognitive structures for communicating in a particular type of setting. I do not wish to claim that the
cognitive processes in language use are identical to the cognitive
processes used in the organization of higher level structures; rather, I
wish to point out that there are a number of interesting similarities.)

An experienced structure can refer to the largest unit under consideration in this study: an entire course. The effect of frequently experiencing a course was acknowledged by one teacher who said, "I could
teach it with my eyes closed". Teachers used previously experienced
ways for breaking down the course goals into major course units and
subunits, for combining activities into themes, or breaking activities
into sets of procedures. For example, Teacher F had an experienced
structure that she used to carry out major conceptual course units,
beginning with a presentation of the new points, then exercises and
writing, then correcting (either by her or sometimes by peers), then
rewriting or copying the corrected parts; there was also an accompanying class organization, starting out with the class as a whole, then
moving to groups, then to individuals which was the culmination of
the process.

The teachers had also developed through experience more local
structures such as ways of checking homework, putting students into
groups, and handing out papers – structures that they did not have to
think through in detail, but could insert freely into the lesson. There
were also experienced structures at yet more local levels. When we
look at teachers' decision-making in the classroom, we can see structures which are activated and inserted into the on-going interactions of
the lesson with little cognitive deliberation on the part of the teacher,
such as ways of addressing and questioning students, things to say to
encourage students, ways of simplifying and altering speed and intonation, and so on.

2.   Experienced structures can be internalized to different degrees

While the emphasis in the literature on routine is the automatic
nature of its use, the verbalizations of the teachers in this study
stressed the importance of having done something before, even if only

once. This non-binary conception of an experienced structure also allows for the structures to be reanalyzed while being carried out, which frequently occurred as part of the assessment process. The teachers' comments suggested that as a structure is used more often in different circumstances, the teacher becomes more skilled at carrying it out, i.e. more fluent at making the connections among levels.

At one extreme is a structure which has been internalized to the point that a greater conscious effort was needed to alter it than to carry it out. A number of the teachers used the term 'habit' to refer to internalized structures that were carried out automatically and sometimes in spite of the teacher's plan. Teacher C's use of the rejoinder 'good' as a routine response to students' contributions was not consistent with her desire to remain a non-judgmental participant in the class; and so a conscious cognitive effort was required not to use this experienced verbal structure (see page 214 for a detailed discussion of this example).

Teacher A, in the comment below, implied a distinction between a conscious structure (the verbal structure "Are there any questions?"), which has a function (although it may not be a deliberately planned structure), and one that is unconscious and has no intended function, which she termed "a mannerism":

A: ... I am conscious of the fact that I do frequently say "Are there any questions?" or "Do you understand?". More often than not nobody stops me at that point. But I really and truly expect them to if they don't understand. Maybe they just think it's a mannerism, and it doesn't mean they should stop me and say "I don't understand".

It is important to note that teachers also discussed the deadening effect of carrying out an identical structure repeatedly, which implies certain desirable levels of internalization. They seemed to want enough familiarity to reduce the pressure of moment-to-moment decision-making, but not so much predictability that there are no decisions to make and the task becomes boring or restricting. This is an important factor to take into account in discussions of the role of automatic processes in teaching.

At the other extreme is a structure which has been experienced only once previously. Simply having the experience of carrying out a structure once seems to give the teacher a feeling for the unknowns that lie between it as a label (such as 'Mrs. Komer's dead dog'), and its implementation in words and actions in the classroom. An excellent opportunity to see the effect of experiencing structures is the case of Teacher A, who taught two sections of the same course, one in the morning and one in the afternoon. In most cases she used the same plan for both classes. In the morning class, the fact that she had not previously experienced the structure led to a number of surprises (both pleasant and unpleasant). In the afternoon class, these surprises (which occurred in terms of specific classroom interactions, and in terms of how long the activities would last) were sorted out.

Early in the course, Teacher A described the advantage of being able to "rehearse" the structures in the morning class for the afternoon class, including particular verbalizations.

A: ... in teaching the second [class], even in giving that mini-lecture today, I found that I could see from the first one what to focus on and what not to, and what I had said that wasn't really going well, and what not to say. So I think that the second class might benefit from the fact that I've already done it once before, like it's been rehearsed ... .

Although having a clearer sense of the substructuring in the afternoon class usually made Teacher A feel more comfortable, it was not necessarily the case that the afternoon class went better. Sometimes the unexpected morning result was considered more positive than the predicted afternoon result when the structure was better planned but seemed more 'contrived'.

It is also a simplification of the concept to state that one experience with a structure makes it immediately more useable. For more complex structures particularly, the process of internalization seemed to be a gradual one, with some aspects of the structure more readily useable than others. Teacher A, in viewing her afternoon lesson on videotape, discussed the fact that she was less satisfied with it than with the morning lesson. She explained that she had tried to recreate her explanations in the morning class but was not able to remember how the class had begun, and "got off on the wrong foot". She stated that a number of factors contributed to this. One was that her awareness of the presence of the camera and researcher again in the afternoon class may have made her want to do the same thing "but differently", i.e. by using different substructures from those used in the morning. She also brought in another factor by saying, "because I've done it before I suppose I'm overconfident", indicating that experiencing a structure once may trick the teacher into wrongly thinking that she or he now knows it and does not have to explicitly reconsider the substructuring. These are all indications that experiencing a complex structure once is not enough to make it useable.

With regard to less complex structures, however, the fact of experiencing a structure once had an obvious impact on subsequent substructuring. For example, Teacher A, in the morning lesson, used the word 'device' as one component of an example which in turn was one component of the lecture introducing the concept of a 'formal definition'. The word 'device' was used in the example definition of a 'watch' to illustrate that, in a formal definition, the term being defined must be put into a 'class' of objects, in this case "a watch is a device that ..." Immediately after giving the example, a student said "What's a device?", indicating that, on some level, he had not understood the point she was trying to accomplish.

A: I really didn't expect anyone to say 'What's a device?' and they kind of caught me off guard because I had never really given much thought to how I would define that for them and well you'll see when I do it but I just gave some general definition and hoped that it wasn't being inaccurate. So/but I had no idea anyone would not know what it meant.

Based on her experience of the morning's interaction, Teacher A incorporated into the afternoon class's lecture on formal definition, and into the example designed to clarify it, a short explanation of the term 'device'.

Experienced versus non-experienced structures

Among the resources available to a teacher are ones which have been passed on verbally from an outside source, ones which are not yet 'experienced structures'. Such structures can involve larger or smaller units. For example, an institutional curriculum or course of study can, for a particular teacher, provide an overall organizational structure of teaching which she or he has never experienced. Similarly, substructures such as thematic units or chapters from a textbook may be resources available to teachers but never experienced. Still smaller substructures, such as an activity, an exercise, a written or taped text to be used as one part of an activity, a way of grouping students, or even a scripted set of instructions, may be found in textbooks or passed on verbally by other teachers or by institutional directives. In this study, teachers had access to many such structures; for example, they had collected in their own files many ideas for structures which they had never used.

However, neither an activity taken from a textbook nor from a colleague nor from an institutional directive fills out the lower level decisions (the moves, the initiations and responses, the actual utterances) required to ground the activity in actual experience. In contrast, with an experienced structure the teacher discovers the links between the activity as a formal element in the lesson, the function of the activity in the accomplishment of higher level conceptual goals, and the specific utterances (or rather sounds and movements) which enact the activity.

There is an important difference between an external structure and an experienced structure. An external structure is where the decisions and subdecisions are laid out for the teacher; it may occur in the form of an imposed curriculum or textbook which specifies the units of teaching and their interrelationships. A teacher working from such an external structure has little feel for how the elements fit together and little flexibility for dealing with new factors that come up in the interactions that make up the classroom teaching and which must be integrated into on-going decision-making. In the case of an experienced structure, however, the teacher has developed an intuitive sense for the role the elements play in the larger picture and the flexibility to alter and improvise. In addition, having experienced a range of higher level structures of a particular type allows the teacher more easily to insert substructures that have not been experienced before; Teacher C did this with the 'conversation circle', an activity that she had collected but never tried before (page 174), but one that was similar in structure to others she had carried out.

Teachers seemed to prefer and trust experienced structures and tended to avoid structures that were completely new to them. Most teachers in the study preferred not to follow a curriculum script if it was not required because it hindered their process of making decisions based on their updated assessment of course events. In fact, Teacher A described an exaggerated version of this type of approach to make her point about its impractibility:

A: ... . the teaching I did before I entered a Master's program, I found that very often I was trying to do what I was told to do when I took my diploma in education but that it was almost impossible to follow all those rules. In theory they were fine, but in practice they didn't work ... [like] being given a prescription. My diploma program was very much "well you stand in front of a class and you ask a question and you wait this number of seconds, and then you don't indicate which student is going to answer until you're sure all the students have formulated the answers in their minds, and then you point to a student so that everybody's ready and,,,"/you know, that kind of approach.

Conclusion

The concepts described in this chapter – the planning at different levels, the prior decisions, the process of comparing expectations and outcomes – are crucial notions. In addition, the importance of the interpretation of events and units at various levels in the assessment and re-planning process has been discussed. However, this chapter has not dealt with how the interpretation of classroom events occurs and what it is based on.

To analyze the teacher's interpretive processes, we have to take into account the teacher's own beliefs, assumptions and knowledge structures. The decisions that the teacher makes in carrying out a unit relate not only to carrying out the activity *per se*, but also to more deeply held beliefs about language, learning, teaching, and even life. For example, the brainstorming activity that Teacher C used as a warm-up for the map activity is a structure that this teacher, involved in recent work on the writing process and sensitive to techniques for including right brain operations in learning, felt particularly comfortable doing. This experience allowed her to fill out some of the relationships connecting the activity to a new higher level node in a way consistent with her underlying views about teaching and learning. The following chapter deals with the role of beliefs, assumptions and knowledge.

7 An integrated view of teachers' beliefs, assumptions, and knowledge

The model developed in Chapter 3 included three main aspects of the teaching process: the events which make up the teaching, the planning processes of the teachers, and the interpretive processes of the teachers. Chapter 4 discussed the structure of classroom events, distinguishing between the *formal* elements or units of teaching (the units which made up the structure of the course, its lessons, activities, exchanges, moves, utterances), and the *function* of those elements or units in the accomplishment of the course. It was demonstrated that an element at any level of the hierarchy functions in terms of the *goal* of the accomplishment of the element or elements which are superordinate to it. Conversely, the subordinate elements in the hierarchy are the *means* by which their superordinate element is carried out. In Chapters 5 and 6, a description was given of the procedures and strategies a teacher uses in order to make the decisions that create the structure that enables the course to be accomplished.

However, with all these strategies available, there are many possible ways that an element or unit of a course can be elaborated into a substructure and carried out. Conversely, for any unit, there are many reasons, beyond the simple accomplishment of the course, that a particular choice is made by the teacher. The question that remains to be answered is why, of all of the possible choices that could be made by teachers, are some selected and others not? A key to answering this question was revealed in the teacher interviews. It is related to the notion that a decision at any level of the hierarchy not only accomplishes superordinate decisions, but also instantiates and signals the teacher's underlying beliefs, assumptions and knowledge. Within the model developed in Chapter 5, the teacher's beliefs, assumptions and knowledge play an important role in how the teacher interprets events related to teaching (both in preparation for the teaching and in the classroom), and thus affect the teaching decisions that are ultimately made.

The first part of this chapter provides a review, primarily of the education literature, of the notions of assumptions underlying teaching, and of teachers' background knowledge (declarative and procedural) and beliefs. These concepts have traditionally been treated separately, but increasingly the distinctions between them are being blurred. This chapter then introduces a hypothetical concept of an *integrated* network of beliefs, assumptions and knowledge (termed BAK). The final sections of this chapter provide support for this concept using data from the teachers' verbalizations to describe a number of features of such a network, and to show how it evolves through a teacher's experiences over time.

Approaching language teaching

At the highest and most abstract level of the learning/teaching process, everybody has the same goal: for the learners to learn the language. As soon as one poses the basic question of classroom language teaching, "what do we now?", issues of what language is, how it is learned and how it should be taught become relevant. The answers to these questions, which guide teachers' approaches to classroom teaching, relate to their underlying beliefs, assumptions and knowledge. This section discusses how these notions have been described in the field of ESL, and uses the data from the teachers' verbalizations to show how these questions are also relevant to the way the teachers in the study approached the teaching task.

An early attempt in the field of ESL to deal with the issue of beliefs, assumptions and knowledge underlying approaches to second language teaching was Anthony's (1963) distinctions: 'approach', 'method' and 'technique'. These terms, which Anthony tried to define, have been and are still used non-technically in the field to describe some of the concepts addressed in this book. Anthony's definitions are as follows:

An approach [is] ... a set of correlative assumptions about the nature of language, and the nature of teaching and learning. (1963:64)

Method is an overall plan for the orderly presentation of language material, no part of which contradicts, and all of which is based upon, the selected approach. (1963:65)

Technique ... is a particular trick, stratagem or contrivance used to accomplish an immediate objective. Techniques must be consistent with a method, and therefore in harmony with an approach as well. (1963:66)

The use of the term 'approach' has generally referred to the assumptions incorporated into teaching materials and teaching directives, entailing a kind of theoretical underpinning, and implying (Anthony notes this explicitly) that the carrying out of a course with these materials and directives would incorporate the same underpinning. Even the current use of the terms, as in phrases such as 'the communicative approach' or 'the process approach' with their definite articles, seem to imply that teachers are all carrying out the 'same' teaching. The assumption is, then, that decisions made to implement a particular curriculum are made in light of these assumptions, and that at each level of the hierarchy, the elements are designed to accomplish the next level in such a way as to be consistent or coherent with the approach.

This point has also been made by Richards (1985) and Richards and Rodgers (1986), who argue that Anthony's distinction does not allow us to examine in a principled way the relationships among these three concepts. These authors propose the terms 'approach' (theory of language and language learning), 'design' (objectives, content selection and organization, and roles of learners, teachers and materials), and 'procedure' (classroom behaviour in terms of techniques and practices). In this analysis, I wish to take this issue one step further, by using the data to examine these relationships as they are manifested during an actual course planned and carried out by a particular teacher. What is the possible range of assumptions that a teacher might hold about language, learning and teaching? How do they affect teachers' decisions made about and in the classroom? First, let us briefly look at the range of assumptions we might expect to find about the nature of the language, the nature of learning and the nature of teaching.

Assumptions about language

Assumptions about language play an important role in a language course, where language is both the means by which the subject matter is taught (as in other courses) and the subject matter itself. People unconsciously internalize beliefs about language throughout their lives, and so the beliefs about what language is, what 'proper' language is, and so on, vary from individual to individual and are often deeply held. The teacher's conception of subject matter in a language class is quite different from, say, one in a history class or a mathematics class (although I would not want to claim that attitudes about history or mathematics do not have an effect on what is taught between the lines in those subjects).

In addition to 'folk conceptions' that are internalized by individuals through their life, language teachers have also been influenced by the many theoretical claims which have been made in the second language literature about what language is, what it consists of and how it works. For example, arguments have been put forward that language is a single unified entity (i.e. with a single underlying basis that underlies all use), that language is a cluster of different entities, types or genres (such as general English, and scientific English, for example). Language has been seen as knowledge (something to be known), but also as abilities (something which can be done), or a combination. Language as knowledge has been considered to consist of phonology, syntax, lexicon, discourse functions, sociolinguistic knowledge, interactional knowledge, and knowledge of communication strategies, as well as strategies for the four skills. Language as an ability has been seen as a single underlying ability, as four discrete abilities (the 'four skills'), and as a large number of microskills (such as guessing meaning from context or articulating sounds) or composite skills (such as notetaking). Beyond these potential ways of viewing language as course content is the question of emphasis – what is the relative importance of all these different aspects of 'language'?

Some of the assumptions evident in the study were ones that derived from the way in which the institution framed the curriculum. Courses A and B were ones devoted to 'academic language', an important aspect of which were a set of rhetorical patterns, and academic language skills, including reading, writing and listening to academic discourse. Courses E and F were part of a curriculum which was divided into core components (Course F, a writing component, was one of these) and optional components (Course E, a vocabulary course, was one of these).

However, in order to begin planning, teachers must make some assumptions about what language consists of. These may reflect deeply held beliefs, or temporary working assumptions. For example, Teacher H, in planning her course (which had the most general institutional focus possible: improving the students' English), made an assumption that the subject matter should be divided into "all six main areas": reading, listening, speaking, writing, vocabulary, and grammar. For Teacher F, the overall conceptual goal of Course F was "to improve their writing", defined for some students as passing the test to enter university, for others as "just better writing". However, underlying this conceptual goal were several assumptions about language and skills. Teacher F's verbalizations, for example, included the notion that students' writing and speaking abilities are independent and can be quite different:

F: Using what I hear from the students on the first day as some kind of guideline to what I expect to see in writing I think is a bit of a fallacy and a trap that one can fall into ... and I try to disregard that as much as possible and concentrate on their writing.

Her assumptions about the nature of writing were primarily discussed in terms of grammatical accuracy. She described improvement in writing ability for her students as being:

F: ... getting the message across, so the reader's attention is moving from the incorrect forms to the message ... because sometimes you know if you have a piece of writing with a lot of errors, I mean you'll start looking so much at the errors, even if you're a non-teacher reading it, that you lose touch entirely with the message that's hidden behind this funny way of writing English ... .

This view is also reflected in the first lesson, where she collected a variety of samples of student writing. She used three separate prompts which required different verb tenses to allow her to check the form and the consistent use of the tenses, as well as spelling errors, punctuation, capitalization, and vocabulary choice (i.e. the use of a range of synonyms to provide, in her words, "variety and style").

Assumptions about language learning

The possible assumptions about language learning are equally complex. They are also related to the above assumptions about language. Is language something we learn through first consciously 'knowing' it, and then transferring that knowledge to application, or something we learn through doing, i.e. through experience? Or is it both, and if both in what proportions? Does learning by knowing occur inductively or deductively? Does learning by experience occur through specific objectives and practice, through exposure, through negotiation and interaction, or some particular combination of these? Are different aspects of language learned in different ways and at different rates? And differently by different individuals? Does learning occur more favourably with the learner's involvement in high level decisions about what and how to learn, or does it occur more favourably with the learner focusing energy exclusively on the tasks which have been set by the curriculum and teacher? Do motivation, attention, fun, time on task, class dynamics, play a role in learning, and if so, what is the relative importance of each one?

Many statements related to learning surfaced throughout the interviews. For example, Teacher F's views about what writing consists of include some assumptions about acquisition, in particular language transfer and fossilization. In the first lesson, she wrote the mother tongue of her students on the attendance record to use when she evaluated their writing.

F: It can help to explain stubborn errors, for instance, errors which show up that we have dealt with but still do not seem to be amended in any one way or the other. If it is a typical problem of a particular language group, it's easier to assume that it's a kind of fossilization that's taken place rather than assume that the student has not paid attention or something like that. So for that reason I like to have that kind of information, to back my own suspicions up perhaps, more than anything else.

Further examples of the assumptions of other teachers, related to issues such as motivation, learner independence and formal learning versus experiential learning, are found throughout this chapter.

Assumptions about language teaching

If teaching is considered to relate to the ways in which classroom activities can be organized so that learning will take place, then considering assumptions about teaching takes the complexity one step further. The assumptions about learning affect the way we assume we should teach the material; and the assumptions about language determine what the material is. We can teach explicitly, implicitly, in relative isolation or relative contextualization. If we can teach explicitly, we can make things explicit before the fact, or after the fact. We can also jump to a level of meta-learning: learning how to learn. In this case, instead of teaching the particular aspects of the language, we can teach strategies for learning those aspects, leaving the direct learning up to the learner. In addition, there are assumptions about teaching related to the role of the teacher and the students, to the organization of the lesson, and to issues such as motivation, discipline and allocation of responsibility.

An important aspect of all this is who is considered to know what. The traditional thinking (as evidenced in audio-lingual methods) is that the learners know neither the target language nor the ways of learning it. The teacher, meanwhile, is considered to know the language (or at least to be able to demonstrate it), but not to know the way that it is to be learned or taught. The method (or the materials which manifest the method) is the authority on the learning (which is generally assumed to be common for all learners), and ultimately on what the subject matter consists of. Motivation for learning is considered to be intrinsically in the learner. But of course, there are many possible alternative assumptions that might be made by any of the participants. Any individual learner may consider him or herself the authority on his or her learning. The teacher may consider him or herself an important motivator. The teacher may consider him or herself an important antidote to the gaps or shortcomings in the method, both in terms of how the target language should be learned and what the appropriate target language is. And so on.

Many assumptions about teaching and the respective roles of teacher and learner surfaced in the interviews. For example, Teacher F's assumptions about the differences in speaking and writing play a role in how she perceived teaching. For her, those who speak well but do not write well need a different kind of help from those who do neither well – the former need help to "transfer existing skills onto paper", while the latter need help in "learning the language from scratch". This assumption underlay her eliciting the students' oral as well as written abilities in the first lesson of the course. There are many further examples of other teachers' assumptions throughout this chapter.

A teacher's priorities in structuring the classroom teaching will therefore depend crucially on that teacher's own assumptions about language, learning and teaching. This argument is a departure from Anthony's (1963:66) statement that in teaching, "techniques must be consistent with a method, and therefore in harmony with an approach", and goes a step further than Richards and Rodgers' (1986:16) statement that "a method is theoretically related to an approach, is organizationally determined by a design, and is practically realized in procedure". This argument is also a departure from the implicit assumption underlying most teaching programs that assumptions about language, learning and teaching have been explicitly taken care of in the curriculum, and are transformed unchanged into the classroom teaching. The assumptions underlying the *actual* teaching that goes on in the second language classroom have remained unexplored. This chapter focuses on that issue.

Teachers' background knowledge and beliefs: the education literature

Although teachers' background knowledge and beliefs have not been investigated in depth in the field of second language teaching, considerable work has been done in other areas of teaching. In the education literature work on these concepts has stemmed from developments in cognitive science such as those outlined in Chapter 3. An extensive review of the education literature in these areas up to the mid-eighties is included in Clark and Peterson (1986). In this work, a number of important theoretical distinctions have emerged. In this section, I outline the distinctions and illustrate that, although crucial in early stages of theory-building, under the closer scrutiny that they have been given more recently, these distinctions break down. It is my contention that finer-grained models are required for the next steps in the development of theories of teaching.

Teachers' background knowledge structures

The concept of the teacher's background knowledge structures has been proposed and refined by a number of educational researchers. Leinhardt and Greeno (1986:75), for example, state that "a skilled teacher has a complex knowledge structure composed of interrelated sets of organized actions" (for which they use the cognitive term 'schemata'). This concept has been described as underlying teach·rs' performance: that knowledge for skilled performance is at different levels of generality, allowing the teacher to construct plans for performing tasks by first choosing global schemata that satisfy general goals, and then choosing the lower level goals and associated schemata required to achieve the higher level.

One important distinction that has been posited within the concept of background knowledge is that of content knowledge versus instructional knowledge. Leinhardt and Smith (1985:247) categorize the knowledge structure of teachers into two "core areas": 'lesson structure knowledge' (knowledge of constructing and conducting lessons, moving through segments and explaining material) and 'subject matter knowledge' (knowledge of the content to be taught). They have developed systems of 'semantic nets' to represent the teacher's content knowledge and 'planning net' to represent lesson knowledge. They acknowledge that "the skills associated with lesson structure knowledge and subject matter knowledge are obviously intertwined", but treat the teacher's use of knowledge in the cognitive aspects of teaching as emerging from these two distinct sources.

The distinction between, on the one hand, subject matter knowledge and, on the other hand, lesson structure knowledge has also been emphasized by Shulman (1986). He used this distinction to argue that, whereas in the medical profession the mastery and use of professional subject matter knowledge was found to be an important factor underlying expert performance, education traditions had primarily looked at teacher behaviour in terms of classroom and course management independent of the teacher's understanding, transformation and use of subject matter knowledge. In redressing this lack, Shulman found that an intermediate category was necessary, producing a distinction between the subject matter knowledge of an expert on the field and the subject matter knowledge of a teacher which has pedagogic characteristics. More recently this set of distinctions has been questioned by MacEwan and Bull (1991) who argue that all knowledge is, in varying ways, pedagogic.

The issue of teachers' background knowledge structures is complicated by a further distinction stemming from cognitive science: that of declarative versus procedural knowledge. This distinction is related to the idea that teachers not only need to know things, they need to know how to do things, and so their decision-making includes decisions about what to do and decisions about how to do it. Leinhardt and Smith (1985:248) state that teachers' knowledge of lesson structure and subject matter have declarative and procedural components. Lesson structure knowledge in declarative form is knowledge of facts about the situation (in this case, knowledge about the materials to be learned, knowledge about the students, knowledge about the resources and constraints of the situation). In procedural form it is knowledge about the classroom procedures. Subject matter knowledge includes facts about a domain of study (declarative) and the "heuristics and algorithms that operate on those facts" (procedural) according to Leinhardt and Smith (1985:248). Increasingly, however, the distinction between declarative and procedural knowledge is being blurred; for example, Leinhardt (1989:146) states "situated knowledge can be seen as a form of expertise in which declarative knowledge is highly proceduralized and automatic...".

Teachers' beliefs and implicit theories

The notion of teachers' beliefs or 'implicit theories' has been discussed by a number of educational researchers. Clark and Yinger (1979:251) describe teachers' implicit theories, stating that "the teacher defines such things as the elements of the classroom situation that are most important, the relationship between them, and the order in which they should be considered". Shavelson and Stern (1981) discuss the notion of teacher beliefs, reporting on a number of studies which hypothesize that beliefs play a role in teachers' decisions, judgments and behaviour. They distinguish between knowledge and beliefs by saying that when information (i.e. knowledge) is not available, teachers will rely on beliefs to guide them. Subsequently, a number of further definitions have been developed to deal with the complex area of types of knowledge and beliefs. For example, Clark and Peterson (1986), in their review of the literature in this area, follow Nisbett and Ross's (1980) distinction of knowledge organized in 'schematic cognitive structures' and beliefs or theories organized as propositions about the characteristics of objects or object classes.

More recently, a plethora of terms has been used to represent and refine the semantic field of knowledge and beliefs. The terms 'conceptions' (Freeman, 1990), and 'preconceptions' (Wubbels, 1992) have been used to combine the two concepts. Leinhardt distinguishes between 'situated knowledge' and 'context-free knowledge' (Leinhardt, 1989). Calderhead (1988) distinguishes between teachers' 'practical knowledge' and 'academic subject matter' or 'formal theoretical knowledge'. Clandinin and Connelly (1986) discuss 'personal practical knowledge' and use the term 'images', which have "strong affective connotations, and are associated with powerful beliefs and feelings about what are 'right' ways of teaching, rooted in past life experiences". Connelly and Clandinin's (1988:14–18) 'meta-paper', examining how twelve researchers used twelve different terms to refer to this concept (comparing the definition of the term, the origin of the idea, the research problem it addressed, the research method used, and the outcome of the research), exemplifies the trend. Through the use of these different terms and the variety of subtle distinctions they imply, the initial straightforward distinction between knowledge and beliefs has also been blurred.

Theoretical issues in the literature: relevance for second language teaching

In this section, I would like to reconsider two distinctions discussed above from the perspective of the field of second language teaching and from the perspective of this study and that data that it has produced. The first distinction is that between content knowledge and instructional knowledge (and the related distinction between declarative and procedural knowledge). The second is the distinction between background knowledge structures and beliefs.

Aspects of background knowledge

The distinctions described above – between declarative and procedural knowledge, and between subject matter knowledge and instructional knowledge – have found currency in educational research. However, making these distinctions in the area of teaching a second language is somewhat more problematic. Attempting to distinguish between declarative and procedural knowledge when the subject matter is language illustrates the complexity. On the one hand, there is a parallel to the distinction made between 'competence' (underlying linguistic knowledge) and 'performance' (which includes the psychological and cognitive aspects of using the language at a moment in time). On the other hand, however, there is a parallel to another distinction – that between 'linguistic knowledge' (knowledge of the language) and 'sociolinguistic knowledge' (knowledge of the appropriate use of the language in particular social settings). In both cases, to complicate matters further, there can be declarative knowledge about procedures.

When we examine the distinctions between declarative and procedural knowledge and between subject matter and instructional knowledge in light of the heterarchical structuring of units of teaching and the relationship between levels, the strict distinctions are not tenable. As was described in Chapter 4, an element at any level is seen as part of content (and, in some sense, declarative) when considered from its own level. However, when looked at from superordinate levels (i.e. how the superordinate level will be taught), it is seen as part of instruction (and, is in some sense, procedural). This implies that teachers' knowledge is not of two distinct types, but can be labelled, accessed and used as one type or the other depending on its relationship to other knowledge being considered.

The important question regarding subject matter knowledge versus instructional knowledge can be framed as follows: what does the teacher need to know about language or language use in order to manage the learning of it effectively? Furthermore, does it need to be known consciously? For example, is having native speaker intuitions about the language necessary or sufficient? In translation approaches to teaching, having declarative knowledge of the subject matter (facts about the target language) was often sufficient to accomplish the goals of the course. Within communicative approaches, where the teacher can orchestrate the exposure of the learners to the language without having to be the source of the language or of explanations about the language, it is conceivable that declarative knowledge of the subject matter (knowledge of the language) is not necessary for the goals to be accomplished. In specialized areas such as English for Specific Purposes, it is not clear what the teacher needs to know about the specific modes of expression of the fields of study of the students, or about the subject matter of the fields themselves.

The relationship between knowledge and beliefs

A further distinction, clear but implicit in the earlier education literature and now becoming increasingly blurred, is that between teachers' background knowledge and teachers' beliefs. In light of the ESL teachers' discussions in this study of their own planning and decision-making, this distinction is not tenable. In many cases it cannot be clearly determined whether the interpretations of the events are based on what the teacher knows, what the teacher believes, or what the teacher believes s/he knows. For example, a teacher who knows/believes that students don't like to work in groups may interpret a particular case of the students' groans at the suggestion of taking up the homework in groups as being caused by the students' attitudes about group work rather than their particular mood that day, or the effects of the class party the previous evening. This event is remembered by the teacher not simply as groans, but in terms of her assumptions about what caused the groans, and is stored as a further abstracted or generalized item of knowledge/belief. From this perspective, it is hard to distinguish between background knowledge structures and belief systems.

This lack of clear distinction between what one knows and what one believes is important for our discussion of teachers' decisions, and

I would like to pursue this notion a little further. There is a sense in which the terms 'knowledge', 'assumptions' and 'beliefs' do not refer to distinct concepts, but rather to points on a spectrum of meaning, even though they have been treated for the most part as separate entities in the literature. We use the term 'knowledge' to refer to things we 'know' – conventionally accepted facts. In our society today, for something to be conventionally accepted, it generally means that it has been demonstrated or is demonstrable. (Some concepts, such as black holes, we treat as knowledge rather than belief because we accept that they have been demonstrated, although not to us, and that they are in principle demonstrable again.) The term 'assumption' normally refers to the (temporary) acceptance of a 'fact' (state, process or relationship) which we cannot say we know, and which has not been demonstrated, but which we are taking as true for the time being. (For example, "I don't know for a fact that he took my book home, but I assume it must have been him.") Assumptions may also refer to 'working assumptions': 'facts' that we may know in a large context are not true, but which we will take as being true for the purpose of carrying out an activity. Beliefs refer to an acceptance of a proposition for which there is no conventional knowledge, one that is not demonstrable, and for which there is accepted disagreement ("I believe that early immersion is good for a majority-language child's cognitive development but my colleague doesn't"). We can take these terms to represent concepts which are situated on a spectrum ranging from knowledge to belief ("I don't just believe it. I don't just assume it. I know it!"), and which in their use, may overlap with each other.

This is an important point surfacing from the data: it was difficult in the data to distinguish between the teachers referring to beliefs and knowledge as they discussed their decisions in the interviews. Their 'use' of knowledge in their decision-making process did not seem to be qualitatively different from their 'use' of beliefs.

BAK: beliefs, assumptions and knowledge

In the literature described above, a large number of terms has been proposed in the semantic domain of knowledge and beliefs, each highlighting certain distinctions, as noted by Clandinin and Connelly (1986) and Connelly and Clandinin (1988). It is perhaps inexcusable then for me to propose yet another one. Nevertheless I am going to do so, but by doing so I do not wish to add to the distinctions that have been made, but rather to reduce them. This is not to say that the distinctions that have been made are not relevant to the issues discussed, or not justifiable. Rather, based on the interview data, it seemed, for the purposes of this study, more justifiable to propose an inclusive rather than exclusive concept.

In addition, I feel that using terms already established for concepts which have different emphases can mask the differences, implicitly carrying the assumption that the same term has the identical referent as in its prior use (a point made by Freeman et al, 1991). When one wishes to highlight different aspects of an issue, it can be advantageous to have a different term, rather than adding a new aspect to an existing term which was developed for another purpose. However, the use of a different term should not be taken to mean that the concept being referred to is necessarily different from that referred to in other studies. Meta-articles such as Clandinin and Connelly's, exploring the underlying meaning of the use of different terms for the same concept, are very valuable (and should also be done in areas where the *same* term is being used by different researchers in different studies). I am drawn to the term I am proposing here precisely because it is difficult to use syntactically – it is hard to know whether the acronym 'BAK' should be used as a count noun (like belief) or a non-count noun (like knowledge). This syntactic ambiguity is consistent with the teachers' verbalizations, where the concept appears sometimes as separate discrete items and sometimes a non-discrete flow.

The hypothetical construct I am proposing, then, is that of *BAK*, a construct analogous to the notion of schema, but emphasizing the notion that beliefs, assumptions and knowledge are included. There is no attempt in this discussion to describe the processes of activation of the BAK, but rather just to note when teachers use it to explain their thinking and their behaviour. Like schemata, BAK networks are structured in the sense that knowledge, assumptions and beliefs can be posited in terms of interrelated propositions, in which certain propositions presuppose others.

Hypotheses about teachers' BAK networks were based on the elicitation of themes, as noted in Chapter 2, and hypothesizing propositions about those themes and the relationships among them, based on the teachers' verbalizations. The first analysis of the data consisted of looking for recurring themes or issues in the stories of each teacher. Many of the themes recurred with a very high frequency and were verbalized strongly. Although in the first examination of a single interview, the themes were not evident, after following a teacher through an entire course, the themes and their relationships emerged with surprising clarity. A subsequent reading of the same interview became rich in subtle instances of these themes. This occurred not only because the instances of the themes were more apparent, but also because the relationships with other themes became apparent. Each instance was not just an instance of that theme *per se*, but also an exemplification of relationships. The notion of BAK, therefore, includes not just 'elements' but also relationships.

A case could be made that some such themes, for example those involving considerations of institutional constraints, are clear expressions of teachers' knowledge of the teaching situation rather than their beliefs or assumptions about language, learning and teaching. However, as the relationships to other themes became more and more apparent, it became evident that they were intimately connected to the teachers' beliefs and assumptions. For example, Teacher C's complaint about the classroom she had been assigned (the size and the type of desks) became much more meaningful in light of her view of the importance of group work (requiring easily movable desks) in the successful accomplishment of her course.

Features of BAK

Initially I attempted to classify types of teachers and types of decisions (in the way that Dias, 1987, did on types of poetry readers, for example) according to patterns arising from the data; however, the data resisted a traditional classification by type as an organizing principle for this study. The themes expressed by the teachers were at different logical levels; therefore grouping into categories what are different levels in a heterarchical organization, would be mixing 'logical types' (as described by Bateson, 1972, using this term) and affecting the validity of the categories. In addition, the most interesting (and explanatory) results are in the relationships among levels: the purpose of an in-context study was to illuminate the relationships among levels and coding and categorizing would have hidden this aspect.

I wish to emphasize that the teachers' verbalizations are the source of the individual propositions posited in their networks of beliefs, assumptions and knowledge. It is through examining the recurrence of these verbalizations, and their relationships to others in the data, that I posited certain features of their BAK systems. I do not wish to claim that such propositions exist in the minds of the teachers as individual entities, but rather that under particular conditions (including both the teaching situation they were involved in and the interview situations in which the data was elicited), they categorized and verbalized aspects of their BAK. In this regard, I am attracted to the cognitive metaphor of PDP (parallel distributed processing) to describe BAK – that the elements do not exist as individual entities but coalesce into patterns in particular situations. The description of Bateson (1979), quoted in Chapter 3, of interconnections of various degrees of density and sparseness I feel also captures the same sense.

Having made this hedge, I wish to elaborate on particular features of BAK, including the interwoven nature of beliefs, assumptions and knowledge, and the relationships among propositions of the teachers' BAK networks.

The interwoven nature of beliefs, assumptions and knowledge

In the discussion in the previous section, a distinction is made between the concept of knowledge and the concept of belief. To determine which of these is relevant in the case of the teachers' verbalizations, we need to examine propositions about teaching. These propositions can be related to Abelson's (1979) article, which posits a number of differences between belief systems and knowledge systems, including the notions that beliefs are non-consensual, that they often involve the 'existence' of abstract entities, that they are evaluative, that they often include anecdotal material, that they have different degrees of strength, and that they have unclear boundaries. All of these points imply that beliefs are not factual.

Comments made by Teacher D while watching the videotape of her lesson, taken in combination with comments in subsequent interviews, allow certain propositions to be posited, ones which represent the knowledge, beliefs and working assumptions that underlie her perception of the teaching. At various moments in the discussion, Teacher D made the following points about her course (this is a partial list of recurring themes in the data).

1. The students are learning English for academic studies.
2. In their academic studies, the students are responsible for making their own choices.
3. In their academic studies, the students have to be able to take in a great deal of information, synthesize it to understand the overall picture, and write about it in an organized way.
4. In their academic studies, specific individual 'facts' are not important.
5. There is no single 'right answer' in the type of work they will be doing.
6. Academic texts typically argue a position.
7. There is a 'correct way of putting things together' in academic texts: a 'formula' by which academic texts are organized using supporting statements to support main arguments.
8. The students often come from previous school settings where specific facts and right answers were important.
9. The ESL class functions as a link between the students' prior educational experience and their upcoming academic studies.
10. In the ESL class, the teacher's role as motivator is important and students will often try to succeed for the teacher before they get to the point of trying to succeed for themselves.
11. The teacher should demonstrate the course expectations clearly.

If we consider knowledge factual, there are a number of ways in which propositions can diverge, in different degrees, from factuality. One way in which this occurs is through abstraction and generalization. In such a case, when something is 'in principle true' or 'generally true', the degree to which the generality is seen to diverge from 'fact' varies from individual to individual, giving it a feature of belief. For example, Statement 1, above, can be considered what Teacher D knows about the students. However, this statement is a generalization in the sense that although it is currently true for most students in the class, it is not currently the case for all of them. For those for whom the statement is currently demonstrable (by asking them), some may well change their minds subsequently. Also, in this case, different teachers may have different points of view on the subject.

Another way in which these propositions diverge from factual knowledge is not that they are true for some cases and not others, but that they are true for all but only to a degree. For example, Statement 2 is factual in the sense that students are to a point responsible for making choices in their studies; but they also have some institutional limitations regarding choices, and they also get (or can get, through strategic means) support in making their choices. This point reflects a course goal that Teacher D has set them. Statements 4, 5, 6, and 7 are also similar in this sense, and Statements 5 and 7 are expressed as statements of existence. Statement 10 is non-consensual (judging from other teachers' verbalizations regarding motivation, below), while Statement 11 is evaluative. In general, the statements above can be considered 'more or less' factual, and therefore located somewhere between knowledge and beliefs.

What is relevant to this study, however, is not a judgment of whether the propositions underlying BAK can be called beliefs or knowledge, but rather how they are used in the decision-making processes of the teachers. The themes in the above statements occurred in virtually every interview with Teacher D. For example, in a discussion of an exam that Teacher D developed to give to her class (one of the course substructures), her choice as to how to structure an exam included, in an intertwined way, several of the points listed above. The view of students' current expectations and attitudes, her goal of students taking on responsibility for the learning necessary for academic studies (where there are 'no right answers', but where there is a correct way of organizing a text), and the teacher's role in that change, are all reflected in her discussion of the exam.

D: Now the reason for making an exam like this is to demonstrate to them that everything they've been doing is a real thing and it's not /... I feel many students come into this level as I've said often with a certain idea about learning the language and with certain expectations about learning and so on and I feel that I have to break those habits or change those expectations ... In trying to break these habits I'm taking a lot of the onus off of me the teacher as guide and director and trying to put it on them and it takes, depending who they are and what their past experiences and their attitude and everything, this takes different amounts of time. And what will happen because the stuff I'm dealing with appears to be simple until they take the responsibility onto themselves and come to realize there is a much greater degree of difficulty here or a greater depth / let me say that, they continue to go on and think this is all very simple and you know they write two sentences when I'm sort of expecting a good, strong healthy paragraph. So what the exam does I think is show them, because it's so long and because there are two quite difficult sections, that if they have, up to this point of exam writing, had the attitude that this is really peanuts, they learn when they do this exam that it ain't so. Does that make any sense? ... [It's] part of the whole academic process / I mean the students who do better when they're in real courses, are those who go out and do a little work on their own. They just don't stick to the bare minimum ... But it's happening. I can see more and more people in the class now are just taking this whole thing more seriously. And just standing in front of them and saying "everybody can have a different answer and all the answers can be right" / they have to live it you know / [otherwise] it's just so many words that the teacher is saying. So it's a matter of what I might call taking their learning seriously or expanding or changing their expectations about learning/ something like that.

A moment later, she discussed the next activity planned, which reflects Statement 7 in the above list:

D: What I am going to do is start working with 'skeletons'. Now presumably they have the idea of "here is a statement and every statement has to be supported, otherwise it's just an opinion" ... I mean if you take a topic like let's say good old television. Okay right away we've got the benefits and the drawbacks. Now under benefits we could probably divide that up into three different things. I would hope that they will understand or approach this thinking that for every area and every sub-area, we are going to have kind a statement and we have to support that and then all these different / you know support a, support b, support c for sub-area a, b, c/ will all lead back to the overall [statement].

Interrelationships in BAK

In the literature on knowledge structures and belief systems reviewed in Chapter 3, an important aspect is the notion that they are not composed of independent elements, but rather structured, with certain aspects implying or presupposing others. This characteristic is supported by the data from the teacher interviews. The example of Teacher G, below, illustrates how, during the interviews over the duration of the course, a picture develops of the teacher's overall approach to teaching in terms of the interrelationships among the recurring themes. There are a number of themes which continually recur, sometimes alone, but more often in combination with others. In cases where more than one theme co-occurs, it is possible to posit particular relationships between the themes, and between the BAK elements that underlie them. Eventually a network of interrelationships becomes discernible in the data. (This point is also demonstrated in the discussion of the evolution of BAK in this chapter.)

Teacher G's statement included the following relationships.

1. The relationship of motivation to success in learning:

G: I think that the biggest thing is how to motivate the students because I'm convinced that students learn best if they want to learn.

2. The relationship of responding to individual student needs to success in achieving motivation:

G: I'm convinced that the more the teaching responds to the needs of the student, the more motivated the student is going to be, and the more motivated and successful he's going to be in his learning.

3. The relationship of an individualized course to success in responding to individual student needs:

G: [The goal of this course is] ... to give them the best English course I can give them for their needs ... trying to make it as tailor-made as possible ... It's basically the students who determine the course.

4. The relationship of a needs analysis to success in giving an individualized course:

G: The needs analysis [an initial needs analysis activity, in which students stated their personal goals for the course] affected very much what we did afterwards.

5. The relationship of learner independence to success in doing the needs analysis:

G: [The first needs analysis is not expected to work because] several students are straight out of high school where they are not trained to think independently, they are trained to accept what they get ... so for several of them it's kind of strange to be asked "What would you like to do?"

G: [A second needs analysis activity is planned a week later after other activities designed to develop their awareness because] they're finding it a little difficult to determine personal goals ... I gave them a short description on independent learning and how to set personal goals and I talk to all of them individually [about their goals].

Teacher G's definition of what English is, and therefore the course content, was defined in terms of what aspects are most important to the students as individuals, and not the class as a whole. It implies that different individuals will have to learn different things. This does not mean that students know best what to learn, because otherwise she would not have had to train them to know what they need. However, it does imply a view that students potentially know best what they need to learn, and that some aspects are not readily accessible to the teacher. This view also implies individualization. It implies a view that students' English will develop more when they are making the decisions about what to learn themselves. One way to individualize effectively is to have students make choices about their learning and take responsibility for these choices, so the teacher does not have to deal with the responsibility for choices and the monitoring of each individual student. Although a consistently recurring theme for Teacher G was learner independence, she stated that the overall goal of the course was not to make the students independent; it was to develop their English. This explicit statement is consistent with the above series of examples. The notions of responsibility, independence and motivation function from one viewpoint as the means to accomplish the course goals, while from another viewpoint they are goals to be achieved via particular activities.

The above themes are interrelated and structured, according to Teacher G's verbalizations in the interviews, and produce a unique whole. Many of the teachers in the study emphasized the importance of motivation in language learning, and its centrality in learning. However, they differed in their views about what produces motivation. Many teachers also indicated the importance of responding to student needs. However, none of the others made the assumption that student needs refers primarily to individual student needs rather than the needs of the group. Several teachers referred to needs analyses, but not as a means to individualize the content. For most of the teachers, learner independence was an emphasized issue (as described in this chapter), but its interrelationships with other concepts differed.

The theme of learner independence also played a role in Teacher G's evaluation of different aspects of teaching and the progress of the course:

G: Students are beginning to come and see me during the break and after the class and they tell me "I'd like to work on this" or "I'd like to work on that".

and was also evident in her criteria for the progress of the students:

G: They indicated that they feel that they've made progress in their chosen areas.

Although there are some generally recognizable entailments in these beliefs (meaning that if a teacher holds belief Z, then it follows that she must hold belief Y), it is important to emphasize that there is an important sense in which these systems are individual, and that the individuality is related to the teacher's particular BAK network. It is easy for an outside observer who observes a single lesson or has one conversation with a teacher to construct a mistaken view based on presumed entailments. For example, the concepts of motivation and needs analysis are ones used frequently in the field of second language teaching and it would be easy to assume that teachers treat them in the same way. In the case of Teacher G, however, we can see a unique pattern: working with the students individually allows them to complete the needs analyses, which allows the course to be tailor-made and individualized, which responds to their needs, which motivates the students, which increases their learning. In other words, it is not just any motivation increaser that is important; it is the motivation related to individual student needs. It is not just any needs analysis, but a needs analysis that allows for individualization.

The evolution of BAK

The development of a network of beliefs, assumptions and knowledge over time is exemplified most clearly in the introductory interview with Teacher B, which is quoted at length in this section. The fact that the other teachers' interviews produced fewer such references may be related to the developing skill of the interviewers (this subject was one of the last in the study), or to the willingness of the subject to delve into background experiences. Choosing a 'best example' to illustrate a phenomenon has an important precedent in the work on the writing processes by Emig (1971). The description below, presented in the form of a narrative (with author commentary), demonstrates how the teacher's BAK evolved over time, how 'hotspots' appeared, and how, under pressure from the teacher's desire to resolve the conflicts, resolutions developed through subsequent experiences.

In the initial interview, the interviewer asked Teacher B to describe any experiences which "had some kind of effect on the way you see yourself as a teacher and the way you view language and learning and teaching". Teacher B discussed several of his relevant previous experiences: (i) his early experiences learning a second language, (ii) his early experiences teaching ESL and his concurrent teacher education program, (iii) his experience in Japan, teaching English and learning Japanese, and finally (iv) his experience in his current teaching setting.

In the following detailed discussion of Teacher B's background, we can see the evolution of his views over time. First we see how some of his ideas and thoughts about language teaching were formed by early experiences as a learner, then as a student of applied linguistics and

ESL teaching, and then as a teacher in practice. An examination of the development of his BAK shows not only the link between the teacher's holistic view of learning and his resistance to teaching grammar, but also how his views about grammar evolved with new teaching experiences with a different clientele. This in turn brought to the surface his beliefs about student needs, student responsibilities and student choice. His experience teaching in Japan and learning Japanese continued this evolution. In the discussion of the course he was currently teaching, we can see the culmination of this evolution.

From the statements made by Teacher B during the interviews, we can clearly discern the issues which were of importance to this teacher, and which arose frequently in discussions of his day-to-day and week-to-week teaching. From these, we can posit clusters of interrelated beliefs or assumptions about language, learning and teaching, including some hierarchical relationships among aspects of his BAK which begin to emerge during these discussions. In particular we can see how certain experiences caused conflicts (or 'hotspots' in the data) in terms of his views at the time, leading to a kind of synthesis of his BAK and the experiences. It is important to acknowledge, however, that these descriptions are not of the past experiences *per se*, but are viewed through the lens of the present. Certain concepts and oppositions may not have been relevant at the time, but are activated retroactively to explain or make sense of the past experiences. These descriptions, therefore, reveal aspects of Teacher B's BAK as well as of the prior experiences.

Early language learning experiences

Teacher B described a number of experiences as a language learner that had influenced his perception of learning a second language. In this description, a number of themes emerge. One is related to learning a language holistically – through communication in context – as opposed to conscious study of individual rules. A second relates to motivation. In his early experiences, these two themes co-exist.

His experience learning French is a case in point. He had taken French as a 'core' subject all through his elementary and secondary schooling, but never felt that he was able to speak French. Once he entered a French environment, however, he found that he was able to speak French very quickly.

B: I guess that was probably an influence for me as far as how language acquisition works was that going through the formal system I learned practically no French, however in the course of about six months of having a French girlfriend or being around French speakers I picked up French very quickly and without much difficulty.

The main reason for this, for him, was that:

B: ... when I was studying French in school, and in university for that matter, was the feeling that there was so much to the language and you were just sort of chiselling away at it and you would never get a grasp of it, rather than with more communicative techniques which really immerse you in a language and you're using it for all intents and purposes, you think that you have a grasp on the whole language when you're only using a small amount of it ... .

As a result:

B: ... that made me feel at the time that the process of learning in the formal education system is not very efficient for one thing, and also that the method used is not very motivating, that it's difficult for students to see the connection between speaking the language and studying the language in class ... .

We see here that his view of learning the formal system of the language in school is contrasted to "getting a grasp on the whole language". This latter idea is a sign of his holistic predilection; and the comment creates an implied link between that and the ideas of communication, learning purpose and motivation.

Early teaching experiences and teacher education

Teacher B discovered, after graduation, that his earlier intuitions about learning a language via grammar were not contradicted by the experiences of his early teaching career:

B: ... I thought having a degree in linguistics would give me all sorts of insights into teaching, especially having done quite a number of courses in grammar, and what was interesting was discovering that it was really of little practical value, especially teaching grammar, that I had to learn pedagogical grammar right from scratch, right from the terminology to how to facilitate the students' understanding of grammar ... .

And, then:

B: ... I think in a very brief time I progressed to the point where I felt that the formal teaching of grammar was of very little value at all ... .

He brings together the notion about "the formal teaching of grammar" and his concern with particular student characteristics in particular circumstances:

B: ... especially because the environment I was teaching in most of the students were immigrants who ... had very little formal education to begin with, so the idea of teaching grammar in a formal way just seemed very inappropriate ... intuitively I just felt that the teaching of grammar was somehow a waste of time,,, you know I'd seen teachers trying to teach students the difference between definite and indefinite articles, students who obviously couldn't grasp the concepts they were talking about let alone the language itself, you know it just seemed futile ... .

Through involvement in subsequent professional development (graduate courses in ESL teaching), he was exposed to the work of Krashen, for which he felt an intuitive affinity:

B: ... I was really pro communicative language teaching because it was in keeping with my intuitions about the way language was and the way language worked ... .

We can see in a number of these comments that his notions about holistic, communicative, purposeful language learning, and his attitudes towards teaching grammar are related to a view about the importance of the characteristics of the students. This issue is implicit in his earlier discussion of his experience learning French and the importance of motivation for learning. However, its role in his view of learning becomes clearer when a conflict occurs between his own view of learning a language holistically and communicatively, and his view of the importance of taking into account students' wishes. This is evident in his discussion of an early teaching experience where the students are not motivated by the same things that he was when he was a learner:

B: ... another thing that happened was that the kind of student population we had at that time changed ... to having a lot of Eastern European immigrants who had more education, more language education, and even the low beginning students expected some kind of grammar, some kind of formal approach to teaching, and if they didn't get it they got really upset, so almost as a placebo sometimes you felt you had to give them some kind of formal presentation, and then you could do whatever you liked as long as they felt they were getting formal presentations,,, so I started to see the formal teaching of grammar or language concepts as a possibly highly motivating thing for a lot of people.

And:

B: ... right from the beginning pretty much, as I said, I didn't teach grammar in a formal way and I didn't feel I had any problems, but when we started to get a lot of Eastern European students I started to feel resistance on the part of the students so I had to really change the way I think.

This conflict was the beginning of a major development in his beliefs about learning and teaching related to who is responsible for what in the management of learning:

B: ... so I started to change my thinking a little bit and started to adopt a philosophy that basically what I as a teacher needed to do was get attuned to the students in the first little while and see how they felt that they should undertake their learning ... .

Later language learning and teaching experiences overseas

These views evolved further during a period of teaching English and learning Japanese in Japan, where cultural assumptions about classroom teaching differed dramatically from his own. His experience as a language learner in Japan had an effect in altering his views about language learning through communication. Based on his interpretation of Krashen, he expected that, simply by being exposed to Japanese in daily life, he would 'acquire' an ability to communicate in Japanese:

B: ... coming from the whole background of ... Krashen's monitor model I really had this idea that if you're in a communicative environment you're going to learn ... I mean that's what it implies, you don't need to make an effort, if you make an effort, that's counter-intuitive, and you should just be in a communicative situation and you'll ... I had this idea ... that if I just placed myself in an environment [where] everybody I knew was Japanese, I was going to learn Japanese ... .

This led to a further step in his beliefs about language learning:

B: ... after about six months when I really didn't have a handle on Japanese ... I wasn't really happy with the way I was communicating in Japanese, so I decided I had to make a more concerted effort to learn, and when I did – when I got some books and some tapes and studied an hour a night or an hour and a half a night and made an effort ... I made a huge leap of progress and within a couple of months I was sitting down and having conversations with people ... I think I came to the realization that effort is needed, if you really want to learn you have to make an effort ... .

He altered his overall perspective to include the notion of putting a concerted effort into the learning, while retaining his former belief in the importance of being in the target language environment and communicating with native speakers. His view about the classroom teaching of formal aspects of the language, although tempered a little, remained: he compared his own abilities in Japanese favourably with people who had learned in formal programs in the United States, in terms of their pronunciation and 'mechanical' way of speaking:

B: ... so in that respect [the mechanical way of speaking] I don't think it's [formal language learning] an efficient way to learn a language, but there's something to be said for it as well.

His experience teaching English in a Japanese high school served to allow this newly developing philosophy to evolve further, as the traditional setting in which he was teaching led toward a particular 'hotspot'. On the one hand, he had strong beliefs about holistic in-context learning and teaching that had evolved through his own experience as a learner and his theoretical affinity for Krashen. On the other hand, his belief in the importance of teaching according to students' expectations and motivations continued to grow stronger.

He began teaching in Japan according to his sense of a communicative, experiential orientation, with the intention of not speaking any Japanese in the classroom (in contrast to the standard use of Japanese for explanations and instructions), and of involving the students in pair work and group work activities. However, his many creative attempts to use English for communication in the classroom were met by silence and what seemed to be lack of comprehension on the part of the students even though they had an adequate level of English to understand. He found that, in their educational subculture, the students were 'obliged' to give answers to questions in a formal exercise, but were not 'obliged' to understand a teacher who attempted to communicate with them in English. As he progressed through a year of difficult teaching experiences, he found he had to "adapt my way of thinking to the Japanese mentality about education".

B: ... they [the students] are obliged in a formal way to understand the language,,, if you ask them in Japanese what does this mean they would have to give you the answer, but if you try to communicate with them it's becoming a personal thing, you're using the language to try and bring them into your world, and that's not part of the education system ... They have a system here and if they did things the way you wanted them to, the students would all fail the exam ... .

Eventually he came to the conclusion that it was more efficient and motivating to base his teaching on the Japanese notion of the 'purpose' of the course – to pass the exam – than on his own notions of authentic purpose and communication. Through these experiences he eventually began to develop a new philosophy for himself, one which superseded his view about the general superiority of holistic communicative learning.

B: ... after teaching there a year I had come to maybe even more than just cope with it,, to feel that I was accomplishing something worthwhile, so that made me realize that every situation should be treated as a new situation and equal challenge ... it made me realize that there is no one way for language to be learned or language to be taught ... .

This led to further refining of his view of the role of the teacher:

B: ... I saw that their system worked for some people for whatever reasons, whether it's just a mental exercise, they worked hard, they were doing something, working hard at it, it made me realize that my job really isn't to know how people should learn but to see how they want to learn that then do whatever I'm capable of doing to help them do that ... .

These comments are not a contradiction of his previous beliefs about how language is learned, but reflect a deeper relationship: his view about learning for communication was in a sense subordinate to his view of purpose and motivation. The view he had formulated earlier, that decontextualized learning of formal language concepts was demotivating and inefficient, was a personalized one based on his own learning experience. When he encountered a 'hotspot' – a situation where *not* having formal presentation of language items was demotivating – it led to an evolution in his BAK. In his experience of learning French he had equated 'purpose' with learning to speak the language, and 'motivation' with seeing that purpose reflected in what is done in class. However, in his experience teaching the Eastern European and the Japanese students, his conception of purpose broadened to include institutional purposes such as passing an exam, and his conception of motivation broadened to include seeing this institutional purpose reflected in the classroom. The idea of learning for communication became only one type of motivation, and only one aspect of purpose. This broader conception of the notions of 'motivation' and 'purpose' is reflected in his use of these terms in the following comment:

B: ... I guess teaching in a [Japanese] high school made me much more aware of the need for being very organized and giving the students a sense of being very organized purely for the sake of motivation, that especially the high school students there really had to feel that you were doing something for a purpose, not just doing it to keep them busy or to babysit them, and to show them that something was headed in a given direction, otherwise it was just chaos ... .

As his BAK evolved, what changed was not his views as to how language should be presented and learned, but rather his views about responsibility for learning and the role of the learner and teacher in the process.

B: ... whereas in the early days of [my] teaching, I always felt that I was the one who knew how people should learn/ it was my job to convince them that I knew and then they would learn/ I started to see more and more that people really had to be responsible for their own learning and that my role as a teacher was more to animate them and to provide them with the tools, if you like, so they could approach it in the way they felt was most appropriate to them.

Current teaching experiences

As Teacher B began to discuss his planning for the course to be taught during this study, especially the content to be learned and taught, the issue of student needs reappeared in relation to his developing notion of purpose and motivation: the students were seen as 'instrumentally motivated'. Since their purpose was perceived as getting through the final exam in order to move on in their own academic programs, his interpretation of the purpose of the course was preparing them to do this. He saw this as the major criterion for success, for them and hence for him:

B: ... when you're teaching English as a second language proper, in the sense that you're teaching people how to communicate in a language, I usually think that objectives in that sense or examinations are more constraints than they are objectives, but in the case of a university course it's the primary thing you're aiming at ... you want to make sure the students know what their objectives are on the exam,, and if you were to say to the students "we're not going to worry about the exam, we're just going to do this", the students wouldn't take that too kindly because most of them when you ask them their purpose for being in the course, they will tell you they have to be there, they need the course for the prerequisite for their program, and while everybody's interested in improving their English, they really want to pass the exam so they can get on with their work at the university.

And:

B: ... if you don't pass the writing portion of the final exam you don't pass the course, so I considered really the most important thing to make sure that they could pass their writing portion of the final exam when they finished ... .

As a result, he considered it important to make explicit what the students had to achieve, and how the structure of the course related to their needs. When discussing an activity being planned by the teaching intern assisting him, Teacher B expressed his interpretation of the relationships among students' motivation, their purpose for taking the course, and the organization of subunits of teaching.

B: ... he [the intern] should gear it [the activity] towards the objectives of the course because the students are pretty much instrumentally motivated, I mean they have a tendency to ask you what does this have to do with the course ... [you have to] make it a little more useful or the students might start to think you're wasting their time ... .

His sense of the purpose of the course even extended to attempting to take into account the characteristics of the teacher of their subsequent ESL course:

B: I'll discuss with other teachers what kind of notation I [should] use for outlining; when I taught [the advanced course] I knew it was the last course they would be doing in ESL so I didn't care what kind of notation I used, but ... I don't know what kind of teacher these people are going to have [in the next course] so I would like to give them some kind of notation or organization for doing a reading outline ... .

When noting a "criticism" of the program or teaching system, he based it on this sense of purpose: what the students want or need:

B: ... one of the criticisms I have of the program here is the exams are never set until a month or two into the course so you always have this real fear that you're going to be teaching something and after two months realize that it was really inappropriate because it's not going to be on the exam ... .

This focus on the instrumental motivation of the students was part of a more general use of student characteristics as a basis for his decision-making. As he began discussing his overall plans for his new class, he made a number of comparisons with his previous class, indicating that his style of teaching, or at least some of the techniques he uses, changed from class to class depending upon its perceived characteristics:

B: ... this class is quite mature and they don't strike me as the type of class that wants to be told everything whereas the class I had before tended to be more 18- and 19-year olds who want you to give them the gospel and then they'll remember it, whereas this class they seem to be more mature and if you tell them something that's fairly obvious they'll go "yeah, yeah, so what?" So I think/ which is pretty good in a way/ to some extent that's changed my feeling about how I'll deal with them, I mean, I'll probably make the classes much more student-centred and do a lot more group work with this class than I did with [the last class] ... what I intend to do is give them more student-oriented work and put them into groups and get them to do more of the/be responsible for more things that go on in the class ... .

In this comment, the respect for students' own purposes and needs becomes intertwined in a complex way with the earlier issues of purposive, in-context, holistic, experiential learning, which extends to a more general view about his relationship with the learners. With regard to his own role as teacher, he frequently indicated that he preferred not to be the one who "knows all the answers" (a point related to his dislike of teacher-fronted classrooms, and also to his preference for experiential learning). He noted that he would not give the students anything to do that he could not do himself:

B: That's always one of my criteria that if I want my students to do something in fifteen minutes in class and I can't do it then it's unreasonable to ask it of them.

He consistently demonstrated a view of course content as relative and negotiated, making comments like:

B: I can also give them the benefit of knowing that not everybody agrees on classification for example, ... that as far as I'm concerned this is what classification is, however, be careful because when you get to [the advanced course], you might get a teacher who feels such and such ... .

He indicated that he did not mind being wrong in front of the students, and that he did not like to supply "right answers" to questions, even questions with straightforward answers. These comments reflect his original orientation toward experiential learning and his explicitly stated assumption that the teacher standing in front of the class presenting already worked out ideas is "not very efficient", now integrated with the notion, stemming from his Japanese experience, that to learn you must make a "concerted effort".

B: I don't think they'll learn very much from it, whereas I think that when students really have to come to grips with it themselves, when they have to make an effort themselves to try and solve some problems, that they will do it a little better.

These comments are consistent with Teacher B's BAK – a perspective about language, learning and teaching that is reflected throughout his structuring of the different levels of the course.

Conclusion

This chapter introduced the concept of an integrated view of beliefs, assumptions and knowledge (BAK). The examples in this chapter show how BAK develops through a teacher's experiences as a learner and a teacher, evolving in the face of conflicts and inconsistencies, and gaining depth and breadth as varied events are interpreted and reflected upon. This chapter has explored the role of experience in the evolution of BAK. The next chapter explores the role of BAK in the interpretation of teaching events.

8 The role of BAK in teachers' interpretive processes

In the last chapter, the notion of an integrated network of beliefs, assumptions and background knowledge underlying teachers' interpretive processes was posited. The case of one particular teacher was described in detail to illustrate how BAK evolves through experience and through the gradual resolution of conflicts arising from novel situations. The more varied experiences the teacher has had, the deeper the resolutions. However, we have not explored the role of BAK in the interpretive process. What kinds of events get interpreted? What is the effect of BAK on the interpretation? This chapter describes the *role* of the BAK network in the teacher's interpretation of teaching events.

The following discussion uses examples from the data to focus on the role of BAK in the interpretive processes of the teachers. These examples illustrate the teachers' interpretations of various types of teaching events: (i) classroom events (including such structures as exchanges and utterances in the classroom), (ii) the curriculum (including higher level teaching structures, such as institutionally-imposed organizational units of a course), (iii) textbook approaches, (iv) texts from the theoretical and research literature, (v) pedagogical concepts, and (vi) approaches to planning. The purpose in this chapter is not to postulate the existence of distinct elements in this BAK network, but rather to explain and exemplify with teacher verbalizations the role that BAK plays in their interpretations of the above types of events.

The focus in this chapter is on the role of BAK in teachers' interpretive processes. Yet, in the data, it was often not easy to separate cases of teachers' BAK playing a role in interpretive processes from cases of teachers' BAK playing a role in subsequent planning and decision-making. Often the interpretation of a particular event had immediate relevance for the teachers' future plans and was framed in that way. In addition, subsequent actions are also an indicator of how a previous event was interpreted. Nonetheless, in this chapter I focus primarily on the interpretive part of the processes, reserving discussion of the role of BAK in the whole cycle of teaching for Chapter 9.

Interpretations in teaching

Interpretation of classroom events

The way in which local level classroom events and verbalizations are interpreted and given significance in light of particular characteristics of the teacher's BAK is illustrated by the following example, taken from Teacher C's lesson. By comparing the teacher's discussions of the particular issues described below, we can gradually posit relationships among these issues.

In the videotaped lesson, Teacher C was eliciting some 'direction words' before the beginning of an activity on 'giving directions' (this sequence of exchanges is transcribed in Chapter 4 page 101). At one point, she said 'good' in response to the contribution of a student. When watching the videotape of this lesson later, the teacher pressed the pause button on the machine at this point and said:

C: Something I'm still trying to get away from in my teaching, which I still do as a natural reflex because it's so deeply ingrained, is to get away from making judgments by saying "good", "that was very good", "that was excellent", and I do that a number of times in this lesson. Each time I do it, you should be able to see my face go ... [she makes a wincing face] "oh I've done it again".

I: Why are you trying to get away from that?

C: Because I don't want to put myself in the position of judging the quality of their/,, what that word does is set me up as a judgmental body and it threatens the position I'm trying to encourage in the class, which is one of facilitator, participant, guide,,, but not judge, and it goes against my notions of trying to encourage their/I don't want them to look upon me as someone who is going to be there to judge the quality of their expression. I want them to look upon me as a receiver of the information.

This is an evaluative comment about a verbal event that occurred in the classroom. It was interpreted and given significance in terms of her BAK network, one in which learning is considered to be enhanced by a particular relationship between teacher and learners. The inconsistency between what she did and what she believes indicates a 'hotspot' in her evolving BAK. She is gaining an awareness of a type of behaviour which had become an 'automatic routine'. Here it could be considered a 'fossilized structure' left from a previous BAK state which is no longer consistent with the evolving BAK structure. (One implication of this argument is that awareness may play a role in the evolution of BAK.)

At a later point in the lesson, the teacher demonstrated to the students how the 'giving directions' activity would be carried out. As part of this demonstration, she asked a student to give a direction, and when she did not understand it and got him to repeat it, she then repeated verbatim what the student had said as a way to clarify the direction. She explained to the interviewer her reason for clarifying in this way (rather than focusing on correct forms), indicating that she wanted to respond in the way an actual native interlocutor would.

I: So your feeling is that it's better [to repeat verbatim] than actually making a correction or actually taking something that somebody said and stating it the right way?

C: Oh absolutely. Definitely,,, because what's really important is the commu-nication. If it works, then there is really no wrong or right way. If it works, it works, and that's it as far as I'm concerned. Also I don't think people learn from corrections. They learn when they are ready to learn something. They absorb it when it's useful for them to absorb it and no amount of/,,, well I suppose we could drill one expression but that's artificial and then all they do is tend to remember the drill and they don't apply it.

This comment is also consistent with the previous one, but illustrates a different aspect of her BAK. In this case, we see that her perception of the teacher's role in a language classroom (i.e. as an interlocutor and not a judge) is related to her view of correction in language acquisi-tion.

After the activity had begun and the students were working in pairs, the room was noticeably noisy. Teacher C stopped the tape and made a comment. In this comment, Teacher C evaluates how the activity as a whole was going. The positive evaluation relates again to her role as an "unessential", and non-judgmental, classroom participant.

C: One comment is that it's nice now. This is the way I like to see the class running. I'm totally unessential here. I try and make myself *appear* useful (laugh), but,,, /and I like the way they're not responding to me when,,, /in the past what happened when I taught was that when I came near a group, the group became aware of my presence, and part of that comes from hav-ing a teacher who is judgmental, who's always correcting and controlling.

Within this perceived event (the pairwork part of the activity), she also picked out a smaller event: "the way they're not responding to me [when I come near a group]". This is a particularly interesting example because in this case perceived event is something that did *not* hap-pen. It is, in a sense, akin to a visual artist's notion of 'negative space': the shape of the empty space between the objects is perceived and used by the artist in the creation of the painting. In this case, the perceived negative event – the *lack* of response – was interpreted as a sign that a higher level goal in the structure which she had created for teaching this class – learner independence from the teacher – was being accom-plished. This example illustrates that what is picked out of the on-going stream of sound and movement, given a label and discussed as an 'event' depends on what is relevant within the teacher's BAK.

Noticeable in the above comments are several important aspects of Teacher C's BAK. One intertwined cluster of themes includes not making judgmental comments, not correcting and accepting the communicative value of the student's utterances. Another cluster includes being unessential, being a co-participant, being a communication partner. Both these clusters are connected to higher level themes for this teacher: students taking initiative for communicating and for their own learning inside and outside the classroom. The teacher being unessential in the classroom helps shift the responsibility to the learners. Developing comfort on the part of the students with group work allows her to be unessential. Focusing on the communicative value of students' language rather than on its correctness promotes the functioning of group work and the students' comfort with it. These themes are consistent with comments made by Teacher C throughout the course.

Interpretation of the curriculum

The second important area of teachers' interpretations is related to the way teachers interpret a curriculum. A curriculum, as discussed in Chapter 4, involves issues concerning the goals of the course, the content to be taught and the ways in which the teaching is expected to be carried out. Information about the curriculum can come in the form of instructions and procedures provided by the institution, the supervisor, the materials, or particular combinations of these, depending on the spoken or unspoken traditions of the institution. The way different teachers interpret these curricular instructions will have an important impact on the structuring of the teaching that takes place; and therefore the teaching decisions reflect the interpretations, and provide additional evidence of them. When we look at the notion of curriculum from the perspective of the heterarchical structure of teaching developed in Chapter 4, we can say that the curriculum is reflected in all the organizational levels of the course, from the overall course goals to the events and verbalizations that occur among the learners and teacher in the classroom. The teacher's interpretations of the curriculum will then be reflected at all these levels.

The role of BAK in teachers' interpretations of a curriculum can be best seen by comparing two teachers in the study who were teaching the same curriculum. (These results have been reported in Woods, 1991.) Teachers A and B taught different classes of students the same course, i.e. what was intended by the institution to be the same curriculum. These teachers, both recommended to me by their director and considered to be teachers of very high calibre, taught parallel sections of a university level academic ESL course. The study actually included three classes of students each based on the same curriculum, as Teacher A taught two sections of the course while Teacher B taught one. We already know a great deal about Teacher B's BAK from the last chapter. Here the emphasis is its role in the interpretation of the curriculum, as compared to that of Teacher A.

The course that these teachers taught had a common set of objectives, a common syllabus, and a common final exam. However, the teachers had a relatively high degree of freedom in implementing the syllabus and achieving the objectives. The objectives of the course, ones that formed the basis for the final exam, included being able to (i) write a paragraph following each of five patterns of rhetorical development (process, comparison and contrast, classification, cause and effect, and definition), (ii) correctly use the related grammatical structures (coordination and subordination of clauses and verb tenses being two major categories), and (iii) correctly identify the patterns of development and correctly identify main points and supporting detail in written and spoken texts. This recently developed curriculum was being implemented for the first time. The actual implementation was new to both teachers (and so they tended to make decisions more consciously and verbalize their decision-making process more readily); however, Teacher A had been instrumental in initiating and developing the new curriculum, and therefore had more familiarity with it and a greater sense of its evolution within the institutional context.

A number of themes that arose in the interviews were common to the two teachers. However, the interaction of the curricular instructions and the beliefs, assumptions and knowledge of these teachers produced very different interpretations of the course to be taught. Analysis of the data revealed, for each teacher, an internal consistency among the decisions they made as they shaped the course, and with the deeper underlying beliefs, assumptions and knowledge about what language is, how it is learned, and how it should be taught. However, the data also revealed consistent differences in the BAK networks of the two teachers, and in their interpretations of the 'what', 'how' and 'why' of the course to be taught. As a result, the classroom events experienced by the learners in Teacher A's two classes were very different from those experienced by Teacher B's class.

Interpretations related to beliefs, assumptions and knowledge about learning

The verbalizations of the two teachers about their teaching included a number of themes related to the way in which languages are learned, and their structuring of classroom events reflected these themes. As noted above, the particular aspects of English to be learned were delineated by the syllabus, and included language and skills for academic study: the relevant grammatical and rhetorical patterns, and the abilities to recognize these patterns in written and spoken texts (articles and lectures) and to use them in writing, specifically in writing a paragraph.

Teacher A's verbalizations indicated a view of learning these target aspects of the language in terms of mastering a progression of items, beginning with the most basic in a simplified and decontextualized form, and leading to the more complex and more contextualized. Her comments reflected a view that learning starts with explicit information, which first has to be consciously understood, and then has to be applied and practised in order to be used in other contexts. Teacher B's verbalizations, in contrast, indicated a gradual but holistic development of abilities, learned right from the beginning in context and with an authentic purpose. His comments reflected a view that learning occurs through the experience of doing, and that information about what is being learned does not necessarily have to be made explicit to the learners by the teacher or the curriculum. Conscious understanding (for example of the grammatical and rhetorical patterns) may occur through reflection or discussion as the language is being used, but it is not a requirement for the language or skills to be learned, and instead often hinders the learning.

In the theoretical literature over the years, arguments have been put forward on both sides of this issue. On the one hand, in the past decade, it has been argued that language does not consist of discrete items and that language learning is not a linear process. These arguments were put forward in reaction to the very structured methodologies of the early 1970's and before, and to the emphasis in linguistics on the phonological and syntactic components of language, and on behaviourist theories of language learning. However, research continues to be carried out on discrete units of language at various levels in linguistics; and it is argued that in learning the mastery of certain less complex abilities is a pre-requisite for more complex abilities. This is not an uncommon conception in language teaching as well – most teachers consider that certain more complex abilities (or activities or texts) are better left until the learners can handle some other pre-requisite abilities comfortably.

These aspects of the teachers' BAK networks are related: items to be taught in a linear fashion can easily be made explicit, and each one can be directly taught and mastered before the next. When the manner of teaching is holistic, students may be learning many things at the same time, and they are not all easily made explicit. I should note, however, that these two views are not the only possible positions on these issues.

For example, in the audio-lingual method of teaching, the argument was made that learning occurs in a linear fashion, not by 'applying knowledge', but rather by imitating and mastering an explicitly organized sequence of grammatical structures. This position is reflected in the buzz phrase 'Teach the language, not about the language'.

Teacher A, early in the course, weighed the pros and cons of having the students first master the appropriate grammatical patterns, and then subsequently work on the patterns of rhetorical development required for the course. (The long quotation describing this decision is included on page 258, as part of the discussion on teacher change.) She indicated her comfort with this procedure, but also her awareness of the 'communicativeness' of the alternative. This conflict between the social currency of communicative teaching and her underlying BAK was a recurring theme in the data for Teacher A. However, her underlying beliefs regarding the progression from simple to more complex concepts surfaced frequently. This progression moved from understanding grammatical patterns, then rhetorical patterns, to manipulating these patterns, to using them in paragraphs, and eventually (in the next course) moving to using them in extended texts. This notion of progression is evident in a log entry made by Teacher A describing her plan for an upcoming lesson in which different sentence types (simple, compound, complex) would be explained and then practised through exercises:

A: Personal intuition that such knowledge is prerequisite for work to be done later on subordination and coordination.

The use of the word 'knowledge' in this log entry also reflects an assumption that gaining an understanding (of a rhetorical pattern, or a grammatical structure) is a required first step in learning, and that this knowledge is transferred to ability through practice. The handouts that Teacher A developed for the class typically started with an explanation of the rules or principles governing the content being presented, followed by examples and exercises to demonstrate and practise applying the rules. The structure of the units, for example those dealing with the five rhetorical patterns, was similar, beginning by a presentation of the concept followed by practice. These interpretations in the course structure are consistent with a comment Teacher A made about her own particular style of learning:

A: ... I'm the kind of person who likes to first figure out how something works and then try and use it,, like I read instructions before I try something. I'm not the type of person who sits down and tries to figure it out.

In contrast to this, Teacher B emphasized the context, audience and purpose throughout the interviews and his structuring of the course.

He resisted dealing with specific items, both for the grammar to be covered and for the patterns of development included in the curriculum. He insisted that grammar should not come before but rather at the same time as the patterns of development were being learned, and the patterns should not come before writing realistic full length pieces for an audience, but concurrently. He said:

B: I'm not going to spend all my time teaching grammar when what we really have to do is learn to write.

He also felt a conflict about isolating the different rhetorical patterns as a basis for teaching on the grounds that there was no 'real' purpose to the activity (other than to do the assignment), and this greatly affected his classroom verbalization to the students. The organization of the curriculum around patterns of rhetorical development and grammar points caused a clash between his view of students' instrumental motivation (to pass the course) and his views about learning. In response, Teacher B developed a number of strategies to resolve the conflict, for example, structuring activities and verbalizations within those activities highlighting 'purpose'. For example, he first presented all five patterns of development in a kind of global overview, and then explicitly pointed out to the students that the patterns of development are "tools" that one uses in particular contexts for particular purposes.

B: ... I'm going to do all the five patterns of development first and introduce them and talk about them as tools that one uses in writing ... .

He indicated that his main goal in dealing with this area is:

B: ... to show that the patterns of development should be seen as tools, not as the focus of the writing; the focus of the writing should be the purpose that you're writing for and the pattern of development should be seen as the tool that you use to achieve that purpose. I found that the students in [the previous course] were really hung up on the patterns of development and they wrote the most inane stuff simply because they were trying to adhere to a definition format or a comparison-contrast format, and it's fairly difficult to get away from that you know because you're constrained or confined by having to teach these patterns of development.

Comments about the difficulty and inauthenticity of teaching abstract 'patterns of rhetorical development' arise frequently during the interviews, even off the cuff. In discussing the help he was giving to a teacher-in-training who was acting as 'class monitor' once a week, he said:

B: ... he didn't understand the patterns of development, which I don't blame him; nobody does unless you teach a course like this or unless you've taken one ... .

There is also a contrast in the treatment of the grammar part of the course, in particular the grammar textbook. Both teachers indicated that the grammar part of the course caused a conflict. However the conflicts were quite different, each being perceived in terms consistent with the teacher's BAK. Teacher A noted in an interview:

A: ... the monitor [teaching assistant] was supposed to go over some grammar exercises with them, and that went off without a hitch, although the students complained that it was boring. Half the students didn't do their homework and so correcting it became a much more tedious process because they all had to figure out the answers first ... .

This 'event' is perceived within Teacher A's views about learning ("explaining", then "check their comprehension" and "practise"), and about the "jobs" and roles of the teacher and learners in the process.

A: ... students are complaining that it's boring, and I can't blame them ... What can I do, I mean the exercises are there for them to practise and to check their comprehension [of the grammar]. I feel it's their job. My job is to explain things to them so they can do the exercises, but if they don't do them that's their problem.

For Teacher A, this interpretation of events suggests that some repair in terms of subsequent restructuring is required, but within her BAK it is not a central problem of the course (and it does not come up again in the interviews). She uses two subsequent structures to repair this problem that occurs in the grammar activities. The first is a "little talk" to the students:

A: ... half of them hadn't done it [the homework]. I just sort of gave them a little talk about, you know, "If you don't do your work you can't really do what I plan to do in class, and other students are complaining that it's boring" ... I just feel bad that they're wasting other students' time, so that's where the whole little talk came in ... .

The second is a restructuring of one aspect of the course: a decision not to structure class time to check the homework ("I'm not going to waste class time going over things half of them haven't done"), but instead to "just give the students the answers and they can check it on their own".

The conflict presented by the grammar part of the course and the grammar textbook created a much more serious conflict for Teacher B, one that arose as a theme many times during the interviews. The statement below has some similarities with those of Teacher A, above; however it includes some crucial differences related to underlying aspects of BAK. The statement indicates both his negative views about practising out of context, and his positive view about students making their own choices:

B: ... I mean I have certain prejudices, like books like [the grammar book] are geared towards a lot of grammar exercises and I've told the students that I don't really find them to be of much use, but if people want to do the grammar exercises ... I mean that's a matter of opinion, some people really feel that they learn a lot from that kind of thing but ... I really don't want to waste time in class doing that because we've got so much other stuff to go through ... .

Instead of interpreting the curriculum as meaning that the students were explicitly to learn the grammar presented in the textbook, he re-interpreted the goal of the grammar section of the course in a way that made sense in terms of his BAK. Since for him grammar was seen as a possible tool rather than a prerequisite, a reasonable goal of the grammar section of the course was to have the students become familiar with the contents of the grammar book so that it could be a resource for later reference. After a great deal of struggle with the problem presented by this institutional constraint, he achieved his goal by coming up with a new sub-structure, one which combined the grammar goal with another course goal, developing 'outlining' skills. His resolution was to have the students practice their outlining skills, and learn where to find the grammatical information contained in the textbook, by outlining its chapters.

B: ... I also had this wonderful idea that/ realizing that the students had bought a $30 grammar text, ... and grammar is only 5% of the entire course so I'm not going to spend all my time teaching grammar when what we really have to do is learn how to write and to read ... so what I said they could do was outline it ... .

Although he initially considered this a 'wonderful idea', the students did not, and several interviews dealt with this question of the students' reaction to the demands put on them by this newly structured out-of-class activity. Eventually he developed a further substructure that succeeded, one consistent with his view of students taking responsibility for their learning by having a role in deciding how the classroom structures should be carried out.

B: ... we've been discussing this thing of them outlining [the grammar book] and I decided to put the ball in their field and say "Okay, you're going to have ten or fifteen minutes ... to get together in groups and come to some common agreement about how you're going to go about organizing this outline" ... .

The unit that both Teacher A and Teacher B did on definition (one of the rhetorical patterns in the syllabus) provided a clear contrast in their interpretations of the curriculum. Teacher A describes the reasons why she chose a particular textbook as a source of information and exercises on definitions, reasons which are consistent with her view of sequencing learning: i.e. learning to write paragraphs should precede learning to write a whole essay; and teaching should involve breaking a learning task into smaller parts to be mastered one at a time.

A: I looked through a variety of books ... And the, reason I chose that one is because it was the only one that dealt with it [definition] on a simple enough level. It's the only one that dealt with it on the level of a paragraph and not on the level of an essay and/ and it also broke it down nicely into the two kinds [formal definition and stipulated definition] ... .

The comment below indicates how a particular concept (for this teacher a concept which is part of the course content) is interpreted quite automatically and subconsciously in a way that is coherent with the individual's BAK, although it can be brought to consciousness and reanalyzed, as triggered by the interviewer's question.

I: Okay. Are there other ways that definition could be broken down besides into the categories of formal and stipulated or do you think that's sort of/

A: I haven't really thought about it to tell you the truth ... I haven't really thought about other ways to break it down. I do know that I'm sure some teachers don't break it down. I'm sure they just teach definition but I think it's important for the students to be able to distinguish between a dictionary type of definition and a personal definition. I think that they should know when they're being completely objective and when they're being subjective in what they/they write and I think this is one of the areas where it comes in.

I: And is that what in this book is the distinguishing characteristic between the two/

A: Objective and subjective? No. That's my interpretation. But because the formal definition is defined as a dictionary type definition to me that means that it's something objective that other people will come up with the same definition and because the stipulated definition is a definition of an abstract term according to a certain group then it's/my interpretation is that it's subjective/

I: /Right. Right/

A: /to that group or person. So/but I just think it's important for them to be able to distinguish between the two. Even when they read one I think it's important for them to be able to say 'Okay this is what the word means or the term means' and everyone would agree or 'This is what the term means according to this author' and we've talked in class about the author's point of view and the author's opinion coming up in the reading and so it comes in there as well.

The teacher's interpretation of the curriculum also influences the order in which the rhetorical patterns are taught, as described in this response to the interviewer's question.

I: Okay. I do have a little question here. Did you have a choice as to how the sequence of the patterns that you would introduce and was there a reason why definition came last?

A: There's no set order. Nobody says you have to do it. There's a recommended order that a couple of teachers thought made sense, you know, starting off with something which was simpler or which would help some other pattern after. I do definition last because I thought that it was really something which you needed to know the other things in order to do it. I know for example that [Teacher B] did it first and I thought that was strange only because of my belief that in order to do definition you really have to understand a little bit about other things that we do, but his approach to it was so different I don't know exactly what he did. He felt it was/ it was good starting point and it was easier. So I guess it's/ it's pretty subjective which just never occurred to me to do it anywhere but last because I always teach it as/ and this is when I taught, you know, the old courses where we still taught these things, but in conjunction with other things. Whenever we did definition I put it at the end ... I just put it last because I felt that it incorporated a lot of the other stuff.

I: So in other words that you can do a comparison and contrast in a definition/

A: /That's it. Yeah. I feel that in order to define something you're going to resort to one of the other patterns or a combination of the other patterns to help define it or you're going to use description. You're going to perhaps compare it to something/ something else, something similar or something different and I even gave on Friday when I talked about the stipulated definitions I gave examples of that to my classes. I think I used love as the word that they would define and show how one person might define it by talking about different kinds of love such as love between members in a family or love between a husband and a wife and define it in those terms and another person might define it by showing how it's different from liking someone and those would both be definitions of what that person considers love but it would be approached in a very different way and it would make use of other patterns that they had looked at. That's why I always put it last.

Teacher A, in the videotaped lesson, focused on formal definition, and the form of a definition. She announced in class her approach of learning things one piece at a time:

A: ... and the second kind of definition, a stipulated definition, is a little more interesting, and we're going to focus more on that, but I want you to understand this one first ... .

She began with a short lecture, giving the students information about the formal properties of a definition, and then gave them exercises to check their understanding of it before moving on to practising writing definitions in a functional way. As a subpart of the lecture, she discussed "traps" (or "problems that you can fall into"), which can lead to producing a "formal definition" which is not technically correct. One of the students, in a brief comment in the classroom interaction, implied that his understanding of the notion of definition was in terms of its function. This, when taken in light of her responses, indicates that his receptive structuring was at variance with her productive structuring:

A: ... But first let's look at the problems you can fall into and then we can look at how we can extend it into a paragraph. Okay. So another problem which you might come across is instead of defining the word you give a synonym for it. Okay?

S: That's a good idea.

A: That might be one way to help your reader understand what the word means. That's not a definition, okay? It might be a technique you use to make sure that your reader understands but it's not called a definition. Okay.

This put Teacher A in a conflict between responding to the student and continuing her planned structure. She stopped the videotape at this point, and indicated that the reason for the particular response was related to content that had been presented previously:

A: The reason I said that and decided to go in that way/ that there are, you know, positive things about doing this [using a synonym] was because she said "That's a good idea" and I had to acknowledge that it was a good idea because earlier in the course when we talked about reading and not understanding what words mean I had gone into a lot on how you can use the context and how there might be a synonym used somewhere else in the sentence or the paragraph and you should capitalize on that and help you, you know, as an aid to understanding and here I was saying that wasn't going to be good so I wanted to maintain its positive aspect to distinguish between that [a synonym] and a real definition.

However, when the issue was pursued by the student, she structured her response in such a way as to follow her planned step-by-step procedure through the larger structure of her organization of the content, in this case a presentation of the "problems" you can have when producing a formal definition, such as using a synonym or an example instead. Her goal as indicated by this example was to have the students succeed in understanding the formal concept.

S: You can give a synonym?

A: First you should give a definition. Later on you might/you might give a synonym,,, Another problem would be using an example.

A's comment: I cut that off and moved on. I decided like I don't want to focus too much on this. It's just sort of/ might confuse the issue especially in some of the students' minds and I thought "Ah, it's better to just keep moving here and we'll downplay that and go on".

Teacher B, in contrast, constantly emphasized the purpose and context of the definition, and based his discussion on the reasons why a person would produce a definition. The comments about using synonyms to achieve the same result as definitions made by the student in Teacher A's class would have fit smoothly into Teacher B's interpretation of the curriculum. Teacher B's examples in the classroom were either technical uses of a word (distinct from normal usage and therefore necessary to define), or humorous (a definition functioning as a joke), as in his example, "a car horn is a device for intimidating pedestrians and other drivers". When a learner, in an assignment, produced a perfect formal definition of a teaspoon, Teacher B's response was:

B: Who would want to define a teaspoon?

This student's response to the task would have been entirely appropriate according to the criteria of Teacher A. Teacher B, in contrast, assessed activities as successful which moved the students away from thinking formally, and towards thinking about 'purposes' and 'context'.

Interpretations related to the role of the curriculum and students in the structuring of the teaching

One clear contrast between the BAKs of the two teachers as reflected in their verbalizations and decisions was whether the superordinate basis of decisions about structuring the course was the pre-determined curriculum (where the decisions had been made prior to the course and which overtly formed the basis for the course), or the characteristics, views and reactions of the particular individual learners in the class.

It is clear that in any teaching situation, there will be a tension between the two: the curriculum is the institutional agenda and perception of what needs to be accomplished; the learners may have different priorities and conceptions, and therefore a different agenda. In a sense the curriculum and the learners each 'know' something about the course goals and how to achieve them that the other excludes, and the teacher is the mediator between these two. In this case, there was pressure on the teachers to follow the set curriculum due to the common final exam which was based on the explicit course objectives. In spite of this pressure, there was a dramatic difference in how the curriculum was interpreted in terms of whether subdecisions were based on the curriculum or the students. Both ways of interpreting and reacting can be defended as being not only legitimate but desirable: objectives are set to be achieved, and allow a progression in a course; yet students' own desires and goals can also be powerful motivators and can be important to follow. They are not necessarily mutually exclusive: it is possible for a teacher to take both into account in any particular course. Both teachers gave indications that they felt both were being taken into account, yet the results were dramatically different.

Teacher A, throughout the taped interviews done over the duration of the course and in the comments on the videotaped lesson, described her decisions in terms of getting the content presented. This does not imply a lack of concern for the students, but rather a particular view of the roles of the curriculum and the students in the instantiation of the course. Specifically, she indicated that she expected the students to treat their ESL course like a regular academic course and follow the set curriculum. Teacher A often discussed the students in the interviews, but primarily with regard to whether they were understanding the material and following what was being presented. For example, during her presentation of the types of definitions in the videotaped lesson, she made an on-the-spot decision to change the order of presentation of examples, and when subsequently viewing the videotape, indicated that this was done in order to give the material a "more logical presentation". At a later point in the lesson, when she indicated a lack of satisfaction with the use of a particular example, it was because she felt she did not explain it as clearly as she had wished.

When carrying out the lecture part of the lesson (her lesson, following the style of a 'regular academic course', as she indicated, consisted of a lecture followed by some problems and exercises), she spontaneously decided to draw the learners into an interaction by asking them some questions. When watching the videotape of the lesson, she interpreted and evaluated this event (and its later occurrence in the afternoon section of the same course) in terms of the accomplishment of the planned lesson and curriculum:

A: I hadn't planned to ask them anything,,, it just came into my head while I was talking ... after I did it [elicited the students' opinions] I was glad that I did it because I thought it worked out well. And the kinds of responses that/,,, the information they provided me with helped lead me to where I wanted to go, although I had to kind of fill out what they said because they were on the right track but they weren't exactly giving me what was necessary. In the afternoon class I did the same thing,,, and that time it didn't work as well because the students didn't give me the kind of information I was looking for.

This comment by the teacher reveals her basis for evaluating an event occurring in the class, one which views the success of an activity and the responses of the students in terms of taking the teacher "where she wanted to go" based on the plan for the lesson and the larger plan provided by the curriculum. She later made this relationship explicit in talking about another student's question:

A: ... it [the student's question] just sort of made me feel like where I was leading was where she wanted to go anyhow, so that was good ... .

In the case of Teacher B, on the other hand, the major methodological decisions were based on characteristics of the learners in his class. He started off his course by handing out, in addition to the required departmental student information sheet, a questionnaire in which the learners described their purpose for taking the course and what they expected from it. Early on in the course, Teacher B assessed the learners in the class as being very "mature", and based on this assessment, he decided to use group work more extensively than his previous term's class, where he had found the learners less independent in their attitude about teaching and learning, and wanting a teacher who provided the 'right answers'. With that group, he decided group work was less appropriate and used it much less frequently.

Based on this assessment of the learners' maturity, Teacher B altered some of the course superstructures to allow the students to have some direct involvement in the substructuring of the course, for example giving the students choices about the criteria for the evaluation of their assignments. In addition, the decisions Teacher B made in dealing with the grammar part of the curriculum resulted in classroom exchanges in which he attempted to bring in learners' opinions about what to do, which he accepted and followed even though they went against his conceptions of how a language is learned.

B: ... I considered either doing a grammar quiz or fitting their mark for grammar into the students' performance in their writing; however, I asked their view on it and they all, or the majority of them, opted for a grammar quiz, so I've decided to go with the grammar quiz ... .

In structuring the overall lesson, he built this notion of student responsibility into a grammar activity in which students researched grammatical points and presented them to one another. His evaluative comments about the activity were based on this notion of student responsibility.

B: ... well, that was my lesson plan, to have a discussion, first the students/ each group would present their verb tenses and give some examples, and the students would [ask questions]. I would generally instigate it and ask if people agreed with it/ and maybe nobody would say anything and I would throw in a question. I tried to make it as much the students getting things going, and once we got going they did pick up on things pretty well, as I said I felt the students were really quite capable of and they really liked being responsible for what happened in that class, it wasn't as if they felt I had abandoned them ... .

His description of an interaction with the students indicates that his attempt to resolve the conflict between the curriculum and his view of learning is also done by relying on student responsibility, as they negotiate together grammar rules and sentence grammaticality.

B: ... and we had a discussion at this point, and one of the students said, "Okay, what about a sentence like 'When I saw him I ran away'?", and he said "That's wrong. You can't have that", and I said "How many people agree with that; what do you think?"

For this teacher, moment-to-moment decisions in the lesson were influenced by the students. In the videotaped lesson, there were many points at which his decisions were affected by a consideration of the learners which overrode the curriculum and his lesson plan. One activity in the lesson had two planned components; but the second one was abandoned when it became clear that the lesson had evolved in a different direction led by the interests of the learners. He made particular decisions on the spot on how to group the students for an activity in order to avoid certain personality clashes, and then he joined the groups in a certain order and dealt with the students in specific ways, decisions which were later elaborated on (while watching the videotape) in terms of his past experiences with these students, in terms of their personalities and working habits, and in terms of the preparation they had done for the activity. All these factors influenced who he sat down with and what issues he broached.

Even at the most local level of his classroom decision-making, his style of speech with the students reflected an attitude of working things out with the students as the lesson proceeded. For example, when a learner brought up a point that he had not planned, he said "Okay, I agree with you there". When he discussed his planning in the interviews as well, the content of his discourse as well as the style revealed a readiness to go wherever the students took him:

B: The discussion will start with a more structurally-oriented thing, looking at the structure of the ideas, and then sort of maybe naturally work in to discussing the ideas themselves and seeing what people feel about it.

In this verbalization, there are many signals consistent with his approach: the lack of precision in his plan ("sort of maybe"), the use of certain words to describe an unplanned evolution ("naturally work in to") and the student-based outcome ("seeing what people feel about it").

At one point when complaining frustratedly about the institutional demands of the curriculum and the final exam, he made his view about this very explicit:

B: I've been putting too much emphasis on the material and not enough on the needs of the student.

This overall comment is consistent with a more detailed comment he made at another point during the course:

B: I'd like to see the students put a lot more into the actual organization of the course. By presenting them with an outline at the beginning that is so pack full, there's very little opportunity for student investment or involvement in the organization of the course. And not only because I think it will help their motivation if they're pursuing things that are of interest to them. I think it will help their understanding if they're the ones who initiate a certain direction in their learning and then end up following it through.

These teachers' overall comments about the curriculum, what it consisted of, and how it was developed, were also consistent with the views described so far. Teacher A, who had worked on revising the curriculum, said that the main goal in the revision was to "correct the problems with the previous curriculum", problems that were mainly related to the organization of the concepts being taught. Teacher B, in contrast, stated that in his view the way to approach curriculum revisions would be to go to the departments that the students were planning to study in, and use information related to their actual studies as a basis for the curriculum.

This comment, above, also begins to bring out the conflict he feels in having to teach the curriculum the way it has been enunciated. One can see, from the development of his philosophy through the background interview, that it is no superficial conflict that can be resolved by a supervisor's decree. A little later in the conversation, he delves into the conflict he feels between interpreting the curriculum in a way consistent with his own BAK and interpreting it in a way more consistent with the institutional system.

B: ... you know, you're given a course outline and ... I did feel a certain responsibility to stick with the outline that was given because the students will go into [the advanced course] and many of the [advanced] teachers have taught the [intermediate course] so they'll be teaching with the understanding that people have learned x, y, z and, as well, I know that especially the patterns of development are a really central part of [the advanced course] for most teachers. Now as I said, if I were teaching [the advanced course] again, I would approach it more from purpose; I would concentrate much more on purpose of writing and try and get a description of all the kinds of purposes that one wants to write for and then maybe do patterns of development in a much more incidental way – because I know [in the advanced course] I'm the last person [English teacher] they're going to see – I feel that that's much more relevant in learning to write. However in [the intermediate course] I know that they're going to [the advanced course] and that's going to be a requirement that they understand those things, so I do feel constrained in that way. I know that I'm betraying the students to some extent if I don't prepare them for [the advanced course] ....

Interpretation of a textbook-based curriculum

There was only one teacher in the study who depended primarily on a textbook for teaching the course. As a result, the analysis presented here of the teacher's interpretation of the curriculum when it is embodied in a textbook is somewhat limited. Whereas most of the teachers expressed a view that a textbook handicaps the teacher by removing flexibility and responsiveness (Teacher G noted: "We have to order a book before we see the students, which to me is a major handicap"), Teacher F's verbalizations suggested an orientation in which the textbook:

F: ... determines an awful lot in terms of how you approach the teaching task, since the methodology employed by the author of the book very much decides the route that you'll be taking when you approach the teaching task.

Teacher F used two different textbooks for her two writing courses (an advanced and a beginning course). The textbooks for the courses were chosen by the master teachers of the institute, and Teacher F indicated that:

F: I could strongly object if I felt really terrible about using a certain book. But pretty much the custom is to stay with the book that you've been suggested, that you've been told to use basically.

I emphasize that this analysis of the teacher's interpretation of the textbook is not meant to indicate that either the teacher or the textbook is more or less 'correct' than the other, but rather to relate the teacher's BAK to ways in which a textbook curriculum is interpreted.
  A number of themes arise in Teacher F's data which can be posited as aspects of her BAK, and as having a relationship to her interpretation of the curriculum. One of these is the issue of using a textbook itself. Beyond that are issues related to her conception of what writing

is, including the role of grammar and errors in learning to write, and the differences between writing and speaking. Another issue is the notion of motivation, discipline and the role of the teacher in a writing classroom. Teacher F's structuring of the textbook curriculum as it is presented to the learners is influenced by these factors.

Teacher F's verbalizations also indicated a grammatical orientation as well as a textbook orientation. It is difficult to say which of these orientations was the stronger because if she was primarily oriented towards grammatical structures, she would have chosen a structural textbook, perhaps, instead of going with the one she was assigned. On the other hand, she did alter the textbooks in the direction of more structures; and she did take issue with some of the aspects of the textbooks.

The textbooks used in the two courses called themselves "process approaches": *Interactions I: A Writing Process Book* (Segal and Pavlik, 1985), and *The Process of Composition* (Reid, 1982). However, the way in which each textbook approached a process approach was quite distinct.

The lower level book, *Interactions*, was organized with a focus on structures throughout. Although the sequential organization of the chapters was thematic, and within each chapter there were a few elements of process: i.e. exploring ideas (by talking to each other or answering questions about the topic), organizing ideas, drafting and editing, within this overall set up there was a major focus on structural aspects of language. As the authors state, "Although the concept of writing as a process is central to the course, traditional areas of instruction such as paragraph form, mechanics, and grammar are practised throughout. The emphasis, however, is on those grammatical and lexical features that serve to unify a paragraph." (Segal and Pavlik 1985:xiv)

The advanced level book dealt with various steps in the process of writing, but also included a more traditional development sequence starting with writing smaller units (paragraphs) and moving to essays and to research papers. The "most basic processes in writing – selection, the topic sentence, supporting techniques, and methods of development" (Reid 1982:x) are included with each of these types of writing, and various stages: prewriting, topic selection, notemaking and outlining, rough draft construction and revision, and writing the final draft. Within these stages, "students are taught to write according to a nearly mathematical set of rules, to write in a very specific format, according to a formula", in order to be able to produce work which uses "the linear and straightforward" structure of American university writing, "that is acceptable to the majority of university professors" (Reid 1982:xii).

Teacher F interpreted the textbooks in the light of her own views about class dynamics, about what language is, about what writing is and about how writing is learned; and she produced lessons – and a course – which emphasized certain aspects of the book and omitted other aspects. Her interpretation of the textbooks first fell within her interpretation of the overall institutional objective of courses F1 and F2: for the students "to improve their writing – for some students it's passing the test into university, for others it just means better writing". Her elaboration of the notion of better writing was based on a view of communication that emphasized structural aspects of language, or "errors".

F: ... getting the message across, so that reader's attention is moving from the incorrect forms to the message ... because sometimes you know if you have a piece of writing with a lot of errors, I mean you'll start looking so much at the errors, even if you're a non-teacher reading it, that you lose touch entirely with the message that's hidden behind this funny way of writing English, and I suppose I tend to look more closely at errors of the type that will jump right at the reader than the errors that would cause them loss of brownie points on the TOEFL test or something like that – I suppose basically what sometimes is called the communicative approach, you know, that the language shall not obscure the message.

Her comparison of the two groups of students, framed in structural terms, is consistent with this view.

F: The overall structure, they [the advanced group] have it. The overall ability to express themselves in the language, they have it. It's more a matter of making them express themselves correctly, to get the reader to focus more on the content than the form in what they are writing, to get rid of things that sort of spring to the reader's eye as something that's inappropriate, that shouldn't be there, and that will distract from the content of the writing. So as the correcting and the adjustments in their writing is getting pickier so to speak, rather than assuming that everybody more or less has a problem with phrasing the past perfect, which you can do in an elementary group because they all do. It's more of a blanket approach there [in the elementary group].

Her view of writing focused on language and grammatical structures, and she viewed the main aim of the course as learning how to write the ideas and not learning how to generate the ideas to write.

F: I see that aim of the course more as being how to write your ideas, not how to come up with the ideas – really it's not a creative thinking course/ or even a talking class could be one where you deal with generating ideas. It's a writing class where it's a matter of putting ideas on paper in a comprehensible and clear form.

The statement that generating ideas is not an essential part of a writing course is also consistent with a further assumption that writing as a skill is clearly separated from speaking. This division between skills is exemplified by her comment, in the videotaped lesson, to a student who suggested that the class discuss the topic they were to write about before beginning to write. Teacher F's response reflected her view that discussing a topic is not directly related to learning the skill of writing; she responded "If I teach a talking class next term, we can discuss the topic then."

Her view of the students writing a first and second draft also reflected a primary focus on language accuracy. After correcting the students' first drafts, she had them carry out the activity of rewriting the parts of their first draft that she had selected as being particularly problematic.

F: It's a little bit along the lines, on the lower levels, of copying writing, but through the copying process you actually also take in what's being copied, but I think it's even more important when you're copying your own corrected writing because you recognize the product as being originally yours even if it's now been spruced up a little bit. That's one thing. Secondly, I think it's important that they get into the habit of considering the first thing they write in a topic as a draft, and not the final product, and I think that this gets best established in their minds if they get into the habit of rewriting what they wrote first, that is not taking their first version as the final version.

There are number of instances where we can see the interplay of Teacher F's beliefs and goals with events that occur in the classroom. She also has a classroom routine, related to her underlying beliefs, of first walking around looking at the students, and then sitting down to watch them. She describes this in terms of her dual role as (i) the person responsible for ensuring that they do what is supposed to be done, and (ii) the person responsible for helping the students with their problems.

F: At certain stages of their writing [I walk round and monitor], if everybody's sort of buckled down and is writing busily and doing what they are supposed to, I usually sit back and monitor them from a distance and try to see if there's any problem brooding under the hair of somebody but [I circulate] until everyone is doing what they are supposed to do.

A comment she made about watching the facial expressions of the students to see if they're having problems – groping for a word or not knowing what to do next, "in which case I would go down and give them a hand ... if I sit down and read a book I may miss something," is also consistent with her view of this role. She made explicit the fact that her role is to teach them the language, not to teach them responsibility or how to learn.

F: And since we don't have the whole academic year with our students, I personally don't want to waste time educating the students how to educate themselves kind of thing, but rather adjust my way of teaching to what they feel more comfortable with, and what they feel they learn best with.

She has also made it clear on a number of occasions that an important priority is having them produce short writings. One reason for this (in addition to the implied workload, as discussed below) is related to the fact that learning to write involves discipline, producing short, concise and organized writing rather than long rambling pieces.

F: I spent about five minutes or so telling them why I thought it was important that they learn to limit their writing, why I did not want them to take everything home and finish it at home, and why I insisted on ... having them write only in the second hour and not always give them a long time slot to write in, because some people have asked me about that during the break, and they've sort of half complained that they felt that they should be allowed to take it home and finish it and so forth, and I said it's not only because if you did that I would do nothing else all night but correct your essays, but it's also that/ some years back when I was a student here I worked in the writing lab, and most students I came across who had severe problems with the organization of their writing were the ones who had to hand in the classical three page essay, not the ones who had to write a thesis. But if you had the maximum two hundred words or three double spaced pages, those were the ones who ended up with a long introduction and half their conclusion and no development. And since this was so consistently appearing, and a lot of the people in this group are geared towards academic studies in English, and I feel that this is an area that they need practice in more than anything else, and even in business I mean you have to be able to do that, you have to limit your reports and things to a readable format for the one you're going to hand it to. I try to make that point that this is a lot more difficult to do than to keep writing at length, once you've gotten over the initial barrier of using the language per se, and secondly it's a requirement that you learn to do this, and that in itself demands strict organization of the writing process. You have to know when you start, not only what you're going to say in the introduction and in the body and in the conclusion, but how much time you have on each, and that will have to decide how much writing you're going to spend on each of the parts. So if I tell you that there's five minutes left and you're still finishing off your introduction, you've got a problem.

To Teacher F, the issue of discipline in writing is also related to buckling down and working quickly. She indicates her ideas about this while watching the videotaped lesson:

F: I've discussed with them previously why I want them to buckle down and get some writing done and do it fast, because this is part of life as well. This is very much a part of reality whether they're in business or in academia. They have to get used to the idea that they cannot sit chewing their pencils until the cows come home. And this is part of one of those practice sessions, if you wish. They hate it like the plague but that's/that's why I've taken some time in the early part of the course to explain why I put them through this kind of torture.

In the data, the issues of writing and discipline also occur together, reflected in her view of writing short pieces. Her view of doing an outline was related both to the issue of discipline and to the issue of short writing. When she circulated "to nudge them into doing their outline", she noticed a student not doing the outline and stopped to question him about it. He was "unwilling to do the outline and had written far more than he was supposed to … I tried to get him to accept the fact that he should have an outline", not in his head, as he claimed it was, but on paper. She relates the outline to being able to write short and concisely, the student "disappears into flowery language that goes in sixteen directions at once". The issue of the outline with this student also relates to discipline in Teacher F's words: "He writes without being forced into the harness of an outline", but she explains, when he uses an outline, "when he disciplines himself", his writing is much better, and "because there is such a difference, I insist."

Teacher F's interpretation of the textbook also led to her making particular decisions in the classroom. Her agenda of wanting short writing resulted in a number of different kinds of decisions designed to support this. For example, she describes the format of the response writing they are doing in advance (150–300 word response, short, just on a couple of the points in the reading, not the whole reading), "so they know this format before they begin writing". As she walked around she noticed that some students were producing outlines that were too detailed, ones that would result in assignments that were way too long. In response to this she put a skeleton of a "brief outline", as she wanted it, on the board: "point 1 + response (for or against), point 2 + response (for or against), point 3 + response (for or against), concluding statement". She explained to the students the message on the board. She then went back and underlined the word 'brief', again to emphasize this main point she was making.

These central issues in the course organization of short concise writing and discipline are not ones which are dealt with explicitly in the textbook. In addition, Teacher F decided which parts of which chapters to include based on her assumptions about writing, for example, downplaying the discussion sections, and focusing more on the structural sections.

Interpretation of theoretical and pedagogical concepts

Although this study was not intended to examine teachers' interpretations of theoretical and pedagogical concepts, there is evidence from the interview data that theoretical and pedagogical information in readings, lectures and discussions was given an interpretation in light of the teachers' own evolving BAK networks, and that the meaning attributed to theoretical and pedagogical concepts taken from these sources was influenced by the teachers' beliefs, assumptions and knowledge. This effect is, of course, predicted by the schema theory of text comprehension, but is rarely acknowledged in discussions of teacher education.

One suggestive, but inconclusive, example of this phenomenon is the case of Teachers A and B, both of whom had recently taken graduate courses in the area of reading in a second language, and were familiar with the current literature on the subject (although there was no attempt in this study to compare the works they were exposed to). Teacher A, on the one hand, voiced a view of teaching second language reading skills that was consistent with her view that learning takes place in a step-by-step manner of increasing complexity.

A: ... it's a feeling that I've had for a while, and a lot of the [graduate] courses that I took pointed to this ... I believe in using unauthentic simplified texts, and I know that's a hotly debated issue these days, but I've built up my own rationale from my reading [for the graduate courses] ... I really do believe that we shouldn't be giving our students completely unadulterated text,,, my feeling is very much that you build them up to that but you don't necessarily start them off with it ... .

Teacher B, on the other hand, discussed reading from a top-down perspective, using knowledge of context and purpose as the basis for developing reading skills, and focusing on authentic texts in the materials that he chose for teaching reading. This perspective of reading was consistent with his BAK, described above.

There were a number of recurring themes that arose in the interviews with many of the teachers, related to such concepts as authenticity, grammar, and communicative teaching, among others. The example of the evolution of Teacher B's BAK, as noted above, demonstrates how the meaning attributed to a certain concept by an individual evolves, in particular, when 'hotspots' occur in the systems of belief. In the case of Teacher B, the conflict that occurred between his sense of how language is learned and his sense of the importance of students' own purposes for learning resulted in the evolution of several notions, including that of purpose and that of authenticity. The initial interpretation of the term authenticity was related to learning language in society in general, and was integrated with his view of holistic learning. Later, because of its subordinate position with respect to motivation and the influence of other teaching experiences, his interpretation of authenticity eventually included the learners' own views and purposes, and even included the formal teaching of grammar.

The concept of grammar also played a wide range of roles in the teachers' BAK, as noted above, both in the contrasting views of grammar held by Teachers A and B, and in the quite different role that grammar played in the course structuring by Teacher F. In the case of Teacher D, the notion of grammar played yet another role. Teacher D (known by some of the students as their favourite teacher because she did correct their grammar) had a particular view of correction in the students' 'exchange journals' – the free writing they did in class. She viewed correction not as a obligatory part of the lesson, but as a "gift" to the students, which they could choose to use if they wished:

D: ... first I correct everything [in their journals]. Now some teachers think "Well we ignore errors". Well I always tell them "This is my gift to you. It's free. Anybody who wants to take the time can use this as a diagnostic", you know, that "you could buy yourself a grammar and you can go home and spend time improving your writing, because you will have a very nice record after twelve weeks of the things that you/ the areas in your writing where you're weak".

She also viewed herself as an intermediary and her approach to correction as part of the process of students' acculturation to the new kinds of classroom learning experiences they would meet in the new setting:

D: ... a lot of students come here and they're I think sometimes a little disappointed when people aren't running around with red pens. And whether or not that's a good approach or a bad approach or neither, I think that if the students have an expectation, to some extent it should be fulfilled, especially I think [this level] is where we or I start off with them doing things they think they should be doing and then bring them to the completely different. Often for many of them the way/ the approach here is very different and it takes them a while to realize that they are learning, even though they're not putting up their hand and, and doing exercise 17 and that kind of thing, so that's all part of what I try and do with them.

As teaching events, curricular instructions and theoretical information are interpreted through teachers' experiences, a number of abstract concepts evolve and are given common labels. A number of these concepts occurred as themes in the data of many of the teachers both in the main study and the pilot study. In many cases, it is possible to see that concepts given the same label are understood differently from teacher to teacher. In some cases, based on these interpretations, different sub-groups or 'subcultures' of teachers develop. An example of this is the pedagogical concept of a 'notional-functional' approach to language teaching. In the ESL subculture represented by a number of British textbooks of the 1970's and 1980's, the term notional-functional implied a specific set of universal functions to be taught in a sequenced, explicit way. In the subculture of English and French second language teachers in the Ottawa/Montreal area, the same term carried the implication of a needs analysis in which learners reveal what they have to be able to do in the target language, which then becomes an implicit basis for the teaching. The comment of one teacher in the pilot study for this project – as she elaborated on the course she was teaching to a group of postgraduate international students – revealed a particular interpretation of the term, including an active role on the part of the learners, that was coherent with the local subculture, but not with the textbook subculture:

T10: ... so in a sense these aren't classes planned by you [the teacher] as much as ones in which they [the students] sort of take the initiative to ask you where their problems are and you try to probe to get them to work it out/,,, notional-functional, you got it, on the nose.

Two of these pedagogical concepts that were particularly prevalent as themes in the interview data are discussed here: (i) learner independence, (ii) motivation (its role in learning, and the role of the teacher in creating it).

Learner independence

One of the frequently stressed themes was that of learner independence. Learner independence is a recurring theme in the data of all the teachers in the study. This is a result that is certainly related to the particular sample of teachers, all coming from a larger social and educational culture where individual freedom and responsibility are important issues, all teaching in university settings where they themselves are given a great deal of freedom, and which most consider an important benefit of their teaching situation.

However, the teachers had different views, in some cases very obviously different, and in other cases subtly different. In the cases where the views seemed similar on the surface, the way learner independence as a concept was interpreted and operationalized in their teaching was quite distinct, and its relationship to other concepts was quite unique.

Teacher B discussed this issue with regard to his course frequently. His notion of learner independence developed over time, from an initial feeling of unease at the type of language teaching he received in school, through his experiences with learners of different types as a teacher. His focus on learner independence related to the larger context of learning as seen as by the learner (and included such things as their view of grammar and final exams). Teacher C also frequently discussed the notion of learners not being dependent on the teacher as a judge, and treated learner independence within her structuring of the teaching as a goal to be achieved by creating communicative classroom interactions. In her case, learner independence is achieved through group work, and through the collective interdependence among students in the class (as opposed to dependence on the teacher). Teacher G focused on the issue of learner independence throughout her course, in the sense of learners' choices and decisions in the content of the course, and through individualization. For her, individualization was a necessary consequence of learner independence (see pages 201–3). Although for Teacher H the concept of 'learner independence' did not arise as a theme in her interviews or as an explicit goal in her structuring of the course, she did allow learners input and choice in the course selection, and focused constantly on their interests and their reactions in her planning and assessment of the structures she chose.

Teacher F, on the other hand, based her decisions about using group work on her perception of the learners' wishes, and used techniques of individualization on this basis.

F: It [working in groups] was not very well received by the students, who I think very much felt like the blind leading the blind when they were working with each other rather than through the teacher, especially with [Asian] students who did not feel comfortable at all with that situation. So with writing, unlike other skills, I feel very much you are better off working with individualized techniques or treating the class as a group as a whole group ... I feel that combination seems to satisfy more students than the group work approach which might look nifty in teacher handbooks, but is not that well received by the majority of the students in the classroom.

Teacher D focused a great deal on the issue of learners becoming independent and responsible; however for her the independence was a product of the power they got from being able to understand the overall picture of texts, tasks, and the course in general. She stated:

D: Basically the first few times we meet I'm going to be talking with them about how the course is structured, what my expectations are, and what their expectations of themselves should be. And I think the message really that I want to get across, say in the first week really, is there's a, a constant/ you have to work constantly, you know, you can't/ for that to be, they will see exactly when everything is due and all the due things are spaced out [so that they have to be responsible for setting out a work schedule]. Now, one of the things that I find these people really have to get a grip on is organizing their time and accepting responsibility, especially these, well as I said, [last summer] we had a lot of younger [students]. I guess their parents send them up here to grow up more than anything else, and they really had no sense of being responsible for themselves or whatever, or for their work or anything. So that's something again in keeping with the preparation for academic study.

However her view of students taking responsibility was not reflected in terms of systematically building student choices into the structuring of the course or making explicit her goal of developing independence in the students.

D: And they may be really confused after the first few classes because I won't have sent them home to, to conjugate a verb and I'll just be talking about all these things/

I: /but will you explain to them why you don't send them home to conjugate a verb?

D: No, no.

I: You don't.

D: No.

I: Uh, why not? You don't, you find that you don't explain your approach to teaching to them? Do you let them sort of come to terms with it themselves, or do you help them by explaining the reasons for not giving them grammatical exercises?

D: No, I don't think that I really have to do that. Um, I don't, hmm, I don't think they really, well I don't know if that's true. I was going to say I don't think they really care, but that may not be fair. But, suppose, suppose I did. So what? They either want the exercises or they're going to trust me, or they don't care. And I can't really change that one way or, you know, that's what it's like. Well I don't know what to compare it to. I just don't think that's necessary.

Teacher E also focused on students' responsibility for learning, and systematically built student choice into her course as a way to achieve this. In this we see clearly one of the paradoxes of teaching: the students have to be "pushed" by the teacher in order to grudgingly accept that they are responsible for their learning.

E: ... in this particular class I have been very much conscious of making students/I want them to realize they are responsible for their own learning, that vocabulary/that's been one of my premises, that vocabulary learning is a very individual thing each person is responsible for/there's only so much somebody else can help you out with it, and the whole course is trying to help them out with it, but there's always been that/ something that I've been trying to push and push and push, you are the one who's responsible.

Motivation

Another frequent theme that occurs in the data is that of motivation. There are a number of views about the role of motivation in learning, and the role of the teacher in motivation. On the issue of the role of the teacher in motivating students, the teachers in the study and in the preliminary pilot study represented a very wide range of views. At one extreme, a teacher from the pilot study stated outright that her job was to teach, not to motivate. At the other extreme, Teacher D indicated that her role in motivating the students was a crucial aspect of the learning process:

D: I spend the first two or three weeks of any course just working up a rapport. What we do is not terribly important. To me it's much more important to establish the rapport and then get down to brass tacks, rather than,,, /I think time is lost and effort is lost if you start right away without taking the time for you to know the students and the students to know you. Because I think that a lot of time / this of course is not always the case, but generally speaking / the effort that they put out is often directly related to the relationship that they have. They're basically working for you as much as for themselves. Often they'll work for you when they wouldn't bother to work for themselves.

She elaborated on what is involved in this teacher aspect of motivation:

D: It doesn't mean just making friends [with them] or getting to know them, it's having them come to realize that I have certain expectations of them and they're high. And that I have expectations of what their expectations of themselves should be, and that's the type of thing I mean when I talk about rapport.

Teacher G also felt that motivation is a very important issue in learning, and also bases much of her teaching around motivation; however, her view was based on her own interpretation of motivation: the students' individual needs. There is a contrast in the relationship between motivation and learner independence in the cases of Teacher D and Teacher G. In the former case, Teacher D uses their dependence as a source of motivation in the sense that "they'll work for you when they wouldn't bother to work for themselves". On the other hand, for Teacher G, the students are motivated when the course responds to their needs; and this occurs when they become independent.

BAK and planning

Another area of influence of BAK on the processes of teaching relates not to beliefs about the content to be taught and learned and how it should be organized, but to the organizational procedures themselves, i.e. the planning process. The planning style is not only relevant to the issue of how teachers plan, but also has repercussions on the way the teaching is carried out. In other words, the teacher's planning practices and beliefs about planning play an important role in determining exactly what the learners face in the classroom. In the case of Teacher A and Teacher B, the issue is the degree to which previously planned decisions function as a basis for subsequent decisions, and the degree to which later decisions negate or replace previous decisions. While Teacher B had a philosophy of avoiding detailed planning, Teacher A planned much more carefully, even if the plans were tentative ones. The difference between the decisions of Teachers A and B of favouring the curriculum or the students as a basis for decisions, noted above pages 226–31, can also be seen as an issue of planning: favouring pre-planned decisions as opposed to favouring spontaneous decisions.

Both positions are pedagogically defensible. It can certainly be argued in specific cases that changing your mind and changing your plan is a wise course of action when things are not working out. On the other hand, it can also be argued that there are cases when sticking something out is a wise course of action, leading to more stability and a greater sense of purpose on the part of the students. Although there are undoubtedly cases in which most teachers would agree that a change should or should not be made, most situations in which a change is being considered are not so clear cut. In such cases, we see dramatic differences between Teacher A and Teacher B.

In many instances in the taped data, when Teacher A had a choice between changing a decision – i.e. interrupting a planned activity to do something else – or carrying on with what she had planned, she indicated that she preferred the latter course of action. This was evident in a number of classroom interactions (noted above), and was made explicit during her interviews:

A: Once I start with something, I finish it even when I'm not happy with it.

On the other hand, for Teacher B the issue of overplanning was a frequently recurring theme. He emphasized the danger of investing too much in the preparation of a lesson – preparing too far in advance and too carefully hinders spontaneity and reduces the flexibility which is required for spur-of-the-moment changes as the lesson is proceeding, creating excessive constraints on his classroom decisions.

B: You know, it's funny, I was thinking about this today writing down/ keeping my log, that if you put a lot/ invest a lot of time into putting together a lesson, along with a certain justification and a certain set of beliefs that this is the way that you learn and this is the way that one should organize it [the content], especially this kind of course, you know, when you start talking about patterns of development ... and if you organize your lesson plan and say "I'm going to teach this pattern of development, I'm going to teach this structure", then you get really stuck there, that you have to sell the students/ that that's/that's *not* the way they're understanding it and you've got to sell them on that's the way they *should* understand it, you know. It's funny.

In another interview, he said:

B: What I mean by what I said before that I don't like to overprepare because I find people who overprepare have a tendency not to want to abandon lesson plans.

His assessment of the events that occurred in a particular lesson are also made on this basis:

B: ... if you really prepare a lot in advance in terms of the content or what things you are going to go through in a lesson,,, I find that if I'm really concentrating so much on that and not what the students are getting out of it and what the students are really understanding and how they're manipulating everything, the process basically, then I get really sort of screwed up, whereas I went into this class/ I immediately started off by listening to what the students had to say and I felt the lesson went better because it was more concentrated on people's problems, what they felt they understood and what they needed to understand better ... .

The teachers in the study exhibited a variety of patterns and methods of planning, which although similar in terms of the characteristics of tentativeness, use of resources and constraints, top-down and bottom-up processes, and experienced structures, differed in ways which had an impact on what the learners faced in the classroom.

BAK, teaching and life

It is also important to emphasize that BAK plays a role not only in terms of teaching itself, but also in fitting the job of teaching into the rest of one's life. Teachers to some degree also make classroom decisions for survival. This is an important factor, as teachers can be inundated, get behind, burn themselves out, and have less time for ideas, for planning, and for the other activities that make up their professional and personal lives, unless they handle their load carefully. This issue was brought up at one point or another by virtually all the teachers in the study.

A number of the verbalizations of the teachers were related to the encroachment of teaching (especially the generation and assessment aspects of the planning process) upon their daily life. This is illustrated by, for example, Teacher C's discussion of planning while shopping (cited on page 161). Idea generation, for example, was a continual process, one that used available resources (including time), and it was clear that this process, and fitting it into one's life, is not only emotionally but also cognitively very demanding. For example, in one interview Teacher C was able to remember where she had left an idea, but not what the idea was:

C: ... I had an idea for the next step,,, now what was it,,, following the party,,, in fact I've got it written down somewhere. Can you stop [the tape recorder] for a second while I think? [click] Well, yesterday afternoon between four and four thirty I had half an hour dead time. I was waiting for my daughter to come out of her choir practice, and there was nothing in the car to write on except a scrap of old newspaper on the floor, so I picked that up and my notes are still written there. Unfortunately the scrap of newspaper is still on the floor of the car. I remember seeing it there this morning but I didn't pick it up.

I: Well, when you rescue it, we'll find out what the missing activity is.

C: Okay,, because it is the major thing [in the next lesson].

Teacher F made a number of decisions about the structuring of the teaching for reasons related to handling the workload: for example, she made very clear limits on how much students could write in the next assignment. This was consistent with the belief she verbalized that one difficulty in writing is organizing and making things short and controlled, but it was also because of the time demands of marking long written assignments. At one point, she made a change of plan in class, partially because of the marking demands.

I: ... you were going to give them a short summary to write on a T.V. program/

F: /Yes, but I want to/I decided to/I rather wanted to give myself the possibility of saving that topic for the longer essay and have a chance to write a longer summary about a longer initial piece of something, whether it be writing or viewing or reading or viewing, and not have them do that paragraph at home. Also I have a built-in reluctance to have them do [such] writing at home because someone always writes several pages even if they are limited by its number of words. And I end up correcting up to three in the morning and who needs it.

This structuring of the activity affected other decisions. When she returned their assignment, she had them trade paragraphs and look at each other's paragraphs and try to correct them.

F: Since I had by then fallen behind a bit with my correcting at home, I did not want to collect any more for correction, and so that's why I did the peer correction stuff.

Both Teachers A and E, who taught two sections of the same course, made attempts to keep the two sections synchronized in order to cut down on the preparation time and on the cognitive load (and potential cognitive confusion) that two sections of the same course at different stages would lead to. Both teachers made classroom decisions in light of this fact. For example, Teacher A said:

A: I guess the aim [of getting the classes synchronized] is pretty selfish. When I plan I want to be able to have them both doing the same thing at the same time. It's going to be very hard for me to teach on the same day two different groups at the same level and to be teaching them two different things. I think I won't know whether I'm coming or going ... so I figure if I can prepare and teach them both the same thing on the same day more or less, it will be easier for me, easier to make photocopies, it will be easier for me to have the appropriate books and materials with me in class ... okay, these are completely pragmatic reasons ... .

Although the examples above illustrate constraints that play an important role in the way in which teaching is balanced in life, the teachers also often mentioned the resources and strengths that come out of a teacher's life that contribute to the teaching. Teacher T05 (one of the teachers in the pilot study) described the importance of taking advantage of her strengths, and of using these in the interpretation of the teaching task and in the decisions that are made to structure the teaching.

T05 ... I would exploit whatever expertise I had accumulated to this time in life in order to create lesson plans that would be really substantial ... because I really believe that teaching anything, but particularly teaching a language, has to be a living, interesting, invigorating experience, because the more interested and relaxed and stimulated people are both intellectually and in a sense I suppose emotionally, then the more readily they're going to convey what they're thinking, because without having the desire to communicate something then you aren't going to be so motivated to work really hard ... I think what I mean is I think people tend to exploit their individual areas of expertise, for example were I a computer programmer or analyst or someone who loves mathematics and science then I would exploit my knowledge of these areas, or sociology or political science. I mean any one of these can be tapped and used to create exciting lessons. For example Ottawa would be a perfect place for a teacher who is interested in political science to incorporate a political science slant into his approach in teaching. I mean it's a very fertile ground because you could take your students to Parliament, you could take them to Question Period and then you could you know teach them the system, the Parliamentary system with questions and answers ... You could give them a class on democracy in Canada and then drag them up the Hill [Parliament Hill]/ I mean teach them about the different political parties and get them to read about/use the newspapers and make them watch Global Sunday Night and Canada A.M. [on television] ... The other area that I exploit personally is Art/ Art and Culture and some of the most exciting and interesting and rewarding lesson plans that I've devised according to my own 'unbiased objective assessment' have been classes that I have oriented around art exhibitions or exhibitions at the National Museum [of Civilization].

I: So did you choose Art because that's something you're interested in?

T05: Well, yes ... If it's good, that provokes people to think and before you communicate anything or before you want to communicate anything you have to think, you have to have an idea, there has to be an idea and then there has to be such excitement or fear or/or I don't know but there has to be a strong emotion involved with that idea so that you will want to communicate it to someone else, and that's where, you know, the sky's the limit. You can choose anything in the spectrum of existence and create really dynamic and exciting lesson plans around it.

Conclusion

The most pronounced characteristic of the underlying BAK network arising out of the analysis of the data is its pervasiveness. The description of the evolution of Teacher B's BAK is an example of how BAK penetrates his discussion. The teachers' BAK is not only pervasive in terms of the frequency of occurrence in the interviews, but also in the effect it has on the teachers' organization of thoughts, decisions, and aspects of the course. There was a notable lack of contradictions in the data. There were certainly contradictions in teachers' remembering facts, and contradictions between what teachers said they did and what they actually did. However, it was not as if they had to 'remember' a particular belief in order to use it in a decision; rather the BAK was part of the perceiving and thinking about the events, and part of the structuring and organizing of the decisions. When a decision was considered, it was considered in the context of BAK, and when it was remembered later it was also remembered in the context of BAK. In a number of cases in the study, there appeared to be contradictions to previously hypothesized aspects of a teacher's BAK. However, in such cases, because of the longitudinal nature of the study, either an underlying element surfaced which made the seemingly contradictory aspects coherent, or there were signals (for example, consideration of different alternatives) which foreshadowed a likely evolution to another stage in the teacher's BAK. (This dynamic aspect of BAK is discussed in detail in Chapter 9.)

It is the notion of evolving BAK networks, with interrelated elements and hierarchical features, that takes us away from the static view of 'approaches' discussed in the field of ESL teaching. This notion also takes us beyond the binary 'transmission' vs 'interpretation' view of teaching described by Barnes and Shemilt (1974), and Barnes (1976). These authors distinguish between two categories of underlying beliefs held by teachers: on the one hand, that learning is a process by which knowledge is transmitted unchanged from teacher to learner and, on the other hand, that knowledge is reinterpreted and recreated by the learner. They present examples to illustrate that misunderstandings in education occur because teachers in each of the two groups interpret the same terms differently (implicitly taking an 'interpretation' view). The present study clearly supports the notion that terms are interpreted differently by different teachers, but suggests, in contrast, that teachers cannot easily be categorized into a simple grouping of two categories. Rather, this study suggests that each teacher has an individual system of interwoven beliefs, assumptions and knowledge, a system which has evolved in an individual and organic fashion when aspects of that teacher's BAK have interacted with experience, especially experiences that resulted in a conflict with the BAK's current state. As a result, each teacher's system differs from other teachers' not only in terms of its individual 'components', but also in terms of the interrelationships among the beliefs, assumptions and knowledge. In other words, this study suggests that categorizing teachers into pre-determined groups hides the dynamic aspects of BAK, and oversimplifies our understanding of the concept and the process of teacher and curricular change, crucial issues in teacher education and educational planning.

If BAK plays a role in the interpretation of events, then, according to the model developed in previous chapters, it must be part of the entire cycle of planning, implementation, and assessment. We have seen in the above case how it evolves over time with the passage – and the teacher's experience – of teaching events. Elements which seem incoherent (i.e. hotspots in the data) may relate to the dynamic evolution of BAK over time and to the developing expertise of the teachers. These issues are pursued in Chapter 9.

9 Coherence in the teaching process

An important aspect of the model developed in previous chapters is related to how the elements function together: how the cycles of planning the teaching, carrying out the teaching, and interpreting and assessing the teaching fit together coherently within a particular course for a particular teacher. In previous chapters, each main aspect of the model was developed separately. Chapter 4 described the structure of the course using the notions of goals, content and method to connect classroom events to overall course goals. Chapters 5 and 6 described how the teacher plans this course structure in an on-going and cyclical fashion. Chapters 7 and 8 described how the classroom structures, as well as other texts, interactions and events related to the teaching, are interpreted according to the teacher's network of beliefs, assumptions and knowledge (BAK).

This chapter focuses on the overall process, first using the notion of coherence to tie these three aspects of the model together. This coherence involves the classroom actions and events, the teacher's interpretation of these actions and events, and the feedback of these interpretations into the on-going planning and decision-making process that leads to further structuring in the carrying out of the course. Then, this chapter looks at the notion of coherence dynamically: the evolving interplay among the teaching events, BAK, and the planning (not only does BAK influence the perception of the event, and thus the planning for the course, but the perception and assessment of the events lead to the evolution of BAK). This notion of dynamic coherence provides a framework for examining the notions of teacher expertise, teacher change and curricular evolution.

The coherent nature of the cycle within a course

This chapter brings together a number of notions developed in the previous chapters. The case of Teacher B exemplified the evolution of a teacher's BAK out of his experiences with language, learning language, learning to teach language and teaching language. The cases of Teachers A and B exemplified the role of BAK in interpreting the curriculum of a course and creating the structure of content, goals and means required to teach it. The case of Teacher C exemplified the role of BAK in the interpreting of classroom events as the teaching of the course progressed. Chapter 6 exemplified how classroom events, and the assessment of those classroom events by the teacher, lead into the subsequent decision-making process, by adjusting on-going events and revising recurring events. Taken together, these different aspects can be seen to fit together into a coherent whole.

The example below illustrates this process at a very local level. In this discussion, Teacher C reports on an interaction between two students in her class engaged in carrying out an activity in which they were giving each other directions in order to fill in the missing locations on two different versions of a map.

C: They were having an argument and I was trying not to take sides. [One student] was saying that he had told her how to do something [find the park on the map] and she was saying "I don't understand a thing!" and I was trying to be very pleasant and smooth feathers and sort of get them back on track. "Okay let's forget what happened about the park" I think it was. "Let's try the Computer Centre. Let's just see how it will go with the Computer Centre." ... .

In Teacher C's description, the interaction between the students was labelled as an event: "an argument". She indicated that it consisted of several components (one of these being the verbalization: "I don't understand a thing!"). The significance of the event for the teacher was related to the goals for this particular activity (completing the map) which was part of one of the units (giving and understanding directions) making up the overall course structure, developed according to her interpretation of course goals and in light of her BAK. Her interpretation and assessment of these events led immediately to an action on the part of the teacher to repair the on-going events in light of the higher level structure.

As the teacher elaborated further, she made explicit the idea that a verbalization can represent a social event, and it is this event that is assessed.

C: ... because she was saying "Oh he can't do this", this is the sort of thing ... I mean she didn't actually say "He can't do this" but that was the obvious communication/that was the message I was receiving, which made me feel "I don't like the way this is developing".

The student's *actual* verbalization (which the teacher does not report) represents a 'message' to which Teacher C gives an interpretation. In reporting the event, Teacher C put her interpretation of the message into a verbal form ("Oh he can't do this"), which was not exactly what the student said (as indicated by her comments "this is the sort of thing", and "I mean she didn't actually say..."). It was this *interpretation* which was assessed by the teacher ("I don't like the way this is developing"), necessitating a repair.

The interpretation Teacher C gave to this event comprises additional levels of complexity that are not evident from an observation of the event by itself. For example, her interpretation of the student's "message" included an additional interpretation of behavioural aspects of different cultures ("in his culture people are very diffident ... and gentle and polite to an extreme"), and an additional interpretation of the student's intentions ("She doesn't mean anything by it. She doesn't mean to be insensitive ...").

C: It's just a cultural thing. She doesn't mean anything by it. She doesn't mean to be insensitive but [the other student] is not receiving that message because in his culture people are very diffident in fact and gentle and polite to an extreme, to his disadvantage because/ so he's taking offense and he's reacting and it's becoming heated and that's why I said "Well let's forget about the park".

This discussion illustrates the organic nature of the overall process. On the one hand, it is partially but not entirely true to say that the planning decisions and classroom actions and events depend on BAK. On the other hand, it is partially but not entirely true to say that BAK depends on classroom actions and events. It is perhaps most true to say that these elements evolve together over time. This takes us to the dynamic issue of how this evolution takes place.

The mechanism for change

The model developed in Chapters 3 and 5 also gives us a framework for understanding two of the dynamic aspects of second language teaching – the process of teacher change and the process of curricular evolution. It is through the cycles of interpretation of events, assessment of what is good or bad about those events according to the interpretations, and input of those assessments in the planning and carrying out of subsequent action, that change – both in a teacher's teaching and in a course's instantiation – occurs. The concepts of teacher change and curricular evolution are actually intertwined: teachers' BAK influences their interpretation of a curriculum and the curriculum (and the experience of carrying it out) influences the evolution of BAK. However, these concepts are discussed separately here.

Teacher change

One of the important issues stemming from this study is that of teacher change. How do teachers evolve over time in their teaching? How do teachers become better teachers? Teacher change involves two interrelated aspects. The first aspect involves changes in 'conceptions' (focused on by Freeman, 1990), or in the terms of this study, changes in BAK. The second aspect involves changes in behaviour: planning, action and the overlap between them. There is a relationship between a teacher's background and the teaching. As noted by Prabhu (1987), over time teachers develop perceptions about how classroom activity leads to desired learning outcomes. As a result, some activities and routines, and their underlying rationales, give the teacher a "sense of plausibility" (1987:104), while others do not. With the experience of teaching, the teacher's sense of plausibility with respect to the particular classroom behaviours is strengthened or weakened or otherwise modified.

However, as noted in Chapter 2, these two aspects – BAK and behaviour – do not necessarily correspond. There may seem to be a contradiction or discrepancy between the actions an individual takes, and the characteristics posited as the aspects of that person's beliefs, assumptions and knowledge, even if we assumed that a completely accurate characterization of an individual's BAK was possible. The discrepancy could occur in a case where some unit of behaviour has become an unconscious routine and carried out as an unanalyzed chunk. In such a case, the individual may not be aware of a particular behaviour which has been internalized previously and reflects the characteristics of a prior state in the evolution of the teacher's BAK. The example of Teacher C's "good" in Chapter 8 is of interest in this regard, as the teacher has begun to be aware that conscious effort is required to bring her behaviour into line with her current beliefs about teaching and learning.

The previously developed model provides a framework for examining the process of teacher change, in terms of the notions of experience, expectations and expertise. The teacher's accumulation of interpretations of events, the dynamic process out of which the BAK network is formed, can also be termed 'experience'. The processes of planning involve expectations, the overlaying of prior experience on an upcoming situation. Out of the interaction of these two concepts with the events that then occur comes expertise, an evolution of the teacher's abilities. Let me demonstrate this process as it occurs in the data.

The expertise underlying a single classroom interaction

The example below is based on a very short interaction between Teacher E and her students, which occurred in the lesson that was videotaped and subsequently viewed and commented on by the teacher. The particular lesson was part of Teacher E's strategy-based vocabulary course, in which the major conceptual unit being covered was 'strategies for remembering new words'. In this section of the lesson, Teacher E had put the students into groups with the assigned task (based on an accompanying worksheet) of figuring out and discussing with each other what strategies they use to remember new words that they come across.

As one group was in the process of discussing the task which had been set for them, Teacher E approached them and sat down. While she sat down, one student was explaining to the other students how he retrieved words from equivalents in his more familiar languages. She asked him a single question, and as he responded she began to rise, acknowledged the response and left the table for another group. The entire interaction took approximately twenty seconds.

[Teacher approaches group and sits down]

S: For me I think about the word, and then/both in French and Arabic, and so/I have to make a prediction and translation from the vocabularies.

E: Can you tell me more about that? What do you mean by 'translate'?

S: I have to imagine the sentence in Arabic or French, and so I look for the word I need. I use it/I found it before in French or Arabic, and I try to translate it.

E: I see. That's one [strategy].

[Teacher rises and leaves group]

Based on the teacher's comments, the sequence can be divided into three segments: first, the approach to the group, second, the verbal interaction, and third, the departure. These segments are discussed as separate entities by the teacher not only while watching this portion of the videotape but also at other points in the interview. Although they seem on the surface to be quite innocuous and to reveal little about the teacher's BAK and expertise, these segments, structured in light of her BAK, are essential parts of the course, and also essential parts of the expertise she has developed in achieving the course goals in ways that are consistent with her BAK.

1.   Approaching the group of students

The first part of this sequence includes both the teacher's manner of approaching the group and the students' response (or rather lack of response), both of which are seen as relevant parts of the event. This event represents for Teacher E part of a gradual process of students learning to treat her as a listener or participant rather than as an authority, part of an evolution which is occurring over lessons as well as in this particular activity.

As the teacher was joining the group on the videotape, the interviewer stopped the tape and asked: "What's your feeling about your role in the group?" Teacher E stated:

E: I was just going to comment about that actually. In this particular case, I wanted to be the listener and a participant ... I do a lot of listening in that course ... I go from one group to another ... and at the very beginning they did not know what my role was, and I would say things like/ well as soon as I'd come, they'd stop [talking] or they'd address me, and I changed that by/ whenever I'd come I'd say "do you mind if I just listen?", and they'd say "oh okay" and then just go on, and so that's how I established being a listener.

This role of the teacher as a listener is consistent with a point she made frequently during the interviews about the importance of students taking responsibility for what and how they learn (for example, which vocabulary strategies they choose to use), which is also a notion that figures prominently in the overall course organization:

E: ... in this particular class I have been very much conscious of making students/ I want them to realize they are responsible for their own learning, that vocabulary/ that's been one of my premises, that vocabulary learning is a very individual thing each person is responsible for/ there's only so much somebody else can help you out with it, and the whole course is trying to help them out with it, but there's always been that/ something that I've been trying to push and push and push, "You are the one who's responsible".

2.   The verbal interaction

The second part of the sequence was the interaction between the teacher and the student, including the type of question she asked, and the student's response. The teacher made this commentary about why she asked the student to elaborate on what he had said:

E: There are two reasons [why I asked him to explain more fully]. One is that I don't want them to get away with something that general. We are trying to get at specific techniques for memorizing words,, ... and I don't want to let them get away with general things and think they understood and think that other students understood. I want them to become very specific, for their own sake and for the other students' sake.

In other words, for this teacher it was very important that the students be very specific in their discussion of the strategies; and the purpose of her question was to encourage this specificity. She described how encouraging specificity in the students' responses was explicit in her choices of verbal structures in the lessons as the course progressed:

E: That was part of my role at the beginning of the course. When I moved from one group to another I would ask those kinds of questions and then I started doing it in a different way. Instead of asking the students "Can you tell us more about that?",,, like "Are you going to let him get away with that?" ... I would look to the other students in amazement and say "Don't let him be that general, you get a lot of information out of this guy!" ... and the gesture I always do is [she makes a 'come on' gesture with her hands] like "Come on! You've got to get a lot out of him". And they know that. In the beginning of the course it was a little bit hard, because they weren't sure where they were going, but it became more and more evident that the kind of interviews they were doing had to be very specific ... because after that we discussed things in very specific terms.

As is evident from these comments, her questions are not isolated events, but a part of a development of ways of answering, and in fact, ways of questioning, that she is trying to teach the students to use. The emphasis on encouraging the students to be specific in their answers, and to question each other in such a way as to get a specific answer, is related partly to an objective underlying the accomplishment of this unit of the course: gaining an awareness of strategies for remembering words. The accomplishment of this unit is directly related to a high level goal of the course: gaining awareness of strategies for learning vocabulary. In addition, her comments on other parts of the lesson indicate that what occurred here was coherent with her own BAK and her view of the course. For example, while watching the group work on the video, Teacher E stopped the tape and made the following comment:

E: A general comment is I thought that there were a lot of good things going on in that group, the far group, a lot of very interesting/

I: /Can you be a little more specific? When you say a lot of good things came out, do you mean a lot of strategies?

E: I mean a lot of strategies, and a lot of "Oh I never do that". A lot of questioning,,, in particular, the Japanese girl with the glasses. She was saying a lot of that "Oh I never do that", "Oh that's a good thing to do", or/ and [another student] as well was saying that she was very aware that she only used two from those [strategies]. And so they were talking a lot about "It's funny how you only use two".

I: So 'good' in a sense means they had an awareness, or meta-awareness of what they do?

E: Yes, yes. Um,, some people are more reflective than others and um,,,

I: And is that something you are trying to encourage?

E: Oh absolutely. Absolutely. And so it's not only that they got to verbalize their strategies, but that they went beyond that. That's what I'm saying.

In this comment, Teacher E reveals her view of the importance of awareness and reflection in this course, and that awareness is considered something "beyond" verbalization. These concepts are related for her, as she indicated at a later point in the interview, while watching a student explain something to another student, when she ponders about the relationship between verbalizing for somebody else, and gaining an awareness of something for yourself.

E: I think he's [the student explaining] doing a very good job, because the difference between learning a word and remembering a word is not that obvious. It's obviously not obvious to that student who came in late because she had a lot of trouble. And I think he was put in the situation of having to explain that. I wonder to what extent making that explicit to someone else made him go further for himself.

These comments include elements from her own view of how students learn: the importance of awareness in learning, the importance of verbalization in gaining awareness. These comments also indicate that the question that Teacher E posed to the student after she joined the group was related to an interconnected conception about what was important to achieve, about how learning takes place, about what is to be learned, and about how what is being learned can be assessed.

3.   Leaving the group of students

The teacher's manner of leaving the table is also related to the above issues. She noted that whenever the discussion becomes centred on her, she gets up and leaves, and that sometimes she asks a question and then gets up and leaves in the middle of the student's answer.

I: Going back to where you left the previous group, do you have a feeling about when it is that you leave them to work on their own?

E: There are some/but it is not obvious from this particular tape, but it would be from other things. I don't know if it will become obvious after, but I leave when I have redirected the conversation and when it is obviously going where I want it but when they start addressing me as opposed to the other students. Sometimes I get up in the middle of their sentence, and their reaction is/ my reaction is if I have the floor and if I really want to talk and the person I am talking to is not paying any attention to me, I am going to get someone else to give my attention to, and that's what usually happens. If I leave and they're in the middle of a sentence, they'll just go on talking to someone else which is exactly what I want them to do. I leave when I think I'm taking on a greater role than I should, and they're starting to see me as an integral part of the group which I don't want to be. It would appear rude to anyone who'd just walk in and look at me, but there is a purpose to that and the rules of the game are clear to everybody.

These strategies and techniques have evolved as an integral part of this teacher's own approach. The technique of 'when a student is answering your question, get up and leave' only makes sense when considered in light of this teacher's BAK, and within the evolved and evolving context of this particular course. The expertise that this teacher has developed to get learners to reflect, to verbalize, and to take responsibility for their own learning is intertwined with her BAK and with the way in which she has created a structure for this course.

This example demonstrates how a coherent BAK underlies a teacher's description of her behaviour in carrying out a particular action within a particular activity, in a particular chronological lesson, in a particular conceptual unit, in a particular course. The coherence is evident not just in terms of this particular instance, but also as part of the dynamic evolution of the course over time. The short sequence analyzed above demonstrates the pervasive influence of the teacher's BAK in her behaviour, strategies and decisions, demonstrating that even the most innocuous of events/action (with or without verbalizations) plays a role, first, in achieving a higher level course goal (as described in Chapter 4), second, in expressing or instantiating aspects of the teacher's BAK, and, third in contributing to the developing expertise of a teacher for whom awareness and verbalization play a crucial role in learning.

The beginnings of change

The case of Teacher A is a good example of a teacher who, according to many indications in the data, was in the beginning stages of change. When, several years later at a conference, she heard a presentation I made that included a description of her interpretation of the curriculum, she noted that the basics were still the same, but that she had come a long way since then. I think it is important to emphasize that teachers are in constant change (some more quickly and more deeply than others); and that the exact teachers described in this study no longer exist – they have all evolved.

Teacher A had recently developed an approach to teaching reading that she was clearly comfortable with, based on her studies and her teaching. However, this had not spread yet to her teaching of listening;

she indicated that this had not been an area she had thought about, but in which there was a 'felt need'. She was also feeling some conflict in certain areas related to separate versus integrated teaching of skills.

In an early interview right at the beginning of the course, Teacher A seriously considered some basic changes in her approach to what she was teaching (what we might call some 'instability' in parts of her BAK). In the following long quotation, she considers two possible overall organizational structures for the upcoming course she was teaching:

A: ... I thought ... "what I can do is work first on grammar and spend a couple of weeks discussing how you join ideas together and how you subordinate and coordinate ... it'll be like the old system where they've got the tools and then after you show them how you apply them in different types of paragraphs". So that was my plan. Then in a discussion with [Teacher B]/ it wasn't anything the person said to me as much as suddenly it came to me that there was another way to approach this. I thought, "Okay, I can have them writing paragraphs right from the beginning and teach the cohesive devices, the subordinators, coordinators, conjunctive adverbs that are appropriate to that type of rhetorical pattern ... and teach subordination, coordination and conjunctive adverbs all together more by theme than by grammatical structure. Okay", I thought, "that'll be good. That'll put things in context and will be real interesting ... much more in with communicative language teaching and all that". These are the kinds of things that were in the back of my mind and then I continued to think about it and I kept changing my mind, going back and forth all day ... Anyhow I tossed back and forth between the two and I tended to feel more secure with my first plan.

I: Why?

A: Possibly because I'm the kind of person who likes to first figure out how something works and then try and use it, like I read the instructions before I try something. I'm not the kind of person who sits down and tries to figure it out, I'm the kind of person who reads the instruction book, and that's probably got a lot to do with it, just my personality. Anyhow I went and called a colleague ... whom I respect, and asked her opinion, and she told me that she had tried the second approach and that the students were confused, that they never really got an understanding of the sentence types as structures. The punctuation was always messed up and it just didn't separate in their minds the difference between the subordinators and the coordinators and conjunctive adverbs, and that it didn't work as far as she was concerned, and she recommended the first one. And because I was already sort of leaning that way and because I respect her opinion I just finally decided on doing it that way.

A frequent theme in Teacher A's data is the notion of relevance to the students, the relevance of the overall course and the way it is structured. However, there is also a recurring conflict in this theme: the relevance is not so evident, and so students have to be "made" to see it.

A: ... I try as much as possible to make them see the relevance of what I'm teaching to their other courses because I feel very strongly that they're taking ESL to help them in their other courses and not as an end in itself and therefore they should be made to realize that there's some value ... .

In attempting to achieve this goal of having the students see the value, Teacher A has developed a number of substructures, or subparts of activities which encourage the students to see this relevance.

A: ... I know that I'm constantly trying to bring in their other courses, and this year more than ever I have tried in giving them topics for paragraph writing which might allow them to use some of the knowledge they have from other courses. Sometimes the topics are more specific than that but at least some of the time the topics are general enough that they can plug in their own experience and their own knowledge and their own expertise into their writing rather than forcing them to write about something which they don't know much about ... .

The expression "more than ever" here implies change, not only in frequency, but also in attitude. It indicates that indeed she had been doing it, but not to the degree that the most recent change did not need to be mentioned, and it implies that there is more change to come. She assessed this aspect of the way she has structured the teaching in a positive way, and contrasted it to her previous approach to structuring the activities.

A: ... and I feel it's quite successful this year. I think I've gotten better paragraphs as far as the content is concerned and the interest level is concerned and I think that giving them more sophisticated things to write about and things that relate to what they're doing has forced them to produce better work than when you give them something very mundane and it's just an exercise in using the language in a certain way rather than really having a message to convey ... when I asked them to write about, for example comparison and contrast and told them to think of something in their own fields that could relate and this woman in art gave me that thing on the two approaches to art and someone else gave me something on different/I think it was approaches to business management. I told them to compare and contrast two approaches to something. That was far more interesting than asking them to/ as I might have done in the past, to compare and contrast I don't know,, something like the climate in this country and their own country which was the kind of thing I might have done a few years ago.

However, this assessment was not without reservations:

A: ... linguistically, well, there are still quite a few language problems, grammar problems ... .

These issues returned in the final interview after the course was over, indicating a further step in the gradual process of change.

A: ... I had that big debate at the beginning about whether to do grammar first and then do the patterns or whether to integrate the grammar with the patterns and all that, and I decided to spend some time at the beginning working on subordination and working on sentence structure, and then using them in the patterns, and it didn't work out. I think I might not do it as much as a separate thing in the future ... .

Nonetheless, her evaluation of the overall process focused on the students' grammatical mastery.

A: ... they wrote more than they ever did in the past ... I found they wrote a lot and the organization wasn't bad, actually they did use the patterns appropriately and they did use the kind of language that was appropriate, but there was something about the structure and the grammar that wasn't/ ... I guess it's not the patterns that was the problem as much as the grammar. I guess I'm disappointed in their ability to deal with the English sentence structures.

As a result, in her consideration of teaching the course another time, her thinking about her structuring of the course (within the institutional restructuring), has evolved. Instead of reducing the communicative focus by moving back away from writing on relevant topics, she has begun to incorporate a new way of dealing with the grammatical aspects of the language that is coherent with her currently evolving BAK.

A: ... I want to spend more time, I think, trying to get them to re-write or proofread or analyze each other's sentences ... I guess part of the problem is the restructuring of the course and I have to figure out how to work that restructuring of the course in without having my students come out with lousy sentence structures.

Expertise and BAK

One of the important aspects of developing expertise is that teachers focused a great deal of attention on problems in areas which were high level issues in their BAK networks. A problem which occurred during the teaching in one of these areas was viewed and treated, not as a failure, but as a current point of an evolutionary path. Moving the students along this path was considered a subgoal of the course, and a necessary one for the teaching to succeed. In order to deal with such areas, each teacher in the study developed an elaborate set of refined substructures.

On the other hand, problems in areas which were not high level issues in their BAK networks were treated as end points, or insoluble problems. In such cases the teachers did not pursue the elaboration of substructures to deal with these areas. An example of this phenomenon was the concept of group work in the classroom. For several teachers, students working in groups was closely identified with their beliefs about learning and teaching, and closely linked to the achievement of the course goals. However, a number of teachers expressed a lack of comfort with group work at various points during the interviews. These teachers generally said that group work did not work in their particular context, with the implication that the current result (that group work does not work) is the generalized end result (that group work will not work).

This contrast is notable, for example, with Teacher F, who put significant creative energy into developing a detailed method to achieve an individualized program for her students of different abilities. She had an elaborate system for categorizing students according to their levels, and for effectively giving each group a different content. She individualized her teaching by giving them differential help in the correction of their writing, and developed a system by which they had to exchange papers with another student at their particular level, and try to make improvements in the other's paper. When problems occurred in this area, for example, when students' behaviour was taken to be resistance, Teacher F took on the role of disciplining them. If the system hit a snag, for example, too many students of one language background who "are kind of blind to [each other's] sentence errors", she pursued various means of substructuring the activity to overcome the problem. For example, she stipulated who traded with who, either as an in-class decision, or a decision planned before the class. She also had a fully developed system of criteria and symbols for types of correction, and spent time at the beginning of the course familiarizing the students with this system.

F: In some cases I indicate what word needs correcting and I indicate in the margin the type of correction needed or sometimes I'll just indicate that somewhere in this line there is a mistake of this kind, find it and correct it, depending on if they seem to be able to do this otherwise and they just sort of slipped in this case, then I will not mark it on the line, I feel they can recognize it themselves. If I feel that it's something that's an inherent problem in their writing, I will indicate the word where the problem is and have the type of correction required indicated in the margin.

On the other hand, the students' behaviour with regard to group work was interpreted by Teacher F as "the blind leading the blind". The lack of success she perceived with group activities was not treated as an impetus to a more refined substructuring of the activities, but rather was simply accepted as a conclusion. Educating the students in the area of group work was not considered a valuable way of spending class time.

F: ... and since we don't have the whole academic year with our students, I personally don't want to waste time educating the students how to educate themselves kind of thing, but rather adjust my way of teaching to what they feel more comfortable with, and what they feel they learn best with.

Teacher F's focus on individualized correction and her avoidance of group work are both consistent with her focus on language form as the basis of writing. They are also consistent with her views that grammar must be learned through practice, and that individual feedback from the teacher and practice and correction at the student's own level are required to avoid fossilization.

Teacher D was not quite so categoric about rejecting group work, as indicated in the answer to this somewhat leading question from the interviewer, yet it was a relatively rare part of her teaching:

I: Okay. Do you, when in a class, do you, is there a lot of opportunity for the students to talk in the classes? Do you do a lot of pair work or group work? Or how, how do you tend to,,,/

D: Oh, yeah. I probably don't do, I always feel a bit guilty about that, and I'm never really sure why. Uh/

I: /guilty about what? Doing it or not doing it?

D: Well, about, I always feel that I should be doing more. Now I don't know if I'm just not good at it, or there's some trick to it that I haven't really grabbed, or if the students, um/ See, my impression is that while that stuff is fine, now and then, I don't think it's the way to operate, so I do it now and then, now I don't know, maybe I don't do it every class. Now maybe I do it once a week, and maybe I only do it twice a month, I really don't know. It depends on what we're doing very much, really. Um, and certainly towards the end, where there's more information exchange and the students all know one another and that, then there certainly would be more, uh, more of this sort of working and sharing. But, not/ less so in the beginning. And my impression is that the students aren't that keen to do this, again not initially anyway. Once they get to be friends and go off to the learning centre together and they/ you know, I think they do this sort of stuff outside of the classroom and you give them the opportunity to do that. Um, but, uh,, I just haven't/ I haven't worked out a way yet where I think a lot of that is necessarily better than/ in terms of learning, than doing what I do. I don't know if I could really defend that very well, but that's the way I feel.

We can see here that even guilt is not an effective means of leading to a change in a teacher's behaviour and BAK. Her comments reveal that part of the issue is knowing the "trick"; yet because success in group work was not a high level aspect of her BAK, she was not actively engaged in the process of refining her attempts to make this type of activity succeed. (Interestingly, this comment indicates some mixed feelings, a mixture of resistance and openness to change. Since the study, I have had the opportunity to observe this teacher, and seen that group work has become an essential and refined part of her repertoire. Unfortunately, the study did not capture this process of change.)

In contrast to this resistance regarding group work, Teacher D placed considerable attention on strategies for getting students to organize their work in a way which they could keep and use for future reference (a recurring theme in her discussions).

D: The one thing I did talk more about [in the class] is the personal writing journals because I always have trouble getting the students to understand I want them to buy a book. A scribbler. And this to me is such a simple thing. And we're weeks into the course and I have always one or two students who are handing in single pages or handing me their book with every other class they're taking all worked into it. And I don't know why this is such a problem. And on the outline I printed in bold type, you know, and I made a special section for each thing, including the journals, and printed this underneath, and uh took a sample book from one of the students. Of course it still took a while, I mean I still, we're at the end of the second week, well, it will be the end tomorrow, and I still have students who haven't bought the book.

This was evidently a matter that led to frustration on her part. She considered it "such a problem", which, in spite of her efforts, "still took a while". Yet it was of such priority, fitting into her sense of organizing being the key to understanding and learning, that she had a fully developed range of substructures to make the activity work in a way that she could consider successful.

Several other teachers in the study, on the other hand, had developed a full blown set of strategies for what to do in cases where group work was unsuccessful, and an evolutionary procedure in order to get it to work over the longer run. Teacher B made this explicit, expressing the conflict between his internalized view of learning through experience and the fact that his current group of students did not take to group work.

B: ... I think I felt a little ill at ease in the past because I wanted to get into more group-oriented things where I wasn't really a teacher, the centre of the class, and I'm thinking I'd still like to do that but they don't work well in groups, or at least I haven't found that they work well in groups. Possibly it's because I haven't orchestrated the group work correctly or adequately ... I don't know, maybe the best thing to do is really try to do as much group work as I can ... to make sure they get some practice ...

for this type of class I don't know how to get away from a teacher-centred class but I'll still work at it. I still think it's a worthwhile thing to do. I really think in writing that you [can] tell somebody a thousand times [but] unless they really practice a lot themselves they're not going to be able to do it.

During the early part of the course, this question of group work remained an unresolved issue. A second unresolved issue was the question of how to deal with the required grammar book, which, as it was intended, did not fit into his BAK, leading to a strong feeling of discomfort. His initial solution was to ask the students to "outline" it, which would give them the required practice in outlining as well as a summary of the grammar book for future reference, but this was initially resisted by the students. At a point much later in the course he was able to resolve both of these issues by finding a sub-activity in which working in groups provided them with an excellent opportunity to solve the problem presented by the outlining task.

B: ... we've been discussing this thing of them outlining [the grammar book] and I decided to put the ball in their field and say "Okay, you're going to have ten or fifteen minutes ... to get together in groups and come to some common agreement about how you're going to go about organizing this outline" ... .

In subsequent interviews, he made clear that, according to his own BAK, he had succeeded in both of these issues – the grammar book outlining turned out to be a great success, and the students became comfortable with group work.

Curricular evolution

The second language literature has become increasingly thorough in its treatment of curricular issues, primarily how the curriculum or syllabus should be designed and implemented and what it should comprise (see for example Johnson (1989), Nunan (1988), White (1988); and Yalden (1987). What is not touched upon are the natural processes of curricular development that occur in social teaching settings. Although the social aspects of teaching were not a focus of this study, the teachers' verbalizations revealed a great deal about how a curriculum evolves in practice.

A crucial result of this study is related to what actually happens in the classroom compared to the planned curriculum. There is an important sense in which the classroom events (what we might call the 'instantiated' curriculum) differs from the planned curriculum. Each time the curriculum is carried out it will have evolved. This occurs especially when it is carried out by a different teacher, but also by the same teacher (whose experience of the course, and BAK, have evolved). When different teachers, who often interact and get curricular advice from each other as part of their planning process, teach the course, there is an evolution over time. In other words, the instantiated curriculum evolves over time even if the curricular guidelines do not evolve.

For example, when Teacher H described a "flop" in the lab activity with her class, she attributed it to her assessment that it was too easy for them, and did not achieve the goal of them thinking that the lab would be a useful and interesting place for them to learn. In response to her comment to this effect, another teacher (Teacher G) suggested her technique of preparing lab activities for the first class at three levels of difficulty, an idea that Teacher H immediately found acceptable.

H: ... Thursday was not a good day ... I took them to the lab, and I did a lab orientation. And I should've chosen something more challenging to do in the lab. I didn't. I thought that their listening was quite poor, and that I'd give them an easy listening to do in the lab. And it was okay as an orientation, in that they now know how to use the lab, but ... in terms of giving them the lab as something challenging to do, [to show them] that the lab is a useful thing, that they will learn through using the lab, it was a flop, because they thought it too easy. And that was silly.

I: How did you know they found it too easy?

H: They finished it in about half the time that I'd expected ... And I spoke to [Teacher G who happened to be in the lab at the same time], and she said that she did things at three different levels. And that seemed to be a really good idea, to say that here's something very easy so that you get used to the lab, and then here's something very difficult, and then here's something sort of at your level, so that they realize that there is challenge involved ... I wish I'd done what she'd done.

For Teacher H, this technique was seen as an excellent way to make the activities of the first lab session achieve their goals. When she said "I wish I'd done what she'd done", however, she was talking only about a specific organizational layer of the teaching structure. For Teacher G, this technique was part of an elaborate system of individualization that represented her view of teaching and learning. The technique could not be passed on to Teacher H as a component of individualization because individualization was not a part (or certainly not an essential superordinate node) of Teacher H's BAK network. For Teacher H, the three-level technique had quite a different purpose: it was not seen as a component of individualization but rather as a way to make the lab introduction more interesting for the students. In addition, if Teacher H did use the technique, it would, in all likelihood, be implemented using quite different substructures (for example, by means of verbalizations which foreground the importance of the challenge that the lab can provide, but not foregrounding the importance of the lab in providing an individualized means of learning what you want to learn). Yet Teacher H enthusiastically took the technique, and fit it into her own system as a part of her growing expertise. For her, this idea may be generalizable only to other orientations, while for Teacher G it is relevant to everything she does.

How does this interaction relate to curricular evolution? The next time Teacher H teaches this course, the curriculum, for her students, may have evolved slightly. On the surface, the change seems to bring the course more in line with Teacher G's course. However, in terms of the underlying structures, this is somewhat of an illusion. The change was triggered by the sharing of a particular activity, but the ramifications on Teacher H's course depend crucially on how the new activity is perceived through Teacher H's BAK and fits into the underlying structure of her course.

The effect of many such interactions and small changes is the natural evolution of the curriculum. This process, which can only be examined empirically by a longitudinal study covering several course offerings, has been noted anecdotally by teachers who return to a teaching institution after an absence and find, even if the courses are nominally the same, that 'things' have changed. This process of change seems to occur for the most part implicitly. On a number of occasions I have noted the difficulty a returning teacher has in understanding precisely how the way of teaching a course has changed. This may be partially because the changes quickly become part of the unspoken and assumed subculture that develops among teachers who interact on a daily basis. (It has always amazed me how quickly teachers begin to say "we've always done it that way", and previous states of the curriculum seem to dissipate). In addition, as in the case noted above, the impact of a shared idea on another individual's BAK is never made completely explicit, which is why these overlapping but non-identical 'micro-cultures' can co-exist. For the same reason, it is also hard for a new teacher to fill in the implicit but definite gap between the curricular guidelines and the curriculum as it is instantiated by its prior and current teachers.

This phenomenon of curricular evolution is illustrated by a case in the pilot study where one teacher left the institution, and a conversation course that she had taught for several terms was taken over by a new teacher. The second teacher had the benefit of the first teacher's materials to use in preparing and carrying out the course. However, after a period of several lessons using the first teacher's materials, she felt the need to reinterpret the course for herself. She discussed her planning process:

T04: I guess I went to the files and I looked at the things that [the previous teacher] had given out, and again it's personal preference in a lot of ways. Some of the things she was doing, I don't like doing. And some of them too I felt for some of the people they/they were getting tired of that kind of activity.

Her interpretation of classroom events was also part of this process of reinterpreting the curriculum. She had a sense of the functional basis of the previous teacher's view of the course which differed from her own emphasis on spontaneous speech.

T04: The second day, or maybe it was even the first day, I was sort of carrying on with these sort of oral skills they're supposed to have like how to introduce somebody, how to request things, those things and one of them was invitations. So I gave them some situations for invitations and some of the phrases you could use to invite somebody and/ informal ones and formal ones, that kind of thing. But it was really flat, you know ... they really didn't respond to it very well. They did it but, I mean, I think for some of them they just/they didn't enjoy doing that any more. So then I started thinking I should just try to get things that were more/ I don't know/ centred around ideas or something that could develop more than that, rather than working on the theme kind of speech. Because I really do think that they can do that. Maybe they don't do it grammatically but they have the sense of how to invite and they do know, you know, that you have to smile at somebody or that you have to be friendlier, whatever, so sort of thinking maybe we could move on to something else or that they could take an idea and develop it and express it or do sort of more thorough questioning.

Later in the interview, it becomes clear that this re-interpretation of the curricular goals is consistent with her view of learning:

I: And what kind of things are, in general say, are you trying to give them or get them to learn or get them to develop?

T04: To think on their feet. Well, just to be able to respond to what's going on and also that they really have a lot of resources,,, you know, in the sense of if they do use a lot of things that are around them they really can learn a lot. Like the newspaper, like the T.V., like, you know.

I: So you're trying to expose them to resources for one thing and as well get them to be able to interact or talk to each other/ deal with things spontaneously?

T04: Yeah. But I think/I believe that if they know what's going/if they know the kinds of things that we're all talking about and if they could give an opinion, well that's half the battle, you know, having something to say. And I think they get so caught up in trying to learn specifics of a language rather than why they want to use it. So I try to give them things they can talk about with people.

The case of team-teaching, which can potentially offer enormous opportunities for sharing and growth, but in practice often produces frustration instead, offers some insights into the process of curricular interpretation and evolution. One of the courses in the study (Course C2) was being team-taught by two teachers (one teacher was a subject in the study and one was not), both of whom were highly respected in the institution and both of whom had high respect for each other. However, the implementation of this course was fraught with misunderstandings and frustrations. The frustrations highlight the importance of experienced structures – the activities and materials that have been previously experienced in use. For example, based on her interpretation of the goal of a subcomponent of an essay writing activity, Teacher C went to her familiar resources.

C: ... Had everything gone according to plan, I would be doing the 'trees' [the tree diagrams] with them. I had a lot of stuff in my 'closet' where I keep my writing process stuff on 'trees', and a couple of other samples of 'trees' that had been developed that I thought would augment the section and be very nice ...

However, a change of plan caused her to have to implement 'non-experienced structures' – activities in the textbook that she had not experienced – with the result that she did not feel well prepared for the teaching.

C: ... as it happened however by the time I got to the lesson, 'trees' had already been done ... so [the other teacher] was well ahead into the unit ... so I tried to carry on from that point but I wasn't as well prepared as I should have been ... I hadn't read that section [of the textbook] with the degree of intensity that I should have ... .

As Teacher C noted, different teachers have "different closets" which contain different sets of structures that can be readily activated and used in a given superordinate structure.

C: ... when she [the other teacher] said ... they [the students] should use [in their essays] a lot of transitions [transition devices], I'm sure that she has something that she has pulled out from her 'closet' that she plugs in at that point when she's dealing with transitions, and I do too. It's just that we have different closets ... .

Although the experienced structures may be intended to accomplish the same superordinate structure in the course (to illustrate the concept of a 'transition device', for example), these structures also signal aspects of the teachers' BAK networks that may differ considerably from teacher to teacher.

An important aspect of coherence in teaching and in teachers' underlying beliefs is the concept of experienced structures. As discussed in Chapter 6, 'experiencing' a structure means experiencing the implementation of a higher order concept in terms of the procedural sub-decisions which carry it out. The teacher interprets the events that occur in the sense of monitoring, assigning meaning to, and assessing the results of the events within the context provided by the teacher's beliefs, assumptions and knowledge. The more a structure is experienced, the greater the sense is of the possible range of types of decisions that may be necessary to implement it in a new context, decisions related to types of course goals, the particular students and their characteristics, and other situational characteristics (for example, the classroom, available resources, and so on). Experienced structures, by virtue of having been experienced, have fewer 'gaps' than structures which have not been experienced, thus requiring fewer local moment-to-moment decisions and reducing the cognitive demands on the teacher in the classroom. When a structure is carried out, it is instantiated, or interpreted (in the performance sense of interpretation) using familiar experienced structures in a way which is coherent with the teacher's BAK. By virtue of this interpretation, the *actual* curriculum – what happens to the learners in the classroom – is different from any planned curriculum. And each subsequent instantiation of the curriculum by this teacher is different – both it and the teacher have evolved.

Conclusion

The focus of this chapter has been the interactions among the three aspects of the model developed in previous chapters: (i) the events which make up the teaching, (ii) the teachers' interpretive processes and (iii) the teachers' planning processes. It is the interaction among these elements that brings us to a dynamic perspective in teaching, including the development of BAK through experience and the role of BAK in creating expectations. These combine to produce teacher expertise, as it is defined above, and curricular evolution.

Contrary to our usual notion of a curriculum which is static unless explicitly changed, in light of this study, curriculum can be seen in a dynamic fashion. When a course is taught, and is instantiated and experienced by the teacher, this instantiation bears signs of that teacher's BAK. In the structuring of the course, the relationship of each level of the structure to its superordinate levels is based not only on the accomplishment of those higher levels, but also on their accomplishment in a way that is consistent with the teacher's BAK. When we take into account the individual ways in which BAK evolves – through the experience and resolution of conflicts and crucial hotspots – and the social ways in which teachers' beliefs, assumptions and knowledge evolve – through interaction with colleagues, with curricular guidelines and directives – and with theoretical information – curricular evolution results. As a course or curriculum is experienced by a teacher it evolves: it is the experience (and storing of that experience) which is used by the same teacher in teaching it again; and it is certain aspects of the way it is taught which are passed on to other teachers. An example of this process is Teacher A's interaction, described above (page 258), with two colleagues, one who encouraged a change in her approach, the other who encouraged her to retain her approach. What is different about the course relates to all the levels on which the course exists as described in Chapter 4 – the verbalizations, the moves, the exchanges, the activities, the lesson units, the multiple lesson units, and ultimately, the course. What is not resolved is the issue of what makes a course 'the same'.

There are many cases in the data where teachers referred to their experiences of prior events as playing an important role in their expectations about what will happen in the upcoming teaching, which in turn provides the basis for assessing the results of what happened. In most cases, there is a discrepancy between the teacher's expectation of potential outcomes and the interpretation of actual outcomes. Sometimes this discrepancy will not be considered critical, and the teacher will consider the results of the teaching structure to have been successful. However, sometimes the discrepancy is related to some critical aspects of success in the view of that teacher (i.e. interpretation of course goals, or own beliefs about success in a classroom activity), and is taken as an indication of lack of success. Most often, success is a relative matter, and adjustments will depend on the teacher's personality and time. However, the discrepancy, if it is an important one for the teacher, provides an impetus for subsequent decisions designed to address this discrepancy, either as an adjustment in the on-going teaching, or a redesigning of certain structures for re-occurrences in other teaching situations. It is through this process of experiencing the outcomes of the structures, and refining them over time, that the teacher develops a repertoire of possibilities for use in other situations. What develops is a very specific kind of expertise in the area considered crucial by the individual teacher. This expertise, however, is developed within the teacher's evolving BAK, since the areas that teachers choose to focus their attention on and develop expertise in are ones related to and coherent with their BAK, and it is there that they have the patience and perseverance to find and develop sub-structures that work.

Contrary to our usual static notion of 'good teachers', in this light expertise can also be seen in a dynamic fashion. Opportunities for developing expertise are always there. There are, however, some teachers who are more open to the discrepancies than others, who see the conflicts, who reflect on the possibilities, and who try out the alternatives. Teachers vary in this regard, some taking advantage of the opportunities more than others. These are the characteristics that distinguish, as the saying goes, between a teacher who has had ten years of experience and a teacher who has had the same year of experience ten times.

10 The structure and process of teaching in context

The model in Chapters 3 and 5 was developed in light of the three research questions posed in the first chapter, and these provided the three poles around which the structures and processes of language teaching were investigated. The goal of the study was to use the verbalizations of the teachers in order to posit patterns and regularities in each of these areas, and then, using the model and the concept of 'coherence', to examine how these three areas fit together.

The three research questions are:

1. What are the structural units of a course of language teaching, and, more specifically, what are the relationships among the more local units such as classroom discourse and the more global organizational units used by the teacher to accomplish the course?
2. What are the procedures that the language teacher uses to structure (plan and carry out) the units of a course of teaching?
3. What are the processes by which a language teacher interprets classroom events and information about teaching, and how do these interpretations influence the teacher's practices?

The relevance of the findings of this study extend beyond the field of second language teaching. They relate to the literature in cognitive science to the extent that this study can be seen as a study in 'applied cognitive science': a number of the concepts (those outlined in Chapter 3) developed in that field and used in theoretical discussions can be seen operating in the 'everyday life' of language teachers. This study suggests ways of looking at relationships among concepts (knowledge and beliefs, procedural and declarative knowledge) that can be explored in more specifically designed cognitive studies. In addition, the findings relate to the education literature to the extent that second language teachers can be seen as representative of teachers in general. In addition, this study suggests a number of important distinctions and relationships that have not been explored in educational studies.

However, the main relevance of the findings in each of the above areas is in providing a perspective on second language teaching that is generally not taken into account in two main aspects of theory and practice. One of these is the area of program development, including both the overall area of planning (curriculum development, and program organization and implementation), and the overall area of assessment (program and curriculum evaluation). The second aspect is related to teacher education and professional development (pre-service and in-service) and teacher evaluation.

This chapter uses the concept of coherence in fitting together the parts of the model to outline the notions of curricular change and teacher change emerging from the study, and then describes their relevance for practice.

The structures of teaching

This study differs in one important way from much of the research that has been reported in the educational literature on teacher decision-making and teacher thinking. Rather than focusing on the identification and categorization of types of decisions and thoughts, it focuses on the relationship of the decisions and thoughts to the *structures of teaching*. Following the literature in cognitive science and artificial intelligence, the study posits a model in which an individual's decisions and actions are seen as being goal-oriented, and the goals are related to each other in a principled, structured fashion. In the case of teaching, the decisions and actions made by the teacher contribute to the events that occur in the classroom, and form what the teacher perceives as a structured organization. This first area of results posits characteristics of these perceived structures using teachers' verbalizations as data.

This study distinguishes between two types of structures. The first type is the conceptual structure: the structure of the units making up the content of the course. The second is the chronological structure: the structure of the bounded time frames making up the course schedule (the weeks and lesson periods, for example). Both types of structure involve sequential and hierarchical relationships: teachers perceive a course as being composed of sequences of units at different levels of generality, with more general, higher level units being made up of more specific, lower level subunits. Although the number and types of levels in the structure are flexible and vary, the form of the overall structure and the patterns of connection operating between levels remain constant.

Of particular importance in the study are the relationships that occur in the conceptual structure. Because the conceptual structure involves multiple or 'tangled' hierarchies, the term 'heterarchy' (following de Mey, 1977) has been used. The units in this heterarchical structure can be seen (and labelled) in terms of their relationship to other units in the structure. These relationships, which are explicit or implicit in most discussions of teaching, include three specific types: goal, means, and content. The term 'goal' (or, in the educational literature, the term 'objective') refers to a higher level unit in the structure from the perspective of its relationship to subordinate units. The term 'means' (or, in cognitive terms, 'procedure' and in pedagogical terms, 'method') is the converse, involving the relationship of a lower level unit to its superordinate units. Units on the same level are related to each other in terms of 'sequence' (and in terms of the educational literature, reference to a unit without reference to higher or lower level units is termed 'content').

The verbalizations of the teachers in the study reflected this type of sequential and heterarchical organization. Specific utterances were discussed in terms of their function of getting particular points across to the learners or in terms of carrying out particular classroom techniques; the points and techniques were used to ensure that activities were accomplished; the activities, in turn, were performed in order to accomplish particular thematic units, for example, which reflected the way in which the teacher had interpreted and structured the overall goals of the course. The levels, then, were connected via the concept of function, a concept that has been used in linguistics and discourse analysis (in this latter case, it explicitly involves the intentions or goals of the speaker): lower levels function as the means to accomplish goals represented by higher levels.

Theoretical relevance

From a theoretical point of view, both in second language teaching and in the field of education in general, the findings are relevant to the areas of syllabus and curriculum, and specifically about the roles of objectives, content and method. Such issues arise frequently in theoretical discussions, for example in the personal communication of a colleague arguing the point that a curriculum involves questions of content (the 'what' to be taught) but not questions of method (the 'how' it will be taught). This study strongly suggests that these concepts cannot be treated as independent entities. Since teaching is described in terms of a structured organization where any items or elements in the structure can be viewed as a manifestation of content or method, or indeed goal, depending on the perspective, discussion of curricular issues by definition includes all three concepts. This theoretical point is relevant to the issues of curricular evolution and curriculum implementation, and is discussed in more detail below.

The analysis of the structures of teaching in this study also takes a different perspective on studies of classroom discourse by virtue of examining the discourse *from the point of view of the teacher*. This perspective makes it possible to relate behaviour at levels of language and discourse to larger event structures; it relates what is said in the classroom not only to what is being done in the classroom but also what is being done in the course. The distinction between chronological structures and conceptual structures in teaching allows us to analyze higher level pedagogical structures in the same terms as lower level discourse structures, and to examine how discourse structures flow into pedagogical structures. The way the 'larger context' of a course is structured in terms of participant intentions and the choice of means used to display and negotiate those intentions may have theoretical relevance for research on event structure in other areas of human behaviour. In this study, I have not pursued the question of event structure outside the field of teaching, however, this is an area where cognitive science, discourse analysis and language teaching can potentially gain mutual benefit from theoretical cross-fertilization.

Relevance for practice

The results in this area also have practical relevance in the area of teacher education, both in pre-service education, where prospective teachers learn to do the things that teachers need to be able to do, and in in-service education, where teachers learn to reflect on and develop their current practice.

For pre-service education, the notion of course structure is relevant to the question of learning how to create and plan teaching structures. One of the tasks given to new second and foreign language teachers in many programs around the world is that of creating and justifying a lesson plan. In many cases, however, this task must be undertaken out of context – without reference to an actual course with its associated sub-structuring of objectives, and without reference to the teacher's beliefs, assumptions and knowledge. Learning how to make decisions (and produce the lesson plans which embody those decisions) in isolation presents a task which is unrepresentative of, and in some ways more demanding than, what practising teachers carry out in their daily work. Such a task is analogous to the language learning activity of practising sentences out of context in order to learn the syntax. As an activity, it may have some formal value in demonstrating the sub-elements of the sentence (or lesson) and how they are structured. However, it neglects the contextual meaning – how the sentence (or lesson) functions within a larger structure of goals and means – and it neglects how this larger structure is used by a teacher in creating the lesson structures.

This point became evident to me when I had presented a paper on this topic to a group of student teachers. Afterward, one explained that, in a recent exam, she had found it very difficult to produce the required sample lesson plan. Her description of the problem was precisely that described above: she had no context to which she could relate the content of the lesson plan. The task set for her was to develop a partial downward structure with no higher level set of structures to provide constraints. She was thrown back into a situation not of showing her understanding of teaching, but rather of guessing the 'correct' context as perceived by the evaluator. As a result, the validity of the task was reduced, as was the likelihood that any ability in structuring teaching activities gained by the student teacher by creating the lesson plan would be transferred to actual practice.

In the case of in-service teacher education, where the student teachers have experience in creating and planning teaching structures, making explicit the notion of course structure may be important in 'debugging' the teaching, i.e. determining more efficiently whether certain elements 'worked'; and when they did not, why not. For example, at the level of classroom structuring of teaching, the notion of the relationships among levels may provide an insight into cases of classroom misunderstanding. When a structure is planned or invoked by a teacher, this does not mean that it will be interpreted by learners in the same way. There may be (i) a misunderstanding downwards in the structure, i.e. a misunderstanding by the student as to the specific means by which a proposed unit of teaching is meant to be carried out, or (ii) a misunderstanding upwards in the structure, i.e. a misunderstanding by the students as to the purpose of the proposed unit.

For example, when a teacher provides learners with procedural instructions, it is done in the form of verbalizations given within the context of a course structure. The teacher giving the instructions can choose at any moment to elaborate the procedural structures at a more detailed level (which the word 'in-struct' itself implies), or allow the students to interpret their own lower level structures for carrying out the higher level course units and accomplishing the associated goal. As well, at any point the teacher may fill in more of the higher levels (purposes or rationalizations for what is being done) so that the students understand better the constraints for carrying it out at lower levels. However, no matter in how much detail instructions are given and rationalized, they are always created by choosing ways and means, and are always open to interpretation by learners. For example, Teacher D in her lesson gave the explicit instruction: "Get into groups of three". The students responded by getting into groups of three, four or five (i.e. 'about three'). In this case, the structure of the activity was such that it also functioned adequately with four or five to a group. In other cases, however, the structure of a task may require exactly three. It is a general understanding of the overall 'what-how' relationship, and a specific understanding of which layers are closed and which left open, that allows a teaching unit to 'work' – to accomplish its superordinate goal. Both new and experienced teachers have to learn what they must do to fill in the missing information to make the activity 'work' effectively and efficiently, and how to check for the required understanding of the intended structures.

In some cases, ones they consider very important, teachers *do* become very explicit. For example, whereas Teacher D's instructions for group work in the example above were slightly ambiguous, her instructions for doing 'writing journals' were extremely explicit. I wish to emphasize, however, that the 'solution' to this question of downward misunderstanding is not absolute explicitness, even if absolute explicitness were possible. First, increased explicitness is costly in terms of time, a commodity that virtually all teachers felt was at a premium. There is not enough teaching time available for everything to be made absolutely explicit. As noted by Leinhardt and others, efficient teaching occurs when unspoken routines develop between teachers and learners. In addition to the question of efficiency, an important aspect of the dynamic and trust that develops between learners and teachers seems to develop through the 'unspoken' – i.e. implicit structures are an important contribution to the success that is felt. For example, Teacher E discussed the extreme satisfaction she felt in accomplishing results that had been implicitly planned and carried out in an unspoken manner. Ultimately, however, when a teacher (especially a new teacher) is aware of the structure of teaching elements, it makes it easier to gauge when new substructures (both higher level organizational structures and classroom verbalization) need to be explicitly inserted in order to make something work. As noted in Chapter 6, this is a process which occurred frequently with the experienced teachers in the study.

Misunderstandings upward – when there is a mismatch between the teacher's sense of the higher level structures and the learner's sense of them – may not directly affect the classroom procedures, but may have an effect on longer term teaching. For example, in a pilot study of teachers and learners (Allwright and Woods, 1992), a teacher created her own materials (rather than using a textbook), designing them carefully and creatively in order to encourage learners gradually to take over responsibility for planning their own learning. At the same time, one learner whose usual approach to language learning was to plan ahead by looking at upcoming lessons in the textbook found it difficult in this particular case because no textbook was used. This example is not an issue about the use of textbooks in teaching, or about the best means to achieve learner autonomy. Rather, it is an issue about the differences between the heterarchy that the teacher has created and interpreted and those that the learners create and interpret, one that suggests the importance of all participants learning how to gain a fuller sense of the higher level structures intended and interpreted by the other participants in the teaching/learning process.

The notion of structures of teaching is also relevant to the issue of assessment of teaching. In addition to such misunderstandings between learners and teachers, there may be misunderstandings that occur in the process of teacher evaluation between teachers and individuals evaluating the teacher. A teaching observation which excludes the context of the higher level structures may result in incorrect assumptions being made about the functions of lower level elements. An awareness of this issue on the part of the evaluator can allow for a much more balanced view, one that takes into account the fact that the observed teaching may have as a major function accommodating the evaluator rather than accomplishing the higher level structures of the course. This issue is also related to processes of interpretation, and is taken up again below.

Teachers' planning procedures

This area of the study deals with the ways in which the teachers in this study planned and carried out their teaching through the process of making decisions. The task of the teacher is seen as one of moving the learners from a perceived current state to a perceived target state via a sequence of classroom events. This overall task includes two parts: (i) developing a conceptual structure linking the overall conceptual goals to a sequence of events, and (ii) mapping these events onto the set chronological structure of the course. The analysis of the data suggests that teaching decisions are made within the context both of the perceived goals of the course and of the current structure which has evolved out of prior decisions. For example, the decisions and ideas that created a lesson plan for Teacher C (in Chapter 6) occurred at a variety of times within the 'problem space' that the objectives and current plan had created.

The planning procedures of the teachers can be viewed in temporal terms – the sequencing and timing of decision-making – or in logical terms – the 'level' of decision-making. The logical aspects of planning, i.e. plans which specify the levels of the teaching structures, are directly related to the logical aspects of the structures themselves. However, the temporal aspects of planning do not directly relate to the chronological aspects of the course since a teacher might make early plans about a late part of the course. These two aspects of planning are intertwined in the process, but it is important to distinguish between them. It is by taking into account the relationship between the temporal and logical aspects of planning that we can account for top-down versus bottom-up planning.

When the relationships among teachers' decisions are examined (rather than just looking at the decisions themselves), and the temporal and logical aspects of decision-making are taken into account, a number of generalizations about the planning process become evident. First is the extreme tentativeness of the decision-making process, an essential feature of the process, permitting the teacher gradually to shape and map the conceptual structure of the course in such a way as to be able to take advance of new information as it arises.

A second generalization is related to the importance of constraints and resources in the decision-making process of the teachers, and the alternation in their use. This point is also related to the issue of relationships among decisions. The teachers creatively shaped the decision-making process (their planning procedures) in order first to increase the constraints gradually (and reduce the unlimited number of possibilities at any moment), and then to expand resources (to find the best possibilities) within those constraints. This cyclical contraction and expansion of possibilities allowed them eventually to get to the point of classroom 'sounds' and 'movement' (things they say and do), yet having had the opportunity to develop a superordinate structure (or underlying structure) that best combines constantly updated information with their interpretation of the requirements and the goals. This notion of constraints and resources connects the temporal aspects of decision-making (which decisions are made before which others) and the logical aspects (the way decisions about an activity, for example, constrain what is said to introduce it).

A third generalization is the use of top-down and bottom-up procedures in planning. This notion also links temporal planning procedures (what a teacher does during the planning process), and the logical relationships among planning decisions. When proceeding in a top-down manner, the teacher starts first (temporally) with higher level tentative decisions (seen first as content, and then as goals to be achieved via lower level structures), and moves downward to make decisions about substructures (first seen as methods to achieve the goals, then as content, and then in turn as goals for their own substructures). When proceeding in a bottom-up manner, the teacher starts with lower level tentative decisions (seen first as content, then as means for achieving something), and moves upward making decisions about superstructures that these subactivities can fit into (first seen as goals, then as content, and then as means to yet higher level goals). These two extreme ways of proceeding are theoretical. In the teachers' planning practices, there was constant movement up and down, starting with what the teacher had available and moving both up and down (both in the direction of goals and of means) to what was not yet worked out. A good example of this is the (lack of) response of the class to Teacher C's question about the news (described in detail in Chapter 6 pages 165–6), which led her into a further discourse substructure (to find out why they did not respond), and subsequently led her to create a new activity, which found an appropriate goal in that class, and in addition became a structure with a different goal in her other class.

A fourth generalization is related to the notion of experienced structures, their importance and use, the distinction between experienced and non-experienced structures, and the gradual internalization of structures as they are experienced. This result departs from the educational literature in that it focuses less on a binary distinction between conscious decision-making and automatic routines, and more on the process of experience in making the unknown substructures of a unit of teaching familiar. A structure (at any level) becomes better understood when it is 'experienced' – in other words, when the teacher has carried out a set of substructures to accomplish the unit, giving the teacher a sense of concreteness (in contrast to the abstractness inherent in the label for that structure, or in a verbalized account of it). This concreteness also includes a sense of the possible reactions that a particular substructuring might provoke. The notion of routine is subsumed under the concept of experienced structure. As a structure is experienced (more often, and perhaps more intensely), some of the details of the substructuring may not need to be considered as explicitly in subsequent implementations. As this happens, the structure is becoming internalized; and at some point there may need to be explicit consideration of the internalized structures in order *not* to implement them.

Theoretical relevance

This study departs from other studies in the field of education in several ways. First, it includes in the model a broader definition of the concepts of planning, decision, and decision-making. In this perspective, decision-making involves considering factors in a dynamic fashion over time, with only certain of those considered factors being conscious at any one time. Therefore a decision can be characterized by varying degrees of consciousness.

This study departs from both educational and discourse studies by distinguishing between the chronological structure (the schedule of lessons in the course, for example) and the conceptual structure (what is taught – and how and why). In the education and discourse literature, there has been an implicit or explicit assumption of a logical link between the chronological structure (such as the 'lesson') and the conceptual structure (such as 'activity structures' or 'interactions'). In much of the literature, a chronological distinction – that between pre-active or planning decisions and interactive decisions – is used in order to account for aspects of conceptual decision-making. In contrast, this study, when considering teachers' conceptual decision- making, did not distinguish in an *a priori* fashion between types of decisions made at different points in time, for example, those made between lessons and those during lessons. It examined the logical connections among conceptual structures, and looked at the process of decision-making by which *the teacher* links these two types of structures.

In addition, traditional studies in the field of education have generally focused on the 'product' of the decision-making process, attempting to identify types of decisions, to classify them and to determine their frequency. The perspective taken in this study, in contrast, is a focus on the *process* of decision-making, i.e. the relationships among decisions. This broader perspective implies that each decision is related to other decisions, either temporally (the relationship between prior and later decisions) or logically (the relationship between more global decisions and more local decisions). An important part of understanding planning is understanding the connection between these two types of relationships. In such a perspective, a single decision cannot be talked about in isolation. What is crucial, then, is not the classification of types of decisions and the occurrences of each of those types, but rather the relationship among decisions, and the process of decision-making that creates those relationships.

The findings have potential relevance to the literature in the areas of cognitive science and education by focusing on the relationships among a number of the theoretical concepts related to human planning developed in the field of artificial intelligence, as outlined in Chapter 3, and used in the field of education, including 'constraints', 'resources', 'routines', and 'top-down' and 'bottom-up' planning. Most studies of teachers' planning have not been longitudinal, and so the distinction between the temporal relationships among decisions and the logical relationships has not been made. It is by taking this distinction into account that we can see more clearly how the teachers' use of constraints and resources are interconnected, and are related to the concepts of top-down and bottom-up planning. In addition, the distinction between 'conscious' planning and 'automatic' routines needs to be explored in more subtle detail, in particular the role of experience in developing fluency in carrying out teaching structures.

In the field of second language teaching, such concepts have scarcely begun to be an issue.

Relevance for practice

There are a number of practical areas of relevance of the results for the planning processes of teachers in the area of teacher education both for learning teachers and for teacher educators. However, it is important to take into account that the results are only suggestive, and can more profitably be taken as a tool or framework for teachers to examine their own practices rather than as content to be taught to learning teachers.

In general, teachers (both those in the study and others with whom I have discussed these results) seem to be only partially aware of a crucial aspect of planning – the extreme degree of tentativeness by which prior decisions gradually narrow possibilities for later decisions, an essential part of the process. Interestingly, several of the teachers themselves felt that a weakness of their planning was the last-minute nature of decisions that they made, which they termed a "lack of organization", and they treated this characteristic as an idiosyncracy – a negative one – of their own teaching rather than an essential part of the process. If nothing else, an awareness of this characteristic of the planning process would have decreased the sense of frustration and guilt they experienced and expressed as they carried out the planning of their courses.

A result of the analysis of planning procedures relevant to teacher education is the use that teachers made of resources and constraints: the alternation between expansion and contraction of teaching possibilities. This is important in two ways. First, it is important that student teachers develop many resources at all levels, including places to find raw and prepared materials, procedures for developing and adapting materials into teachable units, ideas for activities, techniques for carrying out parts of activities, and so on. The implication is that an important function of a pre-service teacher education program should be to allow student teachers to explore and collect as many resources as possible for the types of teaching they may do. A second function is for teachers to experience the art of using constraints to narrow possibilities for teaching. Certainly this seems to occur best within the context of actual teaching, and may be one aspect of the complaint that graduating teachers sometimes make about their programs – that they did not have enough opportunity to gain the practical experience that they need when they begin their first teaching assignments. The framework of resources and constraints can also provide a basis for an inexperienced teacher to observe and categorize the planning processes of more experienced teachers.

Another relevant aspect of the results for planning is the importance teachers place on 'experienced structures'. These play a unique role in their planning process and are a crucial part of their resources, again pointing to the necessity for a significant teaching experience component of a teacher education program, and also to the value of working with experienced teachers. The framework provided by the notion of teaching structures described above can help to make the experience productive in terms of learning what is needed to make a structure work. While for an experienced teacher, such structures are generally implicit, the student teacher can map the structures explicitly (while going through the experience) in order to gain a clearer sense of where the holes are, and what adaptations are possible. One reason why having the experience is so important is because when student teachers themselves have to use the structures, and work through the procedures in order to teach, they will notice and remember most clearly what they are. When they have to teach, the consequences for not filling in or for ignoring gaps in the structure are naturally highlighted for them.

Teachers' interpretive processes

The third area of results of this study is related to teachers' interpretive processes, an important aspect of which is the notion of an interwoven network of beliefs, assumptions and knowledge (BAK) which takes in the context of the teacher's goals, intentions and past experiences. This study focused on a number of characteristics of the underlying BAK network and the role it played in the process of interpretation of events. The events being interpreted include: (i) interactions in the classroom among teacher and learners with each other and with teaching materials, (ii) interactions between teachers and curricular information and directives, (iii) interactions between teachers and verbalized (in articles or lectures) research results and theoretical discussions.

One striking impression resulting from the study is the pervasiveness of the hypothesized BAK in the statements made by the teachers, leaving the sense that it is through this finely and elegantly interwoven design that each teacher viewed the world (or perhaps, it is better said, created a world). In some ways this design was unique to that individual but in other ways it overlapped and interfaced with the worlds of colleagues, and with those represented in curricula, textbooks, and articles. It was not as if teachers' networks of beliefs, assumptions and knowledge were activated in particular cases in order to resolve ambiguous cases or deal with conflicting situations. Rather it seemed to underlie everything that the teachers did and said: as if it was through their individual BAK systems that the teachers structured their perceptions of the curriculum and their decisions as to how to implement that curriculum, from overall organization of the units down to specific classroom activities and verbalizations. In addition, the power of BAK in a conflicting situation was very striking. This was particularly evident in the amount of energy and creativity put by Teacher B into resolving conflict between his BAK and the requirements of the institutional system, described in Chapter 8. (I would like to note that, in this discussion, I am not attempting to make any evaluative comments about any of the teachers or curricula. What I wish to point out is the power and pervasiveness of the individual's BAK in the face of a conflicting teaching situation.)

For the courses in this study, the institutions by and large allowed teachers a great deal of freedom to make their own curricular decisions within the constraints of the overall goals of the program and the course. Although it does not necessarily follow that the interpretive processes would follow the same processes in situations where the curriculum provides much narrower constraints, there is some evidence for this in the literature (for example, Borko et al 1979) and anecdotally (for example, I have heard many teacher trainers recount the difficulty of having teachers follow the narrowly defined procedures of the audio-lingual method). In the cases reported in this study, at any rate, we can see clear signs that the teachers' interpretations of the task that has been assigned to them are coherent with their BAK.

This area of results has both theoretical and practical relevance.

Theoretical relevance

The issue of teachers' interpretive processes in the field of second language teaching has scarcely been touched upon in the literature. However, in the education literature, this issue has had a rapid development; one example of this is the developments in the area of concept mapping (such as Morine-Delshimer, 1991). One of the important differences between this study and many others is the longitudinal focus, with the result that, as this study progressed, the concept of BAK came to be considered not as an object but as a process. In the education literature, many studies do not produce a situation where the aspects of the underlying concepts interact dynamically with decisions and experiences. Even those studies focusing on change tend to compare states, rather than examining the evolving interactions among different aspects of the 'concepts' with each other, and with the actions and events that occur in the teaching.

This study also extends the discussion in the education literature related to concepts of 'knowledge' which implicitly include beliefs, by making this inclusion an explicit part of the concept. It also contributes to the developing sense of the mix of beliefs and knowledge reflected in the work of Calderhead (1988), Leinhardt (1989) and Connelly and Clandinin (1988).

The results of this study have some implication for theoretical findings in previous studies of teaching. For example, the notion of BAK sheds some light on why the unit of an activity has been found to be a central unit of planning in teaching. A unit such as an activity has, to some extent, an explicit downward structure. However, the upward connections to higher level goals and to BAK are often quite implicit. In other words, activities often do not have a unique theoretical allegiance and are transferable from teacher to teacher and situation to situation. As a result, the same activity can be carried out by different teachers with different sets of beliefs for different purposes and still be considered successful. The notion of BAK also provides an insight about the role of constraints in teaching: whereas constraints that are consistent with beliefs are necessary for the functioning of the planning/teaching process, constraints that conflict with beliefs are problematic – a teacher cannot just 'accept' them and carry on teaching. Constraints, however, which are not quite consistent with current beliefs but which are consistent with a desired direction of change seem to be an important aspect of teacher evolution.

These results have analogies in other areas of research in cognitive science and artificial intelligence, especially research on background knowledge structures and related theoretical areas. This study contributes to cognitive work on background knowledge structures by elaborating on the role they play in a specific sphere of everyday activity. In this context, this study extends the notion of the effect of background knowledge on the comprehension of verbal texts (such as written passages) to the understanding of *events*, including both verbal and non-verbal events, where understanding involves identifying, categorizing and interrelating events at different logical levels of organization in light of goals, intentions and background knowledge. This study focuses on events related to classroom teaching, and does not attempt to extend this analogy to other types of structured situations.

Relevance for practice

From a practical perspective, the results on interpretive processes and BAK have relevance for teacher education, both pre-service and in-service. As noted by Anderson et al (1977), our process of education is based on an assumption of learners being responsible for the 'correct understanding' of what has been presented in class; and teachers often do not notice that individual students have developed different interpretations of what has been presented or what has transpired in class. Barnes and Shemilt (1974) have also noted that the normal assumption in education is a 'transmission' model rather than an 'interpretation' model. Teacher education in ESL often follows such a model, as does the literature in the field. For example, methods and approaches are usually assumed to be transmitted intact, and carried out by different teachers in an equivalent manner. However, as noted above, with the complex levels of interacting goals and means inherent in teaching, the number of levels that can be transmitted verbally is only a small proportion of these. Even observing a lesson only shows us a small number of the interacting levels that are part of the observed teacher's conceptualization. It is the individual's own BAK that fills in the levels left implicit. It is for this reason that teachers talking about the same method or approach may be referring to two quite different conceptualizations and therefore quite different sets of structures. Some of these are effects predicted by the 'schema theory' of text comprehension, and yet, interestingly enough, often seem not to be taken into account in teacher education programs even where teachers are reading texts about schema theory.

New teachers also need to gain an understanding of the process of structuring teaching elements, and to learn how teaching techniques can fit into a coherent but evolving 'philosophy' (but that this philosophy never is nor can be perfect: it is always evolving), and to learn a range of strategies for making and testing out decisions. A crucial aspect is the notion that experience plays a vital role in the evolution of BAK. When the impetus for change is exclusively externally motivated (for example, a curriculum that requires 'communicative teaching') there are usually many implicit levels that must be filled in for the change to occur. Experience, on the other hand, seems to provide certain 'hotspots' which highlight gaps in the structure that need to be filled in. In this light, we have to think of teacher education as exploring BAK networks, developing a sense of the aspects which are yet unstable, unelaborated or in conflict, and encouraging the experience of actual teaching events that will permit these aspects to develop. While teaching to teach often focuses on the transmission of information about teaching, learning to teach can be seen as learning how to take advantage of experience so that acculturation as a teacher is enhanced. Often student teachers do not know what or how to observe, what to attend to and how, what they can get out of observing, and how to ask questions about the experience.

Teachers in training typically get theoretical courses in linguistics, second language acquisition, discourse analysis; practical courses in methodology and techniques of teaching; as well as internship and observation. These are all important aspects of teacher training; but, in addition, teachers need to become aware of:

> – how techniques are linked to theoretical issues, issues which are not considered in our traditional categories for dealing with approaches,

but rather ones which are important to teachers as their personal approaches develop and evolve;
- their own assumptions during the period of their training and later as they develop in practice;
- the importance of such issues (those related to assumptions and beliefs) in teaching, and respect for them in other teachers, so that when they observe they are sensitive to what is going on beneath the surface;
- the language that is used to transmit ideas and beliefs in the acculturation of teachers;
- techniques in observation and in interviewing.

Since BAK networks are not always entirely conscious, teachers can become increasingly aware of the role that BAK networks play in their teaching (or, in the case of pre-service teaching, the role that they could play). In addition, it may be that an awareness of one's own BAK make it easier to accept others', to understand how they differ, and to decide that the difference can be worked through in areas of conflict. Teachers who develop an understanding of their own BAK may become more aware of their learners' BAKs and their role in how the classroom operates, and they may also be able to take this into account in their planning.

The notion of BAK and its role in the interpretation of a curriculum also has relevance for research on teaching, especially in cases where the research depends on determining cases where the teaching must be considered the 'same'. In a research project examining the use of computers in process writing classrooms, for example, the researchers found a great deal of variation in the way a process approach to writing was interpreted in the classroom:

> ... our goal was to involve teachers who were all committed to the teaching of writing as process so that the pedagogy would remain constant across all classes. The teachers selected, both on the basis of self-report as well as on the basis of evaluation by their consultants, all seemed to be so committed. Our expectation consequently was that the students involved in the study would all have the same opportunity and encouragement to engage in a complete writing process, whether they used a pen or a computer. Observation of the teaching over the year, however, suggested that the situation was far more complex, that the pedagogy with respect varied in important ways both among classes as well as within the same class over the space of a year. (Freedman and Clarke, 1988:21–22)

Coherence in the teaching process

One of the outcomes of the study is a sense of how the whole picture fits together – the heterarchical structure of course units, the planning processes, and the interpretive processes – in the recursive cycle of planning, action and assessment. This recursiveness, combined with the notion of heterarchy in course structuring has relevance for the way that we view two important areas of change in second language teaching. The first is the area of curricular change, related to issues of curriculum/program planning, implementation and assessment. The second is the area of teacher change, related to areas of pre-service teacher education, in-service teacher education and teacher evaluation. It is the interplay of the teachers' evolving BAKs, their planning processes, and the on-going interpretation of events that lead to teacher expertise in specific areas, to teacher change, and to curricular evolution.

Curricular evolution and evaluation

Borko et al (1979) claim that traditional models of teaching foster the belief that teachers can be programmed to use desirable methods effectively. When this training does not succeed, it is blamed on resistance or ignorance on the part of the teachers. But the failure:

... may result from the erroneous assumption that a particular program or materials will work in any given classroom in any given circumstances. (1979:155)

There is a tradition in the field of second language teaching of talking about teaching in terms of 'approaches', for example, the structural approach, the functional approach, the natural approach, the process approach, among many others. An implicit assumption of this tradition is that these approaches are unified, unambiguous ways of proceeding, with the corollary that teachers basically transmit the content of a planned curriculum unchanged to the students. This tradition is related to another tradition of prescriptivism, that there is a 'correct approach' and that departures from it are to be avoided, a top-down philosophy of implementation and evaluation which implicitly guides programs in many parts of the world (noted by Hutchinson, 1988). A practical consequence of this tradition is found in systems which separate the processes of curriculum development from the processes of teaching, where the individuals involved in one aspect are not involved in the other.

The perspective of this study, describing the interpretive, creative, generative, transformational role played by the eight teachers in linking students' current states to curricular goals, contrasts with this way of talking about teaching and of dealing with issues of curricular change and program implementation. The results of this study suggest that the systems of curriculum/program planning which attempt to implement curricular change uniquely from a top-down perspective, create blocks in the natural evolutionary processes. These results help clarify why such attempts so frequently fail, and also why teachers are so mistrustful of new methods enforced by powers who are not part of their day-to-day classroom realities. This failure is often called a gap between practice and theory; but it can be more constructively seen as a restriction on the two-way flow of evolution in curricular change and development. This study suggests that such 'departures' from a given approach cannot be avoided, but rather that they are an inevitable and essential part of the overall process. There is an indefinite number of ways an approach is instantiated, differing in crucial ways depending on the context in which it is carried out and who is involved in its interpretation in the classroom. If this interpretive process is seen as a normal part of teaching, it can be built into our conception of teaching and means can be developed to encourage its beneficial aspects.

The study also suggests that the separation between curriculum development and teaching, done for reasons of specialization, may hinder the bidirectional flow between levels of teaching. Teachers frequently described how their most useful and applicable ideas for activities, materials and the general development of resources came in response to the constraints of a particular context – i.e. as part of the alternation of constraints and resources that occurred as the teaching was going on. For example, the activity structure developed by Teacher B, one he considered a huge success, of the students outlining the grammar book is also a good example of how ideas arise in the context of the course and the teacher's frame of reference, since this idea developed in response to the events of the course as interpreted through the teacher's BAK.

Clearly the curriculum and syllabus have an important role in the evolution of a program and its curriculum. However their traditional function as the blueprint from which the teaching occurs has been based on a simplified view of the process of change. The curriculum is one source of input to the process of interpretation; however, rather than being considered the ultimate predeterminant of what needs to be achieved, it could play a role which takes into account the dynamic aspect of the curriculum and the relationship of the curriculum and the teacher. This is consistent with the view of a negotiated curriculum discussed by Breen and Candlin (1980). The implication of this view is that the process of curriculum implementation has the potential for a two-way effect with regard to change. The implementation of the curriculum can promote teacher change, and the teacher, through the interpretation of the curriculum, can provide input to curricular change. For this to occur, however, the channels have to be open both ways. For the teacher to be able to feed into the curriculum in a dynamic fashion, rather than struggling against a curriculum which does not suit him or her, the curriculum must be conceived in such a way as to allow multiple interpretations, allowing teacher freedom yet providing support, by requiring teacher input as courses proceed.

A curricular concept that encourages a movement in this direction is the 'retrospective curriculum'. This concept was implemented (not entirely successfully, for what I think are procedural rather than theoretical reasons) as a contrast to the traditional concept of a prospective or implementational curriculum in the development of the Intensive English as a Second Language Courses at Carleton University, and is hinted at in Magahay and Woods (1990). In such a system, course records are kept of the materials, activities and lesson notes of each course taught. These records do not represent what was intended to be done in the classroom, but what was actually done. They act as curriculum guidelines, and are expected to be interpreted differently by different teachers. The goal of such a curriculum is a bidirectional flow of information. The curriculum is to provide teachers with resources, ones developed out of the constraints of the particular course, but not to constrain them in areas which conflict strongly with their BAK. This is, of course, a complex area, as some hotspots are important in the growth of both the curriculum and the teacher. However, it is important to keep the exchange flowing, so there are few 'structural blocks' in the system, i.e. permanent blocks which lead to stagnation rather than growth. In the short run, it is not easy to distinguish between these: something that looks to be a problem may, in the longer run, turn out to be to everyone's benefit. However, when the focus is on using the block in a positive way, the result can support both the teacher and the curriculum. In such an approach, the role of the curriculum can be to set up conditions in which teachers get maximum exposure to tools and skills to take responsibility for their own teaching. The curriculum process, in this sense, is analogous to the reading process where the top-down effects and the bottom-up effects co-occur and interact.

The contrast between a top-down approach and an interactive approach to the implementation of change can be illustrated by two possible interpretations of the results of the analysis of teachers' interpretive processes in this study. These results have themselves been interpreted by interested colleagues as having two quite different implications. One implication is to categorize teachers and learners into types of teaching styles and learning styles based on these interpretive processes (linear vs holistic, teacher centred vs student centred, or transmission vs interpretive), and place them into classes where the styles correspond. This would represent an attempt to effect change in a top-down manner.

An interactive perspective would argue, on the other hand, that learning situations where the styles of the participants differ is desirable, and that confronting a number of styles is an important facet of learning (learning a language, learning to teach and learning to learn). We noted cases in which teachers grew through clashes – i.e. if their expectations were not met, they pursued a number of different means of learning more about dealing with such situations. If learners operate similarly, i.e. if not only teachers but also learners make positive advances from clashes, and if what learners are learning in the classroom is not just the language in the narrow sense but also ways of approaching language use and language learning, then it is not necessarily counterproductive to be in a classroom with teachers and other learners who are different, not just in their knowledge of the language, but also in their style of learning and teaching. It is possible to imagine that a learner who is, for example, grammar-oriented in his approach, may benefit in surprising ways from a teacher who puts him in new kinds of learning situations and gives him new learning strategies, and vice versa. In addition, the teacher may also benefit. This process occurred in the case of Teacher A, who began to think in new ways about a learner in her class with a clearly different learning style from her own.

A: In teaching this year I think that I've for the first time realized that it [breaking things down into parts] doesn't help everybody because I have one student in one class who doesn't see things broken down and she/she has a very hard time with outlining. She has a hard time understanding a lot of things that I'm dealing with because she always sees the global picture and never sees the parts. And so I realize that I might be forcing her to go against her natural way of dealing with something, but because *I* think that way, and because I feel that expository writing in English, and a lot of the things that we're doing, work that way/ by being very,, sort of just sections of things that fit together/

I: /Is this the first time you've had that suspicion that not everybody works that way?

A: Well I think I've sort of had it but I've never really come across a student who's confronted me with it ... [I noticed] partly from one of the paragraphs that she wrote for me which was on a comparison and contrast and she did on two approaches to art. One was the rational view where you learned to copy and imitate what you saw and to focus on all the parts of the painting making each one perfect in itself and the other one was what she called the irrational approach, although I don't really think that that's the word that she was looking for but emotional approach where you saw a total picture and your feelings dictated rather than some sort of reason or logic and then when she/after that I didn't pay too much attention to that but I remembered it and then afterwards when she did an outline for me I realized that she got all the important bits of information but organized them completely contrary to the organization that was in/that was so apparent in the lecture because there were all kinds of markers like "first" and "second" and "there are two things that we have to know" and you know that kind of stuff. And I realized that she just missed all of that completely even though she understood the details of the lecture and so she was unable to/to analyze things that way.

Although it is not clear that this event led directly to a change in Teacher A's teaching, this verbalization occurred during a period when Teacher A was reanalyzing the substructures of her practice of separating the parts and teaching them one at a time, and had begun to encourage students to write about topics of interest and relevance to them. This conflict, and the developing awareness that resulted, may have provided to both participants during the course opportunities for learning that they might not have had if they had been 'streamed' by teaching and learning styles.

However, as noted by Bateson (1972:68) in his discussion of the concept of 'complementary schismogenesis', such interactions have negative results when the differences between the participants lead to yet greater differences (and, in our case, lead to the learner or the teacher simply giving up). There may certainly be counterproductive results if the clashes occur with no respite, if the learner is confronted with a conflicting style all the time. What we probably want is a good variety of experiences – long enough with a teacher to develop an appreciation and understanding, but with enough other teachers to realize the relativity of that style, and the importance of developing across style. (Of course this is enhanced by teachers who also understand the relativity of styles, and the struggles a learner might have when dealing with a teacher with a new style.) One way of promoting the positive change is simply through developing awareness. An awareness, for example, on the part of the teacher about his or her BAK and of the process of change can help him or her to orchestrate the classroom experiences to be positive.

The results of this study also have relevance for program and curriculum evaluation. Since teachers' assessment of events naturally feeds back into the curriculum at levels of course implementation, a natural extension of this is feedback and evaluation of the curriculum. This can occur in an informal manner as addenda to the retrospective curriculum. Having teachers play a role in curricular evaluation also helps to equalize slightly the power inequality between teachers and their supervisors and allows teachers then to invest in the process of curricular development and curricular change. It is important, also, that the teacher may develop an appreciation for the equally complex and sophisticated world of the learner in terms of classroom motivations and behaviour.

The concept of coherence (and the notion of hotspots as a way of pinpointing areas undergoing change) helps us to analyze the data from a single individual; however, this concept can be extended to the broader analysis of program implementation and curricular evolution and evaluation. In teaching situations involving interactions among multiple individuals (learners, teachers, supervisors, and so on), we can also use information from daily activity as data, and use it to determine hotspots. If we take the term 'coherence' to refer to an individual's perception, then in parallel fashion we can use the term 'harmony' (adapting the use of the term by Stevick, 1980) in a technical sense to refer to the interaction of multiple perceptions. It is clear from the complexity of each individual's perceptions that multiple perceptions can be extremely complex, and can have no end of possible disharmonies. In fact, a situation that is completely harmonious is likely impossible; and it would also imply that no change can take place. An important function of research, or new teachers, or new systems of teaching, is to create disharmony, and thus a movement forward. Unfortunately, very often the effect is unproductive disharmony, with frustration and dissatisfaction instead of movement forward. A prime example is that one of the most frequent complaints of experienced teachers is the unproductive disharmonies created by new externally imposed 'methods' or curricula. The notion of teacher change needs to be considered in order to account for curricular change and to encourage productive disharmonies. The notion of 'harmony' is one that implies a dynamic view of teaching in terms of perceptions of the course structures held by the participants. This dynamic view can also affect our view of curricular assessment in terms of a 'larger picture'. Curricular assessment should create positive disharmonies – allowing teachers to see, understand and accept differences in how practice is conceived, and encouraging them to think about practice in an open way. This leads us to the question of teacher change.

Teacher change and evaluation

One of the important issues arising from this study has to do with teacher change: how do teachers change, and in what circumstances are the changes for the better? This issue is tied up with the complex processes of interpretation and planning in teaching. The complexity of teaching has been acknowledged in the literature (Mehan, 1974, Schön, 1983, Whitaker, 1975), but does not seem to have had a major impact on how the process is represented in the training and evaluation of teachers.

As noted in the cases of several teachers in this study, the teachers' classroom behaviour involves carrying out, at different degrees of consciousness, explicitly and implicitly planned teaching structures. These teaching structures, and the teacher's actions which put them into effect are planned and interpreted in light of their BAK network. Each teacher's BAK network is made up of different elements or aspects which are interconnected. This characteristic of interconnectedness means that a change in any one aspect will have an effect on other aspects. A good metaphor for the notion of change with respect to teachers' networks of beliefs, assumptions and knowledge is Lightbown's (1985) discussion of second language acquisition, i.e. change with respect to elements of a language system. Lightbown states that an important reason why externally imposed change (in the form of error correction) often does not work with second language students is because the linguistic knowledge is organized in a cognitive system in which the items do not function independently. Therefore, for one element to change, it means that its relationship to other elements has to change, and other elements will have to change too. The teachers' discussions of their beliefs suggest that an analogous process is in play here. A teacher cannot simply at will 'change' one belief by itself, because each one is part of an interwoven network which includes many other beliefs. In light of these characteristics of teaching, the notion of teachers' 'resistance to change' can be seen in a different light: teacher change can be encouraged but not mandated.

The notion of more closely and loosely bound connections found in the description of parallel distributed processing and found also in Bateson's discussions (cited in Chapter 3) is also a relevant metaphor. We can speculate that where a teacher's belief is very tightly interconnected with other beliefs (and thus more 'central' or 'core'), it will be a much more complex operation to change it. In areas where a teacher's belief is less densely connected to other beliefs (and thus more 'peripheral'), the change will involve a less complex operation, and one that the teacher can be said to be more 'ready' for. This view implies that for change to occur, there will have to be some deconstruction of beliefs before another set can be constructed, and that this can lead to periods of disorientation, frustration, even pain. This metaphor suggests that changes can occur in a number of peripheral areas of a teacher's BAK (as seemed to be happening in the case of Teacher A) with no outwardly visible changes occurring. The result, at a later point, may be what appears to be a very sudden but profound change.

In informal conversations following the study, one of the teachers described changes that she had gone through in subsequent semesters (indicating that they were not due to the study, although a number of teachers stated later that the study had been a catalyst to changes in themselves as teachers). According to her, the changes occurred through her experience with learners during a period in which she interacted a great deal with other teachers, sharing views, ideas and materials, and in which she felt particularly invested in the teaching

she was doing. She noted that the change occurred as a gradual progression, implying that the central aspects of her own approach and
character were at no time threatened (as if there were central aspects
which she identified with, and peripheral aspects that she was more
ready to give up). It seemed that the initiation and the readiness for
change was both internal and external. The internal element included
both an interest in change and a conceptual readiness for change –
akin to Prabhu's (1987:104) 'sense of plausibility'. In addition, there
also seemed to be a social motivation to change. The social system or
'teaching culture' of which the teacher was a part provided both models of and support for the changed state. It seemed for the change to
take place, the characteristics of the new state had to be desirable,
available, plentiful and highlighted in her environment; they had to be
non-threatening to the central aspects that she identified with; and they
needed time to be absorbed.

In this dynamic setting, the issue of teacher evaluation is a complex
one. The examples in Chapters 7 and 8 demonstrate the teachers'
interpretations of a curriculum and the beliefs, assumptions and
knowledge that underlie these interpretations differ in important ways
and are always evolving. The issue of evaluation, or judging which
teachers and practices are 'good', then, is one of deciding, at any point
in time, whose interpretations and BAK is 'right'.

This study emphasizes the difficulty of understanding (and therefore
fairly evaluating) what is going on in the classroom independently of
the broader contexts, i.e. without understanding the functioning of elements observed in the lesson in terms of the larger course structure and
in terms of the teacher's sense of coherence. This phenomenon is illustrated by numerous comments by the teachers on the videotaped
lessons that demonstrate a sophisticated understanding of the
processes and complexities of the teaching that are not at all evident to
an outside observer. Teacher E's discussion of the intricacies of her
ways of approaching and leaving groups and of questioning students
(pages 253–7), and Teacher B's expression of frustration with the curriculum (page 230) both illustrate that when we observe a unit of
teaching, we may have little understanding of how the teacher has
interpreted the same teaching. As a result, we cannot take into account
the interactive process of teacher self-evaluation and evolution that has
led to that class and which will lead to further evolution in subsequent
classes.

The notion of expert teaching arising within the framework of this
study is one that sees expertise as the effective creation and use of substructures to achieve superordinate goals. This study suggests that
expertise develops within the context of a teacher's background and
within the context of a particular course and course goals. This notion

contrasts with our traditional attempts to evaluate teaching based on an external model of effective teaching. Traditional evaluation typically ignores how it is that teachers improve at what they do.

However it is a mistake to suggest that there is no context being brought to bear on classroom evaluation. Rather, it is made within the context brought to bear by the evaluator, i.e. the evaluator's own interpretive processes and biases will play a role in the evaluation process. This phenomenon is exemplified by Fahkri's (1989) discussion of the belief systems of school supervisors doing teacher evaluations in an overseas setting. In an analysis of the evaluations of these supervisors, Fahkri pointed out some firm indications of the beliefs and assumptions underlying the evaluations, and the differences among them from evaluator to evaluator.

These results emphasize the importance of moving from evaluation of teachers' behaviour in the classroom to an evaluation of the whole process in context. What is suggested is a kind of 'triangulation in evaluation', including several types of data and several perspectives. The adaptation of the notion of a 'portfolio' evaluation, as has been developed in the field of written evaluation, would encourage a broader, more contextualized basis. Observation of lessons would be combined with other measurements, including those which would evolve from the criteria for success that the teachers and learners are using in their informal assessments, and including discussions or interviews to explore the teacher's perceptions of the structure of the course and the functions of the classroom elements. Part of the discussion would relate to the planning process: the process of decision-making that led up to the lesson and possibilities that will follow the lesson. Part of the discussion would relate to the teacher's own interpretation and evaluation of the lesson in terms of his or her interpretation of the goals. There are ways in which the teacher could play a role in collecting evidence for and demonstrating excellence in teaching, not just from the single lesson, but over longer time frames and including interpretations of and contributions to the evolution of the institutional curriculum.

However, it is also important to ask ourselves why we want evaluation. There may be cases where institutional decisions such as re-hiring, promotion or dismissal require evaluation; in many other cases in which we carry out evaluation, however, no such decision are at issue. Instead, what is desired is improvement and growth among the teachers who are on staff. In such cases, it may be that evaluation in its traditional sense is counterproductive, and that using negotiated means to achieve teacher change may produce better results.

The results of this study also suggest the importance and value of evaluator training in cases where the evaluation plays an important role in teachers' future job conditions and in the system of education. Evaluators need to be familiar and experienced with methods of inquiring about teachers' plans and activities, about the structuring of a course, about teachers' coherence, so that a discussion about classroom structuring and its role in the course structuring can form a part of the evaluation. In this sense, the methodological aspects of the present study have some relevance to the process of teacher evaluation, if we assume that evaluator effectiveness also develops through structured experience.

Conclusion: exploration and discovery as a catalyst for change

It is tempting to want some specific concrete results about types of teachers or about types of factors that affect decision-making, and to use these to make recommendations for specific changes in how teaching and teacher education should be carried out. However, in a sense this type of 'research-driven' top-down change is precisely what the study suggests does not work effectively. The results of this study suggest not a different way of teaching, but a different way of thinking about teaching. Hunt, in his foreword to Newman's (1991) book *Interwoven Conversations: Learning and Teaching Through Critical Reflection*, states that our normal way of thinking and talking about teaching assumes that "in some fundamental way what happens in different classrooms is similar because we use the same words to describe it". He presents an alternative view which is much closer to that suggested by this study:

Since teaching is something we always do with other people, we don't often think of how isolated and lonely a profession it is. But anyone who has tried to explain to someone else a particular teaching situation, to make clear and understandable some specific incident, has encountered the radical isolation of the teacher. The words we use to describe the acts of teaching are all understood in different ways according to our own backgrounds.

When I use the word 'teach' to one of my colleagues a few doors away, for example, I know very well that the image in her mind is one of me standing at the front of a class, probably behind a lectern, possibly reading from notes, but certainly producing oral language addressed to a group of perhaps twenty or thirty listeners. If I go a few doors down the hall in the other direction, the image would be of me seated on a desk conducting a discussion, acknowledging students with a nod or a gesture, and trying to get students to address each others' concerns rather than directing each contribution to me.

I would have to go all the way down the hall to find someone whose image was a little closer to my reality – which might involve my leaving the room to go to the photocopier while the students, in groups, argued out, in written conversations, strategies for library research. And even he understands only a small portion of the specific circumstances of any teaching situation. (Hunt, in Newman, 1991:vii)

The teachers' discussions in this study indicate that these differences underlie not only our use of the same words but also our assumptions about the same curricula and our observations of the same lessons and activities. The results of this study reveal why, in the anecdote that began Chapter 1, there seemed to be important underlying differences in the classroom teaching I was observing.

However, as much as the data in this study support such a view, the isolation is only one side of the picture. The opposite side is what occurs in moments of teaching when the communication seems total and the connection complete. I suspect that it may be the spark of such moments that draw many individuals into becoming teachers. Newman (1991), in her narrative account of teaching, uses the term 'teachable moments' to describe unpredictable moments of spontaneity, when the 'teaching' seems to occur on its own. Further, these kinds of communicative connections do not occur only with students; they also occur in interactions with other teachers. It is perhaps also the potential of these moments that encourages us to interact with others, and to change.

The results of this study relate more to the notion of reflection and interaction as a catalyst for change than to specific conclusions about how effective teaching takes place. They attest to the centrality of 'situated knowledge' as described by Lave and Wengler (1991) in the process of teacher change. They suggest the value of tools for exploration and discovery such as those described by Connelly and Clandinin (1988), or ones similar to the research methodology used in this study. The use of narrative 'cases' of reflection in action in accounts such as Schön (1988) or Newman (1991) and the use of more informal exchanges of experience among practitioners – as opposed to using abstract generalized 'rules' of teaching – gives the learning teacher the opportunity to see into the underlying structures of the culture they are joining.

One specific result related to methodology has to do with the positive effects of talking about teaching. All the teachers who participated in the study mentioned at some point that being able to talk about what they were doing to an interested observer was very helpful to them. One teacher said "I've never before been able to talk about my teaching as much as I wanted and have somebody *really* listen". As the discussions continued over the weeks, there were many instances during the interviews themselves when teachers came up with ways to deal with a problematic situation: just having verbalized the issues, the procedures, the problems, and the ideas seemed to have a positive effect. The relevance for program planning is the importance of having intrinsically-motivated opportunities to exchange ideas with others, and for building teacher exchange into the curriculum development.

Although it is possible to make concrete suggestions for things that can be done in program implementation to encourage this kind of reflection and interaction, enforcing such exchanges is a top-down directive similar to a specific detailed curriculum. Teachers with heavy work loads often resist meetings and enforced idea-sharings unless these are perceived as having direct benefit for their current teaching situation. Reflective teaching develops out of social environments in which experimentation, being temporarily wrong, reflection and change are not enforced, but rather appear natural. The specific changes must evolve in a way that is appropriate and natural to the practitioners' evolving BAK networks.

As this study progressed, it raised a number of interesting, but unanswered, questions. One of these is the question of the difference between novice teachers and experienced teachers: which aspects of the results of this study would be different? A second question is related to teaching in settings where English is not spoken in the surrounding culture, i.e. where English is taught as a 'foreign language' rather than a 'second language', or indeed where the foreign language being taught is a language other than English. In many such settings, teachers are non-native speakers of the target language, have very little freedom to stray from a required script in a textbook, and may have relatively little training as a teacher. In addition, there may also be aspects of planning and interpretation which are quite culture-specific, and would therefore vary with teachers from other cultures. Which aspects of the results would be different in these situations?

In addition, this study raises the question of the effect of trends in research and education on what we judge to be the central issues for investigation. As the study progressed, I began to realize not only that my own BAK played an important role in determining the teachers whose feelings of success I understood and whose frustrations and problems I empathized with, but also that the socially accepted characteristics of 'good' teachers change as the trend or 'fashion' of education changes and that those whom we judge as the best teachers are those who we judge to be on the front edge of the current trend. Most learners, however, are not aware of what the educational trends are, and their judgments of the teaching that sparks them to greater learning may be quite different from mine, as well as from those considered to be at the cutting edge of the field. The important issues for them may be grounded in the same issues that were primary for the teachers in this study: the balance between support and independence, discipline and freedom, pre-active (decontextualized) and in-situational (contextualized) learning, form and function/meaning. Although some of these issues appear in research in second language acquisition and in second language teaching theory, many do not. In my view, this is a further argument for including the teachers' perspectives in the evolving theoretical work in the field of language teaching.

References

Abelson, R. (1979) Differences between belief systems and knowledge systems. *Cognitive Science 3*: 355–366.

Agar, M. (1975) Cognition and events. In Sanchez, M. and B. Blount (eds), *Sociocultural Dimensions of Language Use*. New York: Academic Press.

Agar, M. (1980) *The Professional Stranger*. New York: Academic Press.

Agar, M. (1982) Toward an ethnographic language. *American Anthropologist 84*: 799–795.

Agar, M. and J. Hobbs (1982) Interpreting discourse: coherence and the analysis of ethnographic interviews. *Discourse Processes 5*: 1–32.

Agar, M. and J. Hobbs (1983) Natural plans: using artificial intelligence (AI) planning in the analysis of ethnographic interviews. *Ethos 11*: 33–48.

Allen, P. (1977) Structural and functional models in language teaching. *TESL Talk 8(1)*: 5–15.

Allwright, R. (1981) What do we want teaching materials for? *ELT Journal 36*: 5–18.

Allwright, R. (1984) Why don't learners learn what teachers teach? The interaction hypothesis. In D. Singleton and D. Little (eds) *Language Learning in Formal and Informal Contexts*. Dublin: IRAAL.

Allwright, R. (1988) *Observation in the Language Classroom*. London: Longman.

Allwright, R. and D. Woods (1992) Making sense of classroom observables: learner, teacher, researcher interpretations. Poster session presented at TESOL Conference. Vancouver, B.C., 1992.

Anderson, J. (1983) *The Architecture of Cognition*. Cambridge, MA: Harvard University Press.

Anderson R. (1977) The notion of schemata and the educational enterprise. In Anderson, R., R. Spiro and W. Montague (eds), *Schooling and the Acquisition of Knowledge*. Hillsdale NJ: Lawrence Erlbaum.

Anderson, R. and A. Ortony (1975) On putting apples into bottles – a problem of polysemy. *Cognitive Psychology 1*: 167–180.

Anderson, R., R. Reynolds, D. Schallert and E. Goetz (1977) Frameworks for comprehending discourse. *American Educational Research Journal 14*: 367–381.

Anderson, R. and Z. Schiffrin (1980) The meaning of words in context. In Spiro, R., B. Bruce and W. Brewer (eds), *Theoretical Issues in Reading Comprehension*. Hillsdale NJ: Lawrence Erlbaum.

Anthony, E. (1963) Approach, method, technique. *English Language Teaching* 17: 63–67.

Arthur, B., R. Weiner, M. Culver, Y. Lee, and D. Thomas (1980) The register of impersonal discourse to foreigners: verbal adjustment to foreign accent. In Larsen-Freeman, D. (ed.), *Discourse Analysis in Second Language Research*. Rowley MA: Newbury House.

Ausubel, D. (1963) *The Psychology of Meaningful Verbal Learning: An Introduction to School Learning*. New York: Grune and Stratton.

Bailey, K. (1983) Competitiveness and anxiety in adult second language learning: looking *at* and *through* the diary studies. In Long, M. and H. Seliger (eds), *Classroom Oriented Research in Second Language Acquisition*. Rowley MA: Newbury House.

Barnes, D. (1976) *From Communication to Curriculum*. Harmondsworth: Penguin.

Barnes, D. and D. Shemilt (1974) Transmission and interpretation. *Educational Review* 26: 213–228.

Bartlett, F. (1932) *Remembering: A Study in Experimental and Social Psychology*. Cambridge MA: The University.

Bateson, G. (1972) *Steps to an Ecology of Mind*. New York: Ballantine.

Bateson, G. (1979) *Mind and Nature: A Necessary Unity*. London: Wildwood House.

Bellack, A., H. Kliebard, R. Hyman and L. Smith (1966) *The Language of the Classroom*. New York: Teachers College, Columbia University.

Borko, H, R. Cone, N. Russo and R. Shavelson (1979) Teachers' decision making. In Peterson, P. and H. Walberg (eds), *Research on Teaching*. Berkeley CA: McCutchan.

Bransford, J. and M. Johnson (1972) Contextual prerequisites for understanding: some investigations of comprehension and recall. *Journal of Verbal Learning and Verbal Behavior* 11: 717–726.

Bransford, J., B. Stein and T. Shelton (1984) Learning from the perspective of the comprehender. In Alderson, C. and A. Urquhart (eds), *Reading in a Foreign Language*. London: Longman.

Breen, M. and C. Candlin (1980) The essentials of a communicative curriculum in language teaching. *Applied Linguistics* 1: 89–112.

Brown, R. (1973) *A First Language*. Cambridge MA: Harvard University Press.

Brown, G. and G. Yule (1983) *Discourse Analysis*. Cambridge: Cambridge University Press.

Bruce, B. (1980) Plans and social actions. In Spiro, R., B. Bruce and W. Brewer (eds), *Theoretical Issues in Reading Comprehension*. Hillsdale NJ: Lawrence Erlbaum.

Bühler, K. (1965) *Sprachetheorie: die Darstellungsfunktion der Sprache, 2. edition*. Stuttgart: Gustav Fischer.

Burt, M. and H. Dulay (1980) On acquisition orders. In S. Felix (ed.), *Second Language Development: Trends and Issues*. Tuebingen: Narr.

Calderhead, J. (1988) The development of knowledge structures in learning to teach. In Calderhead, J. (ed.), *Teachers' Professional Learning*. London: Falmer.

Carrell, P. and J. Eisterhold (1983) Schema theory and reading pedagogy. *TESOL Quarterly* 17: 553–573.

Carroll, J. (1966) The contributions of psychological theory and educational research to the teaching of foreign languages. In A. Valdman (ed.), *Trends in Language Teaching*. New York: McGraw Hill.

Castaños, F. (1984) Las categórias básicas del analisis del discurso y la 'disertacion' *Discurso: Cuadernos de Theoria y Analisis* 2(5): 11–27.

Cazden, C. (1986) Classroom discourse. In Wittrock, M. (ed.), *Handbook of Research on Teaching, Third Edition*. New York: MacMillan.

Cazden, C. (1988) *Classroom Discourse*. Portsmouth NH: Heinemann.

Chastain, K. (1976) *The Development of Modern Language Skills: Theory to Practice, Second Edition*. Chicago: Rand McNally.

Chastain, K. and F. Woerdehoff (1968) A methodological study comparing the audio-lingual habit theory and the cognitive-code learning theory. *Modern Language Journal* 52 268–279.

Chomsky, N. (1957) *Syntactic Structures*. 's-Gravenhage: Mouton.

Chomsky, N. (1965) *Aspects of the Theory of Syntax*. Cambridge MA: MIT Press.

Clandinin, J. and M. Connelly (1986) What is 'personal' in studies of the personal? In Ben-Peretz, M., R. Bromme and R. Halkas (eds), *Advances of Research on Teacher Thinking*. Lisse: Swets and Zeitlinger.

Clark, C. and R. Yinger (1979) Teachers' thinking. In Peterson, P. and H. Walberg (eds), *Research on Teaching*. Berkeley CA: McCutchan.

Clark, C. and P. Peterson (1986) Teachers' Thought Processes. In Wittrock, M. (ed.) *Handbook of Research on Teaching, Third Edition*. New York: MacMillan.

Clark, H. and E. Clark (1977) *Psychology and Language: An Introduction to Psycholinguistics*. New York: Harcourt Brace Jovanovich.

Clarke, D. (1983) *Language and Action: A Structural Model of Behaviour*. Oxford: Pergamon.

Cohen, A. and M. Cavalcanti (1990) Feedback on compositions: Teacher and student verbal reports. In Kroll, B. (ed.), *Second Language Writing: Research Insights for the Classroom*. Cambridge: Cambridge University Press.

Cohen, A. (1984) Studying second language learning strategies: how do we get the information? *Applied Linguistics* 5: 101–111.

Collins, A. and R. Quillian (1972) How to make a language user. In Tulving, E. and W. Donaldson (eds), *Organization of Memory*. New York: Academic Press.

Connelly, M. and J. Clandinin (1988) *Teachers as Curriculum Planners: Narratives of Experience*. New York: Teachers College and Toronto: OISE.

Connelly, M. and J. Clandinin (1990) Stories of experience and narrative inquiry. *Educational Researcher* 19: 2–14.

Cooper, M. and M. Holzman (1983) Talking about protocols. *College Composition and Communication* 24: 284–293.

Corder, P. (1967) The significance of learners' errors. *International Review of Applied Linguistic* 4: 161–170.

Coulthard, M. (1977) *An Introduction to Discourse Analysis*. London: Longman.

Coulthard, M. and D. Brazil (1981) Exchange structure. In Coulthard, M. and M. Montgomery (eds), *Studies in Discourse Analysis*. London: Routledge and Kegan Paul.

Creore, A. and V. Hanzeli (1960) *A Comparative Evaluation of Two Modern Methods for Teaching a Spoken Language.* Seattle: University of Washington.

Dias, P. (1987) *Making Sense of Poetry: Patterns in the Process.* The Canadian Council of Teachers of English.

Dielman, T., S. Leech, M. Becker, I. Rosenstock, and W. Horvath (1980) Dimensions of children's health beliefs. *Health Education Quarterly 7*: 219–238.

van Dijk, T. (1977) *Text and Context.* London: Longman.

van Dijk, T. (1980) *Macrostructures.* Hillsdale NJ: Lawrence Erlbaum.

van Dijk, T. (1981) *Studies in the Pragmatics of Discourse.* The Hague: Mouton.

van Dijk, T. (1983) *Strategies of Discourse Comprehension.* New York: Academic Press.

Diller, K. (1971) *Generative Grammar, Structural Linguistics and Language Teaching.* Rowley MA: Newbury House.

Dulay, H. and M. Burt (1973) Should we teach children syntax? *Language Learning 23*: 235–252.

Edgerton, R. and L. Langness (1974) *Methods and Styles in the Study of Culture.* San Francisco: Chandler and Sharp.

Emig, J. (1971) *The Composing Processes of Twelfth Graders.* Urbana IL: National Council of Teachers of English.

Erickson, F. (1982) Talking down: Some cultural sources of miscommunication in inter-racial interviews. In Wolfgang, A., *Research in Non-verbal Communication.* New York: Academic Press.

Erickson, F. and J. Schultz (1982) *The Counsellor as Gatekeeper: Social Interaction in Interviews.* New York: Academic Press.

Ericsson, K. and H. Simon (1980) Verbal reports as data. *Psychological Reviews 87*: 215–51.

Faerch, C. and G. Kasper (1983) Plans and strategies in foreign language communication. In Faerch, C. and G. Kasper (eds), *Strategies in Interlanguage Communication.* London: Longman.

Fahkri, A. (1989) The language teaching belief systems of three inspectors of English in Casablanca, Morocco. *The University of Michigan Papers in Linguistics 4(1)*: 71–90.

Fanselow, J. (1977) Beyond Rashomon – Conceptualizing and describing the teaching act. *TESOL Quarterly 11*: 17–39.

Fathman, A. (1976) The relationship between age and second language productive ability. *Language Learning 25*: 245–253.

Firth, J. (1957) The technique of semantics. In Firth, J., *Papers in Linguistics, 1934–1951.* London: Oxford University Press.

Flanders, N. (1965) *Interaction Analysis in the Classroom: a Manual for Observers.* Ann Arbor MI: School of Education, The University of Michigan Press.

Flower, L. and J. Hayes (1980) The dynamics of composing: making plans and juggling constraints. In Gregg, L. and E. Steinberg (eds), *Cognitive Processes in Writing.* Hillsdale NJ: Lawrence Erlbaum.

Frake, C. (1968) The ethnographic study of cognitive systems. In Fishman, J. (ed.) *Readings in the Sociology of Language.* The Hague: Mouton.

Frankel, R. and H. Beckman (1982) IMPACT: an interaction-based method for preserving and analyzing clinical transactions. In Pettigrew, L. (ed.),

Explorations in Provider and Patient Interactions. Nashville: Humana Press.

Freedman, A. and L. Clarke (1988) *The Effect of Computer Technology on Composing Processes and Written Products of Grade 8 and Grade 12 Students*. Toronto: OISE.

Freeman, D. (1990) Inter-teaching and the grammar of experience. Plenary presented at the TESOL Mid-Summer Meeting. East Lansing, MI. July, 1990.

Freeman, D., D. Larsen-Freeman, J. Handscombe, D. Allwright and D. Woods (1991) Understanding second language teaching. Symposium at TESOL Conference, New York, April 1991.

Fries, C. (1945) *Teaching and Learning English as a Foreign Language*. Ann Arbor MI: The University of Michigan Press.

Fröhlich, M., N. Spada, and P. Allen (1985) Differences in the communicative orientation in L2 classrooms. *TESOL Quarterly 19*: 27–57.

Garfinkel, H. (1967) *Studies in Ethnomethodology*. New York: Prentice-Hall.

Gass, S. and E. Varonis (1985) Task variation and non-native/non-native negotiation of meaning. In Gass, S. and C. Madden (eds), *Input in Second Language Acquisition*. Rowley MA: Newbury House.

Germain, C. (1990) La structure hierarchique d'une leçon en classe de langue seconde. *Bulletin de l'ACLA 12*: 75–87.

Gregg, K. (1984) Krashen's monitor and Occam's razor. *Applied Linguistics 5*: 79–100.

Goffman, E. (1974) *Frame Analysis*. New York: Harper.

Gumperz, J. and E. Herasimchuk (1972) The conversational analysis of social meaning: a study of classroom interaction. In Shuy, R. (ed.), *Sociolinguistics: Current Trends and Prospects*. Washington: Georgetown University Press.

Halliday, M. (1961) Categories of the theory of grammar. *Word 17*: 241–292.

Halliday, M. and R. Hasan (1989) *Language, Context and Text: Aspects of Language in a Social-Semiotic Perspective*. Oxford: Oxford University Press.

Hatch, E. (1983) *Psycholinguistics: A Second Language Perspective*. Cambridge MA: Newbury House.

Hauptman, P. (1971) Experimental comparison of a structural approach and a situational approach. Unpublished doctoral dissertation. Ann Arbor, MI: The University of Michigan.

Hayes-Roth, B. and F. Hayes-Roth (1979) A cognitive model of planning. *Cognitive Science 3*: 275–310.

Head, H. (1920) *Studies in Neurology*. Oxford: Oxford University Press.

Herrlitz, W. and J. Sturm (1991) International triangulation. Unpublished manuscript.

Hosenfeld, C. (1977) A preliminary investigation of the reading strategies of successful and non-successful second-language learners. *System 5*: 110–123.

Hosenfeld, C. (1979) Cindy: a learner in today's foreign language classroom. In Borne, W. (ed.), *The Foreign Language Learner in Today's Classroom Environment*. Montpelier VT: Northeast Conference on the Teaching of Foreign Languages.

Howatt, A. (1984) *A History of English Language Teaching*. Oxford: Oxford University Press.

Hutchinson, T. (1988) Materials and the system: what role do materials play? Paper presented at the RELC Conference. Singapore, April, 1988.

Hutchinson, T. and A. Waters (1980) ESP at the crossroads. *English for Specific Purposes: 36*: 1–6.

Johnson, K. E. (1992) The instructional decisions of pre-service English as a second language teachers: New directions for teacher preparation programs. In Flowerdew, J., M. Brock, and H. Hsia (eds), *Perspectives on Second Language Teacher Development*. Hong Kong: City Polytechnic of Hong Kong.

Johnson, R. K. (1989) *The Second Language Curriculum*. Cambridge: Cambridge University Press.

Kagan, D. (1988) Teaching as clinical problem solving: a critical examination of the analogy and its implications. *Review of Educational Research 58*: 482–505.

Kant, I. (1963) *Critique of Pure Reason*. (1st edition: 1781) London: MacMillan.

Kelly, G. (1955) *The Psychology of Personal Constructs*. New York: Norton.

Kelly, L. (1969) *25 Centuries of Language Teaching*. Rowley MA: Newbury House.

King, P. (1980) ESP at the crossroads: some points reconsidered. *English for Specific Purposes: 39–40*: 1–2.

Kintsch, W. and T. van Dijk (1978) Toward a model of text comprehension and production. *Psychological Review 85*: 363–394.

Köhler, W. (1947) *Gestalt Psychology*. New York: Liveright.

Knowles, M. (1975) *Self-directed Learning: A Guide for Learners and Teachers*. Chicago: Follett.

Krashen, S. (1981) *Second Language Acquisition and Second Language Learning*. Oxford: Pergamon.

Krashen, S. and T. Terrell (1983) *The Natural Approach: Language Acquisition in the Classroom*. Hayward CA: Alemany.

Labov, W. (1972) *Sociolinguistic Patterns*. Philadelphia: University of Pennsylvania Press.

Lave, J. and E. Wenger (1991) *Legitimate Peripheral Participation*. Cambridge: Cambridge University Press.

Larsen-Freeman, D. (1991) On the need for a theory of language teaching. Paper delivered at the Georgetown Round Table. Washington, June, 1991.

Leinhardt, G. (1989) Math lessons: a contrast of novice and expert competence. *Journal for Research in Mathematics Education 20*: 52–75.

Leinhardt, G. and J. Greeno (1986) The cognitive skill of teaching. *Journal of Educational Psychology 78*: 75–95.

Leinhardt, G. and D. Smith (1985) Expertise in mathematics instruction: subject matter knowledge. *Journal of Educational Psychology 77*: 241–277.

Leinhardt, G., C. Weidman and K. Hammond (1987) Introduction and integration of classroom routines by expert teachers. *Curriculum Inquiry 17*: 135–176.

Lewin, K. (1951) Intentional will and need. In Rapaport, D. (ed.) *Organization and Pathology of Thought*. New York: Columbia University.

van Lier, L. (1988) *The Classroom and the Language Learner*. London: Longman.

Lightbown, P. (1985) Great expectations: Second-language acquisition research and classroom teaching. *Applied Linguistics* 6: 173–189.

Linde, C. (1980a) Investigating language learning/teaching belief systems. Unpublished manuscript.

Linde, C. (1980b) Linguistic analysis of written texts. Paper presented at NWAVE Conference. Ann Arbor MI, October, 1980.

Linde, C. (1980c) Structural semantic analysis of documents. Unpublished manuscript.

Long, M. (1981) Input, interaction and second language acquisition. In Winitz, H. (ed.), *Native and Foreign Language Acquisition.* New York: New York Academy of Sciences.

Long, M. (1983) Conversation and the negotiation of comprehensible input. *Applied Linguistics* 4: 126–141.

Lyons, J. (1968) *Introduction to General Linguistics.* Cambridge: Cambridge University Press.

MacEwan, H. and B. Bull (1991) The pedagogic nature of subject matter knowledge. *American Educational Research Journal* 28: 316–334.

Magahay, W. and D. Woods (1990) (eds), *Carleton Papers in Applied Language Studies 7: The Carleton University Courses in English as a Second Language.*

Maslow, A. (1968) *Towards a Psychology of Being.* New York: Van Nostrand Reinhold.

McCracken, G. (1988) *The Long Interview.* Newbury Park CA: Sage.

McLaughlin, B. (1978) The monitor model: some methodological considerations. *Language Learning* 28: 309–322.

McLaughlin, B. (1987) *Theories of Second Language Learning.* London: Edward Arnold.

Mehan, H. (1979) *Learning Lessons: Social Organization in the Classroom.* Cambridge MA: Harvard University Press.

Mehan, H. (1974) Accomplishing classroom lessons. In Cicourel, A. et al (eds), *Language Use and School Performance.* New York: Academic Press.

Mehan, H. (1979) *Learning Lessons.* Cambridge MA: Harvard University Press.

Mehan, Hertwick, Combs and Flynn (1982) Teachers' interpretations of students' behaviour. In Wilkinson, L. (ed.), *Communicating in the Classroom.* New York: Academic Press.

de Mey, M. (1977) The cognitive viewpoint: its development and its scope. In de Mey, M., R. Pinxten, M. Poriau and F. Vandamme (eds), *CC77: International Workshop on the Cognitive Viewpoint.* Ghent: University of Ghent.

Miller, G., E. Galanter and K. Pribram (1960) *Plans and the Structure of Behavior.* New York: Holt, Rinehart and Winston.

Minsky, M. and S. Papert (1972) *Artificial Intelligence Progress Report: Research at the Laboratory in Vision, Language, and Other Problems of Intelligence.* Cambridge MA: MIT Press.

Morine-Delshimer, G. (1991) Tracing conceptual change in pre-service teachers. Paper presented at the Annual Meeting of the American Educational Research Association. Chicago, 1991.

Moulton, W. (1962) Linguistics and language teaching in the United States, 1940–1960. In Morhmann, C., A. Somerfelt and J. Whatmough (eds), *Trends in European and American Linguistics.* Utrecht: Spectrum.

Newman, J. (1991) *Interwoven Conversations: Learning and Teaching Through Critical Reflection.* Toronto: OISE.

Nisbett, R. and L. Ross (1980) *Human Inference: Strategies and Shortcomings of Social Judgment.* Englewood Cliffs NJ: Prentice Hall.

Nord, J. (1980) Developing listening fluency before speaking: an alternative paradigm. *System* 8: 1–22.

Nunan, D. (1988) *The Learner-Centred Curriculum.* Cambridge: Cambridge University Press.

Nunan, D. (1992) The teacher as decision-maker. In Flowerdew, J., M. Brock, and S. Hsia (eds), *Perspectives on Second Language Teacher Education.* Hong Kong: City Polytechnic of Hong Kong.

Oller, J. and J. Richards (1973) *Focus on the Learner: Pragmatic Perspectives for the Language Teacher.* Rowley MA: Newbury House.

Oxford, R. (1989) Use of language learning strategies: a synthesis of studies with implications for strategy training. *System* 17: 235–247.

Pica, T. (1987) Second language acquisition, social interaction and the classroom. *Applied Linguistics* 8: 3–21.

Pica, T. and C. Doughty (1985) Input and interaction in the communicative language classroom: a comparison of teacher-fronted and group activities. In Gass, S. and C. Madden (eds), *Input in Second Language Acquisition.* Rowley MA: Newbury House.

Politzer, R. (1968) The role and place of explanation in the patterns drill. *International Review of Applied Linguistics* 4: 315–331.

Postovsky, V. (1975) On paradoxes in foreign language teaching. *Modern Language Journal* 59: 18–21.

Prabhu, N. (1987) *Second Language Pedagogy.* Oxford: Oxford University Press.

Reid, J. (1982) *The Process of Composition.* Englewood Cliffs NJ: Prentice Hall.

Reither, J. (1985) Writing and knowing: towards redefining the writing process. *College English* 47: 620–628.

Richards, J. (1985) *The Context of Language Teaching.* Cambridge: Cambridge University Press.

Richards, J. and C. Lockhart (1994) *Reflective Teaching in Second Language Classrooms.* Cambridge: Cambridge University Press.

Richards, J. and T. Rodgers (1986) *Approaches and Methods in Language Teaching.* Cambridge: Cambridge University Press.

Rubin, J. (1975) What the 'good language learner' can teach us. *TESOL Quarterly* 9: 41–51.

Rumelhart, D. (1980) Schemata: the building blocks of cognition. In Spiro, R., B. Bruce, and W. Brewer (eds), *Theoretical Issues in Reading Comprehension.* Hillsdale NJ: Lawrence Erlbaum.

Rumelhart, D. and A. Ortony (1977) The representation of knowledge in memory. In Anderson, R., R. Spiro and W. Montague (eds), *Schooling and the Acquisition of Knowledge.* Hillsdale NJ: Lawrence Erlbaum.

Rumelhart, D., P. Smolensky, J. McClelland and G. Hinton (1988) Schemata and sequential thought process in PDP models. In McClelland, J. and D. Rumelhart and the PDP Research Group, *Parallel Distributed Processing: Explorations in the Microstructure of Cognition.* Cambridge MA: MIT Press.

Rutherford, B. (1979) Notional-functional syllabuses. In Blatchford, C. and J. Schachter (eds.) *On TESOL '78: EFL Policies, Programs, Practices*. Washington DC: TESOL.

Sacerdoti, E. (1977) *A Structure for Plans and Behavior*. New York: Elsevier.

Scherer G. and M. Wertheimer (1964) *A Psycholinguistic Experiment in Foreign-Language Teaching*. New York: McGraw Hill.

Schank, R. and R. Abelson (1977) *Scripts, Plans, Goals and Understanding*. Hillsdale NJ: Lawrence Erlbaum.

Schmidt, R. (1990) The role of consciousness in second language learning. *Applied Linguistics 11*: 129–158.

Schmidt, R. (1994) Deconstructing consciousness in search of useful definitions for applied linguistics. *AILA Review 11*: 11–26.

Schneider, W. and R. Shiffrin (1977) Controlled and automatic human information processing: I. Detection, search and attention. *Psychological Review 84*: 1–66.

Schön, D. (1983) *The Reflective Practitioner*. New York: Basic Books.

Schön, D. (1988) Coaching reflective teaching. In Grimmett, P. and G. Erickson (eds), *Reflection in Teacher Education*. New York: Teachers College, Columbia University.

Schubert, W. (1986) *Curriculum: Perspective, Paradigm and Possibilities*. New York: MacMillan.

Segal, M. and C. Pavlik (1985) *Interactions I: A Writing Process Book*. New York: Random House.

Seliger, H. (1975) Inductive method and deductive method in language teaching: a re-examination. *International Review of Applied Linguistics 13*: 1–18.

Seliger, H. (1988) Psycholinguistic issues in second language acquisition. In Beebe, L. (ed.), *Issues in Second Language Acquisition: Multiple Perspectives*. New York: Newbury House.

Selinker, L. (1969) Language Transfer. *General Linguistics 9*: 67–92.

Selinker, L. (1972) Interlanguage. *International Review of Applied Linguistics 10*: 209–231.

Shavelson R. and P. Stern (1981) Research on teachers' pedagogical thoughts, judgments, decisions and behavior. *Review of Educational Research 51*: 455–498.

Shiffrin, R. and W. Schneider (1977) Controlled and automatic human information processing: II. Perceptual learning, automatic attending and a general theory. *Psychological Review 84*: 127–190.

Shulman, L. (1986) Those who understand: knowledge growth in teaching. *Educational Researcher 15*: 4–14.

Sinclair J. and M. Coulthard (1975) *Towards an Analysis of Discourse: the English Used by Pupils and Teachers*. London: Oxford University Press.

Sinclair, J., I. Forsyth, M. Coulthard, and M. Ashby (1972) *The English Used by Teachers and Pupils*. Final Report to S.S.R.C. Unpublished manuscript, Birmingham University.

Slimani, A. (1989) The role of topicalization in classroom language learning. *System 17*: 223–234.

Smith, P. (1970) *A Comparison of the Cognitive and Audiolingual Approaches to Foreign Language Instruction: the Pennsylvania Foreign Language Project*. Philadelphia: The Centre for Curriculum Development.

Smith P. and H. Baranyi (1968) *A Comparison of the Effectiveness of the Traditional and Audiolingual Approaches to Foreign Language Instruction Utilizing Laboratory Equipment.* Washington: U.S. Department of Health, Education and Welfare.

Spada, N. and M. Massey (1992) The role of prior pedagogical knowledge in determining the practice of novice ESL teachers. In Flowerdew, J., M. Brock, and S. Hsia (eds), *Perspectives on Second Language Teacher Education.* Hong Kong: City Polytechnic of Hong Kong.

Sperber, D. and D. Wilson (1986) *Relevance: Communication and Cognition.* Oxford: Basil Blackwell.

Steffensen, M., C. Joag-Dev, and C. Anderson (1979) A cross-cultural perspective on reading comprehension. *Reading Research Quarterly 15:* 10–29.

Stenhouse, L., J. Rudduck and B. MacDonald (1971) Problems in curriculum research: a working paper. Unpublished paper from Curriculum Development: an International Training Seminar. Centre for Applied Research in Education, University of East Anglia, Norwich, July, 1971.

Stern, H. (1975) What can we learn from the good language learner? *Canadian Modern Language Review 31:* 304–317.

Stevick, E. (1980) *Teaching Languages: A Way and Ways.* Rowley MA: Newbury House.

Stubbs, M. (1983) *Discourse Analysis: The Sociolinguistic Analysis of Natural Language.* Oxford: Basil Blackwell.

Stubbs, M. (1986) "A matter of prolonged fieldwork": notes towards a modal grammar of English. *Applied Linguistics 7:* 1–25.

Tannen, D. (1979) What's in a frame? Surface evidence for underlying expectations. In Freedle, R. (ed.), *New Directions in Discourse Analysis, Volume 11.* Norwood NJ: Ablex.

Tarone, E. (1982) Systematicity and attention in interlanguage. *Language Learning 29:* 69–84.

Terrell, T. (1977) A natural approach to the acquisition and learning of a language. *Modern Language Journal 61:* 325–336.

Varonis, E. and S. Gass (1985) Non-native/non-native conversations: a model for negotiating meaning. *Applied Linguistics 6:* 71–87.

Verloop, N. (1989) *Interactive Cognitions of Student-Teachers: An Intervention Study.* Unpublished doctoral dissertation. Utrecht: Rijksuniversiteit te Utrecht.

von Elek, T. and M. Oskarsson (1972) An experiment assessing the relative effectiveness of two methods of teaching English grammatical structures to adults. *International Review of Applied Linguistics 10:* 60–72.

Walker, R. and C. Adelman (1976) Strawberries. In Stubbs, M. and S. Delamont (eds), *Explorations in Classroom Observation.* Chichester: John Wiley.

Wenden, A. (1986) What do second language learners know about their language learning? A second look at retrospective accounts. *Applied Linguistics 7:* 186–205.

Whitaker, S. (1975) Simulation and stimulation. *English Language Teaching Journal 30:* 1–6.

White, R. (1983) Curriculum development and English language syllabus design. In Johnson, K. and D. Porter (eds), *Perspectives in Communicative Language Teaching.* London: Academic Press.

White, R. (1988) *The ELT Curriculum: Design Innovation and Management.* Oxford: Basil Blackwell.

Widdowson, H. (1978) *Teaching Language as Communication.* Oxford, Oxford University Press.

Widdowson, H. (1979) The process and purpose of reading. In Widdowson, H., *Explorations in Applied Linguistics.* Oxford: Oxford University Press.

Widdowson, H. (1981) English for specific purposes: Criteria for course design. In Selinker, L., E. Tarone and V. Hanzeli (eds), *English for Academic and Technical Purposes: Studies in Honor of Louis Trimble.* Rowley MA: Newbury House.

Wilkins, D. (1976) *Notional Syllabuses.* London: Oxford University Press.

Woods, D. (1984) A process orientation in ESL writing. *Carleton Papers in Applied Language Studies 1*: 101–137.

Woods, D. (1989) Studying ESL teachers' decision-making: rationale, methodological issues and initial results. *Carleton Papers in Applied Language Studies 6*: 107–123.

Woods, D. (1991) Teachers' interpretations of second language teaching curricula. *RELC Journal 22*: 1–18.

Wubbels, T. (1992) Taking account of student teachers' preconceptions. *Teaching and Teacher Education 8*: 137–149.

Yalden, J. (1987) *Principles of Course Design for Language Teaching.* Cambridge: Cambridge University Press.

Yinger, R. (1986) Examining thought in action: a theoretical and methodological critique of research on interactive teaching. *Teaching and Teacher Education 2*: 263–282.

Zamel V. (1982) Writing: the process of discovering meaning. *TESOL Quarterly 16*: 195–209.

Author index

Subject index